European Migrants

Global and Local Perspectives

EDITED BY *Dirk Hoerder and Leslie Page Moch*

Northeastern University Press • Boston

Northeastern University Press

Library of Congress Cataloging-in-Publication Data

European migrants : global and local perspectives / edited by Dirk Hoerder and Leslie Page Moch.

p. cm.

Includes bibliographical references and index.

ISBN 1-55553-242-X. — ISBN 1-55553-243-8 (pbk.)

1. Europe—Emigration and immigration—History. 2. Migration, Internal—Europe—History. I. Hoerder, Dirk. II. Moch, Leslie Page.

JV7590.E953 1996

304.8'094'09034—dc20 95-6506

Printed and bound by Thomson-Shore, Inc., in Dexter, Michigan. The paper is Glatfelter, an acid-free sheet.

MANUFACTURED IN THE UNITED STATES OF AMERICA

99 98 97 96 95 5 4 3 2 1

Contents

Acknowledgments

Grateful acknowledgment is made to the following for permission to reprint previously published material:

"Migration and the Social History of Modern Europe" by James Jackson, Jr., and Leslie Page Moch. *Historical Methods* 22 (1989). Reprinted with permission of The Helen Dwight Reid Educational Foundation. Published by Heldref Publications, 1319 18th Street, N.W., Washington, D.C. 20036-1802.

"The Adjustment of Italian Immigrants in Buenos Aires and New York, 1870–1914" by Samuel L. Baily. *American Historical Review* 88, no. 2 (1983). Reprinted with permission of the American Historical Association.

"Labor Migrations of Poles in Atlantic World Economy, 1880–1914" by Ewa Morawska. *Comparative Studies in Society and History,* Vol. 31, no. 2 (1989). Reprinted with the permission of Cambridge University Press.

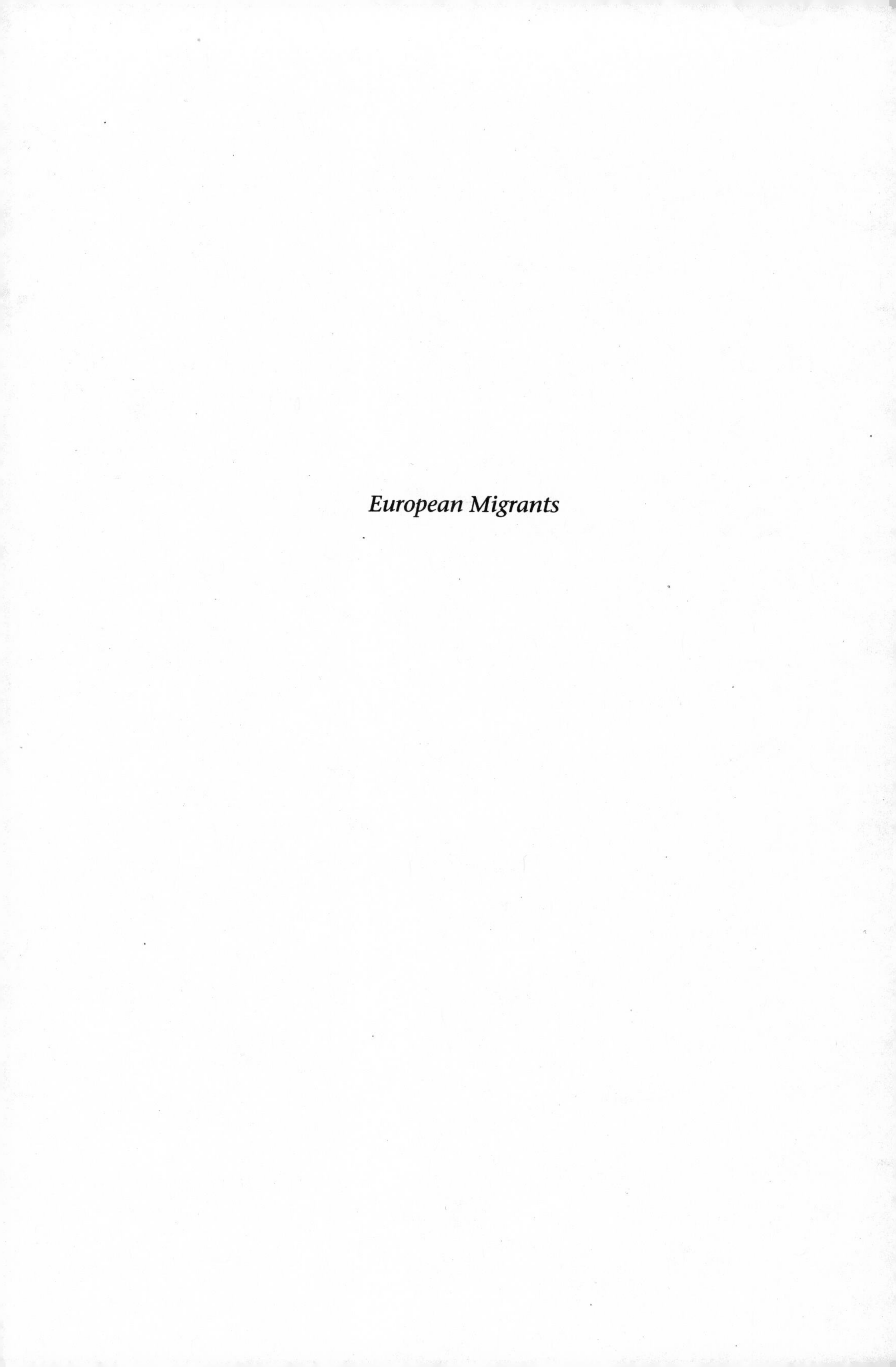

European Migrants

Introduction

LESLIE PAGE MOCH

In the closing decades of the nineteenth century, local conditions propelled Europeans increasingly far from home. Many young men from the village of Valdoria in northern Italy worked in nearby Turin while their brothers and cousins labored in Switzerland and their sisters became domestic servants in Turin. Men from villages to the east of Valdoria traveled to Argentina for harvest work. Likewise, while men in the Polish village of Maszkienice left home to mine coal in a nearby town and women departed to dig sugar beets in Denmark, the men from a neighboring village mined coal in Pennsylvania, and eventually persuaded their countrymen to join them.[1]

The village dwellers of both northern Italy and Austrian Poland sought work away from home because local resources had declined precipitously: populations had grown too large and farm plots too small for the declining agricultural incomes of the late nineteenth century; in addition, other sources of rural income, such as the production of silk or linen, had faded. Villagers felt the negative effects of a worldwide shift in capital and production that enriched large capitalist farms and urban industrial enterprises. Villagers' responses to change depended on the local repertoire of options. Increasingly, those options included leaving the region to work elsewhere for at least a period of several months, if not permanently. Destinations included more prosperous agricultural areas of Europe, the cities of the continent, and the Americas. Some fifty-two million Europeans departed the continent between 1824 and 1924, dwarfing previous transoceanic movements. Many more left their home villages seeking to earn a living in the fields, towns, and cities of Europe.

This volume of essays places these migrations in the context both of local history and of a global perspective, combining new findings on the impulse to migrate within and from Europe with the emerging globalization of migration studies. Imagining a roadmap of research on migrants to the United States, Silvia Pedraza-Bailey identified the roughest of unpaved back roads as "our need to do studies that link the micro and macro levels of analysis more tightly."[2] On the one hand, historical studies of individual migration streams have become very refined, delving into the meaning of chain migration and the experiences of specific migrant groups.[3] Case studies have explored both ends of the journey for migrants by paying increasing attention to home conditions and investigating the varieties of reception and acculturation in North America.[4] On the other hand, since 1980, scholars have increasingly incorporated a global perspective on migration; those studying contemporary migrations, in particular, perceive international mobility as part of a world system in which labor moves among dependent peripheries and dominant cores.[5]

Macro and micro perspectives are profoundly complementary, linking human decisions with the world economic framework. "While the configuration and pressure of forces at the upper structural layers set the limits of the possible and the impossible within which people moved," observes Eva Morawska, "it was at the level of their close, immediate surroundings that individuals made decisions, defined purposes, and undertook actions."[6] The local and international perspectives on migration are mutually informative and together substantially enrich our insights into the process of migration. This complementarity applies not only to migrations in the Atlantic economy, but to movements across the Pacific and the Caribbean, and to contemporary and historical migrations as well.

The essays in this volume focus on European migrations, concentrating primarily on the period of the mass migrations between Europe and the Americas, *circa* 1840–1914. We focus on internal changes in Europe in the context of the world economy, and on links between macroscopic and microscopic change. Systematic studies of this relatively well-documented piece of the global puzzle of historical and contemporary migrations can provide a point of comparison for other movements. Studies of the migrations of Asians to North America in the nineteenth century and of the migrations in the Asian-Australian arena are increasing in number.[7] Historical migrations also foreshadow today's important movements from Latin America and Asia to North America and the Middle East, and from central Europe and the Mediterranean basin to western Europe. Like the European migrations that are the focus of these essays, both contemporary and non-European historical migrations draw people into capital-intensive areas via professional recruiters and personal networks; both include massive temporary movements as well as permanent settlements at destination.[8]

The Essays

The first set of essays in this collection, "Migration Systems: Directions and Issues," addresses overarching questions about the transatlantic migrations. It opens with Dirk Hoerder's "Migration in the Atlantic Economies: Regional European Origins and Worldwide Expansion," which offers a magisterial survey of the migrations of Europeans since the thirteenth century. Hoerder shows how interlocking systems of migration have shifted in this analysis of worldwide European migration in the *longue durée.* James Jackson, Jr., and Leslie Page Moch's essay, "Migration and the Social History of Modern Europe," examines the emerging consensus emphasizing continuities and regional patterns in the history of migration within Europe. They explore the potential of an approach to migration that emphasizes mobility systems, and urge the marriage of economic and social approaches to migration so that neither large-scale change nor migrants themselves are lost. Walter Nugent's "Demographic Aspects of European Migration Worldwide" places the movement of Europeans in a hemispheric perspective; Nugent integrates his analysis of demographic systems both in Europe and at destination to explain the fundamental role in migrations played by population dynamics. He investigates the social and demographic character of the migrants themselves and its impact on the cultures, assimilation, and economic behavior of migrants in the new world. Finally, Donna Gabaccia's "Women of the Mass Migrations: From Minority to Majority, 1820–1930" explores the complexity of women's migrations to the United States from Europe, Asia, and South America. Gabaccia investigates the legal, cultural, economic, and familial explanations for changes in the gender composition of migration groups.

The second section of the text, "Leaving Home," illuminates departures from Europe. Leslie Page Moch's essay, "The European Perspective: Changing Conditions and Multiple Migrations, 1750–1914," surveys the ways in which migration had long been embedded in the family, landholding, and production systems of western Europe. Moch examines the relationship between human mobility and rural industry, which was a benchmark of European economic history and key to subsequent migrations. She then analyzes the nineteenth-century migrations as a socially mediated response to fundamental economic and demographic developments. Steve Hochstadt's "The Socioeconomic Determinants of Increasing Mobility in Nineteenth-Century Germany" is a rich and refined study that pinpoints the countryside as the locus of critical economic and political transformation. Hochstadt details changes in the German countryside that undermined the security of rural life and forced agricultural workers to take to the road. "Labor Migrations of Poles in the Atlantic World Economy, 1880–1914," by Ewa Morawska, demonstrates the value of investigations that work on multiple levels with a model case study. Morawska integrates micro and macro frameworks by setting Polish migrations in a global framework, in the economic and political context of a divided Poland that sent its people to Germany and to the United States, and in the local setting of the village of Maszkienice.

The final section, "Approaches to Acculturation: Comparative Perspectives," provides a sweeping comparative framework for migrants at destination. It opens with Dirk Hoerder's broadly suggestive essay "From Migrants to Ethnics: Acculturation in a Societal Framework." Hoerder surveys the compendium of factors that influence the acculturation of migrants within Europe as well as overseas; he includes neglected issues such as the expectations and voyage experience of the newcomer as well as the structure of the destination economy, society, and political system. He builds a model of migration and acculturation that emphasizes these structural factors, while recognizing the individual agency involved in the decision to migrate and settle abroad. Nancy Green's "The Modern Jewish Diaspora: Eastern European Jews in New York, London, and Paris" applies a divergent analysis to the comparison of migrant groups, challenging the notion that Jewish communities are alike worldwide. Green sets up an investigation of migrants—moving in different-sized groups and by different timing—in significantly different political and cultural environments; her migration systems stretch from eastern Europe into western Europe and across the Atlantic. This section concludes with an exemplary case study by Samuel Baily, "The Adjustment of Italian Immigrants in Buenos Aires and New York, 1870–1914." Baily's comparative perspective allows him to investigate the first stages of acculturation in very distinct contexts to unravel the importance of migrants' social traits, the receiving society, and the nature of the immigrant community.

Perspectives

This collection expands the framework for migration studies in three areas, offering (a) a long-term perspective to explicate the context of mass migrations, (b) a collective view of migration that challenges individualistic push-pull models, and (c) an analysis of gender as a far-reaching consideration in migration and acculturation. In adopting a broad time frame, these essays situate the nineteenth-century mass migrations of Europeans in the history of human mobility from the thirteenth century to the present day. Dirk Hoerder constructs a temporal and geographical framework that begins with the preindustrial European migration system, emphasizing the movements of Germans and Jews that influenced later migrations. Political systems and economics, then, set a variety of mobility patterns for Europeans long before 1800. Hoerder points out the importance of the state in establishing these patterns, noting that many movements resulted from government sponsorship promoting settlement to the east into Hungary, Prussia, and Russia.

During the sixteenth and seventeenth centuries, the countries of Iberia and western Europe emerged as a dominant core in a world system. The movements of small numbers of Europeans in colonial enterprises created a demand for labor that set off migrations of native Asians, Africans, and Latin Americans. Plantations and settlements generated systems of internal movement as well as massive systems of coerced migration of slaves and contract laborers.[9]

In the seventeenth and eighteenth centuries, and as late as the 1830s, relatively few Europeans moved across the oceans in comparison with the millions of people who comprised the tropical slave migrations. In total, about eight million enslaved Africans arrived in the Americas before 1820, compared with some 2.3 million Europeans.[10] The great majority of Africans—an estimated 94 percent—were brought to the Caribbean and South America.[11] The European and African experiences were intimately connected; the European taste for sugar, coffee, and cotton spurred this massive and long-lived slave trade. Then, with the gradual abolition of the slave trade (in the British colonies after 1809 and in Brazil after 1830) and the subsequent abolition of slavery, Caribbean and South American economies recruited European and Asian replacements in the form of contract and free labor. (The migration of Asian contract labor emerged, and its cross-oceanic streams reached East Africa and the Americas.) The abolition of slavery, the end of the Revolutionary and Napoleonic wars, and the sea changes in European society and economy inaugurated a new era in the migrations of Europeans within the continent and worldwide.

Migration was a long-standing part of the family, landholding, and inheritance systems of the continent where free labor prevailed. Teams of harvest laborers had traveled to large farms since at least the seventeenth century. Departure from one's home village had routinely accompanied work as a young farmhand, urban servant, or marriage. Most people moved within their home county in preindustrial England, where rural people moved more than city dwellers, and women more than men. Between 1660 and 1730, over 76 percent of rural women (and 68 percent of rural men) left their village of birth.[12] Throughout Europe, elites worked and married in a wider geographical circle than ordinary people. Finally, the large cities of the continent, such as seventeenth-century Amsterdam, London, and Paris, cast a wide net for rich and poor alike.

A compelling critique of modernization theory is embedded in the long-term and global perspective of these essays. In terms of human mobility, migration theory has associated migration with relatively recent economic developments, rather than with long-standing population and economic systems. In addition, modernization theorists focus on permanent migration from the countryside to the city.[13] Yet not only has cityward migration long been part of European life; rural migration has also enlivened the countryside for centuries. For example, in early modern Europe, three widespread systems of temporary migration brought thousands of workers into the Baltic, the North Sea region (particularly the Netherlands), and Britain; by the end of the eighteenth century, seven systems of long-distance temporary labor migration each moved at least twenty thousand men per year.[14] As Steve Hochstadt points out, all the factors that would promote the expanded migrations of the nineteenth century were in place before 1800.[15] Moreover, migration has been a crucial part of labor systems in Africa, Asia, and Latin America, not simply of the historical core economies. The contention that migration is part of becoming modern—for economies, cultures, or individuals—distorts and obscures geographical mobility rather than illuminates it.

These essays emphasize the collective nature of the migration process. Underlying their discussions of the variety of interlocking and interacting migration systems is an implicit typology of migration systems. Migrations vary both by the extent to which migrants remain in the sending network and by the degree to which the move is definitive. People migrate when they depart or change residence outside their home villages or municipalities. *Local migrations* cover moves within the marriage or labor market that nonetheless historically removed a high proportion of people from their home villages.[16] *Circular migrations* take people farther, but return them home. The harvest teams and temporary urban migrants of seventeenth-century Europe, as well as the Italian "swallows" who made annual grain-harvesting trips to Argentina, were circular migrants because they operated in a regular circuit, retaining their claims and contacts with home.[17] *Chain migration* moves people in a network from home to destination as well, but some of them stay on and tie in with the network at destination, people who provide aid and information to newcomers. Such systems moved Europeans to destinations where many would stay, including cities on the continent and locations in the new world.[18]

Career migration responds to an employing organization and migrant aspirations. This kind of movement took church personnel within (and from) early modern Europe and included more bureaucrats and functionaries like the state-employed schoolteachers of Europe as the nineteenth century drew to a close. More permanent were many *colonizing migrations* that moved groups of people to a new area. The long distance of travel and the high mortality abroad prevented early modern European colonists from returning home. Finally, *coerced migrations* like the slave migrations of the tropical world allowed no return home, generally severing personal contacts between people at home and at destination.[19] Historically, these types of migration have been related. The early colonizing migrations of Europeans, for example, set off chain migration systems of native populations and massive coerced migrations. Chain migrations have in many cases emerged from circular migration systems.

This volume emphasizes changing patterns of local, circular, and chain migration on the European continent as well as chain and circular migrations between Europe and the Americas between 1840 and 1914. The majority of free migrants in systems of chain and circular migration did not make one permanent move, but were at their initial destination only temporarily. By contrast, colonial and coerced migrants were more likely to stay at their destinations than return home. It is for this reason that the term *migration,* rather than *immigration,* which implies permanent settlement, dominates these essays. Permanent stays were a minority phenomenon for the mobile Europeans who moved both on their home continent and to new worlds in the 1840–1914 period. For example, Prussian migration statistics allow James Jackson, Jr., to estimate that the typical migrant in the Ruhr industrial town of Duisburg may have been a man who moved fifteen times in his lifetime, making ten of these moves while single and under the age of thirty.[20] And between 1907 and World War I, an estimated 42 percent of northern Italians and English returned home; moreover, Europeans were more likely to return home from Latin America than from the United States—nearly half of those in Latin America went back to Europe.[21]

These essays accentuate the collective and communal nature of the migration process, embedding the decision to migrate in home conditions wrought by economic, demographic, and political change and mediated by local migration knowledge and traditions. Changes in information and norms about moving were communal changes; for example, the "secularization of hope," the aspiration for improvement in this life rather than in the next, manifested itself in the communal Passover greeting "next year in America" among the Jews of Polotzk.[22] Because migration systems included various members of a community, individual psychological traits do not distinguish movers from stayers; an attempt to categorize German migrants in Australia found that migrants were a heterogeneous group who defined themselves in relational terms as they moved between their sending and receiving network of relationships.[23]

If migration is a collective process, acculturation is as well. These essays confirm the "chilling distance" that separates a collective interpretation of the migration process from both the individualist interpretation of acculturation and the old-fashioned American exceptionalism that claims a distinct story for newcomers to the United States.[24] Rather than define acculturation in terms of individual traits, Dirk Hoerder's largely structural model guides our thinking about the work and accomplishments of newcomers in a new setting. The elements of home culture play a key role; as Samuel Baily demonstrates, they shaped, for example, the levels of literacy, labor skills, and experience in cooperative organizations that distinguished northern Italians in Buenos Aires from southern Italians in New York. Likewise, the structure of housing and employment available at destination yielded different kinds of opportunities, in this case a greater variety of housing and work for northern Italians in Buenos Aires than for the southerners in New York. Similarly, divergent economies shaped a different Jewish immigrant labor force in London, Paris, and New York. Perceptions of and prejudices about migrant ethnicity also shaped opportunity for newcomers. In the case of Italians in the Americas, those in Buenos Aires were welcomed as civilizing Europeans in an uncivilized land while those in New York were viewed as an inferior race that threatened to dilute the population of northern European stock. Native-born Jews in London, Paris, and New York had different attitudes toward their newly arrived eastern European coreligionists, influenced by their own precarious status in the West. The contrast is most extreme among groups: Chinese contract workers, for example, faced regulations and restrictions, while Scandinavian farmers benefited from settlement acts in the Midwestern United States. The welcome mat was not evenly proffered within the continent of Europe either, where members of certain ethnic groups were ill-treated as international migrant laborers; in the nineteenth century, these included the Irish in England and the Poles in German states.[25] In the main, treatment was collective, not individual.

We maintain two caveats for our collectivist orientation. While recognizing the social nature of human movement, which properly replaces an individualistic push-pull conceptualization of migration, it is important to see the place of human agency and perception in migration and acculturation.[26] Migration is a more active, engaged process than the terms "migration flow" or "migration stream" imply; it certainly involves more agency than suggested by the terms commonly applied to immigrants in the United States—"uprooted" or even "transplanted."[27] Historical actors were not helpless automatons; rather they decided among the possibilities known to them whether or not to leave home, to move again, or to return. Moreover, as Dirk Hoerder points out in his essay on acculturation, individual migrants' perceptions of themselves and the world underwent changes that thoroughly altered their interpretations of their own lives.[28] Second, and more obviously, although individualistic considerations are not very helpful in explaining the processes of human migration or acculturation, individual characteristics, such as demographic traits, were absolutely fundamental to migration patterns and migration behavior. For example, every aspect of migrant life—including the propensity to move—was affected by gender, marital status, and age.

The third innovation of these essays is that they begin to correct a fundamental weakness of migration studies by incorporating a systematic analysis of gender. Although discussions of migration were often gender blind until the 1980s, specific discussions of migrants themselves were usually limited to men.[29] Studies of female migrants have since appeared, and are especially well established among investigations of contemporary migrants to the United States and Europe. However, gender has rarely been analyzed in depth as an analytical category for historical migrants.[30] To do so is a taxing enterprise, because women's migrations are both interconnected with and distinct from those of men. Donna Gabaccia reports that the migrations of women to the United States (and return migrations), for example, echoed those of men in terms of numbers and timing, albeit much more strongly for some national groups than others. Likewise, the men and women within national groups had similar literacy and marriage profiles. Women were more important among nineteenth-century migrants from northern and western European nations such as Ireland, where marriage was late and high rates of celibacy were common.[31] In such regions, single European women had migrated for centuries to work as farmhands and urban servants. Productive and reproductive roles shaped the migration of European women, whether within the continent or to the Americas.

In terms of labor, women were rarely interchangeable with men because tasks were assigned by gender both in the old world and the new. Although family migration—migration streams that include women—is associated with farm work, women were more likely to move to American cities than to rural areas. Likewise, a long tradition of migration to the European city for employment made cities female places.[32] And some cities attracted women especially: while young men traveled among mining centers and steel towns for work, country women sought positions as domestics—even in textile centers like Roubaix in northern France or in Verviers in Belgium.[33] Especially when they moved without their families, single migrant women responded to the demand for urban domestic servants on both continents.[34] Those who moved in the company of their families—and who therefore did not need the housing that domestic service provided—were more likely to be seamstresses and factory workers. Married migrant women, from French women in Paris to Japanese picture brides and southern Italian wives in the United States, responded to the demand for female domestic labor, whether or not they also worked for cash.[35] Generally speaking, migrant women's labor has been discounted as an explanation of female movement. This may be in part because migrant women's work (more often in the domestic sphere than more visible men's labor) has been more obscure because it was more privatized and a bit more cushioned from industrial booms and busts than migrant men's employment.[36]

Although the expectation of marriage rarely moved a male, marriage moved many women out of their home villages and small towns. This worked in several ways. Marital relations were the impetus for women leaving Europe to join a spouse or a man to whom they were engaged. Marriage was an explicitly female strategy for the transoceanic migration of thousands of women, who left their homes in order to marry men whom they did not know.[37] The impetus of marriage for women's migration on the continent is important in understanding the age-old movement from one peasant settlement to another with nuptials. Otherwise, marriage played an ostensibly negative role—that is, women left the countryside for the city in the last century to avoid a marriage that would bind them to the barnyard and fields.[38]

Finally, women's capacity for reproduction distinguishes their migration in ways that have not yet been fully researched. The more privatized migration arrangements (as well as religious and charitable institutional supports for single women) reflect in part efforts to protect them from pregnancy. Pregnancies that would not result in marriage provided an impetus for departure from home for some women; in other cases, pregnancies were the result of life away from home without familial social protection. For single women, pregnancy was the palpable manifestation of the poor migrant's social vulnerability.[39]

For the people both back home and at destination (including policy makers), women's capacities for reproduction signaled that when they joined a migration system, male migrants were more likely to stay at the destination of chain migrations and form an immigrant community. For this reason, nations of the Americas and Europe restricted with special care the entry of women and families whom they wanted to exclude as permanent immigrants; this was one impetus to use gangs of male Chinese contract workers in Cuba and the United States. Similarly, the entry of Polish workers in the eastern provinces of nineteenth-century Germany was regulated to prevent family settlement. European women met less prejudice in the United States. They became the majority of migrants when quotas restricting southeastern European migrants were imposed in the 1920s because they joined husbands or came over to marry because men could no longer travel freely back and forth.[40]

Distinctions

State regulation plays a peripheral role in this collection, largely because in the 1840–1914 period, the sweeping migrations within Europe and to the Americas were congruent both with the economics of sending and receiving nations and with the dominant political mode of laissez-faire liberalism. The great periods of religious intolerance that had promoted migrations had passed with the seventeenth century, and the most explicit mercantilist policies that had started up colonial settlements had faded with the era of the American war of independence and the French Revolution. In the revolutionary period of the 1790s, restrictions on immigration were made for political (rather than religious) reasons in Britain, France, Switzerland, Canada, and the United States. The postwar period after 1815 placed relatively few restrictions on departure (except the British ban on emigration of skilled artisans such as machine makers) or immigration to the United States, and several European states had more or less explicit and successful programs to export paupers. The United States warred against its native population, but did not restrict the arrival of Europeans, and even the virulent anti-Catholicism of the Know-Nothing party in the 1850s failed to obtain restrictionist legislation.[41] Supply and demand were allowed to work in relative freedom, between the overcrowded and crisis-ridden regions of the old world and the prosperous regions of Europe and the Americas; the world system of global labor required little state intervention.

When states paid attention to migrants in this period, they first and foremost excluded those whom they considered undesirable. On the European continent, the German states severely regulated temporary Polish workers in the east and German-born Poles in the west in an effort to contain potential Polish nationalism and minimize the presence of Slavs.[42] The pogroms of Russia and the Austrian empire pushed out Jews beginning in the 1880s and 1890s.[43] The United States first acted against Asian migrants, excluding first the Chinese in 1882, and then the Japanese in 1907.[44] As the reaction against southern and eastern Europeans grew stronger in the United States, the quota legislation of the 1920s was passed to restrict disproportionately the so-called "new" immigrants. On the other hand, the United States continued to welcome immigrants from northwestern Europe, and Latin American states pressed for European newcomers after the abolition of slavery; the Brazilian government, for example, subsidized passage fares for Italian workers.[45]

These essays cover a wide range of topics and offer distinct points of view and levels of analysis. Three of them explicitly address the experience of non-Europeans and the movement of Europeans beyond the Americas: Dirk Hoerder's "Migration in the Atlantic Economies: Regional European Origins and Worldwide Expansion," Walter Nugent's "Demographic Aspects of European Migration Worldwide," and Donna Gabaccia's "Women of the Mass Migrations: From Minority to Majority, 1820–1930." Four others focus on the profound changes in life on the European continent and consequent changed migration itineraries: Steve Hochstadt's "The Socioeconomic Determinants of Increasing Mobility in Nineteenth-Century Germany," James Jackson and Leslie Moch's "Migration and the Social History of Modern Europe," Ewa Morawska's "Labor Migrations of Poles in the Atlantic World Economy, 1880–1914," and Moch's "The European Perspective: Changing Conditions and Multiple Migrations, 1750–1914." Morawska's and Moch's essays also straddle the Atlantic, as do Hoerder's "From Migrants to Ethnics: Acculturation in a Societal Framework" and Nancy Green's "Modern Jewish Diaspora."

This collection draws on a diverse body of scholars and scholarship. Dirk Hoerder's contributions on European migration patterns and acculturation reflect his profound acquaintance with immigrant workers at the Labor Migration Project of the University of Bremen. Other essays focus on authors' broader interests. These include Latin Americanist Samuel Baily's comparative essay on migrant adjustment, immigration historian Donna Gabaccia's essay on female migrants to the United States, German historian Steve Hochstadt's essay on rural change in nineteenth-century Germany, German historian James Jackson and French historian Leslie Moch's essay on migration and social history, American historian Walter Nugent's essay on the demographics of migration, Nancy Green's comparative study of Jewish settlements, and Moch's essay on migration in European history. We include three works that have appeared elsewhere because they enhance the coherence and power of the collection. Jackson and Moch's essay on migration in European social history appears in the opening section for its analysis of trends in historical migration studies. The "Leaving Home" section includes sociologist Ewa Morawska's exemplary study of the labor migrations of Poles in the context of the world economy because it is a model of macro and micro approaches. The acculturation section concludes with Samuel Baily's fine comparison of Italians in Buenos Aires and New York.[46]

Within a remarkably similar worldview, a very interesting difference among the essays is their willingness to consider migrant perceptions, choices, and subjective lives.[47] Most of the collection, to be sure, focuses on the absorbing and important task of identifying the structural and collective elements that shaped migration patterns at the global and local levels. Some essays, however, consider the subjective experience of migrants. Both James Jackson, Jr., and Dirk Hoerder ask that the migrant experience be further explored in psychological terms. Dirk Hoerder's essay on acculturation movingly recognizes the broad range of perceptual experiences of migrants. Sociologist Ewa Morawska, who has interviewed migrants extensively in the United States, emphasizes that migrants move within structures while simultaneously creating their own "lifeworlds," making decisions based on local and personal considerations about their movements in the global labor force.[48]

This collection integrates global and local approaches, addressing the present needs of scholars concerned with Europe, the Americas, and the connections between the two—and of those seeking to understand global migration patterns. It attends to the situation and experience of individuals like Rosa—a northern Italian woman who entered the United States at New York harbor to spend years in a Missouri mining town and live out her life in Chicago—placing them in the context of their gender, regional origins, and global itinerary.[49] Together, these essays argue that future research on migrants and migrations must be placed in the more comprehensive frame of reference constructed during the last decade and projected in this volume.

Notes

1. Maurizio Gribaudi, *Itinéraires ouvriers: Espaces et groupes sociaux à Turin au début du XXe siècle* (Paris: Ecole des Hautes Etudes en Sciences Sociales, 1987), chap. 1, esp. 50–51;

Ewa Morawska, "Labor Migrations of Poles in the Atlantic World Economy, 1880–1914," essay in this volume.

2. Silvia Pedraza-Bailey, "Immigration Research: A Conceptual Map," *Social Science History* 14 (1989): 61–62.

3. For exemplary studies, see Rudolph Vecoli and Suzanne M. Sinke, eds., *A Century of European Migrations, 1830–1930* (Champaign: University of Illinois Press, 1992).

4. Many scholars have noted the dramatic shift of paradigm for acculturation between Oscar Handlin, *The Uprooted* (Boston: Little, Brown and Co., 1951), and John Bodnar, *The Transplanted: A History of Immigrants in Urban America* (Bloomington: Indiana University Press, 1985); for critiques of "the transplanted," see James R. Barrett, John Bodnar, John J. Bukowczyk, Nora Faires, Donna Gabaccia, and Dirk Hoerder, "John Bodnar's *The Transplanted:* A Roundtable," *Social Science History* 12 (1988): 217–68; for a model study of a migrant group in the context of home and the new world, see Walter Kamphoefner, *The Westfalians: From Germany to Missouri* (Princeton: Princeton University Press, 1987).

5. The perspective began with the publication of Immanuel Wallerstein, *The Modern World-System: Capitalist Agriculture and the Origins of the European World-Economy in the Sixteenth Century* (New York: Academic Press, 1974); see, for example, Mary Kritz et al., eds., *Global Trends in Migration: Theory and Research on International Population Movements* (New York: Center for Migration Studies, 1983); Alejandro Portes and John Walton, *Labor, Class and International System* (New York: Academic Press, 1981); Virginia Yans-McLaughlin, ed., *Immigration Reconsidered: History, Sociology, and Politics* (New York: Oxford University Press, 1990).

6. Morawska, "Labor Migrations of Poles."

7. See, for example, Lucie Cheng and Edna Bonacich, eds., *Labor Migration under Capitalism: Asian Workers in the United States before World War II* (Berkeley: University of California Press, 1984), and the pioneering essay by Sucheng Chan, "European and Asian Immigration into the United States in Comparative Perspective, 1820s to 1920s," in Yans-McLaughlin, *Immigration Reconsidered,* 37–75.

8. Historical and contemporary migrations are compared in Leslie Page Moch, *Moving Europeans: Migration in Western Europe since 1650* (Bloomington: Indiana University Press, 1992), chap. 5. There are obvious differences between historical and contemporary migrations as well; for example, most of the migrations that are the focus of this volume were settler and labor migrations, rather than part of a "brain drain" or the result of dramatic political turnovers.

9. Kingsley Davis, "The Migrations of Human Populations," *Scientific American* 231, no. 3 (1974): 96; Dirk Hoerder, "Migration in the Atlantic Economies: Regional European Origins and Worldwide Expansion," in this volume.

10. David Eltis, "Free and Coerced Transatlantic Migrations: Some Comparisons," *American Historical Review* 88 (1983): 252–55.

11. Philip Curtin, "Migration in the Tropical World," in Yans-McLaughlin, *Immigration Reconsidered,* 27; Curtin's estimate applies to all slaves between the fifteenth and the nineteenth centuries.

12. Peter Clark, "Migration in England during the Late Seventeenth and Early Eighteenth Centuries," *Past and Present,* no. 83 (1979): 57–90.

13. For an articulation of the modernization theorist's view of migration, see Wilbur Zelinsky, "The Hypothesis of the Mobility Transition," *Geographical Review* 61 (1971): 219–49; for the application of modernization theory to historical migration studies, see Barbara Anderson, *Internal Migration during Modernization in Late Nineteenth-Century Russia* (Princeton: Princeton University Press, 1980).

14. Jan Lucassen, *Migrant Labour in Europe 1600–1900* (London: Croom Helm, 1987), chap. 6; Hoerder, "Migration in the Atlantic Economies."

15. Steve Hochstadt, "The Socioeconomic Determinants of Increasing Mobility in Nineteenth-Century Germany," in this volume.

16. For examples of local migrations, see Roger Schofield, "Age-Specific Mobility in an Eighteenth-Century Rural English Parish," *Annales de démographie historique* (1970): 261–74; Emmanuel Todd, "Mobilité géographique et cycle de vie en Artois et en Toscane au XVIIIe siècle," *Annales: Economies, Sociétés, Civilisations* 30 (1975): 726–44.

17. See Lucassen, *Migrant Labour in Europe 1600–1900;* Michael Piore, *Birds of Passage: Migrant Labor and Industrial Societies* (New York: Cambridge University Press, 1979); J. D. Gould, "European Inter-Continental Emigration—The Road Home: Return Migration from the U.S.A.," *Journal of European Economic History* 9 (1980): 41–112.

18. For examples of chain migration studies to the United States and on the continent, see Bodnar, *The Transplanted;* Leslie Page Moch, *Paths to the City: Regional Migration in Nineteenth-Century France* (Beverly Hills: Sage Publications, 1983).

19. Charles Tilly, "Migration in Modern European History," in *Human Migration: Patterns and Policies,* ed. William H. McNeill and Ruth S. Adams (Bloomington: Indiana University Press, 1978), 51–57; Tilly, "Transplanted Networks," in Yans-McLaughlin, *Immigration Reconsidered,* 88–90. For an entry into studies of the slave trade, see Philip Curtin, *The Atlantic Slave Trade: A Census* (Madison: University of Wisconsin Press, 1969); Eltis, "Free and Coerced Transatlantic Migrations: Some Comparisons"; Paul Lovejoy, *Transformations in Slavery: A History of Slavery in Africa* (Cambridge: Cambridge University Press, 1983).

20. George Alter, *Family and the Female Life Course: The Women of Verviers, Belgium, 1849–1880* (Madison: University of Wisconsin Press, 1988), chap. 3; Steve Hochstadt, "Migration and Industrialization in Germany, 1815–1977" *Social Science History* 5 (1981): 445–68; James Jackson, Jr., "Migration and Urbanization in the Ruhr Valley, 1850–1900" (Ph.D. diss., University of Minnesota, 1980), 169; idem, "Migration in Duisburg, 1867–1890: Occupational and Familial Contexts," *Journal of Urban History* (1982): 235–70.

21. Gould, "European Inter-Continental Emigration," 50–60; Magnus Mörner and Harold Sims, *Adventurers and Proletarians: The Story of Migrants in Latin America* (Paris: United Nations Educational, Scientific and Cultural Organization, 1985), chap. 4, 43, 69–70. Even the best data from the United States may underestimate the rates of return to Britain and the Continent; see Günter Moltmann, "American-German Return Migration in the Nineteenth and Early Twentieth Centuries," *Central European History* 13 (1980): 378–92.

22. Mary Antin, *The Promised Land* (New York, 1912), 141–42, cited by Dirk Hoerder, "From Migrants to Ethnics: Acculturation in a Societal Framework," essay in this volume; James Jackson, Jr., and Leslie Page Moch, "Migration and the Social History of Modern Europe," essay in this volume.

23. Folkert Lüthke, *Psychologie der Auswanderung* (Weinheim, 1889), 130, 192, 329, cited by Hoerder in "From Migrants to Ethnics."

24. Samuel Baily, "The Adjustment of Italian Immigrants in Buenos Aires and New York, 1870–1914," in this volume; Hoerder, "From Migrants to Ethnics"; Virginia Yans-McLaughlin, "Introduction," in *Immigration Reconsidered,* 6.

25. Klaus Bade, "German Emigration to the United States and Continental Immigration to Germany, 1879–1929," *Central European History* 13 (1980): 348–77; Ruth-Ann Harris, *The Nearest Place that Wasn't Ireland: Early Nineteenth-Century Irish Labor Migration* (Ames, Iowa: Iowa State University Press, 1994); Ulrich Herbert, *A History of Foreign Labor in Germany, 1880–1980* (Ann Arbor: University of Michigan Press, 1990), chap. 1; William J. Lowe, *The Irish in Mid-Victorian Lancashire: The Shaping of a Working Class Community* (New York: Peter Lang, 1989); Lynn Lees, *Exiles of Erin: Irish Migrants in Victorian London* (Ithaca: Cornell University Press, 1979).

26. See Douglas S. Massey et al., *Return to Aztlàn: The Social Process of International Mi-*

gration from Western Mexico (Berkeley: University of California Press, 1987); Pedraza-Bailey, "Immigration Research: A Conceptual Map," 62; Tilly, "Transplanted Networks," in Yans-McLaughlin, *Immigration Reconsidered,* 79–90.

27. Barrett et al., "John Bodnar's *The Transplanted,*" 221–63.

28. Hoerder, "From Migrants to Ethnics."

29. See, for example, Piore, *Birds of Passage.*

30. For example, see Donna Gabaccia, *The Other Side* (forthcoming); Annie Phizacklea, *One Way Ticket: Migration and Female Labour* (London: Routledge and Kegan Paul, 1983); Janet Nolan, *Ourselves Alone: Women's Emigration from Ireland* (Lexington: University Press of Kentucky, 1989); Rita J. Simon and Caroline B. Brettell, *International Migration: The Female Experience* (Totowa, N.J.: Rowman and Allanheld, 1986).

31. Donna Gabaccia, "Women of the Mass Migrations: From Minority to Majority, 1820–1930," essay in this volume; for the "European marriage pattern," see John Hajnal, "European Marriage Patterns in Perspective," in *Population in History: Essays in Historical Demography,* ed. D. V. Glass and D.E.C. Eversley (London: Edward Arnold, 1965), 101–43.

32. Roger Mols, *Introduction à la démographie historique des villes d'Europe du XIVe au XVIIIe siècle* (Louvain: Publications Universitaires, 1954–1956), vol. 2; the exceptions to this rule are garrison towns such as old-regime Berlin and the coal-mining and metalworking towns that boomed in the nineteenth century; these had a majority of males, quite unlike administrative, commercial, and textile cities; see, for example, Jackson, "Migration in Duisburg, 1867–1890."

33. Leslie Page Moch, " 'Infirmities of the Body and Vices of the Soul': Migrants, Family and Urban Life in Turn-of-the-Century France," in *Essays on the Family and Historical Change,* ed. L. P. Moch and G. D. Stark (College Station, Tex.: Texas A&M University Press, 1983), 35–64; Alter, *Family and the Female Life Course,* 84–96; Dudley Baines, *Migration in a Mature Economy: Emigration and Internal Migration in England and Wales, 1851–1900* (New York: Cambridge University Press, 1985), 235–37.

34. Abel Chatelain, "Migrations et domesticité feminine urbaine en France, XVIIIe siècle–XXe siècle," *Revue d'histoire économique et sociale* 4 (1969): 506–28; Gabaccia, "Women of the Mass Migrations"; Rachel Fuchs and Leslie Page Moch, "Pregnant, Single, and Far from Home: Migrant Women in Nineteenth-Century Paris," *American Historical Review* 95 (1990): 1007–31.

35. Gabaccia, "Women of the Mass Migrations"; Hoerder, "From Migrants to Ethnics"; the story of *Rosa,* which concludes Hoerder's essay "From Migrants to Ethnics," relates the arrival of a married immigrant woman who came to the United States specifically to provide domestic labor for her husband and his coworkers in a Missouri mining town; see also Marie Hall Ets, *Rosa: The Story of an Italian Immigrant* (Minneapolis: University of Minnesota Press, 1979).

36. Donna Gabaccia, "Interpreting Sex Ratios: Immigrant Women before 1924" (paper delivered at the meetings of the American Historical Association, San Francisco, December 1989); see also Lars-Göran Tedebrand, "Remigration from America to Sweden," in *Labor Migration in the Atlantic Economies,* ed. Dirk Hoerder (Westport: Greenwood, 1985), 374.

37. See Donna Gabaccia and Christiane Harzig, "Female Migration" (Mercy College and University of Bremen); Dirk Hoerder, Inge Blank, and Horst Rössler, eds., *Roots of the Transplanted: East Central and Southeastern Europe,* 2 vols. (New York: Columbia University Press, 1993), pt. 4, "Women's Roles and Socio-Economic Status under the Impact of Migration"; Simon and Brettell, *International Migration: The Female Experience;* Phizacklea, *One Way Ticket.*

38. Moch, *Paths to the City,* chap. 2.

39. Fuchs and Moch, "Pregnant, Single, and Far from Home."

40. Chan, "European and Asian Immigration into the United States"; Gabaccia, "Women of the Mass Migrations"; Hoerder, "From Migrants to Ethnics."

41. For an overview, see Aristide Zolberg, "International Migration Policies in a Changing World System," in McNeill and Adams, *Human Migration: Patterns and Policies,* 241–86.

42. Bade, "German Emigration to the United States and Continental Immigration to Germany"; Herbert, *A History of Foreign Labor in Germany, 1880–1980,* chap. 1.

43. See, for example, Michael Marrus, *The Unwanted: European Refugees in the Twentieth Century* (Oxford: Oxford University Press, 1985).

44. The Chinese Exclusion Act was enacted in 1882; the Gentlemen's Agreement was signed in 1907; for the role of the state, particularly in Asian migrations, see Chan, "European and Asian Immigration into the United States"; Ronald Takaki, *Strangers from a Different Shore: A History of Asian Americans* (Boston: Little, Brown and Co., 1989). Likewise, the Chinese government forbade contract labor to Brazil after seeing the virtual slavery to which its people were subjected elsewhere in Latin America; see Mörner and Sims, *Adventurers and Proletarians,* 26–29.

45. Mörner and Sims, *Adventurers and Proletarians,* 29, 41–42, 89–91.

46. These were originally published as Samuel Baily, "The Adjustment of Italian Immigrants in Buenos Aires and New York, 1870–1914," *American Historical Review* 88 (1983): 281–305; James Jackson, Jr., and Leslie Page Moch, "Migration and the Social History of Modern Europe," *Historical Methods* 22 (1989): 27–36; Ewa Morawska, "Labor Migrations of Poles in the Atlantic World Economy, 1880–1914," *Comparative Studies in Society and History* 31 (1989): 237–72.

47. For comments on this aspect of the treatment of immigration by historians, see Virginia Yans-McLaughlin, "Metaphors of Self in History: Subjectivity, Oral Narrative, and Immigration Studies," in *Immigration Reconsidered,* 254–90.

48. Ewa Morawska, *For Bread with Butter: The Lifeworlds of East Central Europeans in Johnstown, Pennsylvania, 1890–1940* (New York: Cambridge University Press, 1985), and "The Sociology and Historiography of Migration," in Yans-McLaughlin, *Immigration Reconsidered,* 187–238.

49. As mentioned (note 35), Rosa's story is related in Hoerder, "From Migrants to Ethnics."

PART I

Migration Systems: Directions and Issues

Migration in the Atlantic Economies: Regional European Origins and Worldwide Expansion

DIRK HOERDER

The most important early formulation of the connections between the economies of the two sides of the Atlantic is Brinley Thomas's seminal work, to which Frank Thistlethwaite later added his own call for a new approach to migration research.[1] Several international conferences on migration (Wuppertal 1974, Paris 1975) and a session at the Eighth International Economic History Congress in Budapest in 1982 pursued the theme.[2] Contrary to some approaches to worldwide migrations, we argue that tribal, pastoral, and labor migrations cannot simply be added to show a world population in motion but that groups of connected migrations have to be integrated systematically into smaller or larger networks or "migration systems." The approach has to be more dynamic and sophisticated than Ravenstein's "laws" of migration, still used as a point of reference by some authors.[3] Migration systems are empirically observable interconnected migrations that continue over time. The earlier paradigm of the singularity of the transatlantic migration to the United States lacked analytical rigor[4]—for ideological reasons and because of the dream-like image of "America" shared by many migrants.[5]

The concept of migration in the Atlantic economies presented a new paradigm in migration research, but it was limited to the core of what by the nineteenth century had become a world system.[6] Therefore, in this comprehensive overview we will try to restate concisely the origins of the European migratory system in the period before industrialization, 1200–1800, well aware that other unrelated or only thinly related migratory systems existed in other parts of the world. This is the period of rural and protoindustrial migrations supplemented by "outwork," that is, home production distributed over areas of labor surplus. Second, this essay deals with the migration to rapidly developing areas within Europe before industrialization, and third, it considers colonial migrations into areas outside Europe. The fourth phase is the nineteenth-century migration in the (North) Atlantic economies, which is paralleled by moves into the more distant parts of the imperialist world system. These phases overlap in time. From the reorganization of the European political map in 1918 and the emergence of the United States as main creditor nation, through the depression decade after 1929, to the emergence of independent states in the former colonial areas in the 1950s, a phase of restructuring of migrations followed. Since the 1950s, new systems of capital and labor movements have established themselves.

In this study, the emphasis will be on economic developments and migratory flows. The changes in socioeconomic relations from feudal to capitalist, from rural to urban, and from artisanal to proletarian will be taken for granted. Aspects of natural demography are treated elsewhere in this volume as are the experiences of migrants in their cultures of origin, during their voyages, and in their processes of acculturation.[7] What is still lacking is an approach that sees through the eyes of the actual women and men who migrated, an approach from the bottom up, relying on letters, autobiographies, and other life writings.[8]

The Background: Europe from the Thirteenth to the Sixteenth Centuries

From about 1300 to 1648, power relations among European states changed profoundly, and the basis for new forms of production was laid.[9] In the Southeast, the Ottoman empire began its expansion, dislodging the Venetians from predominance in the eastern Mediterranean, and thereby inducing the westward exploration that soon turned into expansion. The European-Asian connections mediated by Arab merchants and navigators declined, and the coast-bound African and transatlantic American connections began to be established. The older interregional trading regimes, apart from dynastic territorial units, declined by the end of the sixteenth century or earlier; these were the Italian seaborne empires of the merchant cities Genoa and Venice, the family trading networks of the Medici in Florence and of the Fugger and Welser families in Augsburg, and the merchant cities' "Hanse" league in northern and north-central Europe.

Accumulated mercantile capital permitted an increase in manufactory production. The Medici, for example, employed about ten thousand persons in textiles around 1400. The resulting urban social stratification led to tensions and to artisanal revolts in Flanders (from 1280), in Paris, in Italian cities—particularly Florence—and in Prague (1419–36). At the same time, the increasing urban demand for provisions for the growing populations and primary materials for production led to changes in agriculture in western and southern Europe, which in turn resulted in numerous peasant uprisings and wars.

By 1500, the center of economic activity shifted from the Baltic area in the North (the cities of the Hanse) and the Mediterranean basin in the South (the Italian cities) to the "New West," the Atlantic shores. From there, overseas connections were established in 1492 to West India (America) and in 1498 to East India. Geographical and astronomical discoveries and concepts using a new view of the world preceded and accompanied the move outward from Europe, Asia, and North Africa. Large-scale economic organizations emerged: new administrative councils (*casas*) under the crowns as well as private or chartered merchant (adventurers') companies that traded with or exploited the new colonial territories rather than conduct business across Europe as the earlier trade networks had done. Production became increasingly market oriented.

Two large-scale migrations—of Germans and of Jews—deserve mention since they influenced later migrations up to the present. The German migrations eastward, first as movements of conquest or colonization, and then upon invitation by rulers in need of a skilled and commercially active population, established a central-European, German-language culture. This facilitated later artisanal and skilled worker migrations, furthered the commerce that linked eastern European markets to the West, and finally, in the nineteenth century, led to a secondary migration of some of these Baltic, Russian, and other Germans across the Atlantic.[10] Second, economic competition, the devastating plague epidemics, and consequent anti-Jewish pogroms as well as the expulsion of the Jews from the Iberian peninsula and elsewhere resulted in the formation of eastern European Jewish settlements. They, too, established a separate Eastern culture, that of the *shtetl*. Persecution from the 1880s led to secondary migrations.[11] Both groups, for different reasons, remained separate culturally, linguistically, economically, and socially from the surrounding population.

A third migration was that of the nobles who replaced the local feudal lords.[12] As a result, social stratification became also ethnic stratification. Centuries later, in an age of emerging national consciousness, tensions, out-migrations, and expulsions resulted from these earlier in-migrations.

In Europe, three regions can be discerned whose socioeconomic structures and political administrations produced different patterns of migration. In western, northern and southwestern Europe the influence of mercantile capital and more or less centralized courts and bureaucracies produced specific forms of migration.[13] In southeastern Europe, the Ottoman conquest, with its distinctive economic development, resulted in different population movements and patterns of mixed ethnic living.[14] In northeastern and east-central Europe, the emergence of the large estates and the sinking of peasants into serfdom around 1500 retarded migrations. Connections between the three sections of Europe and their migration systems grew only slowly.

Superimposed on these three regions and types of migratory potential were demographic, ideological-religious, and political-economic developments. The population decline from about 73.5 million in 1340 to 45 million or less in 1400 due to the plagues slowed down any expansionist impulses. Only in the early sixteenth century did the total population of Europe again reach and then surpass the level of the early fourteenth century.[15]

Rural and Protoindustrial Migrations in Europe, 1650–1800

From 1650 to the period of the French Revolution and the political reorganization of Europe, migration in the most developed section of Europe consisted of many different types. The Thirty Years' War (1618–48) reduced the population of the German territories from about 20 to 7 million (or from 15 to 10 million, according to other estimates). Internal migration, international in-migration, and recruitment of religious refugees occurred in the subsequent decades. Involuntary rural mobility was necessitated by the enclosure movement in Great Britain (as well as the colonization of Ireland) and the demise of serf or free tenant systems in Spain and Italy and in German, Polish, and Russian areas east of the Elbe River. This involved the replacement of peasant holdings (subject to rents and dues) by direct management of manorial lands and a consequent impoverishment of the rural populations (sixteenth and seventeenth centuries).

It was a reaction to religious intolerance and mercantilist policies that first combined to mobilize people. Religious refugees (500,000 Huguenots from France, 60,000 Protestant Dutch from the Spanish provinces, 32,000 Protestant Salzburgers, 150,000 Bohemian dissenters, and thousands of Pietists, Puritans, and Quakers) turned into economic migrants almost at the time of their crossing of the borders after the host states offered subsidies for settling down and privileges for practicing trades. These usually highly skilled migrants were sought-after producers and revenue payers. The situation was more complex for the Jews expelled from the Iberian peninsula (160,000 in 1492) and other parts of Europe. Early privileges granted them in Poland were later withdrawn.

Second, the retreat of the Ottomans under Hapsburg attacks caused resettlement and in-migration in southeastern Europe. The mixed patterns of settlement and the interaction of peasant, church, mercantile, and administrative languages brought about a rudimentary multilingualism that was reflected, in the late nineteenth century, in the immigrant quarters to which people from the Hapsburg empire migrated.

Third, the opening of the plains of southern Russia for settlement induced Russian nobles to move there with their serfs, and soon people of different ethnicity began to arrive. From 1763 to the 1820s, German peasant families came, forming rural colonies and developing a Russian-German (in the Hapsburg areas, a Danubian-German) culture that was socially different as well as geographically distant from the urban central-European German-language culture of the earlier migrations, and from the postunification German national culture after 1871.

Fourth, a Baltic migration system existed, from the 1650s to the 1720s, during Sweden's hegemonial outreach. It included Finnish peasants, German administrators, miners from several areas, French investors with their craftsmen, Scottish merchants, and mercenaries from all over Europe.

In addition to these visible migration flows, five different types of everyday migration involved larger numbers and covered much of Europe. First of all, a part of the rural population either had to leave or wanted to leave subsistence agriculture and migrate from naturally unproductive to naturally productive regions. Seasonal movements followed the harvest cycles, or, in times of population expansion, the direction reversed; hillsides were cultivated, and backwoods areas became populated. Migrants in this category remained within rural society. Estimates for France assume that about one-fifth of the population migrated, while estimates for England reach beyond the 50 percent mark.[16]

Second, a constant flow of male laborers and female domestics from rural areas to provincial and central towns can be observed.[17] Frankfurt on the Main grew from 11,500 inhabitants in 1500 to 20,000 in 1600; then it declined by more than 3,000 until 1650, increasing again until it reached 27,500 by 1700. In these two centuries, natural increase contributed to population growth only during two decades. In 1600, several thousand migrating journeymen artisans, 3,000 middle-class Dutch Protestant in-migrants, and 2,500 Jews accounted for more than 40 percent of the inhabitants ("Stadtluft macht frei").[18] Third, a circulation of urban populations between towns took place: a study of seventeenth-century Nördlingen (Germany) found between 10 and 20 percent of the population to be in-migrants, most of these men and women belonging to the middle classes. This urban circulation often was a "transfer of young people between distant cities."[19]

A fourth type of migration involved the movement into areas of planned establishment or the expansion of mines and urban centers. Cosimo I Medici granted duty-free port facilities to Livorno in 1565, and freedom of settlement and religion in 1593. Jews and Moriscos came singly or with their families as did entrepreneurs and artisans. In 1603 Gothenburg was founded. Although it was originally intended as a Dutch colony, other in-migrants, including Swedes, soon settled there. Its Council consisted of four Swedes, three Netherlanders, three Germans, and two Scots. Further east, the modernizing policies of Czar Peter and the founding of Petersburg in 1703 led to an in-migration of Finnish workers and craftsmen, German artisans and burghers, and many others, and the expanding town became a prosperous center for shipbuilding, production, and commerce. Similarly, rapidly expanding mining areas received skilled labor (and the initial capital) from afar. For example, the mines in Zips, Slovakia, had been worked by miners from Saxony from the end of the twelfth century, and throughout the thirteenth century there were Bavarian miners and men from the metalworking trades.

The fifth form of migration—of recently married women into patrilocal households—has received the least attention of all. Though not a migration in the strict sense of the term if the movement remained within the parish or village borders, with the crossing of these boundaries it became part of the general micromobility in Europe.

The urban migrations were complex. A portion of the migrants included members of the middle classes who sought better chances outside the places where they lived. Often their movements were intended to establish commercial links; in an age of slow communications and limited legal means to remedy the breaking of contracts, for example, the personal connections between firms and their partners in other towns were of supreme importance. But the vast majority of migrants belonged to the poorer levels of society. These were not only journeymen artisans but day laborers and persons who provided menial help of any sort. Migration for these people was more than just for economic improvement—it was for their basic subsistence. Amsterdam grew from 35,000 inhabitants in 1557 to more than 100,000 in 1622, Paris from 200,000 (1590) to 412,000 (1637).[20] The migration of women into the towns as domestics and, in some highly developed manufacturing areas, as workers in (cloth) production was also part of the rural-urban population movement.[21] The frequency of migration for women was low during the child-rearing period of their lives. Almost totally neglected as a field of study is the influence of female migrants on the nurturing patterns, eating habits, and other aspects of child-rearing.

The research situation is better for the study of the migrations of journeymen artisans under guild regulations. These migrants later influenced the nineteenth-century intra-European migration patterns of skilled workers. Journeymen artisans traveled in the Northeast via Prague and Warsaw to Petersburg, in the Southeast to Budapest, and further on to Constantinople and even into Egypt. In the West they established separate quarters in Paris and London. While the guild system had intended this mobility to facilitate the transfer of skills between distant areas and the improvement of each migrant's capabilities, it also became a means to spread the political and social consciousness of journeymen. Because they radiated from German-language areas, German became the lingua franca among artisans and later among migrating skilled workers in central and eastern Europe. By the end of the eighteenth century, the system had degenerated into a means for established master artisans to keep journeymen on the move, and this movement became a precursor of the later labor migrations.[22]

Parallel to the migrations of female domestics, male artisans, and the middle class in general, a continuous small migration of persons with special expertise brought drainage experts from the Netherlands, dairy experts from Switzerland, and cabinetmakers from Germany to wherever this expertise was in demand.[23] In this context, it deserves mentioning that much of the exploration of the Atlantic was accomplished by migrant experts from Italy—navigators and captains who, like Columbus, found no profitable employment in Italy's declining economy.[24]

Migration in modern Europe was thus inter-rural, rural-urban, and inter-urban or towards (small) centers of intense (but often short-term) investment and expansion. It involved particularly female domestics, male artisans, and skilled experts who had had the experience of paid work and, in their home regions, of the emergence of new systems of production. During protoindustrialization, the alternative to migration was to move work to surplus labor forces, to cottage production. This reduced the original need for capital accumulation since the cottagers provided their own means of production in the form of looms, potter's wheels, or other special tools. Because of possibilities for family formation independent of the scarce resources of cultivable land and independent of the transfer of land ownership from parents to children, marriages came earlier and cottage production was often followed by population increase. When further mechanization led to centralized production, surplus cottage workers provided a large potential for migration.[25]

Two regional migration systems will exemplify the complex flows. The Baltic system, which flourished from the 1650s to the 1720s, when Sweden had reached the zenith of its power, involved most of the coast of the Baltic Sea. The crown instituted an efficient central administration, which was able to raise and allocate large sums of money; it integrated the nobility into this administration and then began to explore the available natural resources, particularly iron and copper. Crown and nobility embarked on a construction program for castles and residences, and soon the wealthy town burghers followed suit. To fill the demand for labor, master builders and journeyman masons, stonecutters, and sculptors came from all over Europe, and particularly from the German-speaking areas. Dutch, Walloon, Jewish, French, and Scottish migrants came mainly with capital or special skills, Baltic nobles joined the Swedish aristocracy, and Finnish peasant migrants settled in central and northern Sweden or worked in the iron industry. Demand for mine labor increased with ore exports. German miners, who had been migrating to Sweden since the Middle Ages, now came in increasing numbers. The military system, following the Dutch model, had recruited twenty-five thousand mercenaries by 1699. When foreign architects and entrepreneurs started new enterprises or erected buildings, they often hired masters and journeymen from their own place of origin, for example French potters for a faience manufactory. By the 1750s, internal labor migration networks near coastal and lumbering areas had also developed. Stockholm exerted a pull on skilled and unskilled workers from Finland (ruled by Sweden until 1809).[26]

In Great Britain, English rural socioeconomic relations underwent substantial changes. Long-term leases (for a period of three generations or "lives") were reduced to seven-years, and enclosure by farmer-entrepreneurs pushed masses of rural people off the land. The population of London increased from 50,000 in the first half of the sixteenth century to 200,000 at the beginning of the seventeenth and to 600,000 by the end of that century. "In the early eighteenth century . . . England was moving steadily towards a society of great landowners, large farmers and a proletarianized labour force."[27] Cloth production began to be specialized and become concentrated by 1700. The iron industry was encouraged because of its importance to the navy. Population increase accelerated during the second half of the eighteenth century: from 5.5 million in 1700, the population grew to almost 6 million in 1751, to more than 7 million in 1771, and to 8 million by 1791. Given its early commercialization and the development of its industrial centers, its insular position, and its imperial orientation, England did not connect with other European migration systems except for an influx of artisans and skilled workers from the continent into London and an in-migration of Dutch and Protestant refugees. Its regionally differentiated internal migrations were supplemented by the migration of people from its colony Ireland into the rural and urban economies. Out-migration went overseas and included the marginal Celtic areas of Scotland, Wales, and Cornwall.

Europe's main empires still followed different patterns of migration. In the Northeast, Ivan IV granted a patent in 1558 to the Stroganoff merchant family to colonize Siberia. Only a quarter-century had passed since Spain had conquered Central and South America. Half a century was to go by before the British moved westward and settled permanently in North America, and then eastward to develop a colonial base in India (1612-13), and before the Dutch founded their East India Company. In Siberia, as in the Ukraine, Cossacks, that is, escaped serfs from Great and Little Russia, founded independent quasi-military settlements and were recognized by the Czar in return for military service. They became sable hunters and were followed by traders, merchants, and finally by settlers.[28] As in the Americas, native people were subjugated. Siberia was made a penal colony for criminals, political opponents, and, from 1760, for rebellious serfs. It became integrated into the world economy as a result of the fur trade, as was North America by this time.

In the Southeast, until the Peace of Karlovac (1699), Ottoman domination of the Balkan region had brought about ethnically mixed settlement patterns. Urban populations often differed from those of the surrounding countryside, the town patriciate from the urban journeymen, and one village from the next. The *millet* system permitted ethnic and religious coexistence. Ethnic groups kept their own religions, and church heads became the spokesmen in negotiations with the Islamic authorities. Within towns, ethnic segregation was high, and ethnicity determined faith and profession. By 1800, these ethnically diverse areas remained untouched by industrialization, and the penetration of mercantile capital was only at a rudimentary stage.

Up to about 1800, the largest part of the continental international migration came from the economically and politically weak German-speaking areas that continuously exported experts, artisans, and settlers and whose princes sold soldiers by the regiment to foreign armies. Its economic development was delayed because of its fragmented political structures. Division of inherited land among all sons in central and southern Germany forced smallholders to leave. While the southeastern routes, now established for a century and a half, were less frequented from the early 1800s, the first migrants to America ventured west after the 1680s, about ninety thousand setting out between 1680 and 1790.

With the coming of the American and French revolutions and the subsequent wars to maintain North America in its colonial status, liberate other European peoples from their hereditary monarchs and aristocracies, and expand the influence of France under Napoleon, migration seems to have come almost to a standstill, though detailed studies of the period are lacking. But the mobilization of millions of soldiers probably had an effect on further migrations.

Before turning to the new patterns of migration in the Atlantic world after 1815, we must examine the colonial migrations from the seaborne empires based along the Atlantic coast.

Expansion I: The Seaborne Empires and Colonial Migrations Overseas, 1400–1800

European expansion should be analyzed in terms not only of migration flows but also of capital flows. Native populations were displaced or exterminated when their existence was detrimental to the interests of the invaders (or their biological resistance capabilities were not adapted to European diseases). Where existing local production was of commercial interest, indigenous economic systems were partially linked to Europe (e.g., the production of spices and silk). Where Europeans planned to introduce new crops or production methods, native labor was mobilized. Throughout the world, migration systems existed and either these were tapped or new ones were established by force, economic pressure, and administrative fiat. Such new systems of involuntary migration could be extended over large distances by the transport of laborers from subjugated populations into distant parts of the respective colonial empires. In the case of lifetime slavery, large sections of local populations were transported into areas where labor demand could not be met by local labor forces or voluntary in-migrants. Labor migration, whether voluntary, under administrative regulation, or by enslavement, involved larger numbers of people than the primary European out-migration into the colonial possessions before the nineteenth century.[29]

When expansion commenced from the Iberian peninsula, the Arab settlements and trade routes that linked Venice and India and dominated the African coast had to be conquered.[30] One example will show the limitations on this expansion. After 1500, Southeast Asian spices could be sold in Lisbon for one-fifth the price demanded in Arab-supplied Venice. However, since Portugal had no distribution network, the profitable commerce in these spices fell to urban centers in the North, especially to Antwerp. As for the numbers of people involved and the volume of trade, in 1504 only twelve ships left Portugal for the east.[31]

The way west was more crowded. On his second trip, Columbus took along about 1,500 workmen and artisans. Within half a century, tens of thousands of slaves had been transported from Africa to the New World. Small bands of European soldiers destroyed the existing high cultures of Central and South America, and imported European diseases destroyed much of the population. The survivors were subjugated and were used as auxiliary troops and mine and plantation labor. French corsairs, English sea dogs and merchant adventurers, and Dutch privateers operated throughout the Caribbean region.[32] They were later given the official support of their respective governments. The subsequent rise of the urban Netherlands and the centralization of France and Great Britain brought about a shift of power to the northwestern Atlantic.[33]

The growth of the European population from about 70 to 90 million (or 80 to 105, according to other estimates) between 1500 and 1600 necessitated the cultivation of less fertile lands. Populations expanded up mountain slopes, into wet marshes, and along stony hillsides. The combination of price increases and inflationary trends led to the "price revolution"—only the cost of labor remained virtually unchanged. Thus, in the course of the seventeenth century, a growing population was facing a decreasing real income.[34] Socioeconomic and demographic conditions combined to provide the base from which a different kind of expansion began, the movement of settler populations into the conquered territories. By 1600, a network of sea lanes as well as new Spanish and Portuguese colonies had been developed that provided the thoroughfares and prototypes for new worldwide migrations.

This expansion will be analyzed according to the patterns of migration, rather than according to the nature of European power or of the destination involved. Of course, the patterns are related to physical and climatic as well as social and political structures in both the areas of origin and of arrival.

The establishment of a trading network by the Portuguese along the coasts of Africa and eastern India involved the migration of sailors, soldiers, and merchants in small numbers. Colonial administrators joined them later. The merchants were often employees of the large companies that were chartered by the government, rather than independent entrepreneurs, and they may thus be regarded as precursors of the later governmental administrators. Since this migration was almost exclusively male and since Portuguese society harbored few racial biases, Creole populations emerged along the Portuguese trading routes. This was the first new pattern of migration to develop. The Dutch, on their course to Africa and Southeast Asia, followed the pattern set by the Portuguese, but strongly discouraged any ties between Dutch administrators and native populations, except, of course for the purely economic nexus. In Southeast Asia, the English, too, had followed this pattern since the seventeenth century. Their main base in India, Madras, acquired in 1639, counted about 375 white persons, including a garrison of 200 white men, as opposed to 10,000 Indian residents.[35] This constituted the *trading post expansion and migration* pattern.

European commerce and the emerging migratory networks came into contact with indigenous local and regional migration systems as well as with stable populations. These links and the increasing demand for the products of India, Ceylon, Cochinchina, China, and the islands of Southeast Asia brought about changes in labor force requirements. In these "connected territories," economic incentives, force, or the mediation of local rulers created new migration systems or increased the volume of existing ones. In Goa, cotton plantations and cloth manufactories were established; in Ceylon, cinnamon production increased. In Java, the Dutch induced local rulers to develop coffee plantations, on which native labor had to work for defined periods of time without recompense. In China, export-oriented industries developed during the sixteenth century when the Portuguese and Spanish opened their trading stations: sugar, textiles—especially silk—porcelain, metal wares, and teas.[36] This *plantation expansion and migration* pattern was usual for the large-scale production of food, stimulants, or crops for industrial use. A variant of this pattern was the control and development of the *extractive sector* (including the mining and guano industries).

Finally, the populating of relatively empty (from the European point of view) or newly emptied areas by farmers constitutes the *settlement expansion and migration* pattern. These three types were supplemented, fourthly, by the semi- or involuntary *labor migration* of indentured servants or convicts. The European in-migrants mobilized local labor, labor from the surrounding areas or from other, densely populated, distant colonies for plantation work, extractive labor, or hired farm labor. According to the process of mobilization, we distinguish between (a) slave transport, (b) the deportation of convicts, (c) the emigration of contract, *mita,* bound laborers, and (d) free migration. The latter was undertaken by persons with no savings (laborers), or with limited means (settlers, small businessmen), or with large amounts of capital (merchants, plantation owners). Later, Indian, Chinese, and other Asian migrants joined the limited-means migration streams.[37]

The colonizers of the Caribbean, Central America, and South America conquered vast territories rather than simply establishing coastal trading posts.[38] Since the existing cultures were militarily helpless against European firepower, few soldiers had to be sent to deal with them. Once these areas were secured (the last, Peru, by 1533), Spanish, Portuguese, English, Dutch, and French migrants arrived—surplus sons of the lower nobility, fortune seekers, entrepreneurs, artisans, mining experts, and overseers for the latifundia. While the top administrative posts were reserved for Spanish-born officials, a colonial landed nobility and Creole population developed, urbanization began, and cities quickly grew.

The newcomers relied on native migratory labor or on imported African slave labor. In the Spanish colonies the *mita* system of forced temporary labor migration to mining areas led to involuntary population concentrations (extractive colonies).[39] The silver city of Potosi in Peru, founded in 1546 at an altitude of 4,000 meters, became the second largest city in the Atlantic world after London by 1600.[40] The *encomienda* system, by which grants of land, along with its inhabitants, were awarded to the conquistadors, tied the native population to the Spanish or Creole agrarian upper class without reducing them to slavery. This system was later replaced by the *repartimiento* of able-bodied males from the native villages among the Spanish landholders. Beginning in 1510, African slaves were imported to the Americas. The basic pattern was characterized by migration from Spain, the development of a Creole population, and the involuntary labor of the surviving native population.[41]

In the areas of South America ruled by Portugal and in the West Indies, economic and migratory development was different. Local population density was low and much of the indigenous population had been annihilated. The Portuguese succeeded in transferring Mediterranean crops to the West Indies and Brazil. Sugarcane plantations emerged, and to meet the demand for labor, slaves were transferred to the New World via the Portuguese trading posts along the African coast. Within half a century after colonization, at least one hundred thousand slaves had been imported to the Caribbean and South America. This type of colonization thus rested on the immigration of a limited number of Europeans, the large-scale, forced migration of Africans, and the development of Creole populations.[42]

Further to the north, the British colonists from the Carolinas to Virginia followed a similar pattern, with tobacco, rice, and indigo as the staple plantation crops. Because of strict racial separation, no Creole population developed. The offspring of white fathers and slave mothers remained slaves. The white, American-born population considered itself "English," but was treated by the imperial center as a subservient colonial people in a way that was similar to the Iberian treatment of its own colonial offspring.

Patterns changed from about 1600 with the emergence of colonies of settlers in British and French North America. From the Chesapeake Bay region to Maine, British migrants developed farming colonies. In the St. Lawrence valley, about ten thousand French settlers attempted in 1690 to replicate the old-world social system: *seigneurs* ruled over dependent *habitants*. The pattern was also adopted by the Dutch in South Africa after 1652, and by the British in Australia (New South Wales) after 1788, originally with transported criminals.[43] Settlement migration and the emergence of colonial Creole populations shaped the economies and communities on the North American side of the Atlantic.

From 1607 to 1775, English settlers and plantation owners as well as a laboring population of indentured servants and redemptioners—several hundred thousand migrants in all—colonized North America from Maine to Georgia, and fur traders moved in from the North through the Hudson Bay after 1670, thus tying Native American economies and social systems to European demand. The English, fighting off the weak colonization schemes of the Swedes and Dutch/Walloons, admitted to the areas under English control about 90,000 German migrants (starting in 1683, in larger numbers after 1714), 25,000 Scots, and 250,000 Scotch-Irish (from 1689, in larger numbers after 1710), as well as Welsh (from 1682), French Huguenots (from 1685), and a few others. By 1790, the population amounted to 3.9 million,[44] including 60,000 free Negroes and 700,000 slaves. The southern plantation colonies and the northern farming colonies became, through their commercial activities, part of the imperial trading patterns, tied to the core by the Navigation Laws and political checks. North of Maine, the French population of about 80,000 had, by 1763, developed a fur-trading system and explored the continent along its inland waterways.[45]

Thus, by the 1760s, much of the world had come under European dominance, and four different regional patterns of European overseas migration and procurement of labor had developed: (1) the usually temporary migration of sailors, soldiers, merchants, and administrators, who mobilized the labor of native populations through local rulers, thus intensifying existing systems or creating new migratory systems in the areas of arrival (Africa, India, Southeast Asia); (2) the migration of conquistadors, merchants, and landowners, with some artisans and other lower-class groups, who established control over and mobilized large native populations as the local labor force (Central America and western South America); (3) the migration of the same groups, but who relied on enslaved African workers (Brazil, the Caribbean, and, in a socioracial variant, the southern British North American colonies); and (4) the migration of settlers and indentured servants (French and British northern North American colonies).

Toward the end of the eighteenth century and at the beginning of the nineteenth, decisive political changes and rearranged power relationships influenced migration, while demographic changes vastly increased its volume.[46] The outcome of the continental European wars after 1792 gave Britain, the dominant maritime power, occasion to take over the colonies of declining empires. In India, the British parliament changed the private East India Company into a governmental administrative body. In some areas, the unsettled political situation in Europe permitted colonial peoples to reach for independence. Following the British North American colonies, the African population in Haiti did so in 1804, forming the second independent republic in the Western Hemisphere. The Spanish and Portuguese possessions in Central and South America gained their political independence by 1824. But the entire American hemisphere remained connected to the European core by cultural and economic ties.

Forced migration also changed. In 1807, the slave trade was abolished in the British empire, and in 1808 legal importation to the United States ended. By 1870 Britain had effectively brought about an end to the transatlantic slave trade of all other nations.[47] From 1550 to 1870, ten million Africans had been transported to the American colonies; three to ten million more died on the way to being sold.[48]

From the period of imperial reform after 1763 to the legal end of the slave trade and the reordering of Europe, migration slowed down. The complex eighteenth-century migration systems did not survive the age of democratic revolution. Economic changes within Europe as well as the increasingly integrated world economy and improvements in transportation systems brought forth new patterns of migration.

The Development of the Atlantic Core and Its Migration System, 1815–1914

The one hundred years from 1815 to 1914 is the classical period of migration in the Atlantic economies. Eastward the Russo-Siberian migration system developed. But at the beginning of the nineteenth century, seven regional migratory systems still ringed the western Mediterranean and the North Sea.

The Dutch core and the North Sea system functioned from 1600 to 1850. This most commercialized region of Europe consisted during this period of more than two hundred towns and provided Spain, its imperial center until the revolt in 1568 that resulted in independence in 1648, with seven times the income in tax revenues compared to the silver income it received from the Americas. By 1800, the region attracted an annual seasonal in-migration of some thirty thousand workers for grass mowing, haymaking, peat digging, ditch and canal construction, dike building and repair, brickmaking, and work in bleacheries. The migrants came from a pull area that stretched from Calais, via Cologne and Hannover, to Bremen. Brickmakers arrived in March, peat diggers in April, and mowers in June. Female domestics stayed for the whole year. The percentage of foreign-born among the total population increased from less than 2 percent in 1530 to more than 10 percent in 1620; then it remained stable at 6 percent from 1700 to 1780, after which a decline set in. From 1550 to 1800, a number of unskilled occupations in Amsterdam had a proportion of foreign-born ranging from 25 to almost 50 percent. Out-migration of skilled experts took place at the same time.[49]

Eastern England, Lincolnshire, and East Anglia, as well as London, attracted migrants from western Ireland and from Wales and Scotland. A third system, centered on Paris and the surrounding départements, involved about sixty thousand workers annually. Most of the migrants came from the Massif Central, and others from the Alps and the western part of France.[50] Like the Dutch cities and London, Paris also attracted skilled workers and artisans from the German-speaking regions of central Europe.[51]

In the western Mediterranean, Madrid and Castile drew migrants for harvesting and construction from Galicia, the northwestern corner of the kingdom. The fertile coastal areas between Catalonia and Provence attracted about thirty-five thousand migrants from the mountainous areas of the Pyrenees, the Massif Central, and the Alps. Marseille was the destination of a constant stream of in-migrants, many of them artisans. In northern Italy, agriculture in the Po Valley was short about fifty thousand workers annually, and the cities of Milan and Turin attracted additional men and women. Again, people came from the surrounding hilly areas. The pull of the cities, however, was not comparable to that of Paris or London in the North. Finally, the largest pull areas were the central Italian provinces of Tuscany and Lazio, with an annual in-migration of about one hundred thousand agricultural workers for the harvesting of grain and other crops. The pull of the cities, especially Rome, must also be recognized.[52]

Intercontinental migration resumed after the Congress of Vienna and was pushed further, during the hunger years, in the traditional emigration areas of southwestern Germany. This developed into the Atlantic migration system. Eastward, a separate migration system, the Russo-Siberian one, came into being. The dividing line between the systems extended from Lake Peipus, via Smolensk along the Dnieper, to Odessa. With the exception of the Jewish westward migration from the Pale of Settlement, migration was to urban centers, especially to Petersburg, Moscow, and to the Donets basin, the three areas of industrialization. Southward it was directed into the more fertile agricultural areas. Czech artisans moved into this Eastern system, and into the 1820s western and central European settlers were still destined for the areas from the Dniester to the Donets and in particular along the Volga. Large-scale settlement in the South and East began with the building of the Trans-Caspian Railroad (1883–86) and the Trans-Siberian Railroad (1892–1905). About ten million persons had gone east by World War I. The Russian population grew from 98 million in 1880 to 175 million in 1914.[53]

From 1800 to the 1880s, the population in the Ottoman empire remained relatively stable. Then the Balkan peoples joined the Atlantic migration system. East of that line, separate migration systems began, and only occasionally would particularly hard-pressed groups, for example the Armenians, enter the westward migration routes.

Throughout the nineteenth century, seasonal agrarian migrations continued. Movement into the cities increased and women continued to migrate—usually over short distances—into farmwork as servants, into towns and cities as domestics, and toward centers of textile production as factory workers. Garment and shoe production began to be centralized, compelling women to leave the complex work arrangements of the home and join the factory labor force.

A new stage of economic activity involved the large amount of construction work that was needed to establish infrastructures: canal digging, railroad building, river regulation. The navvies came from surrounding peasant populations or (in the case of the Italians and Poles) over long distances.[54] Often expertise had to be imported, too, for example English engineers and Dutch drainage experts. Railroad lines extended for a mere 332 kilometers in 1831, but by 1876 they reached a total length of more than 300,000 kilometers. The European ports which had accommodated sailing and steam vessels with a tonnage of 32,000 in 1831 were receiving 3.3 million tons in 1876.[55]

The economies of scale achieved by mass production not only led to a slow decrease in prices, but also to a new awareness concerning the time-consuming nature of home production. Women became dramatically aware of the futility of their labors when certain goods—cloth for example—could be bought cheaply at the village grocery. With the introduction of farm machinery and new crop varieties, men often lost their jobs just as home production was declining and when cash came into great demand as a medium of exchange. The resulting cash crisis forced not only families but whole populations to reorient their economic behavior in very basic ways. Cheap goods and machine production made special skills and earning capacities obsolete. The search for wages pushed populations into the regional and international labor markets. The consequent increase in cash incomes then led to increased demand, thus intensifying pressures on worldwide raw-material and finished-goods production systems. As a result, more human labor resources were drawn to centers of production.[56]

Local and regional migration became increasingly international. About fifty million Europeans left the continent between 1800 and 1914.[57] The vast majority turned to North America, partly in search of cultivable lands (settler migration) but mostly in search of wage work (labor migration), and even larger numbers moved within Europe.[58] Labor migrants included many small landowners, who migrated to industrial centers for a few years, planning to return home and invest their savings in more land. An already precarious existence in agriculture was extended by a temporary, voluntary proletarianization to avoid a permanent one. Artisans and skilled workers, threatened by mechanization, moved to a labor market where their skills were still in demand to avoid social descent into the class of unskilled workers. Those miners and workers who were just one or two generations removed from landowning peasant status hoped for a return to independent farming. Toward the end of the century, large migrations of unskilled workers from both rural and urban areas turned into a proletarian mass migration.

Within Europe, England, Germany, France, and Switzerland became the main labor-importing core. Great Britain and Germany exported labor (and settlers) to North America at the same time, while emigration from France and Switzerland was low. England drew workers mainly from its Irish colony, Switzerland from Italy, Germany from Poland and Italy, and France from most of its neighboring countries and Poland. Belgium and the westernmost industrializing sections of Austria, particularly the Vienna region, attracted considerable numbers of migrants but experienced heavy out-migration at the same time. The Scandinavian countries exported settlers and workers to North America and, in much more limited numbers, to Germany. The core attracted labor whenever demand exceeded supply.

The periphery consisted of the labor-exporting countries: Ireland, Italy, the eastern parts of Austria-Hungary, Poland and the Jewish Pale of Settlement, and the settler- and labor-exporting northern European countries. By the 1840s, only one-third of the migrants to North America were settlers, one-third were artisans and skilled workers, and the last third consisted of unskilled workers, agrarian laborers, and domestics. Southeastern and northeastern Europe began their mass export of an unskilled, mainly rural, working-age population in the 1880s, with some "pioneer" and political migrations dating back to 1848 and the 1850s.[59] By the end of the century, the northeastern and north-central United States (as far as Chicago) had joined western Europe to form the industrial core. Internal migrations in the United States and in-migration did populate the western parts of the continent, but the West did not serve as a safety valve.[60] Rather, urbanization attracted the surplus rural population.[61]

By the 1880s, competition for European workers became more acute internationally and led to a consideration of bringing Asian workers into the Atlantic core. Chinese and Japanese contract labor came to the western

United States and Canada, while the plans of Junkers to substitute "coolies" for their emigrating German and new Polish laborers in the eastern Elbe region came to nothing. European labor movements bitterly polemicized against Asian workers, and the United States and Canada also eventually closed their doors to them.[62]

"Connected" territories in Central and South America, South Africa, and Australia—many of which ultimately achieved their political independence—remained within the political and economic sphere of the core. They continued to import settlers and, more importantly, laborers. Italians from the Mezzogiorno moved to Argentina by the millions, while European emigration in general to Brazil increased. On the other hand, the transportation of persons who, by the standards of the times, were criminals came to an end. Much of Britain's fortification and trade establishments around the world had been built by them. After having served their time they usually remained in the area of destination as free persons. According to Shergold's findings for Australia, they did not differ substantially in social composition from voluntary migrants.[63] Migration into the connected territories provided a range of opportunities for migrants of little means that was broader than in the more capitalized North American extension of the European core.

Developments in Italy provide a good example of the impact of world markets and power relations on local populations and their migrations.[64] Imported grains from the United States and Australia wrought havoc in the relatively backward agriculture of Italy—as elsewhere in the world—during the 1880s. Faster and cheaper transportation brought other competition. India exported rice—competing with the profitable Italian Piedmont production, while China and Japan drove Italian silk from its customary markets. Other Mediterranean countries competed with Italy's trade in citrus fruits, dried figs, almonds, and oil. The agrarian surplus population, almost fourteen million in the four decades from 1876 to 1914, moved to the industrializing areas of western Europe, to industrial centers in North America, and to the agricultural and mining areas of Latin America. By 1900 the Americas received more than half the emigrants from Italy, with Brazil and Argentina being the favored destinations, with less than one-third of the America-bound migrants going to the United States. Those who could afford the passage to Latin America went there: prospects were better, language problems less difficult, and cultural adjustment easier. Those with little money went to the United States: tickets were cheaper, and industrial jobs with quick cash income and rail and road construction permitted seasonal employment, allowing a return home for the harvest. Others, for example skilled masons, annually followed the traditional routes to France and Germany. Later, some went to the new African colonies.[65]

During the last quarter of the nineteenth century, three-fifths of all migrants came from northern Italy. The economically backward Venetian region lost 13 percent of its population. Remittances from emigrants, if they were not used to support relatives, were largely deposited in banks. These remittances financed the take-off of industry in the Milan/Turin/Genoa triangle, which could not otherwise absorb its own agrarian surplus labor.

The migratory system by 1900 consisted of an Atlantic importing core, an eastern and southern European exporting periphery, a western North American importing periphery, and an appendix of South American connected economies and isolated pockets of investment or settlement elsewhere, for example in South Africa and Bombay. Capital flows and resulting labor demands annexed the colonial areas of the world to the Atlantic core. In the core, the war-induced interruption of migration after 1914, the changed power relationships after 1918, and particularly the demands of industry for cheap (and segregable) labor resulted in a restructuring of migration patterns after World War I.

Expansion II: The Imperialist World System

During the nineteenth century, European dominance over the rest of the world changed in significant ways. The replacement of hand manufacture by machine manufacture brought about the demand for huge supplies of raw materials. Since most of these were agricultural products, the tropical plantation system expanded rapidly all over the world, along with mining operations.[66] The trading-post system became obsolete and was replaced by colonial dominance over entire regions. Populations laboring in subsistence economies had to be forced into wage work. Tax collection became a means to force native populations to supply themselves with cash and thus to leave village economies for wage work. Debt bondage, forced labor, vagrancy laws, and duty-to-work codes were other means to this end.[67]

The quest for sources of supply for raw materials necessitated an increase in the size of military organizations and colonial administrations. Soldiers, especially in India, were recruited from native populations, transported elsewhere, and used under European officers against natives of different ethnic backgrounds. The recruitment of administrators, plantation managers, and factory overseers from among educated natives led to the emergence of mercantile and administrative elites who were often supplemented by small intelligentsias—and these were to become an important group in the reassertion of ethnic consciousness and national aspirations.

While the process of colonial expansion from 1500 to 1800 involved small numbers of migrants and small amounts of goods, the nineteenth century is conspicuous for the vast extent of worldwide operations and manpower needs.[68] Mining operations (silver, gold, and diamonds), the production of raw materials or industrial crops (cotton, rubber, and palm oil), and the large-scale growing of food crops (wheat, rice, and bananas) and of stimulants (sugar, coffee, tea, cocoa, and opium) demanded the long-distance migrations of professional and technical personnel and caused the emergence of regional labor migration systems to mining and plantation areas.[69]

To facilitate commercial exchange, huge construction operations were necessary. The building of the Isthmian railroad in Central America, the Uganda railroad, and the Suez and Panama canals repeated earlier European labor mobilizations for the construction of earthworks, but on an international scale. About twenty thousand conscripted Egyptian fellahin labored for four years on the Suez Canal, while European immigrant laborers dug the Panama Canal from 1904 to 1914.[70]

The large-scale production of stimulants had begun in the seventeenth century, or in some cases earlier.[71] The sugar plantations of the West Indies had relied on massive importations of slave labor, 1.34 million slaves in the seventeenth century and 6 million in the eighteenth.[72] Production underwent a decline when Napoleon closed the European continent to British imports, when the slaves in Haiti fought for their independence, and when slavery was abolished in British Jamaica. The spread of a substitute plant for sugarcane—the sugar beet—in Europe changed the requirements for a European labor force and induced further migrations there. For their plantations overseas, the British tapped two new sources of labor supply: indentured laborers from the East Indies were brought in to cultivate sugarcane in Mauritius, Trinidad, and Guyana, and Melanesian workers from the New Hebrides were imported to Queensland, Australia (from 1863), and to Fiji (from 1864). The Dutch, on the other hand, began to cultivate sugarcane on the islands of Indonesia in the 1830s, utilizing the local labor supply by forcing villagers to pay taxes in kind (sugar and coffee) and by allocating one-fifth of village lands to sugarcane. They invested in sugar-processing factories, continuing to draw their labor from the rice-growing village populations and imposing on the local peoples a European elite of land and factory managers.[73]

Coffee, introduced to Europe from Ethiopia through Ottoman mediation, was originally grown in Yemen. At the beginning of the eighteenth century, the Dutch brought coffee cultivation to Java; by 1825, one million coffee trees had been planted, and by 1850, three hundred million. The local economies had to meet the massive demand for labor. In Brazil, slave labor was used on coffee plantations, but the abolishment of slavery in 1888 prevented expansion. Subsistence and food farmers could not be expropriated or lured by wages into the plantation economy because this would have endangered food production. As elsewhere in the world, the importation of Chinese laborers was discussed. But an alternate reservoir of labor offered itself. Since the 1870s, southern Italian peasants had begun to migrate in large numbers, and between 1880 and 1890 a million and a half

European migrants came, most of them Italians. The basic worldwide pattern during the nineteenth century was the parallel existence of "plantations producing a cash product and subsistence-oriented 'labor reserves' " and migration between the two.[74]

By the second half of the nineteenth century, production of some basic foods was also centralized. Wheat was grown for world markets in four areas: (1) Migrants to the American Midwest and West and later to Canada cultivated crops on a large scale, supported during the harvest period by migrant laborers. Production was increased through the use of agricultural machinery, and exports brought about a decline in prices and an agricultural crisis throughout Europe in the 1880s. (2) In the large landed estates of the eastern Elbe, the Junkers drove out their tenants, setting off a new migratory flow to North America, and relied on cheaper Polish seasonal migrant laborers. The plains of southern Russia had been cultivated by in-migrating foreigners, especially Germans, and by a much larger number of internally migrating Russians, in the nineteenth century. Finally, Argentina joined the ranks of the large wheat-producers in the 1880s, filling its plains with European immigrant colonists and Italian seasonal harvest workers.[75]

Under British and French control, rice-producing areas expanded in Southeast Asia: internal migrants in Burma and rice mills in Rangoon prepared the crop for export. Burmese rice was used to feed East Indian indentured-labor migrants in other parts of the British empire. In the rice-producing areas around Bangkok in Thailand, canal construction linked the eastern with the northern plains. These areas were settled with Chinese and Thai migrants, with Muslim Malay and Laotian prisoners of war, and with freed urban slaves. The third area of production, Cochinchina, was under French domination from 1861. It produced largely for the Chinese market, with Chinese merchants acting as intermediaries.[76]

Industrial crops included rubber, palm oil, and cotton. Rubber was first collected in Brazil by migrant laborers and natives, and, in the Congo of Leopold II, by forced native labor. Subsequently, in the region between Singapore and Malacca, it was cultivated by the ubiquitous planters, who were then replaced by the managers of larger farms. The labor force here consisted of Tamil work gangs from southern India. The Dutch developed rubber plantations on Sumatra, working the growing areas with Javanese and Chinese laborers, where "local villages gave way to company towns."[77]

The industrialization of cloth production and the cultivation of raw materials, mostly cotton and wool, in Australia became the prototype for new factory and plantation systems elsewhere. In England, Manchester grew from 24,000 inhabitants in 1773 to 250,000 in 1851. Of these, more than two-thirds were in-migrants, about 130,000 coming from nearby countries and 40,000 from colonial Ireland. The factories there first received raw materials from cotton plantations in the West Indies (50 percent), Smyrna, and the Ottoman empire (25 percent). By 1860, 60 percent of the raw cotton came from the slave-labor areas of the U.S. South. The shift in production from the earlier coastal plantations to places farther inland led to another forced migration of slaves to Alabama, Mississippi, Louisiana, and Texas. This labor supply was increased by systematic slave breeding in the earlier coastal plantations. In the 1870s, Egypt, then part of the Ottoman empire, began to increase cotton production and to supply English factories. The main secondary supply and factory center was the area around Bombay. Coming under British rule in 1665, the town's ten thousand inhabitants increased to 180,000 around 1800, including voluntary and involuntary recruits from the neighboring provinces and skilled Zoroastrian migrants from Persia. Labor migration to the cotton mills came from within a circle with a radius of up to three hundred kilometers from the city, but the distance grew larger during the twentieth century. Finally, after 1890, cotton was also imported from plantations in Uganda, which had by then been added to the British possessions in Africa.[78]

The intrusion of Europeans and, by the 1860s, of Americans, whether through financial capital or military power, resulted in an increased demand for some forced labor but mainly for semivoluntary labor from surrounding areas. Long-distance migration by contract laborers supplemented migrations of short and medium range. The "initial movements toward capitalist industry" over short distances in Europe were followed by a "second flow [which] sent Europeans overseas" and African slaves mainly to the Americas. A third wave of migration "carried contract laborers of diverse origins to the expanding mines and plantations of the tropics."[79] After the abolition of the slave trade from Africa in 1807, India became the main source of supply for contract workers. The term "coolie" came to symbolize cheap labor among the capitalists and working-class organizations in the core. It translated as "bitter strength" in Chinese and meant "wages" in Tamil.[80] From Bihar and the South, one to two million Tamil workers were shipped off to other parts of the empire between 1830 and 1870. They worked in Mauritius, South Africa, the West Indies, and British Guyana, and were fed rice produced in Burma.[81] A second reservoir of labor was China. Workers contracted out through Portuguese Macao or Singapore into mining in South Africa and railroad construction in North America.[82] In 1906, the South African mines employed 18,000 Europeans, 94,000 Africans, and 51,000 Chinese. From a third area, the islands of the South Pacific, especially the New Hebrides, Melanesian contract workers were transported to plantations in Fiji and Queensland. In the 1890s "*contadini*" from southern Italy migrated in large numbers.

These migrations in turn set in motion secondary migrations, helping to fill vacated jobs or pushing people into less fertile areas. These and the penetration of capitalism influenced other relatively closed economic regions and migration systems like the Russo-Siberian, the Chinese, and the Japanese systems.[83]

Migration Flows in the Northern Hemisphere: The 1920s to the 1940s and since the 1950s

After the war-induced break in transatlantic migration, from 1914 to 1918, decisive changes occurred in the worldwide and especially Northern Hemisphere migration flows. While the economic ties between the Atlantic economies, except with Russia in Europe, remained intact, and while the center of economic power shifted from Britain to the United States, migration weakened to the point that transatlantic migration to and from North America became merely one of several movements. Racist feelings in the United States and increasing fear of a radicalization of the immigrant population resulted in the passage of the quota laws. In-migration, which had averaged one million annually from 1905 to 1914, was cut to an annual maximum of 357,000 in 1921 and further reduced to 164,500 in 1924. The worldwide depression, 1929 to 1939 reduced in-migration even further. In some years, more people left the United States than arrived in it. The transatlantic migration link was finally broken.[84]

Within the United States the demand for labor was satisfied by a large South-North migration of Black workers, beginning in the early years of the century and reaching massive levels during the manpower shortages of the war years. Furthermore, changes in job structure led to the increased recruitment of women for service and administrative jobs. As yet, Pacific in-migration, mainly of Filipinos, remained small, and migration from Mexico was not only discouraged but checked through deportation drives in the depression years. The planned change from European migrants to Black migrants as a labor reservoir prevented a radicalization of the labor force, permitted easy segregation of southern Blacks in the ghettos of northern cities, kept wages low, and depressed the intermarriage potential of foreign eastern or southern European white stock with Anglo-German, northern European white stock.[85]

Canada became the newest recipient of migrants on a large scale, taking some of the peoples who were prevented from entering the United States. Before 1900, annual averages of immigration to Canada had stayed below the 50,000 mark for most of the time. It reached almost 300,000 in 1900 and remained between 100,000 and 150,000 through the 1920s.[86]

Return migration to Europe increased after the end of World War I, especially to the new east-central, Baltic, and southeastern European states. Return migrants who had hoped for improved economic conditions after the yoke of the decaying German, Russian, Austro-Hungarian, and Ottoman empires had been broken were disappointed by what they found. During the depression years, return migration did remain high, however, since the support provided by family networks at home was often considered a better alternative to the chances for aid in the original receiving societies, especially the United States.[87]

Within Europe, the involuntary post–World War I population movements (ca. five million) were politically and ethnically induced. Though these were not labor migrations, the migrants did join the respective labor forces of the areas of arrival. A permanent source of labor had been one of the German war aims: control over eastern Europe would open a vast reservoir of what was considered cheap and docile labor.[88] Since the plans for German continental domination came to naught, and since the German economy remained slack after 1918, only very limited in-migration occurred up to the depression. About two-thirds of the approximately four hundred thousand Polish miners in the German Ruhr district moved on to French mines, hoping to meet less discrimination there. In Germany, the recruitment of foreign labor was ended for racist and nationalist reasons after the seizure of power by the Nazis in 1933, but was reinstituted shortly afterwards to increase industrial and military production. During World War II, a system of forced labor was instituted that was much worse than that of the previous world war.[89]

France continued to recruit Italian and Polish workers (about 1.1 million from 1919 to 1939). In the Scandinavian countries, out-migration ended and a balanced labor market emerged in the years before World War II. Limited in-migration (seventy to eighty thousand) took place in the industrializing Soviet Union, with some migrants pursuing the dream of going to an ideal workers' republic, comparable to the earlier expectations of migrants of an ideal "America."[90] The new socialist system, the ongoing eastward migration, and internal industrialization kept this part of Europe and its colonized Northeast Asian territories apart from migrations in the rest of the continent.

The end of World War II brought about another large-scale involuntary migration of refugees, expellees, and displaced persons (eighteen million). They, too, entered the labor markets of the arriving areas, some of them in the United States and Canada.

By the mid-1950s, after decades of stagnation, the North Atlantic migration system came to an end. Instead, two significant South-North migration systems developed from Mexico and Puerto Rico to the United States, and from the Mediterranean basin to the highly industrialized northern European countries. In Europe, about twelve million men, women, and children had moved north by 1973 (the net figure for resident aliens) when the economic downturn and restrictive governmental regulations stopped most of the movements except for the in-migration of dependent women and children. This cut-off was instituted for racist and labor-market reasons.[91] In the cases of France, the Netherlands, and Great Britain, the dissolution of their colonial empires temporarily led to in-migration.[92]

The migration patterns of the period from the late 1950s to the 1970s resembled those of the three decades before World War I in the sense that migrants from peripheral areas migrated in large numbers to the cores. The earlier colonial/imperialist migrations came to an end, and capital export and indigenous development induced internal migrations consequent upon urbanization and industrialization processes in sections of the "Third World." It is beyond the scope of this chapter to summarize the development of the resulting numerous migration systems in these parts of the world, but as labor migrations they remained independent of the core's dual South-North labor migration systems. They were connected to the core not only through capital flows but also through the temporary elite migrations of students, police and military officers, and economic and technical experts who arrived for training purposes, both professional and ideological.

In the 1970s, a Pacific migration system to North America began to take sizeable form, though its beginnings date back to the 1860s. Other new regional and hemispheric migration systems include an Asian system, with Japan as the dominant economic power, and the Middle East migration system centering on the oil-producing states. Whether new East-West movements will develop out of the former socialist countries and whether North African migrations to southern Europe will reach sizeable proportions remain open questions. It is apparent that hunger, international and civil wars, ecological deterioration, and population increase are compelling millions—hundreds of millions—of people in the Southern Hemisphere to move north.

Notes

This essay has benefited from comments by Elliott Barkan, John Bukowczyk, Walter Kamphoefner, Leslie Page Moch, Walter Nugent, my colleagues of the Labor Migration Project, and many others.

1. Brinley Thomas, *Migration and Economic Growth: A Study of Great Britain and the Atlantic Economy* (Cambridge, 1954); Ralph Davis, *The Rise of the Atlantic Economies* (London, 1973); Frank Thistlethwaite, "Migration from Europe Overseas in the Nineteenth and Twentieth Centuries," in *XIe Congrès International des Sciences Historiques, Stockholm: Rapports,* vol. 5 (Göteborg, 1960).

2. *Les migrations internationales de la fin du XVIIIe siècle à nos jours* (Paris, 1980); Charles Tilly, "Migration in Modern European History," in *Human Migration: Patterns and Policies,* ed. William H. McNeill and Ruth S. Adams (Bloomington, 1978), 48–72; Ira Glazier and Luigi de Rosa, eds., *Migration across Time and Nations: Population Mobility in Historical Context* (New York, 1986). See also the earlier and still invaluable compilation of Walter F. Willcox and Imre Ferenczi, *International Migrations,* 2 vols. (New York, 1929, 1931).

3. E. G. Ravenstein, "The Laws of Migration," *Journal of the Royal Statistical Society* 2, no. 48 (1885): 167–227, and no. 52 (1889): 241–301. See Nancy L. Green, "L'histoire comparative et le champ des études migratoires," *Annales: Economies, Sociétés, Civilisations* 6 (1990): 1335–50.

4. Relevant publications of the Labor Migration Project include Dirk Hoerder, ed., *Labor Migration in the Atlantic Economies: The European and North American Working Classes during the Period of Industrialization* (Westport, Conn., 1985). On interethnic cooperation in the receiving culture, see idem, ed., *"Struggle a Hard Battle": Essays on Working Class Immigrants* (De Kalb, Ill., 1986). On the press of labor migrants, see Dirk Hoerder and Christiane Harzig, eds., *The Press of Labor Migrants in Europe and North America, 1880s to 1930s* (Bremen, 1985); Dirk Hoerder, Inge Blank, and Horst Rössler, eds., *Roots of the Transplanted,* 2 vols. (New York, 1994).

5. Migrants did not go to the United States of America but to a specific labor market in a mental construct "America." See Dirk Hoerder, "German Immigrant Workers' Views of 'America' in the 1880s," in Marianne Debouzy, ed., *In the Shadow of the Statue of Liberty: Immigrants, Workers, and Citizens in the American Republic, 1880–1920* (Paris, 1988); Dirk Hoerder and Horst Rössler, eds. *Distant Magnets: Expectations and Realities in the Immigrant Experience* (New York, 1993).

6. Immanuel Wallerstein, *The Modern World-System,* 2 vols. (New York, 1974, 1980); Samuel Baily, "Comparative Migration History and the Use of Models: Italians in Buenos Aires and New York City, 1875–1925," and Peter R. Shergold and Stephen Nicholas, "The Convict as Migrant: An Australian Perspective" (papers given at the Conference "A Century of European Migrations 1830–1930 in Comparative Perspective," Immigration History Research Center, St. Paul, 6–9 November 1986); Rudolph J. Vecoli and Suzanne M. Sinke, eds., *A Century of European Migrations, 1830–1930* (Urbana, 1991); Walter Nugent, "Frontiers and Empires in the Late 19th Century," in *Religion, Ideology and Nationalism in Europe and America* (Jerusalem, 1986), 263–75; idem, "Atlantic Populations in the 1880s" (unpublished paper, 1986).

7. See essays by Walter Nugent and Dirk Hoerder below.

8. Publications of the letters include Walter D. Kamphoefner, Wolfgang Helbich, and Ulrike Sommer, eds., *News from the Land of Freedom: German Immigrants Write Home* (Ithaca, 1991; German original 1988); Salvatore J. LaGumina, ed., *The Immigrants Speak: The Italian Americans Tell Their Story* (New York, 1979). See also Donna R. Gabaccia, comp., *Immigrant Women in the United States: A Selectively Annotated Multidisciplinary Bibliography* (Westport, Conn., 1989), chap. 11, "Autobiography."

9. Even before 1300, the center of power in Europe had shifted from the German empire to France, while the population decline began only by 1348. The movement of the economic core from the Iberian peninsula to France, then to the Dutch provinces, and then to Great Britain lasted until 1700. By 1648, the end of the Thirty Years' War, geographical movements of people were no longer either hindered or forced by military action, and the depopulated areas had to be filled with settlers.

10. Walter Schlesinger, "Die geschichtliche Stellung der mittelalterlichen deutschen Ostbewegung," *Historische Zeitschrift* 183 (1957); Walter Kuhn, "Die deutsche Ostsiedlung vom Mittelalter bis zum 18. Jahrhundert," in Göttinger Arbeitskreis, ed., *Das östliche Deutschland* (1959).

11. Pogroms began during the first crusade (1096); the Church Councils of 1179 and 1215 decided upon exclusionary measures; England expelled the Jews in 1290; mass pogroms in Germany followed the Great Plague (1349); expulsion from France took place in 1306 and 1394; and finally, expulsion from Spain and Portugal occurred in 1449 and 1492–97. The eastward migration of Jews began during the crusades, and Polish rulers granted privileges from 1264 (autonomy and freedom of commerce) to further economic development. With the mass movement from the end of the fourteenth century, social conflicts with urban merchants and artisans developed, and separate living areas (ghettos) began to be forced on Jews. See Martin Gilbert, *Jewish History Atlas* (London, 1969), 29ff.

12. Two other movements seem to have had little subsequent impact: the crusades from 1096 to 1270 (the last crusade) and 1291 (the end of the last crusader state), and the

Arab expansion into Spain (the Reconquista, 1063–1492), as well as the expulsion of the Moriscos (250,000 from 1609 to 1614). See also Janet L. Abu-Lughod, *Before European Hegemony: The World System, A.D. 1250–1350* (Oxford, 1989).

13. Leslie Page Moch, *Moving Europeans: Migration in Western Europe since 1650* (Bloomington, 1992).

14. Kemal H. Karpat, *An Inquiry in the Social Foundations of Nationalism in the Ottoman State* (Princeton, N.J., 1973).

15. Carlo M. Cipolla, ed., *The Fontana Economic History of Europe,* 6 vols. (Glasgow, 1972), 1:25–70, 2:15–82. A summary of population growth and migration is given by Karl F. Helleiner, "The Population of Europe from the Black Death to the Eve of the Vital Revolution," in *The Cambridge Economic History of Europe,* vol. 4, *The Economy of Expanding Europe in the Sixteenth and Seventeenth Centuries,* ed. E. E. Rich and C. H. Wilson (Cambridge, 1967), 1–95.

16. These differences are partly due to different methods, lack of data for short-term migration, and varying time-spans (migration per year or migration during lifetime). See Pierre Goubert, *L'Ancien Régime,* 2 vols. (Paris, 1969), vol. 1; Abel Chatelain, *Les migrants temporaires en France de 1800 à 1914,* 2 vols. (Lille, 1976); Peter Clark, "Migration in England during the Late Seventeenth and Early Eighteenth Centuries," *Past and Present,* no. 83 (1979): 57–90. One large-scale migration of unskilled male peasant offspring out of agriculture was the movement into the European armies of more than half a million Swiss in the sixteenth and seventeenth centuries.

17. Paul M. Hohenberg and Lynn Hollen Lees, *The Making of Urban Europe 1000–1950* (Cambridge, Mass., 1985), chap. 3, esp. 90–98.

18. Friedrich Bothe, *Geschichte der Stadt Frankfurt am Main* (Frankfurt am Main, 1966), 359–84.

19. Christopher R. Friedrichs, *Urban Society in an Age of War: Nördlingen, 1580–1720* (Princeton, N.J., 1979).

20. Cipolla, *Economic History,* vol. 2 (chap. 1 by Roger Mols) and vol. 3 (chap. 1 by André Armengaud); Richard van Dülmen, *Entstehung des frühneuzeitlichen Europa 1550–1648* (Frankfurt am Main, 1982), 19–28.

21. Abel Chatelain, "Migrations et domesticité feminine urbaine en France, XVIIIe siècle–XXe siècle," *Revue d'histoire économique et sociale* 4 (1969): 506–28; H. Heulenbroek, "De Duitse dienstmeisjes," *Vrij Nederland,* 13 November 1982, Bijlage 28, 28–47.

22. Klaus J. Bade, "Altes Handwerk, Wanderzwang und Gute Policey: Gesellenwanderung zwischen Zunftökonomie und Gewerbereform," *Vierteljahrschrift für Sozial- und Wirtschaftsgeschichte* 69 (1982): 1–37; William H. Sewell, *Work and Revolution in France* (Cambridge, 1980); Cynthia M. Truant, "Solidarity and Symbolism among Journeymen Artisans: The Case of Compagnonnage," *Comparative Studies in Society and History* 21 (1979): 214–26.

23. These migrations are usually mentioned only in local histories. No overall studies have come to my attention. For one group, see Dolf Kaiser, *Fast ein Volk von Zuckerbäckern? Bündner Konditoren, Cafetiers und Hoteliers in europäischen Ländern bis zum ersten Weltkrieg* (Zürich, 1985).

24. For the African route to India, the Portuguese explorer Vasco da Gama relied on experts from another declining empire along the Mediterranean, the famous Arab navigator Ahmid ibu-Majid.

25. Van Dülmen, *Entstehung,* 19–101, on the general economic framework; Peter Kriedte, Hans Medick, and Jürgen Schlumbohm, *Industrialization before Industrialization* (Cambridge, 1981; German original 1977); Jan Lucassen, *Migrant Labour in Europe 1600–1900: The Drift to the North Sea* (Beckenham, England, 1986; Dutch original 1984). Only rarely were the skills of cottage workers in demand at the place of arrival.

26. Michael Roberts, ed., *Sweden's Age of Greatness, 1637–1718* (London, 1973), 58–131;

Claude Nordmann, *Grandeur et liberté de la Suede, 1660–1792* (Paris, 1971), 285–326; S. Montelius, "Recruitment and Conditions of Life of Swedish Ironworkers during the 18th and 19th Centuries," *Scandinavian Economic History Review* 14 (1966): 1–17; Göran Rosander, *Herrarbete* (Uppsala, 1967); Hans Norman and Harald Runblom, "Migration Patterns in the Nordic Countries," in Hoerder, *Labor Migration in the Atlantic Economies,* 35–68.

27. Davis, *Rise of the Atlantic Economies,* 202 (quote), 289 passim in what follows.

28. By 1610, western Siberia to the Yenisey was known, and three decades later central Siberia to the Lena, and shortly after that, eastern Siberia. The first European-Chinese Treaty established the border along the Amur (1689), and in 1727 a trade agreement was concluded with China. By 1742 the North Cape was "discovered" and the exploration of Alaska began (it was annexed 1791 and sold to the United States in 1867).

29. This section is based on David K. Fieldhouse, *Die Kolonialreiche seit dem 18. Jahrhundert* (Frankfurt, 1965); Dülmen, *Entstehung;* John Horace Parry, *The Age of Reconnaissance, Discovery, Exploitation and Settlement 1500–1650* (London, 1963); C. Verlinden, *Les origines de la civilisation atlantique* (Neuchâtel, 1966); James D. Tracy, *The Rise of Merchant Empires: Long Distance Trade in the Early Modern World, 1350–1750* (Cambridge, 1990); Peggy K. Liss, *Atlantic Empires: The Network of Trade and Revolutions, 1713–1826* (Baltimore, 1983); Stanley Lieberson, "A Societal Theory of Racial and Ethnic Relations," *American Sociological Review* 29 (1961): 902–10. The best summary concerning the impact of capital flows on local laboring and peasant population remains Eric R. Wolf, *Europe and the People without History* (Berkeley, 1982), 127–261.

30. The Portuguese established their (fortified) trading posts along the African coast between 1450 and 1500, in India from 1498, and in China first in 1516, in Canton. After 1580, when Portugal became linked to Spain by personal union, it lost much of its overseas influence to the Dutch and English.

31. Charles Ralph Boxer, *The Portuguese Seaborne Empire* (London, 1969).

32. Franklin W. Knight, *The Caribbean: The Genesis of a Fragmented Nationalism* (New York, 1978); David Watts, *The West Indies: Patterns of Development, Culture and Environmental Change since 1492* (Cambridge, 1990).

33. No expansionist moves were yet made by the Dutch (who fought for their independence from 1581 to 1648), the French (who were occupied with religious wars and the 1598 Edict of Nantes), or the English (beset with succession and religious struggles). By the end of the Thirty Years' War (1648), Germany had divided itself off the political map.

34. Eric Hobsbawm, "The Crisis of the Seventeenth Century," *Past and Present* 6 (1954): 44–65.

35. Wolf, *Europe and the People without History,* 241.

36. Fieldhouse, *Kolonialreiche,* 96–113; Wolf, *Europe and the People without History,* 255–58. While profits were extremely high, the volume of trade remained limited. The French East India Company, from 1725 to 1756, reached profit margins of more than 90 percent, but trade was limited to between sixteen and twenty-five ships annually.

37. A survey from the British point of view is A. J. Youngson's "The Opening Up of New Territories," in *The Cambridge Economic History of Europe,* vol. 6, "The Industrial Revolutions and after: Incomes, Population and Technological Change (I)," ed. H. J. Habakkuk and M. Postan (Cambridge, 1965), 139–211.

38. John Horace Parry, *The Spanish Seaborne Empire* (London, 1966); Magnus Mörner, *Adventurers and Proletarians: The Story of Migrants in Latin America* (Pittsburgh, 1985).

39. The *mita* system (from 1570) required each village to send one-seventh of its adult male population annually for work in the mines or in public projects. Work lasted between eighteen weeks and six months, the trip taking up to two months in each direction. Families accompanied the workers. After return—of the survivors—the other villagers had to provide for their subsistence until they could harvest their own crops again.

40. Wolf, *Europe and the People without History,* 136–37; P. J. Bakewell, *Silver Mining and Society in Colonial Mexico* (Cambridge, 1971); Lewis Hanke, *The Imperial City of Potosi* (The Hague, 1956).

41. Tim Guldimann, *Lateinamerika: Die Entwicklung der Unterentwicklung* (München, 1975).

42. Walter Nugent has suggested that the term "Creole" be expanded to "Eurocreole" so as to include all colonial-born descendants of Europeans. We prefer a distinction according to patterns of racism and the gender composition of the migration, thus separating Portuguese and Spanish colonial populations from British, Dutch, and French descendants of migrants. Both groups were, of course, dependent on the hegemonial "home" culture. See Nugent, "Frontiers and Empires," in *Religion, Ideology and Nationalism,* 263–75.

43. Transport of criminals was also part of the Russo-Siberian system.

44. Of the white population (3.2 million), 60 percent were of English origin, and 8 to 9 percent each of Scottish, Irish, or German origin.

45. Bernard Bailyn, *The Peopling of British North America: An Introduction* (New York, 1986); D. W. Meinig, *The Shaping of America: A Geographical Perspective on 500 Years of History,* vol. 1, *Atlantic America, 1492–1800* (New Haven, Conn., 1986).

46. An attempt to reform historically grown structures by enlightened, rationalized modes of thought in the Habsburg, the British, and the Ottoman empires brought about resistance to centralization.

47. In the peace of Utrecht (1713) at the end of the war of the Spanish succession, Britain had been granted a monopoly of the slave trade with the Spanish colonies. Abolition of slavery came later: Great Britain in 1833, the British colonies in America in 1838, the United States in 1863, the Spanish colonies in America in 1883, and Brazil in 1888. For a summary see Wolf, *Europe and the People without History,* 195–231; David Brion Davis, *The Problem of Slavery in the Age of Revolution, 1770–1823* (Ithaca, 1975), and *The Problem of Slavery in Western Culture* (Ithaca, 1966).

48. Philip D. Curtin, *The Atlantic Slave Trade: A Census* (Madison, 1969); Nathan I. Huggins, *Black Odyssey* (New York, 1979).

49. Lucassen, *Migrant Labour in Europe;* idem, *Quellen zur Geschichte der Wanderungen . . . zwischen Deutschland und den Niederlanden vom 17. bis 19. Jh.* (1986); Jan Lucassen and Rinus Penninx, *Nieuwkomers, Immigranten en hun nakomelingen in Nederland, 1550–1985* (Amsterdam, 1985).

50. Lucassen, *Migrant Labour in Europe,* chap. 6; Chatelain, *Migrants temporaires en France.*

51. This migration received additional impetus when the reactionary German political systems forced liberal and freethinking men and women into exile.

52. Lucassen, *Migrant Labour in Europe,* chap. 6 and Appendix 2, esp. 108–13.

53. Roger P. Bartlett, *Human Capital: The Settlement of Foreigners in Russia 1762–1804* (Cambridge, 1979); Donald W. Treadgold, *The Great Siberian Migration: Government and Peasant in Resettlement from Emancipation to the First World War* (Princeton, 1957).

54. See, for example, Terry Coleman, *The Railway Navvies* (London, 1965); Runo B. A. Nilsson, *Rallareliv* (Uppsala, 1982).

55. Eric J. Hobsbawm, *The Age of Capital, 1848–1875* (New York, 1975), 310; George R. Taylor, *The Transportation Revolution 1815–1860* (New York, 1951).

56. Donna R. Gabaccia, *Militants and Migrants* (New Brunswick, N.J., 1989), 20–30.

57. André Armengaud estimated sixty million from 1700 to 1914. See also Carlo M. Cipolla, ed., *Europäische Wirtschaftgeschichte* (= *Fontana Economic History of Europe*), vol. 3 (Stuttgart, 1985), 39; Franklin D. Scott, ed., *World Migration in Modern Times* (Englewood Cliffs, N.J., 1968).

58. See the essays in Hoerder, *Labor Migration in the Atlantic Economies,* and Willcox and Ferenczi, *International Migrations.*

59. Thomas J. Archdeacon, *Becoming American: An Ethnic History* (New York, 1983), 134.

60. The argument has been summarized by Ray A. Billington, in *The American Frontier Thesis: Attack and Defense* (Washington, D.C., 1958; reprint, 1971).

61. For reasons of space, the internal migrations in the receiving countries cannot be dealt with in this essay.

62. Klaus J. Bade, " 'Preußengänger' und 'Abwehrpolitik': Ausländerbeschäftigung, Ausländerpolitik und Ausländerkontrolle auf dem Arbeitsmarkt in Preußen vor dem Ersten Weltkrieg," *Archiv für Sozialgeschichte* 24 (1984): 91–162. The German Junkers' attempts to attract Dutch or Italian workers, to replace the—from the chauvinist German point of view—"inferior" and politically "undesirable" Polish workers, led nowhere. Dutch migrants never considered going to Germany, and the Italians preferred Argentina to the regions of the eastern Elbe.

63. Anna Maria Martellone, "Italian Mass Emigration to the United States, 1876–1930: A Historical Survey," *Perspectives in American History,* n.s., 1 (1984): 379–423; Peter R. Shergold and Stephen Nicholas, "Convicts as Migrants: An Australian Perspective" (paper presented at the symposium "A Century of European Migrations, 1830–1930," Minneapolis, November 1986).

64. See Martellone, "Italian Mass Emigration," and Dino Cinel, "The Seasonal Emigration of Italians in the Nineteenth Century: From Internal to International Destinations," *Journal of Ethnic Studies* 10 (1982–83): 43–68.

65. Marie Hall Ets, *Rosa: The Life of an Italian Immigrant* (Minneapolis, 1970); John Potestio, ed., *The Memoirs of Giovanni Veltri* (Toronto, 1987).

66. Philip D. Curtin, *The Rise and Fall of the Plantation Complex: Essays in Atlantic History* (Cambridge, 1990).

67. Willemina Kloosterboer, *Involuntary Labour since the Abolition of Slavery: A Survey of Compulsory Labour throughout the World* (Leiden, 1960; reprint, Westport, Conn., 1976); Leslie Raymond Buell, *The Native Problem in Africa,* 2 vols. (New York, 1928).

68. See, e.g., Leland Jenks, *Migration of British Capital to 1875* (1927; reprint, New York, 1973).

69. Agricultural mass production also emerged in the core, where geographical conditions and property distribution were favorable, e.g., the plains of North America, the eastern Elbe, Hungary, and Russia.

70. For an eyewitness account of a migrant worker, see "John D. Chessa," in LaGumina, *The Immigrants Speak,* 25–27.

71. For this section see Wolf, *Europe and the People without History,* esp. chap. 12.

72. Curtin, *The Atlantic Slave Trade.*

73. Wolf, *Europe and the People without History,* 196, 333–36; Sidney W. Mintz, "Time, Sugar and Sweetness," *Marxist Perspectives* 2 (1979): 56–73.

74. Wolf, *Europe and the People without History,* 338. See this work for details on other crops.

75. Ibid., 318–19.

76. Ibid., 319–21; H. Tinker, *A New System of Slavery: The Export of Indian Labour Overseas, 1830–1920* (London, 1974).

77. Wolf, *Europe and the People without History,* 330.

78. Ibid., 287–90.

79. Ibid., 362–63; Morris D. Morris, "The Recruitment of an Industrial Labor Force in India. . . ," *Comparative Studies in Society and History* 2 (1960): 305–28.

80. Joan M. Jensen, *Passage from India: Asian Indian Immigrants in North America* (New Haven, Conn., 1988), 9.

81. In 1917, the government of India induced the British government to prohibit contract labor.

82. Persia Crawford Campbell, *Chinese Coolie Emigration to Countries within the British Empire* (London, 1923).

83. Wolf, *Europe and the People without History,* 379–80.

84. From 1908 to 1915, emigration from the United States, mostly return migration to Europe, came to 283,000 annually plus a similar number of temporary departures annually (250,000). From 1920 to 1929, annual permanent departures averaged 128,000, registering a decline by almost 150 percent from 1922 to 1923 and remaining low thereafter. (Temporary departures remained high: 157,000 annually.) During the depression years, from 1930 to 1939, out-migration averages came to 49,000 annually, or more than two-thirds of the in-migration, leaving an annual net in-migration of 18,000 per year. See *Historical Statistics of the United States* (Washington, D.C., 1960).

85. Florette Henri, *Black Migration: The Movement North, 1900–1920* (Garden City, N.Y., 1976); John Higham, *Strangers in the Land: Patterns of American Nativism 1860–1925* (New York, 1963); Roy Garis, *Immigration Restriction* (New York, 1927).

86. *Historical Statistics of Canada,* ed. F. H. Leacy (Ottawa, 1983).

87. Dirk Hoerder, "Immigration and the Working Class: The Remigration Factor," *International Labor and Working Class History* 21 (Spring 1982): 28–41; Mark Wyman, *Round-Trip to America: The Immigrants Return to Europe, 1880–1930* (Ithaca, 1993); Neil Shumsky, "The Silver Saddle: Return Migration from the United States, 1870–1930" (manuscript, 1992; forthcoming).

88. Lothar Elsner, "Foreign Workers and Forced Labor in Germany during the First World War," in Hoerder, *Labor Migration in the Atlantic Economies,* 189–222.

89. Ulrich Herbert, *Geschichte der Ausländerbeschäftigung in Deutschland 1880–1980* (Berlin, 1986); Lothar Elsner and Joachim Lehmann, *Ausländische Arbeiter unter dem deutschen Imperialismus, 1900–1985* (Berlin, 1988); Tilly, "Migration in Modern European History," 48–72.

90. Andrea Graziosi, "Foreign Workers in Soviet Russia, 1920–1940: Their Experience and Their Legacy," *International Labor and Working Class History* 33 (Spring 1988): 38–59; Reino Kero, "The Canadian Finns in Soviet Karelia in the 1930s," in Michael Karni, ed., *Finnish Diaspora* (Toronto, 1981).

91. For a brief, worldwide survey of major migratory movements, see Francis Wilson, *Migrant Labor in South Africa* (Johannesburg, 1972), 120–44, which deals with the United States, Latin America, China, Western Europe, West Africa, East Africa, and Central Africa; Mary M. Kritz, Charles B. Keely, and Silvano M. Tomasi, eds., *Global Trends in Migration: Theory and Research on International Population Movements* (New York, 1981); Stephen Castles et al., *Here for Good: Western Europe's New Ethnic Minorities* (London, 1984); R. B. Craig, *The Bracero Program* (Austin, Tex., 1971); Robin Cohen, *The New Helots: Migrants in the International Division of Labour* (Aldershot, England, 1987).

92. See, e.g., Jean Anglade, *La vie quotidienne des immigrés en France de 1919 à nos jours* (Paris, 1976); Colin Holmes, *John Bull's Island: Immigration and British Society, 1871–1971* (London, 1988); Lucassen and Penninx, *Nieuwkomers.*

Migration and the Social History of Modern Europe

JAMES JACKSON, JR., AND LESLIE PAGE MOCH

Since 1700, Europe has been transformed from a sparsely settled rural society to one that is characterized by densely populated urban centers and significant overseas settlements. Europe's population recovered to its early-fourteenth-century levels, and growth accelerated after the mid-eighteenth century, due apparently to declining mortality rates and changes in marriage patterns.[1] What is not so clear, however, are the causes of population concentration and the social meaning of city growth. More specifically, in what ways were human migrations responsible for this change from a rural to an urban society, and how were these movements played out? The answers to these questions are central to the way historians view the European past as well as the way they understand the contemporary world.

The original answer to the questions of migration and urbanization was formulated by observers of the society of the late nineteenth and early twentieth centuries who saw the shift in population from the agricultural countryside to the crowded and alien worlds of the city and the factory as the root cause of contemporary social problems.[2] These critics of urbanization perceived an increase in the total volume of migration and thus assumed that more individuals were suffering from the effects of residential dislocation. Seen from this perspective, migration was an irreversible phenomenon that enabled the demographically moribund and decaying city to exist by draining the vitality from rural migrants, leaving them hollow vestiges of their former robust selves. Within this context, the situation fraught with contemporary urgency, governmental agencies continued to collect descriptive information that enabled scholars, such as the English statistician E. G. Ravenstein and the German social scientists Rudolph Heberle and Fritz Meyer, to sketch a basic outline of migration behavior in the nineteenth and early twentieth centuries.[3] Ferdinand Tönnies, Georg Simmel, Max Weber, and Friedrich Engels created powerful stereotypes of community and society that continued to animate and circumscribe sociological research well into the twentieth century, partly because they did not view migration merely as a problem of demographic calculus.[4] Rather, they helped to set our research agenda by focusing attention on the social meaning of migration for individual lives and for the collectivity.[5]

Since the nineteenth century, migration has been viewed as a hallmark of modern life. Indeed, geographic mobility has been incorporated into the modernization paradigm. The hypothesis of a "mobility transition" distinguished premodern sedentary societies from modern ones and articulates the idea that migration is an important component of modernity.[6] A corollary argument asserts that individuals who are willing to move are more "modern" than those who do not leave home.[7]

An Emerging Consensus

The conventional analysis of the link between migration and urbanization declared that city growth in the nineteenth century was caused by the movement of rural dwellers, who were irreversibly drawn from their sedentary villages into the city, and that this signaled a transition to the modern urban-industrial era. A new perspective on migration is emerging, however, that is profoundly different from the modernization paradigm. Neither the presumed destructive power of migration nor the irreversibility of rural-urban moves plays an important role in the alternative view. Rather, this view emphasizes the continuities and regional networks in migration history.

The origins of a new analysis of migration are to be found, first, in an ideological and methodological reaction to the modernization paradigm. Critics have pointed to the ethnocentric social and political assumptions of such theories of development, as well as to the imprecision of the presumed tension between the major variables of "tradition" and "modernity."[8] Students of migration are particularly disturbed by the ignorance of rural lifeways displayed by modernization theory, which reads sedentary qualities into rural life and overlooks rural migration patterns.

A second source of alternative assessments of classic migration theory springs from studies of contemporary migration in the Third World. Using survey techniques as well as census data, researchers have placed the assertions of the conventional wisdom into a cross-cultural perspective and have begun to reveal the complex interplay of migration, social mobility, housing, and employment. For example, Janice Perlman's investigation of the migrant shantytowns of Rio de Janeiro reveals networks of kin and friendships that created a vital urban community where outsiders saw only poverty and disorientation.[9]

The third source of this revision of the conventional wisdom includes a plethora of case studies and a few surveys of broader bodies of data, which are based on newly explored migration records, including the population registers of Sweden, Belgium, and Italy, and the impressive German migration statistics.[10] Population registers and migration records provide the most accurate information about the levels and flows of human mobility in the past. Scholars of other areas of Europe that have no such migration records, such as England and France, are also contributing to a new analysis of migration by asking new questions of traditional sources, such as parish records or bureaucratic surveys—questions that are not bound by assumptions about the presumed sedentary nature of premodern life or about the necessary connection of migration and social disorder.[11]

The clearest conclusion of this new analysis of migration is that Europeans have always moved in considerable numbers. European populations have never been as sedentary as we once thought; rather, several distinct kinds of movement have characterized the countryside since at least the seventeenth century. Most closely tied to the agricultural seasons were the great annual migrations undertaken by groups of harvest laborers, construction workers, and peddlers within the powerful reaches of Rome, Milan, Paris, and, to a lesser extent, London, the North Sea Coast, Provence, and Madrid.[12] In addition, many men traveled long distances within their own nations, such as the northern English who flocked to London for apprenticeships and less certain fortunes in the seventeenth century.[13] The movements of seventeenth- and eighteenth-century Europeans appear to have been particularly intense between mountain and plain, city and hinterland. Poor mountain areas, hard-pressed to support their residents year-round, quickly developed traditions of temporary out-migration. They could spare the manpower needed for the most onerous and difficult lowland tasks, especially in the winter months.[14]

Besides these long-distance movements, many of which were seasonal and temporary, rural Europeans regularly traveled shorter distances. Those most likely to do so were cultivators who moved from one large estate to another; in such cases, the majority might leave their home villages.[15] Sharecroppers moved by a similar pattern—entire families moved together to work for a new landlord.[16] Although landowning peasants were less likely to move, they also disappeared from parish records at a much greater rate than was once thought.[17] The most important form of rural migration primarily involved single persons. Young men and women—even those who would eventually inherit a farm or be a mistress of one—worked as farmhands, hired out by the year. From as early as age ten until their mid-twenties, many young peasants moved annually from one service position to another.[18] In the eighteenth century, in areas where farm servants were commonly used, as many as 70 percent of the young men aged twenty to twenty-four (and half of the women) moved to a new parish annually as they changed masters.[19]

Many of those who did not go into rural service worked in the nearest market towns as day laborers, domestics, or apprentices. Families in areas surrounding cities could spare their daughters; cities attracted these young women to work in urban kitchens, shops, inns, and alehouses.[20] Extant urban records from seventeenth- and eighteenth-century cities in Germany, England, and France unanimously show that men—from elite and wealthy merchants to apprentices—also came to the preindustrial city from surrounding regions.[21] It is important to note that even in the seventeenth and eighteenth centuries, cityward moves were not necessarily permanent. French studies have shown, for example, that even among the most sedentary group—couples with more than one child—migration was commonplace in the late seventeenth and eighteenth centuries, during which between one-fifth and one-third of these families departed from their respective cities.[22]

Thus a multitude of case studies suggests that the modernization paradigm, which characterizes migration as a comparatively recent phenomenon, fundamentally distorts the historical experience of Europeans. Both temporally and socially, migration appears to have been an established pattern; it is part of all recorded periods in early modern and modern Europe and was experienced by elite bureaucrats and peasants, by the landless and unlucky, by women as well as men. After 1750, when the demographic pattern of the old regime began to break down, geographic mobility enabled European societies to adapt to changing growth patterns and to adjust their labor forces to new opportunities in agriculture and manufacturing. The implications of this new research on preindustrial migrations suggest that a reassessment of the relationship and social meaning of migration and urbanization in the nineteenth century is essential—a revaluation that recognizes the continuities of human mobility.[23]

Problems and Unsolved Puzzles

In light of this accumulating evidence, we can no longer view geographic mobility as a unilinear and mechanistic phenomenon. Clearly, a preoccupation with only one piece of migration—whether that is movement into a city or departures from a rural area—seriously truncates our understanding of the process and its central place in European history, both before and after 1750. In addition, the tendency to use "migration" interchangeably with "urbanization" has obscured our understanding of both city growth and migratory behavior. A thorough reconsideration has been stimulated not only by a growing body of research but also by colleagues who suggest that social historians strive to "illuminate the complex interplay between large structural changes . . . and routine social life," including mundane geographic wanderings.[24] Several problems and unsolved puzzles stand in our way, however.

Formidable technical and source problems present the greatest difficulty in discovering the volume and rhythms of historical migration. Necessity forces us to depend upon varying bureaucratic definitions of migration, which makes comparisons difficult. The second quandary results from the quality of migration data. Few major sources allow the reconstruction of an individual's migration history over an entire life course. Information about migration in most European countries has been culled primarily from censuses that, until recently, reveal present residence and perhaps birthplace but little or nothing about the duration of residence or places of previous residence.[25] This kind of cross-sectional information tells us only about selected migrants and net population flows. Church records from nations such as France and England vary enormously in quality from parish to parish, and the availability of civil status records from the past hundred years remains problematic in France.[26] The high-quality migration statistics for Germany apply only to cities and smaller administrative districts, leaving rural movements for large areas of the country unclear. Moreover, German migration statistics reflect the particularistic history of Germany in the nineteenth century—they began as Prussian statistics recording migration in the lower Rhine area, a practice extended to Berlin in 1838. Between unification in 1871 and World War I, cities outside Prussia were added one by one to the list of those gathering migration data.[27] Population registers offer clearly superior data because they cover rural and urban areas, but they were not instituted until the mid-eighteenth century in Sweden, the 1840s in Belgium, the 1850s in the Netherlands, and the 1860s in Italy.[28] As a consequence, it is possible to discern migration rates for only a few historical populations, and, unavoidably, our understanding of geographic mobility is bound to fall short of what we would wish.

More difficult than determining the magnitude of historical migration, which better sources would allow, is the task of defining the mechanisms and social meaning of geographic mobility. For the purposes of this essay, we have organized this analytical task into five interrelated questions: How did migrant selectivity operate? What motivated people to leave their homes and take a chance on new surroundings? What was the character of migration streams? What was the impact of migration on places of origin and destination? Finally, how did individual migrants respond to residential change?

First and most fundamental, our knowledge of the operation of migrant selectivity is sketchy. Migrants were not a random sample of either their places of origin or their destinations. Rather, migration was selective on a wide range of variables, particularly age, gender, landholding status, education, and income. Young males, the landless, and the educated were generally the most likely migrants in historical Europe. It is clear, however, that this selectivity worked differently in one labor market and geographic location compared to another. On the question of gender, for example, Ravenstein stated that "woman is a greater migrant than man," but he also observed that women moved shorter distances within Britain than did men.[29] Indeed, during the nineteenth century, women moved in droves—many of them to commercial cities where they could find work as domestics. Other migration streams were clearly male; for example, men were more likely than women to make their way to coal-mining towns, and the great majority of seasonal harvest labor—both in modern Africa and in historical Europe—was male.[30]

Migration selectivity by demographic and social traits, such as education or landholding status, is fairly clear and relatively easy to analyze. It is more difficult to analyze individual migrant psychology and attitudes, specifically the degree to which a person is an innovator or open to change.[31] From the standpoint of the sending communities, the migration of their more innovative citizens may deprive them of future social leadership. Migration does not necessarily require a pioneering spirit, however. Those interested in preserving a traditional way of life do migrate; indeed, the desire to finance land purchases in order to maintain peasant families sent European rurals temporarily to both distant fields and cities to earn cash. Moreover, well-established migration systems forged by leaders carry their share of followers.[32]

A second area of migration research concentrates on the motivation for geographic mobility.[33] Historical studies suggest that landholding and demographic patterns, seasonal organization of work, migration traditions, political upheaval, and religious intolerance all caused people to migrate. Clearly, we must scrutinize a broad range of perspectives in order to understand why people moved and how they chose a destination. Migration patterns respond primarily to a need for labor and to political and religious persecution. Within this framework, the social organization of migration explains the impetus to migrate, the timing, and the destinations for a large proportion of historical actors. Indeed, the flow of information among migrants offers the best explanation for such large-scale movements as migration from Britain to North America.[34] In the view of many migration scholars, the perceptions of migrants about opportunities in different places are more significant in the decision to move than objective economic reality.[35] The personal information field that each potential migrant possesses about possible destinations, employment opportunities, and social support explains why people are attracted to certain destinations and jobs.[36] Information is exchanged within many kinds of institutions. Occupational traditions and employing organizations weighed heavily in determining the peregrinations of traveling apprentices and bureaucrats.[37] In addition, students of the family economy have found that the family, rather than the individual migrant, made migration decisions in its economic interest.[38] Migrants tend to go where neighbors have gone; therefore, traditions of migration have been created between home towns and particular destinations.[39] Chain migration thus linked the Auvergne to Catalonia and Westphalia to Holland in the seventeenth century, and Sicily to North America and Anatolia to Germany in the twentieth century. Although it appears that information flows and social contacts create migration systems, this insight has yet to be integrated into a broad theoretical understanding of migration and historical change.

A third area of geographic mobility research concerns flows of movers within a migration system. Based on published statistical sources, some migration studies have focused on the impact of net population movements on gross population characteristics and have analyzed the biased character of flows between sending and receiving areas.[40] Other studies have recognized the relationship between distance and the character of the migration stream and have employed various gravity models to describe the friction of distance.[41] Additional research has attempted to delineate the patterns of inter-area population flows and to identify hierarchies of migration destinations.[42] What is most lacking in studies of migration streams is an analysis of return migration and multiple moves.[43] These factors offer keys to the lives of proletarians in Europe and to their struggles with economic dislocation, as well as to the peregrinations of bureaucrats and church officials. If we could better understand multiple moves and returns home, migration would be integrated more realistically with the social history of Europe.

A fourth theme of migration studies emphasizes the impact of geographic mobility on the places people left and on their destinations. This is tied directly to the compositional effects of migrant selectivity. The young male migrants who flooded Paris before 1848 created a concern regarding urban social problems such as prostitution, drunkenness, and theft.[44] The experience of the Austrian city of Graz, with its heavy influx of retiring civil servants during the late nineteenth and early twentieth centuries, illustrates the ways in which the demographic and occupational structures as well as the political life of a town can be deeply influenced by migrants. Likewise, rural areas underwent demographic restructuring when they lost young people to urbanization; these regions lost some of their most highly educated children.[45] Intriguing questions remain about the impact of migration on historical populations at origin and at destination. Studies of villages from which young men migrated in great numbers in times of economic stress, for example, show a boom in the number of unwed mothers.[46] How typical are these Portuguese and French parishes, and what other social effects might such villages illustrate? The answer to these questions would tie migration more realistically to the social history of Europe.

The fifth and final area of migration studies focuses on the consequences of migration for the individual mover. Much of this work responds to studies of urban crime and to nineteenth-century observations that migrants became disoriented and uprooted people, prey to revolution and mental disorders. The pessimistic view of the conventional wisdom has been challenged by scholars whose work attempts to explore the social context or auspices of migration.[47] From Marseilles and Nîmes in southern France, from Duisburg in the Ruhr Valley, and from London and Preston across the English Channel come reports that migrants found structures of stability that cushioned their adjustment to the urban world.[48] On the other hand, one recent analysis of criminal convictions reports that not everyone who left home became a social and economic success; thus, although not all migrants were criminals, a disproportionate number of urban criminals were migrants.[49] As Olwen Hufton observed, it is unlikely that the poor could always stay on the right side of the law in their efforts to survive.[50] Thus, the issue of social deviance lingers, often becoming embroiled in insoluble definitional disputes: is migration disorienting simply because a typical nineteenth-century migrant might change residences fifteen or sixteen times during a lifetime; or, because two-thirds of these moves are made during the young adult years and permit a migrant long stretches of residential stability, does migration lack disruptive power?[51]

The division of migration analysis into these five basic emphases is useful in order to set our research agenda. Nonetheless, this topical compartmentalization must not obscure the fact that the most significant historical issues in the study of geographic mobility encompass all five categories. Historical questions are multifaceted in another sense as well: their resolution requires the perspectives of sociologists, geographers, social psychologists, and economists, as well as historians. The three primary *historical* issues in European migration studies illustrate these scholarly axioms. They deal with the relationship between migration and social change—first with cottage industry, then with the development of factory production and the concomitant urbanization, and finally with the transition from one to the other.

The implication of cottage industry for migratory behavior is the central conundrum for the eighteenth and early nineteenth centuries. A growing body of evidence suggests that long-run shifts occurred in migration trends in the eighteenth century. The relationship between these shifts and simultaneous economic and demographic change has yet to be established, however. In England, long-distance migration slowed, and levels of migration decreased in the countryside. The expanding rural industry that employed people at home, the declining rates of population increase, and the implementing of strict residency requirements for poor relief are three factors that slowed migration, but the role of each has yet to be determined.[52] The continent, on the other hand, exhibited contradictory patterns during a time of relative peace and population increase following 1750. Population pressure forced increasing numbers of long-distance migrants to leave mountainous regions and find temporary work in provincial cities and prosperous countrysides; some would never return home.[53] Areas of expanding rural industry are said to have absorbed their own prolific populations, but there are no investigations to confirm this. In some of these areas, rural mobility seems actually to have increased as protoindustrial villages were infused with newcomers.[54] These contrasting patterns have not been adequately confirmed; nor have they been analyzed as part of a continental system of mobility.

A second historical problem is the nature of the connection between migration and urbanization in the time between the onset of factory industry and the outbreak of World War I. How much migration was there? Did it increase to previously unreached levels? The best German data show that a peak of migration in and out of cities was reached in the decades preceding World War I, but there are no reliable comparisons with migration rates of earlier times. Moreover, a simulation of migration and urbanization from 1500 to 1800 suggests that the nineteenth-century migration rates may not have been unprecedented.[55] Did migration make the cities grow? To a degree, yes; but cities were less deadly than they had been in the seventeenth and eighteenth centuries, so that migration may have been much less important to the growth of some important administrative and commercial capitals than contemporary observers believed. This is partly true because many people departed from the cities as well as entered them, and these departures have rarely been recorded. German sources that recorded the actual volume of migration (as opposed to net migration figures) reveal large numbers of moves in and out of cities for every person permanently added to the urban rolls.[56]

In addition, the existence of long-standing regional and local exchanges of population illustrates the complex relationship of migration, industrialization, and urban growth in the nineteenth century. This finding suggests that the people who came to industrial cities were not strangers from alien rural cultures. Miners alternated between agricultural pursuits and ore extraction; factory workers moved between fields and workshops, as long as employers tolerated or required seasonal absences.[57] Clearly, in many areas, rural dwellers balanced themselves between urban life and the fields. Researchers must try to disaggregate earlier preindustrial fluctuations of population and newer patterns that accompanied the commercial and manufacturing revolutions of the nineteenth century.[58] Moreover, we must explain new and unexplored patterns within the nineteenth century, such as the precipitous decline in overseas migration and the simultaneous unprecedented acceleration of internal migration in Germany in the 1890s.[59]

The issues of migration that surround rural industry and the growth of urban production do not fall neatly into separate temporal categories. On the contrary, it is increasingly obvious that some forms of domestic production persisted long after the 1840s; in many regions, domestic rural industry existed simultaneously with factory production. The relationship between these two becomes the third major issue of European migration studies. What kinds of population movements did the deindustrialization of the countryside mobilize? What role did the collapse of rural industry and the resulting agricultural crises play in rural-urban migration? There are some indications that rural residents left home only when necessary and that they balanced their lives between urban and rural areas as long as possible, but there is little direct evidence of this.[60]

Thus, the links between migration, industrialization, and urbanization remain sketchy. They will be clarified by interdisciplinary work that acknowledges a variety of perspectives while allowing the historical picture to be complicated by a variety of insights into issues such as selectivity, the social organization of migration, and the melding of human motivation and social consequences with large-scale change. If these issues can become part of historical studies of migration, the social history of Europe will be enriched.

A Systems Approach

The application of a systems framework to the migration experience suggests one means to meet the need for a comprehensive perspective by providing a strategy to overcome topical compartmentalization.[61] By seeing migration as a circular, self-modifying system and a complex of interacting elements, individual movers can be placed in the context of their places of origin and destination, the structural context can be specified, and the long-term implications of migration for that structural environment can be defined.[62] Systems analysis can (1) demonstrate how interrelated social, political, economic, and technological forces converge to stimulate geographic mobility; (2) uncover the social tensions unleashed by this mobility; and (3) show how countervailing migratory trends emerge.

The potential and the hazards of an integrated systems approach are illustrated by Jan Lucassen's treatment of seasonal migration between Holland and northern Germany at the turn of the nineteenth century.[63] From diverse and problematic, yet remarkable, data sources, Lucassen demonstrates how structural features of the receiving economy on the North Sea coast of Holland—demographic patterns and the nature of typical work cycles for casual laborers and small farmers in a capital-intensive agricultural system—created opportunities for outside laborers. He notes the decline of the regional population and the shrinkage of the scope of major construction projects after 1680 that broke down the local work cycle and created a demand for seasonal migratory labor in Holland. In the German regions of Westphalia, Oldenburg, and Hannover, on the other hand, the growing population could neither be accommodated on existing farms nor supported by expanding cottage industry. Drawn by the higher wages along the North Sea coast, northern German migrant workers took seasonal employment that was considered menial by native workers—work as haymakers or grass mowers, for example—and that fit into their own work cycles. When some of these fundamental demographic and economic structures changed, as they did in the first decades of the nineteenth century, these systems of seasonal migration began to deteriorate.

Lucassen is also able to describe how particular migration streams developed between Holland and northern Germany and to explain how the particular boundaries of the North Sea basin migration were set. This is accomplished through (1) an analysis of migration routes via the location of peat bogs, rivers, and gathering places where migrants converged to share information; (2) an estimate of numbers and rhythms of movement from examining passenger ship schedules on the Zuider Zee; and (3) a consideration of labor availability by exploring the significance of serfdom east of the Elbe.

Lucassen's study suggests some of the ways in which predominantly young male seasonal laborers affected the receiving area on the North Sea coast by briefly analyzing housing practices and patterns of residential segregation. Ideally, a more comprehensive investigation that takes an integrated systems approach would examine the structural modifications wrought in Westphalia, Hannover, and Oldenburg as well. What happened to fertility levels, consumption patterns, and employment trends at home? Attention to such feedback mechanisms, which cause structural change in both the sending and receiving areas, would help to illustrate how unequal economic growth in the two areas was perpetuated and how migration became a long-term social and economic fact of life.

The systems framework is not the only logical method of investigating the impact of migration. Moreover, there are problems in collecting the varieties of data that are needed for an analysis of changes in social and economic structures. Lucassen, for example, found it necessary to exclude the social and psychological aspects of migrant workers' lives from the study. Nonetheless, the systems approach does provide a strategy of analysis and also has the virtue of forcing us to deal with the feedback aspects of migration systems, requiring that we see the effects and causes of migration as well as the long-term structural concomitants in combination. Although we may continue to analyze general notions about migration by studying its individual components, the systems approach can help us identify the significance of our particular study in acquiring an understanding of a larger social process.

Conclusion

Our brief survey offers fundamental observations about European migration studies. First, many descriptive studies of migration still need to be done. Second, scholars from many disciplines can fruitfully contribute to this task—geographers, with their grasp of spatial matters; anthropologists, with their understanding of values; demographers, with their expertise at specifying impacts; and economists, with their perceptions regarding flows of labor and capital. Such disciplinary and interdisciplinary endeavors will enrich our understanding of the fundamental processes of social change in the past three centuries, challenging conventional views of cultural, economic, and institutional change since 1700. The high volume of preindustrial mobility, for example, conflicts with the durable stereotype of premodern society as being immobile, a stereotype that distorts both historical research and findings. The fact that movement into urban industrial jobs did not necessarily involve disorienting changes adds an important perspective to our concepts of industrial labor force formation. In addition, we can attempt to unlock a basic dilemma of human society: how can individual stability exist simultaneously with aggregate disruption? In this view, migration is the motor force behind the creation of subcultures that offer supportive networks and at the same time create social friction.[64]

Nonetheless, we cannot allow our concern for understanding migration as a core historical phenomenon to blind us to its link with distinct regional and national histories. If migration is a significant connector of social processes, we must link it to the most important questions of social history in each nation of Europe: what is the link between France's migration experience and its relatively limited development of factory production? Can geographic mobility help us to understand the unique elements of German social and political development during the nineteenth century? In seeking to comprehend migration as a historical process, we must also see it in relation to the polity and national history.

Finally, our view of migration will be impoverished if we neglect the fact that it is a human process—not the shuffling of economic atoms but rather the movement of historical actors embedded in systems of family, politics, religion, education, and sociability. If we ignore the experiences of ordinary people and attach ourselves instead to the passive implications inherent in the language of migration "flows" and "streams," of "push" and "pull," we will be neglecting an excellent opportunity to deepen our understanding of the historical process.

Likewise, common people can be obscured from view by the haze of ideological and methodological controversy.[65] Our assessment of migration increasingly is following the same patterns as the debate concerning the standard of living during the Industrial Revolution. Pessimists—from Friedrich Engels, Barbara Hammond, and John L. Hammond to Eric J. Hobsbawm and Edward P. Thompson—have used literary evidence to describe the pernicious qualities of early industrial life and indict industrial capitalism.[66] Optimists, including George R. Porter, Thomas S. Ashton, Ronald M. Hartwell, and Arthur J. Taylor, have assembled statistical data in order to explore the concrete dimensions of workers' lives, demonstrating the material benefits of capitalism.[67] This debate can serve as a warning to migration scholars, partly because it demonstrates the limits of both quantitative and literary evidence and the powerful undertow of ideology. The contentiousness of these optimists and pessimists also illustrates how easily we can isolate the economic and social sides of migration from one another. Only by embracing such complexity can ordinary citizens of the past be endowed with their role as active agents of change in the urban-industrial world we have gained.

Notes

1. A general discussion of these developments can be found in Adna Weber, *The Growth of Cities in the Nineteenth Century: A Study in Statistics* (Ithaca: Cornell University Press, 1965; reprint, 1899); Frank Thistlethwaite, "Migration from Europe Overseas in the Nineteenth and Twentieth Centuries," *XIe Congrès International des Sciences Historiques, Stockholm,* vol. 5 (Gŏteborg, 1960), 32–60; E. Anthony Wrigley, *Population and History* (New York: McGraw-Hill, 1969); Janet Roebuck, *The Shaping of Urban Society: A History of Urban Forms and Functions* (New York: Scribner's, 1974); Andrew Lees and Lynn Lees, eds., *The Urbanization of European Society in the Nineteenth Century* (Boston: Heath, 1976); James Vance, *This Scene of Man: The Role and Structure of the City in the Geography of Western Civilization* (New York: Harper's, 1977); W. Robert Lee, ed., *European Demography and Economic Growth* (London: Croom Helm, 1979); E. Anthony Wrigley, "The Growth of Population in Eighteenth-Century England: A Conundrum Resolved," *Past and Present,* no. 98 (1983): 121–50; Hans Jürgen Teuteberg, ed., *Urbanisierung im 19. und 20. Jahrhundert: Historische und Geographische Aspekte* (Cologne: Bohlau Verlag, 1983); Jan de Vries, *European Urbanization, 1500–1800* (Cambridge, Mass.: Harvard University Press, 1985); Paul M. Hohenberg and Lynn Hollen Lees, *The Making of Urban Europe, 1000–1950* (Cambridge, Mass.: Harvard University Press, 1985); N. L. Tranter, *Population and Society, 1750–1940* (London: Longman, 1985).

2. For a review of these ideas, see Carl Schorske, "The Idea of the City in European Thought: Voltaire to Spengler," in *The Historian and the City,* ed. Oscar Handlin and John Burchard (Boston: M.I.T. Press, 1963), 95–114; Claude S. Fischer, *The Urban Experience* (New York: Harcourt, Brace, Jovanovich, 1976); Brian J. L. Berry, *Comparative Urbanization: Divergent Paths in the Twentieth Century* (New York: St. Martin's Press, 1981); Michael P. Smith, *The City and Social Theory* (Oxford: Basil Blackwell, 1980).

3. Ernest G. Ravenstein, "The Laws of Migration," *Journal of the Statistical Society* 48 (1885): 167–227, and 52 (1889): 241–301; Rudolph Heberle and Fritz Meyer, *Die Grossstädte im Strome der Binnenwanderung* (Leipzig: Hirzel, 1937).

4. Ferdinand Tönnies, *Community and Society* (East Lansing: Michigan State University Press, 1957); Georg Simmel, "Die Grossstädte und das Geistesleben," in *Die Grossstädte: Vortrage und Aufsatze zur Städteausstellung,* ed. Thomas Petermann et al. (Dresden: Zahn und Jaensch, 1903), 183–206; Max Weber, *Die Lage der Landarbeiter im ostelbischen Deutschland,* Abteilung 1: "Schriften und Reden," Band 3, in *Max Weber Gesamtausgabe,* ed. M. Riesbrodt (Tübingen: J.C.B. Mohr, 1894); Max Weber, *The City* (New York: Basic Books, 1958); Friedrich Engels, *Zur Wohnungsfrage* (Frankfurt am Main: Marxistische Blätter, 1974).

5. See the work of the Chicago school of sociology, especially that of Robert E. Park,

"The City: Suggestions for the Investigation of Human Behavior in the Urban Environment," *The American Journal of Sociology* 20 (1916): 577–612; idem, "Human Migration and the Marginal Man," *The American Journal of Sociology* 33 (1928): 881–93; Louis Werth, "Urbanism as a Way of Life," *The American Journal of Sociology* 44 (1938): 1–24. For a review of these perspectives, see Claude S. Fischer, "Toward a Subcultural Theory of Urbanism," *The American Journal of Sociology* 80 (1975): 1319–41.

6. Wilbur Zelinsky, "The Hypothesis of the Mobility Transition," *Geographical Review* 61 (1971): 219–49.

7. See, for example, Barbara A. Anderson, *Internal Migration during Modernization in Late Nineteenth-Century Russia* (Princeton: Princeton University Press, 1980).

8. The most recent critique of modernization theory from a migration scholar is Steve Hochstadt, "Temporary Migration and Rural Social Science History" (paper presented at the annual meeting of the Social Science History Association, New Orleans, October 1987); see also Andre Gunder Frank, "Sociology of Development and Underdevelopment of Sociology," *Catalyst* 3 (1967): 20–73; Joseph R. Gusfield, "Tradition and Modernity: Misplaced Polarities in the Study of Social Change," *American Journal of Sociology* 72 (1967): 351–62; D. C. Tipps, "Modernization Theory and the Comparative Study of Societies: A Critical Perspective," *Comparative Studies in Society and History* 15 (1973): 199–226.

9. Janice A. Perlman, *The Myth of Marginality: Urban Poverty and Politics in Rio de Janeiro* (Berkeley: University of California Press, 1976); Michael P. Todaro, *Internal Migration in Developing Countries: A Review of Theory, Evidence, Methodology, and Research Priorities* (Geneva: International Labor Office, 1976); Alan Simmons, Sergio Diaz-Briquets, and Aprodicio A. Laquian, *Social Change and Internal Migration: A Review of Research Findings from Africa, Asia, and Latin America* (Ottawa: International Development Research Center, 1977).

10. de Vries, *European Urbanization*; Myron Gutmann and Etienne van de Walle, "New Sources for Social and Demographic History: The Belgian Population Registers," *Social Science History* 2 (1978): 121–43; Steve Hochstadt, "Migration in Germany: An Historical Study" (Ph.D. diss., Brown University, 1983); Steve Hochstadt and James Jackson, Jr., " 'New' Sources for the Study of Migration in Early 19th-Century Germany," *Historical Social Research/Historische Sozialforschung* 31 (1984): 85–92; Ann-Sofie Kalvemark, "The Country that Kept Track of Its Population," in *Time, Space, and Man: Essays in Microdemography,* ed. Jan Sundin and E. Söderlund (Atlantic Highlands, N.J.: Humanities Press, 1979), 221–38; David Kertzer and Denis Hogan, "On the Move: Migration in an Italian Community, 1865–1921," *Social Science History* 9 (1985): 1–24.

11. Among the best studies are David Souden, "Movers and Stayers in Family Reconstitution Populations, 1660–1780," *Local Population Studies* 33 (1984): 11–28; Michel Térisse, "Méthode de recherches démographiques en milieu urban ancien (XVIIe-XVIIIe)," *Annales de démographie historique* (1974): 249–62.

12. de Vries, *European Urbanization;* Steve Hochstadt, "Migration in Preindustrial Germany," *Central European History* 16 (1983): 195–224; Jan Lucassen, *Migrant Labour in Europe, 1600–1900: The Drift to the North Sea* (London: Croom Helm, 1987); Abel Poitrineau, *Les espagnols de l'Auvergne et du Limousin du XVIIIe au XXe siècle* (Aurillac: Malroux-Mazel, 1985).

13. Peter Clark and Paul Slack, *English Towns in Transition, 1500–1700* (London: Oxford University Press, 1976), 64–65; Peter Clark and David Souden, "Rural-Urban Migration and Its Impact in Early Modern England," *Proceedings of the Eighth International Economic History Congress, Budapest* B8 (1982): 1–7.

14. Raoul Blanchard, *Les alpes françaises* (Paris: Colin, 1925); Olwen Hufton, *The Poor of Eighteenth-Century France* (Oxford: Oxford University Press, 1974); Abel Poitrineau, *Remues d'hommes: Essai sur les migrations montagnardes en France aux XVIIe et XVIIIe siècles* (Paris: Aubier Montaigne, 1983); Alfred Perrenoud, "Les migrations en Suisse sous l'ancien régime: Quelques problèmes," *Annales de démographie historique* (1970): 251–59.

15. David Gaunt, "Pre-industrial Economy and Population Structure," *Scandinavian Journal of History* 2 (1977): 183–210.

16. Emmanuel Todd, "Mobilité géographique et cycle de vie en Artois et en Toscane au XVIIIe siècle," *Annales: Economies, Sociétés, Civilisations* 30 (1975): 726–44.

17. Alan Macfarlane, "The Myth of the Peasantry: Family and Economy in a Northern Parish," in *Land, Kinship and Life-Cycle,* ed. Richard M. Smith (Cambridge: Cambridge University Press, 1984); Souden, "Movers and Stayers in Family Reconstitution Populations."

18. Ann Kussmaul, *Servants in Husbandry in Early Modern England* (Cambridge: Cambridge University Press, 1981); Roger Schofield, "Age-specific Mobility in an Eighteenth-Century Rural English Parish," *Annales de démographie historique* (1970): 261–74.

19. Todd, "Mobilité géographique et cycle de vie," 730.

20. Abel Chatelain, "Migrations et domesticité féminine urbaine en France, XVIIIe siècle–XXe siècle," *Revue d'histoire économique et sociale* 4 (1969): 506–28; Jean-Pierre Poussou, *Bordeaux et le sud-ouest au XVIIIe siècle: Croissance économique et attraction urbaine* (Paris: Editions de l'Ecole des Hautes Etudes en Sciences Sociales, 1983); David Souden, "Migrants and the Population Structure of Late Seventeenth-Century Provincial Cities and Market Towns," in *The Transformation of English Provincial Towns, 1600–1800,* ed. Peter Clark (London: Hutchinson, 1984), 133–68.

21. Clark and Slack, *English Towns in Transition;* Hochstadt, "Migration in Preindustrial Germany"; Poussou, *Bordeaux et le sud-ouest au XVIIIe siècle.*

22. Jean-Pierre Bardet, *Rouen aux XVIIe et XVIIIe siècles: Les mutations d'un espace social* (Paris: Société d'Edition d'Enseignement Supérieur, 1983), 1:216; Terisse, "Méthode de recherches démographiques en milieu urbain ancien," 259.

23. Hochstadt, "Migration in Germany"; James Jackson, Jr., "Migration and Urbanization in the Ruhr Valley, 1850–1900" (Ph.D. diss., University of Minnesota, 1980).

24. Olivier Zunz, *Reliving the Past: The Worlds of Social History* (Chapel Hill: University of North Carolina Press, 1985), 6.

25. See, for example, Richard Lawton, ed., *The Census and Social Structure: An Interpretive Guide to Nineteenth Century Censuses in England and Wales* (London: Cass, 1978); E. Anthony Wrigley, *Nineteenth Century Society: Essays in the Use of Quantitative Methods for the Study of Social Data* (Cambridge: Cambridge University Press, 1972).

26. Michel Fleury and Louis Henry, *Nouvel manuel de dépouillement et d'exploitation de l'état civil ancien* (Paris: Institut National des Etudes Demographiques, 1965); Leslie Page Moch, *Paths to the City: Regional Migration in Nineteenth-Century France* (Beverly Hills: Sage Publications, 1983), 212; Etienne van de Walle, *The Female Population of France* (Princeton: Princeton University Press, 1974); E. Anthony Wrigley, *An Introduction to English Historical Demography from the Sixteenth to the Nineteenth Century* (London: Weidenfeld and Nicolson, 1966).

27. Steve Hochstadt, "Urban Mobility in Germany, 1850–1914" (Bates College, 1987); Hochstadt and Jackson, " 'New' Sources for the Study of Migration"; James Jackson, Jr., "Population Registers and the Study of Migration for Nineteenth-Century Germany" (Point Loma College, 1987).

28. Gutmann and van de Walle, "New Sources for Social and Demographic History"; Kertzer and Hogan, "On the Move"; Kalvemark, "The Country that Kept Track of Its Population." For a complete description of population registers, see United Nations, "Methodology and Evaluation of Population Registers and Similar Systems," *Studies in Methods,* ser. F (1959), no. 15.

29. Ravenstein, "The Laws of Migration," 48:196.

30. Morag Bell, "Past Mobility and Spatial Preferences for Migration in East Africa," in *The Geographical Impact of Migration,* ed. Paul White and Robert Woods (London: Longman, 1980), 84–107; Lucassen, *Migrant Labour in Europe.*

31. Galtung suggests that innovators can only be identified in terms of their communities of origin and may be very traditional in the context of destinations; Johan Galtung, *Members of Two Worlds: A Development Study of Three Villages in Western Sicily* (Oslo: Universitetsforlaget, 1971).

32. William Peterson, *Population,* 3rd. ed. (New York: Macmillan, 1975); Charles Tilly, "Transplanted Networks," in Virginia Yans-McLaughlin, ed., *Immigration Reconsidered: History, Sociology, and Politics* (New York: Oxford University Press, 1989), 70–90.

33. For a general overview of this problem, see Gordon F. De Jong and Robert W. Gardner, eds., *Migration Decision Making* (Elmsford, N.Y.: Pergamon Press, 1981).

34. Dudley Baines, *Migration in a Mature Economy: Emigration and Internal Migration in England and Wales, 1861–1900* (New York: Cambridge University Press, 1985).

35. Julian Wolpert, "The Decision Process in a Spatial Context," *Annals of the Association of American Geographers* 54 (1964): 537–58; idem, "Behavioural Aspects of the Decision to Migrate," *Papers and Proceedings of the Regional Science Association* 15 (1965): 159–69; Walter Isnard, *Location and Space Economy* (Cambridge, Mass.: Harvard University Press, 1960), chap. 3; Donald J. Bogue, "A Migrant's-Eye View of the Costs and Benefits of Migration to a Metropolis," in *International Migration: A Comparative Perspective,* ed. Alan A. Brown and Egon Neuberger (New York: Academic, 1977), 167–82.

36. Thorsten Hägerstrand, "Migration and Area," *Lund Studies in Geography,* ser. B13 (1957): 27–158.

37. For an analysis of the migration of artisans, see Joan W. Scott, *The Glassworkers of Carmaux* (Cambridge, Mass.: Harvard University Press, 1974). Discussions of the geographical mobility of bureaucrats can be found in Charles Tilly, "Migration in Modern European History," in *Human Migration: Patterns and Policies,* ed. William H. McNeill and Ruth S. Adams (Bloomington: Indiana University Press, 1978), 48–72; Georges Dupeux, "Immigration urbaine et secteurs économiques," *Annales du Midi* 85 (1973): 209–20; Moch, *Paths to the City,* chap. 5; William H. Sewell, Jr., *Structure and Mobility: The Men and Women of Marseilles, 1820–1870* (Cambridge: Cambridge University Press, 1985). For an overview of economic problems in migration analysis, see Kenneth George Willis, *Problems in Migration Analysis* (Lexington, Mass.: Saxon House, 1974), chap. 2; Charles F. Mueller, *The Economics of Labor Migration* (New York: Academic, 1982), chap. 2.

38. Lutz Berkner and Franklin Mendels, "Inheritance Systems, Family Structure, and Demographic Patterns in Western Europe, 1700–1900," in Charles Tilly, ed., *Historical Studies of Changing Fertility* (Princeton: Princeton University Press, 1978), 209–23; Leslie Page Moch, "The Family and Migration: News from the French," *Journal of Family History* 11 (1986): 193–203; Leslie Page Moch et al., "Family Strategy: A Dialogue," *Historical Methods* 20 (1987): 113–25; Louise A. Tilly and Joan W. Scott, *Women, Work and Family* (New York: Holt, Rinehart and Winston, 1978).

39. See, for example, Caroline Brettell, *Men Who Migrate, Women Who Wait* (Princeton: Princeton University Press, 1986); Poitrineau, *Remues d'hommes*. Transatlantic migrations are best known; see Baines, *Migration in a Mature Economy;* Josef J. Barton, *Peasants and Strangers: Italians, Rumanians, and Slovaks in an American City, 1890–1950* (Cambridge, Mass.: Harvard University Press, 1975); Erich Franke, *Das Ruhrgebeit und Ostpreussen: Geschichte, Umfang und Bedeutung der Ostpreussen-Wanderung* (Essen: Walter Bacmeisters Nationalverlag, 1936).

40. Wolfgang Köllmann, *Bevölkerung in der industriellen Revolution* (Göttingen: Vandenhoeck und Ruprecht, 1974).

41. Hägerstrand, "Migration and Area."

42. Philip E. Ogden and S.W.C. Winchester, "The Residential Segregation of Provincial Migrants in Paris in 1911," *Transactions, Institute of British Geographers* 65 (1975): 29–44.

43. Dirk Hoerder, ed., *Labor Migration in the Atlantic Economies: The European and North American Working Classes during the Period of Industrialization* (Westport, Conn.: Greenwood Press, 1985).

44. Louis Chevalier, *Laboring Classes and Dangerous Classes in Paris during the First Half of the Nineteenth Century* (New York: Fertig, 1973).

45. William H. Hubbard, *Auf dem Weg zur Grossstädte: Eine Sozialgeschichte der Stadt Graz, 1850–1914* (Munich: R. Oldenbourg, 1984). For a historical view of rural loss, see Jean Pitié, *Exode rural et migrations intérieures en France* (Poitiers: Norois, 1971). For current studies of migration, see Harley L. Browning and Waltraut Feindt, "Selectivity of Migrants to a Metropolis in a Developing Country: A Mexican Case Study," *Demography* 6 (1969): 347–57.

46. Brettell, *Men Who Migrate, Women Who Wait;* Gay Gullickson, *Spinners and Weavers of Auffay: Rural Industry and the Sexual Division of Labor in a French Village, 1750–1850* (Cambridge: Cambridge University Press, 1986).

47. A. Gordon Darroch, "Migrants in the Nineteenth Century: Fugitives or Families in Motion?" *Journal of Family History* 6 (1981): 257–77.

48. Michael Anderson, *Family Structure in Nineteenth Century Lancashire* (Cambridge: Cambridge University Press, 1971); James Jackson, Jr., "Migration in Duisburg, 1867–1890: Occupational and Familial Contexts," *Journal of Urban History* 8 (1982): 235–70; Lynn Lees, *Exiles of Erin: Irish Migrants in Victorian London* (Ithaca: Cornell University Press, 1979); Moch, *Paths to the City;* Sewell, *Structure and Mobility.*

49. Sewell, *Structure and Mobility,* chap. 8.

50. Hufton, *The Poor of Eighteenth-Century France,* 367.

51. Jackson, "Migration and Urbanization in the Ruhr Valley."

52. Clark and Slack, *English Towns in Transition;* Clark and Souden, "Rural-Urban Migration and Its Impact in Early Modern England"; de Vries, *European Urbanization;* Rabb Houston and Keith D. M. Snell, "Protoindustrialization? Cottage Industry, Social Change, and Industrial Revolution," *The Historical Journal* 27 (1984): 473–92; David Levine, *Family Formation in an Age of Nascent Capitalism* (New York: Academic, 1977); Souden, "Movers and Stayers in Family Reconstitution Populations."

53. Poitrineau, *Remues d'hommes;* Poussou, *Bordeaux et le sud-ouest au XVIIIe siècle.*

54. Pierre Goubert, *Beauvais et le Beauvaisis de 1600 à 1715* (Paris: Service d'Edition et de Vente des Publications de l'Education Nationale, 1960). For an overview of the theory of protoindustrialization, see Leslie A. Clarkson, *Proto-Industrialization: The First Phase of Industrialization* (London: Macmillan, 1985).

55. de Vries, *European Urbanization;* Hochstadt, "Urban Mobility in Germany."

56. de Vries, *European Urbanization;* Steve Hochstadt, "Migration and Industrialization in Germany, 1815–1977," *Social Science History* 5 (1981): 445–68.

57. Michael Hanagan, "Agriculture and Industry in the Nineteenth-Century Stephanois: Household Employment Patterns and the Rise of a Permanent Proletariat," in *Proletarians and Protest: The Roots of Class Formation in an Industrializing World,* ed. Michael Hanagan and Charles Stephenson (New York: Greenwood, 1986), 77–106; Heilwig Schomerus, "The Family Life-Cycle: A Study of Factory Workers in Nineteenth-Century Württemberg," in *The German Family: Essays on the Social History of the Family in Nineteenth- and Twentieth-Century Germany,* ed. Richard J. Evans and W. Robert Lee (London: Croom Helm, 1981), 175–93; Scott, *The Glassworkers of Carmaux.*

58. Michael Anderson, *Family Structure in Nineteenth-Century Lancashire;* Louis Chevalier, *La formation de la population parisienne au XIXe siècle* (Paris: Presses Universitaires Françaises, 1950); Kertzer and Hogan, "On the Move"; Leslie Page Moch, "The Importance of Mundane Movements: Small Towns, Nearby Places, and Individual Itineraries in the History of Migration," in *Migration in Modern France: Population Mobility in the Nineteenth and Twentieth Centuries,* ed. Philip E. Ogden and Paul E. White (London: Unwin Hymen, 1989), 97–117.

59. Klaus Bade, "Die deutsch überseeische Massenwanderung im 19. und frühen 20. Jahrhundert: Bestimmungsfaktoren und Entwicklungsbedingungen," in *Auswanderer-*

Wanderarbeiter-Gastarbeiter: Bevölkerung, Arbeitsmarkt und Wanderung in Deutschland seit der Mitte des 19. Jahrhunderts, ed. Klaus Bade (Ostfildern: Scripta Mercaturea Verlag, 1984), 259–99; Hoerder, *Labor Migration in the Atlantic Economies.*

60. Steve Hochstadt, "Urban Migration in Imperial Germany: Towards a Quantitative Model," *Historical Papers / Communications Historiques, 1986* (1987): 197–210.

61. Ludwig von Bertalanffy, "An Outline of General System Theory," *British Journal of the Philosophy of Science* 1 (1950): 134–65; idem, "General System Theory," *General Systems Yearbook* 1 (1956): 1–10; idem, "General System Theory—A Critical Review," *General Systems Yearbook* 7 (1962): 1–20.

62. A few studies have taken this approach; see George J. Demko, *The Russian Colonization of Kazakhstan, 1896–1916,* Uralic and Altaic Series (Bloomington: Indiana University Press, 1969); Akin L. Mabogunje, "Systems Approach to a Theory of Rural-Urban Migration," *Geographical Analysis* 1 (1970): 1–18; John Walker Briggs, *An Italian Passage: Immigrants to Three American Cities, 1890–1930* (New Haven: Yale University Press, 1978); Michael J. Piore, *Birds of Passage: Migrant Labor and Industrial Societies* (New York: Cambridge University Press, 1979).

63. Lucassen, *Migrant Labour in Europe;* see also Eva Morawska, "Labor Migrations of Poles in the Atlantic World Economy," essay in this volume. For use of a systems framework in discussions of international labor migration to Europe after World War II, see Piore, *Birds of Passage;* John Berger and Jean Mohr, *A Seventh Man: A Book of Images and Words about the Experience of Migrant Workers in Europe* (London: Writers and Readers, 1975); Stephen Castles and Godula Kosack, *Immigrant Workers and Class Structure in Western Europe* (London: Oxford University Press, 1973); White and Woods, *The Geographical Impact of Migration.*

64. Fischer, *The Urban Experience.*

65. For example, there is the history workshop movement in England and the controversy among German social historians regarding the relative merits of "structural" and "experiential" history. See Raphael Samuel, ed., *People's History and Socialist Theory* (London: Routledge and Kegan Paul, 1981); Gerhard Paul and Bernhard Schössig, eds., *Die andere Geschichte* (Cologne: Bund-Verlag, 1985); Hannes Heer and Volker Ulrich, eds., *Geschichte entdecken* (Reinbek bei Hamburg: Rowohlt, 1985); Jürgen Kocka, "Sozialgeschichte zwischen Strukturgeschichte und Erfahrungsgeschichte," in *Sozialgeschichte in Deutschland, I,* ed. Wolfgang Schieder and Volker Sellin (Göttingen: Vandenhoeck und Ruprecht, 1986); Peter Borscheid, "Alltagsgeschichte—Modetorheit oder neues Tor zur Vergangenheit?" in *Sozialgeschichte in Deutschland, III,* ed. Wolfgang Schieder and Volker Sellin (Göttingen: Vandenhoeck und Ruprecht, 1987).

66. Friedrich Engels, *The Conditions of the Working Class in England in 1844,* trans. William O. Henderson and William H. Chaloner (Oxford: Basil Blackwell, 1971); Barbara Hammond and John L. Hammond, *The Rise of Modern Industry* (London: Methuen, 1926); Eric J. Hobsbawm, *Labouring Men* (New York: Basic Books, 1964); Edward P. Thompson, *The Making of the English Working Class* (New York: Pantheon Books, 1963).

67. Thomas S. Ashton, "Economics Responsible for Living Conditions," in *Capitalism and the Historians,* ed. Friedrich A. Hayek (Chicago: University of Chicago Press, 1954), 33–155; Ronald M. Hartwell, "The Rising Standard of Living in England, 1800–1850," *Economic History Review* 13 (1961): 397–416; George R. Porter, *The Progress of the Nation* (London: John Murray, 1847); A. J. Taylor, "Progress and Poverty in Britain, 1780–1850: A Reappraisal," *History,* n.s., 1960, 16–30.

Demographic Aspects of European Migration Worldwide

WALTER NUGENT

Introduction: European Migration in World Context

Despite the huge extent of "European migration worldwide," the term does not encompass all human migration, for to migrate has probably been a more normal human activity than to stay in one place.[1] Certainly Europeans have not had a monopoly on migration, although they did dominate intercontinental migration flows during the "age of steam," the period from about 1870 to 1914, when steamships replaced sailing vessels and railroad networks replaced travel by foot and horseback in Europe and in the Americas. Steam transportation greatly extended migration targets until World War I, the 1920s, and the 1930s, when war, restriction laws, and economic depression interdicted the process.

At other times, however, migration did take place. European migration was no new phenomenon before 1870. Princes and landlords commonly interfered with migration before the abolition of serfdom, while from the 1920s many Western democracies kept their virtues to themselves and restricted free entry well past 1950, despite the desperate needs of Jewish and other eastern European refugees. But when restriction eased, as it did with a new immigration law in the United States in 1965, migration resumed almost in flood tide. The post-1965 movement was, as before, to a more prosperous United States from less prosperous regions. Migrants also continued to flow from less developed areas of Europe to more affluent ones—Irish to England, Yugoslavs and Turks to Germany, Portuguese to France, and eastern Europeans to Germany after the fall of the Berlin Wall in 1989, for example. For the United States, however, the sources of immigration after 1965 were not Europe but rather Mexico, Central America, South Asia, the People's Republic of China, Korea, Taiwan, and the Philippines. The imminence of the British departure from Hong Kong promoted migration from there to the United States and, dramatically, to Vancouver in Canada.

Europe, then, was not the only source of migrants; millions of Asians migrated across national borders in the nineteenth and twentieth centuries.[2] But American and European scholarship has focused on transatlantic,

Europe–to–North America migration. Most of the transoceanic migrations of the past century and a half were in fact undertaken by Europeans; their sheer numbers warrant attention. During the nineteenth and early twentieth centuries, including "the age of steam," Europeans occupied most of the migration stage while Asians, Africans, and Latin Americans played less prominent roles.

From the middle of the nineteenth century, legal restrictions on a European's decision to migrate loosened or disappeared. Industrialization both destroyed older cottage industries and local markets and created opportunities for land seekers and wage seekers. Steam-powered transportation on land and sea did indeed, as the cliché says, abolish time and distance. For a little less than half a century, from about 1870 to World War I, Europeans migrated as never before or since. Probably fifty-five million of them went westward across the Atlantic to the United States, Argentina, Canada, Brazil, Cuba, Australia, New Zealand, and (in lesser numbers) other receivers. Perhaps 40 percent returned to Europe, and some crossed the ocean a number of times. In a legal sense these crossings were voluntary. Although economic duress and harsh labor contracts were often part of the explanation, slavery, serfdom, and military force were not.[3]

Migration and Age-Sex Structures of Populations

Linkages between migration and the concerns of demography—fertility, mortality, family size, age and durability of marriage, nutrition and disease, sex and age structures, and other characteristics of population—have been made in limited cases but not for the entire Atlantic region. The central concerns of demography are fertility, mortality, and migration, because these (and the balance among them) account for the growth or decline of populations. All three should be understood as historical and not simply contemporary phenomena. A few linkages (hardly exhausting the subject) are as follows.

Europeans during "the age of steam" migrated selectively rather than uniformly across age and sex groups. As a consequence, migration had a selective impact on the populations from which the migrants came, and those to which they came. If, as was true of nearly all European countries during the period 1870–1914, out-migrants are disproportionately male and young (most of them aged fifteen to forty), then fertility rates should fall and mortality rates should rise in the areas they came from. In other words, if the old and very young remain home, and others leave, higher mortality is virtually inevitable because the very young and the old are always more at risk of dying—more so a century ago than now (water and milk were less often pure, no cure existed for widespread tuberculosis, etc.).

Before 1914, upwards of three-fourths of all migrants to the United States, and more than half of migrants to Brazil (even though Brazil actively recruited whole families) were young men. Eventually these migrants produced a native-born second generation whose age and sex distribution approached the biological norm.

Age-sex pyramids help reveal these changes, dividing a population into five-year cohorts, stacking them from the youngest upward to the oldest, and placing them by sex on either side of a perpendicular axis (usually placing males on the left, females on the right). Pyramids representing populations undisturbed by migration or wars, or interference with natural mortality through sanitation, good nutrition, and health care, have wide bases and smooth sides. The widest bars (the zero-to-four age group) are at the bottom, narrowing steadily up the pyramid to the oldest and smallest group at the top. Bars extend about equally to the left and right of the vertical axis, showing a nearly even sex ratio in every age group. The pyramid of a preindustrial, "Third World," isolated population, now or in the past, has a wide base and a low peak, reflecting a low median age, because of high mortality and brief life expectancy within that society. Sanitation and other controls on endemic and epidemic disease have lengthened life. Pyramids of societies that benefit from them become taller, representing more people living longer: a higher proportion appears in the older cohorts, near the top.

In historical reality, the sides of population pyramids have always exhibited dents and bulges reflecting events that have interfered at some point with natural life courses. Age and sex pyramids for France, Germany, and Britain ever since 1920 have had deep indentations on the male side (and a less deep yet visible dent on the female side) for the cohorts who were then in their twenties and were disproportionately killed during the 1914–18 war. Similar reductions in a later cohort in their twenties became apparent after the 1939–45 war. As those cohorts grew older, they climbed to higher levels on the pyramid and took their reduced numbers—and thus dents in the sides of the pyramid—with them.

Such deep indentations do not appear in pyramids of the U.S. population. Deaths related to World War I numbered 117,000, and to World War II, 405,000—hardly inconsiderable but much lower, absolutely or proportionately, than those suffered by the major European belligerents.[4] A far more lethal event, the influenza epidemic of late 1918 and early 1919, killed over ten times as many Americans—550,000—as died in France in 1917–18. But since the influenza killed young and old, male and female alike, it made virtually no impact on the shape of the pyramid although it produced a huge if momentary surge in the national death rate. Dents and bulges in European age-sex pyramids in the twentieth century resulted largely from wars, while the American pyramids changed more from economic swings between prosperity, depression, and recovery, together with cultural forces still not clearly explained.

Migrations have also dented age-sex pyramids, notably among the cohorts aged fifteen to forty. Many of the migrants in the "age of steam" were young males. Among the Irish and the eastern European Jewry, many females left, too. These departures meant large indentations about halfway up the sides of those societies' pyramids. Conversely, in the four American countries receiving the bulk of the migrants (the United States, Canada, Brazil, and Argentina), pyramids briefly took on odd fir-tree-like shapes, narrower at the age zero-to-fifteen base than just above it, while the cohorts from fifteen to about forty were abnormally wide, especially on the male side. Then the pyramids flattened, reflecting the scarcity of people over forty-five. These irregular shapes persisted until after 1930. After that, restrictive laws and economic depression kept away new migrants; the earlier arrivals grew older and died, or returned to Europe; and their children restored the national pyramids to biological normality.

Links between migration, fertility, and mortality have generally meant lower fertility and higher mortality when young people leave, and a rise in fertility but lower mortality in places where the migrants arrive and stay. But relationships have seldom been as clean and uncomplicated as these rather arithmetical statements suggest. In the past, the connections have always been mitigated and skewed by social, economic, and cultural forces. In Italy, for example, the birthrate after 1900 remained high despite high out-migration, as if those who remained struggled to make up for the loss of those who emigrated.[5]

Family and Individual Migration, Land-seeking, and Labor-seeking

Changes in the nature of the migrating group, from families to individuals, deserve further exploration, as do changes in sex ratios, both among those who left Europe and among the many who returned. In the historiography of American immigration, pre-1880s migrants have been thought of as coming from northern and western Europe, seeking land, and traveling as families, while migrants from the 1880s to 1914 have been seen as coming from southern or eastern Europe, seeking wage-paying industrial jobs, and traveling by themselves or in work teams. There is some truth in all of these statements, but they obscure many exceptions. The shift from land-seeking to labor-seeking, on the face of it, seems to have coincided with the simultaneous onset of agricultural depression and the expansion of factory, construction, and mining jobs in the United States in the late 1880s—that is, the "closing of the frontier." Urban-industrial opportunities in the United States expanded at that very moment, as they also did in Germany.[6]

This account involves serious problems, however. Nearly twice as many homesteads were patented after 1900 than before; new entries peaked during 1901–10, and final patents during 1911–20—*not* before 1900.[7] Between 1902 and 1921, in virtually every year, would-be homesteaders entered claims for over ten million acres (four million hectares). Not once before 1902 was that level of settlement reached. Sales of railroad land, state-held land, and former Indian allotments under the 1887 Dawes Severalty Act, together with the distribution of federal lands, disproved conclusively the idea that the frontier ended in 1890 or any year close to it. Over seven hundred thousand additional farms were created in the United States between 1900 and 1920.[8]

This immense amount of new farm settlement was hardly undertaken exclusively by native-born Americans. In the Dakotas and Montana, into which settlers swarmed in the first dozen years of the twentieth century, the newcomers prominently included Ukrainians, Norwegians, Volga Germans, Scots, Irish, English, and a sprinkling of Polish Jews, Syrian Melkite Christians, and African Americans. The population of the Western census region (the eleven Mountain and Pacific states) more than doubled between 1900 and 1920, from four million to nine million, and that number included hundreds of thousands of migrants born in every country that sent people to the United States from Europe or Asia. They entered the entire occupational range from farming and ranching to mining, construction, railroading, public and private services, and many more categories. Ethnic America did not stop at the Mississippi River, nor did the migrants' farming frontier close in 1890.

Ethnicity was even more a feature of settlement in western Canada. In the prairie provinces of Manitoba, Saskatchewan, and Alberta, the frontier of settlement lasted until 1930, when Ottawa's "Dominion Lands Policy" ended, and it encompassed vast acreages as far as the northernmost limits of arability. Scots and English arrived, as well as Americans (many of Canadian background). The Ottawa government and the Canadian Pacific Railway also aggressively recruited Ukrainians, German Russians, and other Europeans after 1906, with much success—indeed more than was wise given the difficulty of making a living from homesteads in the colder and more arid locations.[9] Well into the twentieth century, in short, migrants to Canada sought western land as well as wage-paying jobs in eastern Canada. Europeans also continued land-seeking, not only labor-seeking, in Argentina: Italians surged into the pampas after this area opened to settlement in 1880. Although few migrants became owner-occupants after the mid-1890s, and although they were restricted to various forms of tenancy, they continued to arrive and become agriculturists.[10]

Brazilian history also demonstrates that land-seeking continued to be an activity involving European migrants well beyond 1900, and not just in the period following the abolition of slavery in 1888, when the greatest immigration surge began. Poles, Germans, Japanese, and others—but especially northern Italians—went there. As in Argentina, relatively few became landowners. The Italians were usually wage earners (i.e., sharecroppers paid at least partly in wages as well as their own produce). But they were rural wage earners, not urban. They were recruited, they arrived, and they worked in family groups rather than as independent individuals, from 1889 to 1902, when the Italian government forbade further further assisted migration of families because of bad conditions in Brazil.

Thus, northern Italians in Brazil contradicted three stereotypes: they settled on the land—the coffee plantations—rather than in towns; they earned wages; and they worked in family groups, with parents and children all contributing.[11] Their male-female ratio was consequently more balanced than was usually true of European immigrant groups of that period. That and the contribution of small children to family survival and success in the coffee-growing regions helped maintain Brazil's high fertility rate well beyond 1950.[12]

The stereotypical shift among European migrants from land-seeking to wage-seeking was, therefore, neither complete nor clear-cut. The degrees of dependence and the levels of tenancy among migrants to rural Argentina, Brazil, Canada, and the United States were as complicated and personally significant as the levels among European peasants, although local terms differed. The "agricultural ladder" from hired hand to sharecropper to tenant did include a top rung in Canada and the United States—freehold ownership—that was normally missing in Brazil and Argentina after the 1890s, but even there some migrants did reach it.

To some degree, then, the American receiving nations were all lands of opportunity for Europeans, whose chances of ownership in Europe were essentially nil except for first sons who inherited.[13] Even in Brazil, where freehold ownership was more difficult to achieve than in any other New World receiver, some migrants did achieve it. How easily remains in doubt.[14] Very probably, independent land ownership in Brazil or Argentina was never easy to achieve except for the favored few who arrived early and were rewarded by the crown or by conquerors. A small number—tens of thousands among millions—of Italian and German settlers in state-sponsored nuclear colonies in southern Brazil or parts of the Argentine pampas achieved it. By contrast, in Canada and the United States after 1900, small proprietors numbered in the hundreds of thousands or the millions.

What made the difference? Many things, no doubt; but a system of precise survey and public sale of land, and retention of it by the central government until it was sold, was critical. Despite well-intentioned and inspiringly worded land laws, Brazil and Argentina lacked such a system. The United States and Canada had that system. It underpinned land-seeking family migration in the United States until about 1913 and in Canada until 1930. Sponsored family migration to Brazil ceased abruptly in 1902; opportunities for migrant families in Argentina hardly survived the 1890s. In North America, however, family opportunities continued. Rural fertility, therefore, remained high, and the peopling and plowing up of prairie land proceeded more rapidly and thoroughly after 1900 than before.

Sex Ratios among Migrants: Women as Migrants

Sex ratios among migrants, and how they changed over time and among nationality groups, also reward study. Ratios of females to males obviously were more nearly equal when families rather than individuals dominated migration flows. National-level statistics from most European countries in the 1870–1914 period reveal that males were more likely to migrate than females, and to return home more often. Sex ratios can affect social behavior, as was often revealed in the different behavior of male-dominated gold rushes all over the American West, and in family-centered copper-mining towns, very strongly Irish, such as Butte, Montana.

Families, however, have not been the only explanation for balanced sex ratios. Women have not migrated solely as family members in the roles of wives and mothers. Females have, in fact, outnumbered males among migrants to the United States in most of the years since World War I. The United States Department of Labor reported in 1985 that "the traditional working-age immigrant male has accounted for only a third of all immigration to the United States," with women and children providing the other two-thirds. This has been true unvaryingly since the 1930s. Part of the explanation is that American law has encouraged the reuniting of families. Women have arrived, often with children, to rejoin husbands, and women have arrived as widows to rejoin children. As on expert wrote in 1985, "the overwhelming majority of immigrants who enter the United States today come to complete a family, rather than to work."[15] This suggests that World War I marked a sharp discontinuity in the sex ratios of migrants, and probably in people's reasons for migrating to the United States from Europe, since males predominated before 1914 and females since 1919.

Single women migrants were hardly unknown before 1914, however. Among Irish migrants, one of the three largest national groups going to North America, females outnumbered males at least as early as the 1870s. Many young Irish women migrated to become domestic servants.[16] Facing only a minimal language barrier and coming from the society with the highest celibacy rate in Europe, single Irish women often became teachers in public schools while others arrived as members of religious orders, becoming teachers in the proliferating Catholic parochial schools or nurses in Catholic hospitals. Among the eastern European Jewish migrants to the United States, women were almost as numerous; that is, the sex ratio was closer to equal than in most other groups. Many Jewish women brought skills and made contacts that led to jobs in the garment industries of New York, Chicago, and Philadelphia. Immigrant Jewish women "moved in and out of work and politics," and "turned the garment industry upside down with a wave of militant strikes and shop-floor activism and helped build the two major clothing workers' unions."[17]

Among other immigrant groups, sex ratios were higher—roughly 65 to 70 percent male among non-Jewish eastern Europeans (Slavs and Magyars), over 70 percent among Italians, and upwards of 90 percent among Balkan peoples. Women from these groups less frequently or visibly worked outside the home. They were nonetheless active in a broad range of activities that were domestic but not familial; they participated in the money economy as shopkeepers, dressmakers, laundresses, boarding-house operators, and in other ways.[18] During the "age of steam," the proportion of women among the gainfully employed in the United States rose from less than 15 percent to over 21 percent, and the actual number from under two million to over eight million.[19] Immigrant women were very much part of that growing labor force.

Sex ratios among people leaving Europe were not always the same as sex ratios among ethnic groups after arrival and settlement in the United States and other receiving countries, because in this period men left home more often than women, but also returned more often. Married or single, women migrants (more than men) stayed in North America once they got there. Reasons were abundant. One needs only to read of the unappetizing situations of young Norwegian or Irish farm women to appreciate why they would have been eager to migrate and not return.[20] Rates of reverse migration varied from group to group among women, as they did for men. Fewer than 10 percent of Jewish and Irish women (or men) returned, while over half of the Bulgarian and Romanian men and women did so.[21] Among all nationalities, women returned less often than men regardless of the overall migration rate for the group, its sex ratio, or whether they were married or single.

The rate of repatriation, and the sex ratios among migrants, returnees, and persisters, bore directly if not always predictably on the ease or difficulty of a group's assimilation into the receiving society, whether that of the United States or that of another country. Economic and cultural factors were always important, but so was demography: the increasing presence and greater persistence of females, over time, promoted the formation of families, social stability, and a second generation, born in the New World, with a biologically balanced sex ratio. Immigrant groups with male-skewed sex ratios could and did establish themselves through either intermarriage with women of other groups or endogamous marriage if that option was open. But among groups in which females were largely absent—the most extreme case in the United States being the Chinese, who were well over 90 percent male in the first generation—assimilation and growth were very slow. Self-sustaining demographic regimes obviously could not happen without women. As long as endogamy was the norm, as it was for most newly arrived migrant groups, and as long as females either did not migrate with the males or frequently returned home, the position of such groups in the receiving country remained unstable.[22]

Source Problems in Establishing Numbers of Migrants

Migration historians are indebted to demographers for establishing concepts such as fertility, mortality, and age-sex ratios, defining them precisely, devising techniques for measuring them, and assembling time-series data on them. Demographers have, however, focused much more on fertility and mortality than on migration in measuring changes in the sizes of populations or in explaining changes. One probable reason for such different emphases is greater confidence in the statistical raw materials about fertility and mortality as compared to migration. For there are some annoying problems with the data on European and New World migration.

To begin with, even the national and supranational totals of migrants are uncertain and arguable. Four recent estimates of the gross number of people who left Europe do not fully agree. One claims that 55 million left between 1846 and 1924, of whom perhaps 25 percent returned, leaving a net east-to-west flow of about 41 million. Another estimates 55 to 60 million westbound migrants between 1820 and 1830. A third estimates westward flow at 65 million gross, 50 million net, between 1800 and 1914. And a fourth finds 35 million between 1871 and 1915.[23] The fourth figure is almost certainly too low; a recent estimate of total arrivals in the four major receivers alone—Argentina, Brazil, Canada, and the United States—puts them at 42 million for 1871 to 1914. Of that number, 70 percent went to the United States, 11 percent to Canada, just under 11 percent to Argentina, and 8 percent to Brazil.[24]

As for specific countries, departure figures for given national groups often do not match, even closely, the arrival figures for the same groups. For example, the records of Argentina, Brazil, and the United States show more Italians arriving than the records of Italy show Italians leaving, for most years from 1876 through 1900; and for 1901 through 1913, Italy recorded more departures than the Argentine, Brazilian, and U.S. recorded arrivals.[25] Discrepancies also appear in the records of other migrant groups. Spanish authorities, in a volume published in 1916, noted that their own figures for 1911–15 counted 403,000 Spaniards departing for Argentina, while Argentine figures showed 484,000 Spaniards arriving. The authors attempted to explain that some migrants left from non-Spanish ports in Europe, and others arrived in Argentina overland, presumably from Uruguay.[26]

Although German and American figures correspond better than most, between 1871 and 1928 German emigrant figures were 20 percent lower than American immigrant figures for Germans, with a particularly severe undercount (less than half of the American figures) for one decade.[27] Many Germans did, in fact, take ship from non-German ports such as Antwerp, Rotterdam, or Le Havre, and thus missed being counted. For other countries that received Germans, discrepancies are considerably greater than for the United States.

Since the gross and net estimates for the entire Atlantic region are compilations of statistics like these, totals inevitably must be somewhat uncertain. Other kinds of records, such as national censuses, mitigate the problem when they provide place of birth and, at times, place of previous residence. Careful compilation has led to estimates of gross and net European migration that are reasonable, if not exact. Ferenczi and Willcox (a fifth estimate, close to Pounds's given above) added up the official figures for the sending and receiving countries, and put the total of departing Europeans, 1820–1924, at 50 million, but of Europeans who arrived in the New World, 1846–1924, at 55.5 million. Since the average annual transatlantic migration between 1820 and 1846 by anyone's count was much smaller than it was after 1846, the discrepancy between sending and receiving totals, for the same years, becomes about 10 percent.[28] If so, we are justified in about 90 percent confidence—that is, confidence within a range of 10 percent either way—in gross and net totals for the entire emigration, and by country, with the understanding that in certain years the figures may be well inside or outside that range. The discrepancies have never been thoroughly explained; changes in visa requirements, in record-keeping, and in definitions of who was a migrant account for some of them, but we will probably never have all the correct figures.[29]

Destinations of European Migrants

Although the migration statistics are therefore problematic, the size and direction of flows are not seriously in dispute. As suggested earlier, the United States undoubtedly took in 60 to 70 percent of the people who left Europe, with Canada and Argentina each absorbing 10 to 15 percent, and Brazil 7 to 10 percent. Other countries in the New World, and other receiving areas such as Africa and Australasia, absorbed smaller numbers. Differences between gross and net migration—the separation of all the migrants into those who left Europe permanently and those who went back—were, in general, more explainable by conditions in Europe than in the receiving locations. In other words, the tendency of Irish, for example, to stay in the United States (which took in around 90 percent of them) or Canada or Australia rather than return, or conversely of southern Italians to return in many cases rather than stay in Argentina or Brazil or the United States, was more a function of Irish and Italian conditions than of New World conditions. In a major receiving country, and the United States is the best example, rates of persistence or return varied widely among groups; as noted above, female migrants in high-return groups went home much more frequently than male migrants in low-return groups.

Destinations varied among European groups, for many reasons. Similarity of language and culture assured that a majority of Portuguese went to Brazil, or Spaniards to Cuba, or Scots to Canada. A faster voyage (meaning wages earned more quickly) and cheaper steamship tickets directed the choice very often. So did prepaid tickets sent from America; as one writer put it, the decision to emigrate was often made in America, when someone there sent a ticket to someone at home. The presence or lack of a social-occupational "roof," as Samuel Baily has shown, sent many Italians to Argentina (or kept them there instead of returning home) because they enjoyed much greater upward mobility, occupational choice, and acceptance in Argentina than in the United States.[30] Chain migration—the presence of kinfolk or townfolk already on site—played an enormously important role for members of all groups. Temperate climate helped. Laws, welcoming or discriminatory, shaped people's choices. And there were other reasons.

Migration to Latin America was in no sense evenly spread. Between 1900 and 1930, Argentina's population grew almost four times as fast as Mexico's, Brazil's more than twice as fast: European in-migration accounted for 44 percent of Argentina's growth, and virtually none of Mexico's.[31] As one authority explains,

> Only a few Latin American countries benefited from mass European migration. In order of importance, these were Argentina, Brazil, Cuba, Uruguay and Chile. Approximately 4 million Europeans settled in Argentina, followed by 2 million in Brazil. . . . A little less than 600,000 people settled in Cuba and the same number in Uruguay. . . . Net migration to Chile probably amounted to about 200,000.[32]

Brazil overtook Mexico in the late nineteenth century as the most populous country in Latin America, as Mexico failed to attract Europeans, and in many years (especially 1910–20) saw thousands of its own people depart for the United States.[33]

Besides Italians, who went to both countries in large numbers, Brazil drew Portuguese and Argentina drew Spaniards, because of language affinity. From 1891 to 1914, over eight hundred thousand people left Portugal (according to Portuguese figures), and of these, 81 percent went to Brazil,

13.5 percent to the United States (mostly from the Azores), 3.4 percent to Africa (which included Angola, Mozambique, and other colonies), 1.2 percent to South American countries other than Brazil, and less than 1 percent to Asia and Oceania.[34] Of Spanish migrants in the years 1910–13 inclusive, 67 to 76 percent went to Argentina, 15 to 29 percent to Cuba, 5 to 9 percent to Brazil, about 1 percent to the United States, and the remaining 3 to 5 percent to all other countries of Latin America plus Canada.[35]

During the period 1881–1910, 2.15 million Germans emigrated (officially, at least), and of those, 1.99 million, or 92.5 percent, went to the United States. Brazil and Argentina each received 1.6 percent, Canada 0.9 percent, Australia and Africa 0.6 percent, and Asia 0.1 percent. The receiving countries' figures on arriving Germans are substantially higher, but still show the vast majority coming to the United States.[36] The Reich's official colonies—Southwest Africa, German East Africa, various Pacific islands, and other places—attracted a few thousand, while the Missouri Valley and Great Plains of the United States, attracting hundreds of thousands, functioned as its real, de facto colonial sphere. Over 90 percent of migrating Scandinavians chose the United States, the remaining few Canada or, less likely, Latin America.[37]

Italian migrants' targets fluctuated considerably over time—leading choices were France in the 1870s, Argentina in the 1880s, Brazil in the 1890s, and the United States in the 1900s and 1910s; but at no time did any significant number migrate to Italy's African colonies of Libya, Eritrea, and Somaliland.[38] Of the nine million people who left England, Wales, Scotland, and Ireland between 1871 and 1914, 5.6 million went to the United States, 2.1 million to Canada, 1.3 million to Australia and New Zealand, and a handful to Britain's many other colonies.[39] More than half of the emigrant Scots chose Canada, but the Irish overwhelmingly went to the United States,[40] as did roughly two-thirds of the English. One point is very clear: overseas colonies—whether of Portugal, Spain, Germany, Italy, or even Britain (aside from Canada, Australia, and New Zealand)—did not attract migrants from their "parent" countries in even remotely the numbers that went to Argentina, Brazil, and, most of all, the United States. The European overseas empires, so visible at the close of the nineteenth century, have long since reverted to home rule; and from a demographic perspective it is easy to see why. There were never enough "mother country" emigrants to establish a self-sustaining demographic majority.

Demographic and Mobility Transitions: A Critique

Certainty about numbers does not improve as one deals with groups at subnational levels. Trustworthy information is scarce regarding the age and sex composition of populations, family and individual living arrangements, and other desirable demographic statistics. Fertility figures are fortunately now available for Europe throughout the mass-emigration period. The Princeton European Fertility Project under Ansley Coale and his associates has established precise levels and changes in European fertility, appearing in a series of monographs of which the summary volume came out in 1986.[41] These volumes constitute a critically important contribution to European demographic history. The results, curiously, undermine the hypothesis that the project set out to verify, namely, the theory of demographic transition. Historic European fertility patterns, when established by the group's research, did not support that conventional wisdom.

Two uses of "demographic transition" need to be distinguished here. No one denies that in European (and New World) societies, both birth and death rates have declined, often sharply, from higher levels in the past. Somehow, sometime, suddenly or gradually, births and deaths declined in Europe, much of the Americas, and some other parts of the world. In that simple sense, the transition from high rates to low certainly occurred. But the paradigm statement of "transition" went well beyond that. It posited a sequential pattern of fertility and mortality changes. The English social scientist A. M. Carr-Saunders first expounded this idea in 1925, based on what was then known of English population history.[42] In 1971 the American geographer Wilbur Zelinsky gave it a classic restatement, writing that demography has only two "axiomatic items":

> the theory of the demographic transition and the so-called laws of migration [set forth by E. G. Ravenstein in the 1880s]. The first is the assertion that, on attaining certain thresholds of socioeconomic development, every community will pass from a premodern near-equilibrium, in which high levels of mortality tend to cancel out high levels of fertility, to a modern near-equilibrium, in which low fertility almost matches low mortality *but with the decline in births lagging far enough behind the decline in deaths to ensure a substantial growth in numbers during the transitional phase.*[43]

"Premodern" high fertility and mortality have indeed given way to "modern" low fertility and mortality. But was there typically a lagged response of lowered births to lowered deaths? Was there any "transitional phase"?

Zelinsky declared that the "demographic transition" he regarded as axiomatic should more properly be termed a "vital transition," since he also saw a "mobility transition" taking place in societies as they progressed from premodern to modern. The two transitions, vital and mobility, together constituted in his view two sides of "demographic transition." This idea fell on deaf ears, however, which was probably just as well since neither of these putative transitions correspond at all closely to the historical record. The Princeton demographers, after their enormous efforts to trace European fertility changes, had to conclude that,

> Given the rough coincidence of modernization and the demographic transition, and the persuasiveness of the stories that were told to explain their relation, it is surprising that, in country after country, the tests of the hypotheses embedded in demographic transition theory [the lag in fertility decline] produced *no certain confirmation of the theory.*[44]

The historian Steve Hochstadt, reviewing the Coale and Watkins summary volume in the *American Historical Review*, reported that

> Perhaps the most significant finding is that the original theory of the demographic transition, a variant of post–World War II modernization theory, cannot explain differences either in the timing of the [fertility] decline or in levels of fertility.

Hochstadt also noted that the relation "of declining fertility to declining mortality, one of the primary causal connections claimed by demographic transition theory [is] rejected in this volume."[45]

Facts played strange tricks on this once-persuasive, indeed in Zelinsky's words "axiomatic," theory. The paradigm of demographic transition, in its classic sequential form, failed its most elaborate historical test. Historians nonetheless owe the Princeton demographers a great debt for their work on historical fertility trends; the real record is much more complex and nuanced than Carr-Saunders and his many followers ever suspected. A similar massive effort to discover historic mortality patterns would be most welcome.

A word may also be said about Zelinsky's "mobility transition"; it relates even more directly than fertility and mortality to the history of migration. Yet here, too, lie problems. Zelinsky assumed that the late-nineteenth-century English statistician E. G. Ravenstein and the more recently developed modernization theory were correct.[46] Mobility, wrote Zelinsky, is "an essential component of the modernization process"; it invariably accompanies modernization; it increases as societies undergo fertility and mortality transitions; it changes in orderly ways; and this mobility transition is irreversible. All of these characteristics were standard elements in modernization theory as it was elaborated from the 1940s through the 1970s. In theory—though it is not a historically sustained theory—they accompany the changes undergone by societies, over time, as they progress from "traditional" to "modern."

In discussing mobility, Zelinsky described the starting point, the traditional end of the continuum, as "sedentary peasant societies." As their fertility and mortality shifted downward, mobility (i.e., migration) increased.[47] Unfortunately, however, "sedentary peasant societies" have proved hard to find in the histories of Europe and the Americas. As Leslie Moch, Dirk Hoerder, Caroline Brettell, and others have demonstrated about Europeans since the eighteenth century (indeed by Fernand Braudel about

Europeans living around the Mediterranean since ancient times), mobility and migration have always been part of European peasant life.

Europeans have always migrated—in preindustrial as well as industrial periods, for all sorts of reasons—to improve their economic condition, to gain psychological satisfaction, to raise their status, to make good marriages or escape bad ones, to avoid jail or conscription, to join mercenary armies, to achieve "freedom" in any number of ways. If there has been a "mobility transition" it has been going on for a very long time, far too long to account for a stage "from which" and a stage "to which." There never was a "traditional European peasantry" that fitted the pattern variables of conventional modernization theory. Europeans in Europe, the Americas, and the South Pacific have not behaved as the theory says they must have.

As for Ravenstein's laws, the economic historians Donald and Jo Ann Parkerson have evaluated them recently. They note that, writing nearly thirty years before Carr-Saunders announced the idea of sequential demographic transition, Ravenstein laid a basis for it. Ravenstein "minimized individual, class and ethnic variations" in migration, and, "by arguing that the increase in the volume of migration essentially was a linear one . . . he tied migration to later modernization models of society." But Ravenstein based his "laws" almost exclusively on nineteenth-century English and Scottish data. With much more information now known about trans-European and transatlantic migration, few would now claim, as Zelinsky did, that Ravenstein's laws are "axiomatic."[48]

Demography, Empires, and Settlement Frontiers

The alternative to a false transition theory of the sequential kind is further research of the high caliber of the Princeton European Fertility Project—but on mortality—and continuing research on migration patterns. One such pattern provides an answer to why some European implants on other soil took firm root, while others withered. The answer lies in migration and numbers of migrants. "Settler societies," as the Australian historian Donald Denoon called Australia, New Zealand, Chile, Argentina, Uruguay, and South Africa, took root because Europeans went to those places in numbers, stayed long enough to create a second generation balanced in age and sex structure, and pushed aside the aboriginal inhabitants.[49] Of the six, South Africa is the only one in which native peoples have outnumbered people of European stock, and there, following the peaceful shift from F. W. de Klerk to Nelson Mandela, the story is still being written. In the other five, the likelihood that indigenous people will ever push aside those of European stock is remote.

A similar rooting of Europeans took place in Brazil, Canada, the United

States, and virtually all of the New World including Oceania. As indicated earlier in this essay, it did not take place in other "outposts of empire" where Europeans gained footholds in the eighteenth and nineteenth centuries with so much travail, conflict, and bloodshed on all sides—India, Indo-China, most of Africa, and parts of the Middle East. The motivations and mentalities underpinning settlement frontiers and "outposts of empire" had much in common, not least the Europeans' assumption that it was permissible, even laudable, to intrude upon and "make better use" of territory—territory that was already occupied, but by people they considered primitive. The main difference between frontiers of settlement and imperial outposts is that migrants did not follow the military and the civil servants to the outposts in any numbers; they flocked to frontiers of settlement whether or not government and soldiers opened the way. Examples abound in U.S. history of settlers or miners crossing into Indian country regardless of treaty lines, and similar activity still takes place in Amazonia, the last great frontier of both settlement and resource exploitation.[50]

The linking of migration history with traditional "frontier history" in the United States and Canada has only recently begun. But both are essentially demographic movements. Frontiers of settlement mean mass migrations, as do the more volatile frontiers of exploitation such as the gold rushes to California, Victoria, and the Yukon, or the seizure of land for cattle ranching in the North American Great Plains, the Argentine pampas, and Amazonia. The history of settlement and migration has sometimes involved exploitation and a pessimistic historiography—and sometimes opportunity and success, with an optimistic historiography, as in the American Turnerian tradition. In many migration histories lies an unspoken major premise—that the fundamental burden of the story is *either* one of exploitation *or* of opportunity, perceived or achieved. The dichotomy is seldom complete, nor the direction perfectly plain. Few Turnerians (certainly not Turner himself) have been so blinkered as to ignore exploitation; few of the pessimists have wholly ignored the element of opportunity. The middle ground is vast, and specific cases require their own emphases. Each historian must decide whether—or more likely, to what extent—opportunity or exploitation better describes the history of European migration worldwide, or any specific part of it.

Notes

This essay, in a different form, was first given as a paper at the Bremerhaven Conference (see note 1 below). In revising it the author has benefited greatly from remarks by commentators Rudolph Vecoli and Nora Faires as well as several of the conference participants.

1. Kathleen Neils Conzen, Comments on the session, "Cultures of Origin: The Ger-

manies," at the Conference on "Continental European Migration and Transcontinental Migration to North America, A Comparative Perspective," Bremerhaven, Germany, August 17, 1991.

2. Examples of helpful works on Asian migration eastward across the Pacific include Yasuo Wakatsuki, "Japense Emigration to the United States, 1866–1924: A Monograph," *Perspectives in American History* 12 (1979): 387–516; Joan M. Jensen, *Passage from India: Asian Indian Immigrants in North America* (New Haven: Yale University Press, 1988); Yuji Ichioka, *The Issei: The World of the First Generation Japanese Immigrants, 1885–1924* (New York: Free Press, 1988); Arlinda Rocha Nogueira, *A Imigração Japonesa para a Lavoura Cafeeira Paulista, 1908–1922* (São Paulo: Universidade de São Paulo, 1973). An excellent general history of Asians in the United States is Roger Daniels, *Asian America: Chinese and Japanese in the United States since 1950* (Seattle: University of Washington Press, 1988). See also Peter Corris, *Passage, Port and Plantation: A History of Solomon Islands Labour Migration 1870–1914* (Melbourne: Melbourne University Press, 1973); Geoffrey Blainey, *The Tyranny of Distance: How Distance Shaped Australia's History* (New York: St. Martin's Press, 1968); J. W. McCarty, "Australia as a Region of Recent Settlement in the Nineteenth Century," *Australian Economic History Review* 13 (1973): 148–67.

3. For a more extended discussion of many of these points, with more detailed reference to specific countries and national groups, see Walter Nugent, *Crossings: The Great Transatlantic Migrations 1870–1914* (Bloomington: Indiana University Press, 1992).

4. United States Bureau of the Census, *Historical Statistics of the United States from Colonial Times to 1970* (Washington: Government Printing Office, 1975), 2:1140.

5. B. R. Mitchell, *European Historical Statistics, 1750–1970* (New York: Columbia University Press, 1975), series B5, pp. 86, 93; Unsigned essay, "Sviluppo della Populazione Italiana da 1861 al 1961," *Annali di Statistica* (Roma: Istituto Centrale di Statistica), Serie VIII, vol. 17 (1965):18.

6. The frontier thesis of Frederick Jackson Turner, which he announced in his essay "The Significance of the Frontier in American History" (1893), colored the thinking of the next two generations of American historians, including historians of migration. In his essay, Turner's point of departure was the observation of Census Bureau officials that the 1890 Census revealed so much new settlement in the western half of the country that no meaningful "frontier line" could be drawn on the map. Turner translated this into the statement that the frontier had ended, four hundred years after Columbus and a hundred years after the American Constitution, and that this meant the end of the first great (frontier) phase in American history—leading to an uncertain future.

7. Strictly speaking, a "homestead" was a 160-acre (64.75-hectare) tract of public domain made available to actual settlers under the Homestead Act of 1862. Later acts expanded the tract size to 320 acres (129.5 hectares) or more. Much government land was never disposed of under these acts, but continued to be sold at land offices. Railroads for decades sold land granted them by the government as an inducement to extend their lines westward. Thus "homesteads" were free, while other land cost money. "Homestead" is often used, more loosely, to refer to any new farm regardless of the means by which it was acquired.

8. Paul W. Gates, *History of Public Land Law Development* (New York: Arno Press, 1979), chap. 18 and Appendix A; United States, *Historical Statistics,* 1:457, series K4.

9. "Homesteading" is the accurate term for Canada although the precise details differed from American homesteading. Settlers frequently combined 160 free acres of government land with a contiguous 160 acres purchased from the Canadian Pacific. For Canadian frontier settlement after 1900, see Gerald Friesen, *The Canadian Prairies: A History* (Lincoln: University of Nebraska Press, 1984), and Chester Martin, *'Dominion Lands' Policy* (Toronto: McClelland and Steward Ltd., 1973).

10. On Argentina, very helpful works are Ezequiel Gallo, *La Pampa Gringa: La Coloniza-*

ción Agricola en Santa Fe (1870–1895) (Buenos Aires: Editorial Sudamericana, 1982); James R. Scobie, *Revolution on the Pampas: A Social History of Argentine Wheat, 1860–1910* (Austin: University of Texas Press, 1964); Carl E. Solberg, *The Prairies and the Pampas: Agrarian Policy in Canada and Argentina, 1880–1930* (Stanford: Stanford University Press, 1987).

11. On migration to Brazil, see Lucy Maffei Hutter, *Imigração Italiana em São Paulo (1880–1889)* (São Paulo: Universidade de São Paulo, 1972), and idem, *Imigração Italiana em São Paulo de 1902 a 1914: O Processo Imigratorio* (São Paulo: Universidade de São Paulo, 1986); Warren Dean, *Rio Claro: A Brazilian Plantation System, 1820–1920* (Stanford: Stanford University Press, 1976); Paul Hugon, *Demografia Brasileira: Ensaio de Demoeconomia Brasileira* (São Paulo: Universidade de São Paulo, 1973).

12. Pedro Calderon Beltrao, *Demografia: Ciencia da Populaçao, Analise e Teoria* (Pôrto Alegre: Libraria Sulina Editora, 1972), 173; Girogio Mortara, *Pesquisas sobre Populações Americanas,* Estudos Brasileiros de Demografia, Monografia No. 3 (Rio de Janeiro: Fundação Getulio Vargas, 1947), 86–90; Giorgio Mortara, "The Development and Structure of Brazil's Population," in Joseph J. Spengler and Otis Dudley Duncan, *Demographic Analysis: Selected Readings* (Glencoe: The Free Press, 1956), 653.

13. Stefan Kieniewicz describes the different levels of peasantry in postemancipation eastern Europe in *The Emancipation of the Polish Peasantry* (Chicago: University of Chicago Press, 1969). For tenancy contracts in Argentina, see Gallo, *Pampa Gringa,* 80–81, 88–94; James R. Scobie, *Argentina: A City and a Nation* (New York: Oxford University Press, 1964), 117–19; Mark Jefferson, *Peopling the Argentine Pampas* (New York: American Geographical Society, 1926), 168–71; Robert F. Foerster, *The Italian Emigration of Our Times* (Cambridge: Harvard University Press, 1924), 243–46.

14. For differing views, see Thomas H. Holloway, *Immigrants on the Land: Coffee and Society in São Paulo, 1886–1934* (Chapel Hill: University of North Carolina Press, 1980), 173–74; Manuel Diegues Junior, *População e Propriedade da Terra no Brasil* (Washington: União Pan-Americana, 1959), 45; Dean, *Rio Claro,* 192.

15. *New York Times,* 9 September 1985.

16. Hasia Diner, *Erin's Daughters in America: Irish Immigrant Women in the Nineteenth Century* (Baltimore: Johns Hopkins University Press, 1983).

17. Susan A. Glenn, *Daughters of the Shtetl: Life and Labor in the Immigrant Generation* (Ithaca: Cornell University Press, 1990), 242 and jacket. Also helpful is Sydney Stahl Weinberg, *The World of Our Mothers: The Lives of Jewish Immigrant Women*) (New York: Schocken Books, 1988).

18. The scholarly literature on immigrant women as workers continues to grow. Donna Gabaccia, in her extremely useful *Immigrant Women in the United States: A Selectively Annotated Multidisciplinary Bibliography* (Westport, Conn.: Greenwood Press, 1989), lists 470 items in two chapters on "Work" and "Working Together." More research is needed on recent migrants and on European women who migrated to South America.

19. From 1870 to 1910. United States, *Historical Statistics,* 1:129, series D26–D28.

20. Jon Gjerde, *From Peasants to Farmers: The Migration from Balestrand, Norway, to the Upper Middle West* (New York: Cambridge University Press, 1985), esp. 38; Kerby Miller, *Emigrants and Exiles: Ireland and the Irish Exodus to North America* (New York: Oxford University Press, 1985), esp. 405–8; Robert E. Kennedy, Jr., *The Irish: Emigration, Marriage, and Fertility* (Berkeley: University of California Press, 1971), esp. 84.

21. Donna Gabaccia, "Female Migration and Immigrant Sex Ratios, 1820–1928" (unpublished paper, November 1989), table 3 for 1908–28. I thank Professor Gabaccia for permission to cite this, and also her "Women of the Mass Migrations: From Minority to Majority 1820–1930." Also valuable is Joanne Meyerowitz, "Autonomous Female Migrants to Chicago, 1880–1930," *Journal of Urban History* 13 (February 1987): 147–68, and idem, *Women Adrift: Independent Wage Earners in Chicago, 1880–1930* (Chicago: University of Chicago Press, 1988).

22. Intermarriage did take place between European migrants and native-born women at certain times and places, for example French in eighteenth- and nineteenth-century Canada (producing *métis*), Spanish in Mexico and Central America, Scotch-Irish and Cherokees, and the many permutations of European-African-Indian mixtures in Brazil. Endogamy seems to have been the rule, however, among European migrants in the "age of steam." But more research is needed on sex ratios, marriage patterns, and assimilation-acculturation.

23. These sources are, respectively, Norman J. G. Pounds, *An Historical Geography of Europe, 1800–1914* (Cambridge: Cambridge University Press, 1985), 79; Huw R. Jones, *A Population Geography* (New York: Harper and Row, 1981), 254; Charles Tilly, "Migration in Modern European History," in *Human Migration: Patterns and Politics,* ed. William H. McNeill and Ruth S. Adams (Bloomington: Indiana University Press, 1978), 58; United Nations, Department of Social Affairs, Population Division, *The Determinants and Consequences of Population Trends* (New York: United Nations, 1953), 100.

24. B. R. Mitchell, *International Historical Statistics: The Americas and Australasia* (Detroit: Gale Research Company, 1983), series B7, 138–42. Why Brazil received relatively few migrants despite its size is discussed in Nugent, *Crossings,* chap. 15.

25. Anna Maria Ratti, "Italian Migration Movements, 1876 to 1926," in Imre Ferenczi and Walter F. Willcox, *International Migrations* (New York: National Bureau of Economic Research, 1931), 2:440–70.

26. Spain, Consejo Superior de Emigración, *La Emigración Española Transoceánica 1911–1915* (Madrid: Hijos de T. Minuesa de los Rios, 1916), 97–98.

27. Friedrich Burgdörfer, "German Migration," in Ferenczi and Willcox, *International Migrations,* 2:336. For a more detailed discussion of this problem, and Burgdörfer's treatment of it, see Nugent, *Crossings,* 64–66. Much of Burgdörfer's essay appeared in English in the second volume of the massive and authoritative compilation by Ferenczi and Willcox, *International Migrations,* 2:313–89. The original version is Burgdörfer, "Die Wanderungen über die deutschen Reichsgrenzen im letzten Jahrhundert," *Allgemeinisches Statistisches Archiv* (Jena: Verlag von Gustav Fischer), 20 (1930): 161–96, 383–419, 537–51.

28. Ibid., 1:82.

29. A good discussion of this problem is Max Lecroix, "Problems of Collection and Comparison of Migration Statistics," in Milbank Memorial Fund, *Problems in the Collection and Comparison of International Statistics* (New York: Milbank Memorial Fund, 1949), 71–105.

30. Samuel L. Baily, "The Italians and Organized Labor in the United States and Argentina: 1880–1910," *International Migration Review* 1 (Summer 1967): 56–66; idem, "The Adjustment of Italian Immigrants in Buenos Aires and New York, 1870–1914," essay in this volume.

31. Nicolas Sánchez-Albornoz, "The Population of Latin America, 1850–1930," in Leslie Bethell, ed., *The Cambridge History of Latin America* (Cambridge: Cambridge University Press, 1986), 4:136.

32. Ibid., 4:129.

33. Ibid., 4:124–25; Lawrence A. Cardoso, *Mexican Emigration to the United States, 1897–1931* (Tucson: University of Arizona Press, 1980).

34. Fernando Emygdio da Silva, *Emigração Portuguesa* (Coimbra: Franca and Armenio, 1917), 192.

35. Spain, Consejo Superior de Emigración, *La Emigración Española Transoceánica,* 78–79.

36. Wilhelm Mönckmeier, *Die Deutsche Überseeische Auswanderung: Eine Beitrag zur deutschen Wanderungsgeschichte* (Jena: Verlag von Gustav Fischer, 1912), 192–93.

37. Nugent, *Crossings,* 57.

38. Italy, Istituto Centrale di Statistica, *Sommario di Statistiche Storiche dell'Italia, 1861–1965* (Roma: Istituto Centrale di Statistica, 1968), 29.

39. N. H. Carrier and J. R. Jeffery, *External Migration: A Study of the Available Statistics, 1815–1950* (London: Her Majesty's Stationery Office, 1953), 95–96.

40. Michael Flinn et al., *Scottish Population History, from the 17th Century to the 1930s* (Cambridge: Cambridge University Press, 1977), 449–51; W. E. Vaughan and A. J. Fitzpatrick, *Irish Historical Statistics: Population, 1821–1971* (Dublin: Royal Irish Academy, 1978), 55.

41. Ansley J. Coale and Susan Cotts Watkins, eds., *The Decline of Fertility in Europe: The Revised Proceedings of a Conference on the Princeton European Fertility Project* (Princeton, N.J.: Princeton University Press, 1986).

42. A. M. Carr-Saunders, *Population* (New York: Oxford University Press, 1925), esp. 39–43.

43. Wilbur Zelinsky, "The Hypothesis of the Mobility Transition," *Geographical Review* 61 (1971): 219; italics added.

44. Coale and Watkins, *Decline of Fertility in Europe*, 435–36; italics added.

45. Steve Hochstadt, review of Coale and Watkins, *American Historical Review* 95 (February 1990): 152–53.

46. See E. G. Ravenstein, "The Laws of Migration," *Journal of the Royal Statistical Society* 48 (1885): 167–227; 52 (1889): 214–301.

47. Zelinsky, "The Hypothesis of the Mobility Transition," 221–22, 224.

48. Donald Parkerson and Jo Ann Parkerson, "Unresolved Issues in Migration Research: A Re-examination of Ravenstein's Laws" (paper presented at the Social Science History Association annual meeting, November 1986).

49. Donald Denoon, *Settler Capitalism: The Dynamics of Dependent Development in the Southern Hemisphere* (Oxford: Clarendon Press, 1983).

50. For development of these points see Walter Nugent, "Frontiers and Empires in the Late Nineteenth Century," *Western Historical Quarterly* 20 (November 1989): 393–408.

Women of the Mass Migrations:

From Minority to Majority, 1820–1930

DONNA GABACCIA

Women participate in every human migration, but far more actively in some than in others. Women outnumbered men in cityward migrations in Europe in the nineteenth century,[1] but in international movements, male migrants usually predominated. Even the United States, which attracted proportionately more women than other countries, saw the numbers of female immigrants rise to equal and then surpass males only at the very end of the mass migrations.[2]

Historians of migration routinely acknowledge that they can never estimate with total confidence migration totals, even for specific migration streams and specific periods of migration.[3] Figures for emigration from sending countries often differ significantly from figures for immigration into receiving countries like the United States. At the same time, no scholar has ever suggested that the registration of female migration—in either sending or receiving nations—poses unique problems. In this essay, immigration data from the United States is the main source. Data about women who migrated is found in U.S. government publications and in the monumental and widely used critical compilation by Walter F. Willcox and Imre Ferenczi, *International Migrations*.

Table 1 charts the female component among migrants arriving in the United States from 1820 to 1979.[4] From a small minority, the proportion of women initially increased along with migration totals. For about forty years after 1850, through otherwise extreme fluctuations in total migrations, women were roughly 40 percent of arriving migrants. Between 1895 and World War I, as both total migrations and the numbers of women bound for the United States reached their historical peaks, the proportion of women dropped sharply to one-third. Finally, as the century of mass migrations closed and total immigration fell, the proportions of women again rose—to 50 percent in 1930. Since 1930, by contrast, women have dominated migrations to the United States.[5]

Women's representation as immigrants varied considerably by ethnicity and decade. Overall, women were less than 30 percent among migrants

Table 1
Percentage of Female Migrants to the United States, by Decade, 1820–1979

	Percent Female	Total Immigration
1820–29	31.0	128,502
1830–39	37.6	508,381
1840–49	44.5	1,497,277
1850–59	41.2	2,670,513
1860–69	39.8	2,123,219
1870–79	39.0	2,742,137
1880–89	38.8	5,248,568
1890–99	38.4	3,694,294
1900–09	30.4	8,202,388
1910–19	34.9	6,347,380
1920–29	43.8	4,295,510
1930–39	55.3	699,375
1940–49	61.2	856,608
1950–59	53.7	2,499,268
1960–69	55.6	3,213,749
1970–79	53.0	4,336,001

from Asia and the Mediterranean, and more than 40 percent among a diverse group of northern Europeans, central Europeans, and migrants of African descent from the Caribbean.[6] Table 2 summarizes this data.[7] Groups with the lowest representation of women prior to World War I usually had the highest representation by 1930.

To understand why minority became majority requires attention to female migration and to female migrants. Until quite recently, however, scholarship on international migration avoided special attention to women as "reductionist."[8] Feminist research on contemporary migrations has expanded throughout the 1980s,[9] but historical studies of international female migration scarcely exist.[10]

This essay offers a preliminary survey of a large topic. With its focus on the sex ratios of the mass migrations, it does not claim to offer a systematic analysis of female migration itself. Based on readily available U.S. sources, this essay can only hint at homeland influences on women's migratory behavior. Still, first steps must be taken. My purpose is to offer some hypotheses about how gender worked to differentiate migrant from nonmigrant over the course of an important century of migration, resulting in fluctuating sex ratios among those arriving as immigrants in the United States.

Thomas Archdeacon has argued that some combination of culture (e.g., toleration of female emancipation from the family) and the changing pull of U.S. land and labor markets caused variations in immigrant sex ratios in the nineteenth century—a theme elaborated by Hasia Diner in her study of Irish women.[11] In sharp contrast, studies of contemporary female majorities

Table 2
Percentage of Female Migrants to the United States, by Ethnic or National Background, 1820–1928

Asia	
Indian	1
Chinese	5
Korean	17
Japanese	33
Southern and Eastern Europe	
Bulgarian	10
Dalmatian	12
Romanian	18
Croatian	22
Greek	23
Italian	25
Portuguese	37
Russian	31
Ruthenian	31
Hungarian	32
Lithuanian	34
Polish	34
Slovak	35
Hebrew	46
Northern and Western Europe	
Belgian	36
Dutch	37
Finnish	37
Swiss	37
Norwegian	38
Scandinavian	38
Swedish	40
Welsh	40
English	42
German	42
Scottish	42
Irish	48
The Americas	
Mexican	32
Cuban	33
Spanish American	34
West Indian	34
Canadian	39

instead attribute them to provisions of U.S. immigration law.[12] General historical studies of migration differ from both in seeing changes in the home country as the most important determinants of migration patterns.[13]

This essay considers law, the differential impact of pushes and pulls on the two sexes, and the differing structural positions of men and women in worldwide systems of production and reproduction as factors in migration.

It is the differences between men and women, not their many (and significant) similarities, that begin to explain women's varying participation in the mass migrations.

Men and Women in U.S. Immigration Data

Overall, trends in male and female migration to the United States were very much alike during the century of the mass migrations. Male and female migrations rose and fell in close tandem, but women's migrations varied less, causing changes in sex ratios over time.[14] Each of the forty ethnic and national groups traceable in immigration statistics exhibit this pattern. Trends in return migration were also alike for both sexes, with men's and women's rates of return rising and falling together (see table 3).[15] In the twentieth century, groups with higher than average rates of male return usually had higher than average rates of female return, too, although women's rates were usually lower than men's of the same background.[16]

For the twentieth century, when better information becomes available, reports of the Commissioner of Immigration reveal additional similarities. Men and women were about equally literate (or illiterate).[17] The age and marital status of both sexes were also roughly similar in each migrant group: when most men were working-age and unmarried, the same was true of women (Irish, Finns, Bohemians); in other groups (southern Italians, Mexicans, Russians), most adults of both sexes were married.[18] Ethnicity and background mattered more than gender in determining many dimensions of migration.

Still, other data do document significant differences in male and female migration. For example, at the turn of the century, women's migration followed a different annual rhythm than men's. The majority of men arrived in the period March through June. These were peak months for female migration, too, but half of women immigrants arrived July to December—months when less than a third of male arrivals disembarked.[19]

Not surprisingly, the largest gender differences in American immigration data are those of destination and occupation. Women were more likely to arrive in East Coast ports, especially New York.[20] Women arrivals, more than those of men, also gave New England and the Northeast as their destination.[21] Census data confirms that women followed through on these preferences. In 1890, women were over half the foreign-born population of New Hampshire, Massachusetts, Rhode Island, New York, and Maryland, while they were less than a quarter of the immigrant populations of Montana, Wyoming, and Nevada.[22] In addition, women migrants of every background were less likely to return to their homelands than were men; in combination with differential mortality rates, this produced a much more

Table 3
Estimated Rates of Return, by Sex, 1868–1924

	Men	Women		Men	Women
1868	14%	9%	1894	76%	53%
1870	15	7	1895	95	69
1871	22	10	1898	65	45
1872	13	7	1899	44	35
1873	16	9	1900	30	31
1874	31	19	1901	33	32
1875	54	36	1902	24	31
1876	52	42	1908	68	19
1877	59	43	1909	31	16
1878	51	31	1910	21	16
1879	33	20	1911	41	18
1880	11	6	1912	52	19
1881	9	5	1913	31	14
1882	10	5	1914	30	15
1883	16	8	1915	89	26
1884	25	12	1916	59	20
1885	50	24	1917	28	15
1886	42	21	1918	115	48
1887	24	17	1919	121	39
1888	24	15	1920	96	28
1889	39	20	1921	42	16
1890	33	14	1922	96	35
1891	28	20	1923	18	12
1892	30	20	1924	14	7
1893	34	24			

balanced census population (46 percent of the foreign-born were female in the period 1860–1920) than immigration data.[23]

Like women wage earners in most nations in the nineteenth century, immigrant women clustered in a very few female-dominated occupations. Unfortunately, U.S. immigration records identify the occupations of women arrivals only for 1896.[24] Domestic service was the most important and most exclusively female occupation, given by 87 percent of women with occupations. Seamstresses and dressmakers (also exclusively female) and spinners, weavers, and teachers (40 to 50 percent female) were the only other occupations given by sizable numbers of women.

Women migrating to the United States were increasingly likely to claim an occupation over the course of the nineteenth century. (Data about the largest female occupations in 1896 are available for 1872–90, and for 1898–1928—without breakdown by gender[25]—allowing estimates of the numbers of women with occupations.) From about 10 percent of female arrivals in the 1870s, women with occupations increased to 30 percent by 1900. After World War I, however, proportions of women workers again decreased slightly, to less than a quarter.

The proportions of adult women with occupations varied considerably

Table 4
Migration Type and Women with Female Occupations in 1910

	Percent Family Migrants*	Percent Women with Occupations	
		All Adult	Adult Single
Japanese	96	1	16
Chinese	92	11	125
East Indian	86	33	200
Bulgarian	81	34	175
Lithuanian	81	59	86
Mexican	73	7	32
Dutch	73	21	57
Romanian	72	22	91
Cuban	68	6	8
Russian	68	31	82
Italian, Southern	66	30	80
Hungarian	65	28	83
Italian, Northern	64	37	89
French	61	37	74
Welsh	61	31	69
Korean	60	—	—
Portuguese	60	55	117
English	60	38	77
Turkish	59	27	75
Syrian	59	26	73
Spanish American	58	24	49
Spanish	58	33	74
Hebrew	58	31	61
Armenian	57	38	90
Scottish	55	32	62
Greek	55	44	87
Dalmatian	55	40	77
German	53	41	78
Croatian	52	43	83
West Indian	50	43	77
Slovak	50	45	80
African	49	72	108
Bohemian	49	50	85
Polish	39	60	89
Finnish	34	69	96
Scandinavian	32	78	104
Ruthenian	31	60	83
Irish	22	80	98

*Married women and girl children as percentage of total female migration for the year.

by background and type of migration, as table 4 shows.[26] Still, for women of all groups, domestic service was the most common or the only female occupation. Domestic servants predominated among migrant women workers continuously from the 1870s through the 1920s. This finding may be somewhat misleading, however, as European sources list departing female emigrants as either lacking employment or as farm laborers rather than servants.[27] Occupational terminology (which increasingly equated work with wage earning) was changing during these years, and it is likely that Europeans and Americans also differed over who counted as a domestic servant.[28]

Gender did matter, then. While we need not segregate the study of female migration as either too unimportant or too different from male migration, men and women were not interchangeable as immigrants. Differences in male and female migration, and thus in immigrant sex ratios, can be traced both to the gender assumptions of the homeland and to those of the American labor market.

Women and Their Homelands

Historians of immigration have increasingly looked to migrants' homelands to explain the timing and extent of migration to the United States. But whether they attend to "pushes" or to the capitalist transformation of agricultural societies, few have explored changes in the homeland as influences on male and female patterns of migration. Existing studies do permit limited speculation, however.

Severe homeland crises of any sort pushed both sexes to migrate permanently. Famine and pogrom did not discriminate on the basis of sex, and they also discouraged return migration. Indeed, women were well represented among the Irish and the Jews of eastern Europe, the most "pushed" migrants, and rates of return for both groups were also low. Still, the relationship between homeland crisis and sex ratio is not ironclad. Irish women were less well represented in the 1850s than they were after the famine, and Irish sex ratios during the famine were not markedly more balanced than in other United States-bound groups during the same decade. While it is difficult to determine Jewish sex ratios during the 1880s and 1890s—when the threat of pogrom was most severe—it seems that Jewish women were better represented after 1900 than before.

A number of scholars have argued further that severe homeland crises like famine and pogrom pushed migrants out in family groups.[29] This view clearly needs modification. Eastern European Jews sometimes fled their homelands in nuclear family groups, but the Irish instead left as young unmarried women. As the Irish case indicates, the presence of women alone is not a sufficient indicator of family migration.[30]

Scholars less concerned with pushes than with the economic transformation of migrants' homelands have pinpointed declining rural industry,[31] differing forms of agricultural organization,[32] and patterns of local and regional migration systems[33] as keys to the development of migration to the United States. Attention to variables like these can move analysis of migrant sex ratios beyond simple assumptions about cultural support for female emancipation or levels of patriarchal control of women—both of which are impossible to measure systematically. The impact of economic transformations on female migration requires that we explore the complex division of labor by sex in rural families and kinship groups.

Agriculture organized by family groups, partible inheritance, and the widely distributed but "dwarf" farms that resulted from it, are often associated with migration to the United States. Migrations from northern Europe[34] and from China prior to 1880[35] came from agricultural areas like these, as did migrations from southeastern Europe after that date.[36] Sex ratios varied considerably in migrations from such areas: Dutch, southwestern German, and Scandinavian women were about 40 percent of the permanently migrating family groups, while southeastern European and Chinese migrations were heavily male-dominated and temporary.

Cultural explanations help little in this case, since they require us to view northern European women migrating with families as "more emancipated" than the Chinese or Bulgarian women who remained behind. But other factors can be identified. Readily available land in the United States influenced the decisions of northern Europeans (see below), while during the latter period, migration to the United States was more often undertaken to earn cash for the purchase of land at home.

Scattered evidence suggests that the organization of family agriculture and the division of labor by sex within it may also have been quite different in the two cases. Agriculture in parts of southern and eastern Europe and China was still organized by kin groups larger than the nuclear family,[37] meaning that women and children were not directly dependent on husband/father "breadwinners." (One study of Chinese migration even argues that kin groups held wives hostage to ensure that migrated sons returned.[38]) In addition, the cultivation of staple food crops was often a female task in southern and southeastern Europe; men were more involved in rural industry, herding, or the cultivation of cash crops.[39] (In northern Europe, by contrast, dairying and the sale of milk and butter loomed large among most women's agricultural tasks, while the staple crop—usually grain—remained men's responsibility.[40]) The extended kin group and female subsistence cultivation may have guaranteed the economic well-being of families, allowing men to migrate, pursuing cash intended for land purchase or upward mobility at home.[41]

Impartible inheritance, proletarianization, and the state regulation of marriage, as well as large-scale commercial agriculture, became more prevalent across the nineteenth century. These changes seemed to have created new patterns of migration for both sexes. In many parts of northern Europe[42] and in Japan[43] by 1900, children of both sexes sought work away from home as farm maids and laborers during their early teen years. Families with little or no land could neither feed nor employ teenagers; even in propertied families, noninheritors had to seek new places in the world, and they began this search early. As a result, Germany's, England's, and Sweden's early, relatively balanced migrations of families gave way to migrations of unmarried individuals, among whom women were still relatively well represented.[44] Thus, proletarianization, and restrictions on marriage through law or inheritance, constructed the structural basis for female autonomy and independent female migration in these regions.

Many scholars have noted that international migration grew out of local and regional ("step") migrations; these, too, developed from traditional agricultural practices which expelled children early from family work groups. Migration to distant agricultural workplaces (Polish women to Germany),[45] to industrial workplaces (Japanese and northern Italian women to regional centers of textile production),[46] and to the kitchens of nearby cities (Swedish women to Stockholm, Slovaks and Czechs to Vienna or Budapest)[47] were all common by the late nineteenth century. Of these three, employment in the middle-class urban house proved the most important for girls: As Theresa McBride concluded, "The history of domestic service in the nineteenth century *is* the story of urban migration."[48] It is no accident, then, that high representations of women, low proportions of family migrants, and high proportions of farm laborers / domestic servants correlate positively in U.S. migration data.[49] The search for work in Europe continued as domestic servants traveled across the ocean. Women were most likely to become international migrants in areas where local urban middle classes were already well developed and drawing rural girls out of their families to work as domestics in nearby cities.

It is striking, too, that by 1900, European agricultural organization, female migration, and migrant sex ratios correspond roughly to the demographic delineation of two continental marriage systems—with late age at marriage and a high incidence of celibacy characteristic of northern and central Europe, and early and nearly universal marriage characteristic of southern and eastern Europe.[50] Women of the south and east could marry in their homelands in part because they still found work there in family-based subsistence. By contrast, for the women of northern and central Europe the pursuit of work was inseparable from the search for marriage partners: neither could be had close to home. Migration resulted not only in jobs, but in marriages.[51]

Thus, while it is true that Asians and southern Europeans tolerated less female independence than northern and central Europeans, these cultural constraints did not exist in a structural vacuum. Female autonomy and mobility emerged within specific types of agricultural organization and divisions of labor, linking marriage and work in differing ways. In Asia and southeastern Europe, marriage and work in households pursuing subsistence resulted in female rootedness. In northern Europe, by contrast, both female work and female marriage required migration away from the family of origin at an early age.

The Pull of the United States

Like the homeland division of labor, the attraction of the United States became quite sex-specific. During the mass migrations, land and jobs were the major forces pulling migrants to the United States. Gender mattered in both cases: men and women were not interchangeable laborers on family farms or in the eyes of U.S. employers.

U.S. land, scholars have usually argued, attracted migrants traveling in families in order to guarantee sufficient labor for permanent settlement on frontier farms. Settlement on the land seems logically associated with balanced sex ratios among immigrants.[52] But there are problems with this association. Before 1890, when land still lured many to the United States, women were not best represented in immigrant groups settling in rural areas. Women were consistently better represented in the period 1850–80 among the Irish (49 percent), who were more likely to settle in cities, than among the Dutch (32 percent) or the Swedes (40 percent), who more often farmed.[53] (The presence of children correlated far better with farming: 16 percent of the Swedish and 24 percent of the Dutch migrants of the 1870s were children, but only 10 percent of the Irish were.[54])

In addition, foreign-born women were not present in above-average proportions in areas where one would expect to find farmers in 1850–90.[55] In 1860, immigrant sex ratios in rural farming districts of Wisconsin, Missouri, or Iowa (40–44 percent female) fell below those for Boston and New York (55 and 52 percent female).[56] However important women's labor was to farm families—and this is not in doubt—farming regions attracted more men than women, probably to work as seasonal farm laborers.

In the United States, as in Europe, migrating women gravitated toward cities, not the land. The reasons were the same in both cases: female jobs, especially in domestic service, could be found there.[57] Still, scholars have disagreed about the influence of U.S. labor markets on female migration. Some argue that women, like men, responded primarily to the economic pull of labor markets.[58] Others point out that female migration was less sensitive to the swings of the U.S. business cycle than male migration.[59] Attention to the linkage of labor and family concerns helps clarify this apparent contradiction.

Clearly, migrant women were responsive to the pull of the U.S. economy. As the size of the U.S. female workforce expanded,[60] the numbers of female arrivals increased to their historic peak, and the proportion of female migrants with an occupation more than tripled. Foreign-born women and

Table 5
Impact of Depression and Recovery on Male and Female Migration

	Percentage Change in Arrivals	
	1879–80	1906/07–1908/09
All Men	+157	−39
All Women	+157	−27
Women with Occupations	+191	−35

their daughters became a sizable proportion of the female workforce of the United States;[61] they dominated domestic service in the north and factory work everywhere. (Three-quarters of migrant women worked in these jobs.[62]) Jobs influenced female patterns of settlement, too. Textile jobs and garment production were concentrated in New England and the Mid-Atlantic states, where three-fifths of foreign-born women lived.[63] Migrant women in these regions had the highest rates of employment (25–34 percent in 1900[64]) in the nation. The draw of particular city economies was also gender-specific: while servants scattered more widely, and men preferred heavy industry and mining centers like Pittsburgh,[65] the upper Midwest,[66] or Buffalo,[67] over half of all immigrant dressmakers and seamstresses headed for New York with its garment industry.[68]

Scholars have viewed women migrants as less influenced by the U.S. business cycle in part because they have ignored differences in demand for male and female labor in the late nineteenth century. Demand for domestic servants varied little over the course of the year, explaining in part why women migrants arrived continuously throughout the year. As table 5 suggests, however, the migration of women with occupations demonstrated as much sensitivity to swings in the U.S. economy as the migration of men. As with men, too, women's rates of return to the homeland always increased during periods of depression.

Demand for female labor did not expand as rapidly as demand for male labor in the late nineteenth century, influencing migration patterns in predictable ways.[69] U.S. employers complained incessantly about a "servant crisis,"[70] yet demand for domestics increased only slowly in the period 1870–1920, and lagged well behind the growth of the female labor force generally.[71] Growth in the female workforce during these years originated largely with the increasing demand for white-collar workers, and jobs in this category were not open to foreign-born women.[72] Consequently, even as the numbers and proportions of servants arriving in the United States increased, domestic servants became an ever smaller component of the female workforce, and immigrant women's place in the workforce actually dropped from the nineteenth century to the twentieth.[73] This, too, helps explain the supposed insensitivity of female migration to the U.S. business cycle.

Female migration to the United States, furthermore, reflected more than a demand for female wage earners: the formation, reunification, and completion of families—in economistic terms, migrant men's demand for women's domestic or family labor—also motivated much female migration. Because women worked both with and without pay, inside and outside families, it is not possible to differentiate simply between the female "labor migrants" of northern and central Europe—responsive to the demand for domestic service—and the economically indifferent female "family migrants" of southern and eastern Europe and Asia. Irish, Finnish, and Scandinavian female "labor migrants" also knew they would have their pick of husbands in the United States. And unmarried women from southern and eastern Europe, although migrating with families, also expected to work for wages in the United States: table 4 shows that they claimed occupations almost as frequently as northern Europeans. Rates of employment among single immigrant women of all backgrounds were likewise relatively high in the United States.[74] The major variation among female migrants was not the importance or necessity of work, but rather the location and type of work sought. Married women of all backgrounds worked at home, combining family with paid labor as boarding-house keepers and sweated workers.[75] Unmarried women traveling independently to the United States were more likely to work as domestic servants than their counterparts in family migrations—who preferred industrial work.[76]

The association of female migration with permanent settlement, especially on the land, has obscured considerable similarities between regional and international female migrations during the nineteenth and early twentieth centuries. Not only did regional migrations of women in Europe generate female migration to the United States: the United States was also attractive to women because it offered them the opportunity to work, and most female jobs, as in Europe, were in cities, not on the land. The demand for female labor seemed as much an influence on individual "labor migrants" as on unmarried "family migrants." Ironically, however, the most emancipated female migrants took the most traditional female jobs in domestic service, where relative demand was declining, while unmarried "family migrants" entered the more modern—and still expanding—industrial sector.

The Influence of Law

Sociologists usually find an explanation for present-day female majorities in the provisions of U.S. immigration law, a factor historians rarely consider when noting women's changing representation in the mass migrations.[77] Yet beginning with the Chinese Exclusion Act of 1882 and continuing through the restrictive laws of the 1920s, U.S. immigration policy has routinely promoted family reunification. If we assume that women more often than men migrated for family reasons, then these provisions might have influenced migrant sex ratios before the 1930s, too.

The Chinese Exclusion Act of 1882 and the 1907 Gentlemen's Agreement (limiting the migration of Japanese laborers) contained the earliest provisions for family reunification in U.S. immigration law.[78] Under the Chinese Exclusion Act, only merchants and their wives and children were allowed to accompany or rejoin men who had migrated earlier; the Gentlemen's Agreement extended this privilege to the dependents of Japanese laborers. Table 6 demonstrates that provisions for family reunification had differing outcomes in the two cases.[79] The Gentlemen's Agreement resulted in the picture-bride era of Japanese migration—when female migrants significantly outnumbered males.[80] While the representation of women also increased slightly and temporarily among the Chinese, there was no comparable picture-bride era for this group. Among the Chinese entering for family reasons, 90 percent were the children, usually the sons, of merchants—not their wives.[81] That proportionately more Japanese than Chinese women entered the United States under restrictive laws thus requires reference to factors other than provisions for family reunification.[82]

Beginning with the Literacy Act of 1917, the U.S. Congress attempted to reduce migration overall and to stem migration in particular from southern and eastern Europe. Like earlier restrictions applying only to Asians, the Literacy Act provided for reunification of families separated by migration: illiterates were allowed to enter the United States if their purpose was to rejoin a naturalized parent, husband, or child.[83] Almost 90 percent of the illiterates admitted under this provision were women.[84] But their numbers remained quite small. In 1921, for example, the exclusion of twenty-four thousand illiterate women would have lowered the sex ratio among arrivals by less than one percentage point.[85]

Wives and children of some migrants were also exempted from the restrictive quotas introduced for southern and eastern European groups in 1921 and tightened further in 1924.[86] But their numbers, too, remained low enough in the 1920s that they did not affect annual sex ratios. In 1925, the first full year under the most restrictive quota law, for example, only 7,200 persons (of a total migration of over 500,000) were admitted outside the quotas for family reasons. Of these, just over half were wives; the rest were children of naturalized citizens.[87]

The impact of changing immigration policy on women's representation among migrants after World War I was a complex one, for the restrictions of the 1920s were highly selective. Congress imposed no restrictions on migrations from the Americas. The new laws allotted northern Europeans such generous quotas that they normally went unfilled; migration from this area, too, remained, in effect, unregulated.[88] The same laws excluded

Table 6
Percentage Female among Japanese and Chinese Migrants, before and after Restrictive Legislation

	Japanese	Chinese
1880	—	1
1881	—	1
1882*	—	0
1883	30	1
1884	5	14
1885	14	45
1886	18	38
1887	5	20
1888	9	19
1889	13	24
1890	13	18
1891	10	8
1892	—	—
1895	—	—
1896	9	4
1897	1	7
1898	5	0
1899	7	1
1900	3	1
1901	7	2
1902	27	3
1903	20	2
1904	11	3
1905	11	4
1906	10	6
1907**	9	8
1908	25	7
1909	55	7
1910	67	10
1911	69	14
1912	69	15
1913	62	16
1914	63	13
1915	56	12
1916	54	12
1917	53	15
1918	53	19
1919	55	16
1920	63	20
1921	58	18
1922	58	19
1923	56	20
1924	55	20
1925	46	11
1926	29	14
1927	32	21
1928	31	—

*Chinese Exclusion Act
**Gentlemen's Agreement

Table 7
Percentage of Female Migrants during the Era of Immigration Restrictions

	Southeastern Europe	Northwestern Europe	New World
1910	25	39	35
1911	32	42	35
1912	34	45	34
1913	29	46	41
1914	32	43	44
1915	41	45	44
1916	31	45	46
1917	36	45	46
1918	36	50	41
1919	25	45	37
1920	40	47	35
1921	43	49	42
1922	53	53	43
1923	45	42	30
1924	40	41	35
1925	53	46	31
1926	57	46	24
1927	52	45	29
1928	47	47	35

Asians and set severely restricted quotas for migrants from southern and eastern Europe.

Table 7 summarizes women's representation in unregulated (New World), effectively unregulated (northern European), and heavily restricted (southern and eastern European) migrations before, during, and after the passage of restrictive immigration laws in the period 1917–24.[89] Among southern and eastern Europeans, women's representation was already increasing prior to regulation, but the law of 1924 resulted in occasional female majorities. Women's presence increased but little among the effectively unregulated northern Europeans, and among unregulated New World migrants the proportions of women actually dropped.

Rising proportions of women among restricted southeastern Europeans cannot be traced exclusively to provisions for family reunification. By 1910, the proportions of women in these groups was increasing irregularly, as total migration peaked. More generally, however, whenever the total volume of these migrations dropped sharply (as a result of reduced demand for male labor, as in the depressions of 1907 or 1921, or with the onset of war in 1914), the percentage of females increased. Restricting migration exaggerated this pattern.

As the numbers of southern and eastern European migrants fell, New World migrants entered the United States in ever increasing numbers, filling a void in the male labor market. Not surprisingly, the proportions of women entering the United States from Mexico and other Caribbean and

Latin American countries fell to levels resembling those of prewar migrations from southern and eastern Europe.

Provisions for family reunification probably do encourage female majorities in contemporary migrations. But that was true before 1930. The differing impact of the Chinese Exclusion Act and the Gentlemen's Agreement suggests that culturally varying definitions of family ties and the options for female labor in the United States independently influenced whether males or females took advantage of unification provisions. As late as 1930, large numbers of potential immigrants remained unaffected by restrictive laws and thus in little need of special provisions for reunifying their families. The women from southern and eastern Europe who entered the United States during and after World War I often came to reunify families, but their numbers were insufficient to produce general female majorities as long as male labor migrations from the New World continued unrestricted in response to market conditions in the United States.

Conclusion

Given the changing and complex influence of the homeland, and U.S. land and labor and law, it is not yet possible to explain with complete confidence all the swings we can document in women's representation during the mass migrations. Evidence presented in this essay does, however, provide some clues to three critical transitions in the change from female minority to female majority—the low representations of women prior to the 1840s, the decrease to small female minorities after 1890, and the emergence of female majorities in the twentieth century.

Culture cannot be ruled out as an independent influence on female migration, but neither does it seem the best explanation for any of these three transitions. Women were no more than a small minority during the earliest years of every migration, regardless of attitudes toward female autonomy.[90] The representation of women among the Dutch, Swedes, and Germans prior to 1840 was often as low as among the Italians and Balkan migrants after 1890. (Women may have been better represented among Irish, English, Scottish, and Welsh migrants in the 1820s and 1830s because these were among the oldest continuous migrations to the United States.[91]) Northern and southern European societies certainly differed in their tolerance of women moving independently of their families, but neither allowed much room for women as pioneering migrants.

Heavily male-dominated pioneer migrations seem to have generated their own corrections within about twenty years: this was true of both northern European migrations after 1840 and southeastern European migrations after 1910. It is harder to explain why this correction in the nineteenth century should have resulted in a long period of relatively high and quite stable female minorities in the period 1850–90. More research on the relation between female migration and rural settlement, and greater attention to female wage earning during the "old immigration" may help explain this transition.

The drop in immigrant women's representation between 1890 and 1914 was not a by-product of southern or eastern European opposition to female autonomy as these migrations grew in size. As new migrations, we would expect the representation of women in them to be low in any case. But other factors, too, were at work. Sex ratios in long-established northern European migrations also dropped off during these years, further evidence that the United States simply demanded more male than female wage laborers, regardless of background. With demand for domestics stagnating, southern and eastern European women did not find jobs as domestic servants—even though domestic service was the most frequent female occupation given by Jewish, Italian, and Polish women migrants alike. It may also be true that some of these new migrant women did not seek work in domestic service: subsistence agriculture in the homeland continued to employ much female labor, and in the New World the demand for factory "girls"—not domestics—was increasing.

Finally, provisions for family reunification were only one factor in the development of female majorities by 1930. In fact, it is likely that there would have been female majorities by 1930 even without provisions for family reunification in the 1921 and 1924 immigration laws. When the depression of the 1890s reduced the demand for male laborers, women temporarily outnumbered men among the Bohemians, Irish, Mexicans, Swedish, and Swiss. The proportions of women among southern and eastern European migrants had begun to increase already by 1910, in a spontaneous adjustment to earlier male-dominated migrations. World War I had the same impact on migration patterns as the depressed demand for male labor, and female representation increased to over 40 percent, with female majorities appearing in a variety of migrant groups. The passage of restrictive laws strengthened an already existing trend, especially for southern and eastern Europeans. But ultimately it was the Great Depression and the plummeting demand for male labor that finally transformed the female minority into a female majority.

Notes

1. E. G. Ravenstein, "The Laws of Migration," *Journal of the Royal Statistical Society* 48 (1885): 167–277.

2. Walter F. Willcox and Imre Ferenczi, *International Migrations* (New York: National Bureau of Economic Research, 1929), 2:212.

3. Walter Nugent, *Crossings: The Great Transatlantic Migrations, 1870–1914* (Bloomington: Indiana University Press, 1992), 29–30.

4. The source for the years 1857–1930 is Marion F. Houstoun et al., "Female Predominance of Immigration to the United States since 1930: A First Look," *International Migration Review* 28 (Winter 1984): 908–63, appendix table A-1. For the years before 1857, see Willcox and Ferenczi, *International Migrations,* vol. 1, tables V and VI.

5. Besides Houstoun et al., "Female Predominance," see Andrea Tyree and Katharine M. Donato, "A Demographic Overview of the International Migration of Women," in *International Migration: The Female Experience,* ed. Rita James Simon and Caroline Brettell (Totowa, N.J.: Rowman and Allanheld, 1986), 21–44; Richard Easterlin, "Immigration: Economic and Social Characteristics," in *Harvard Encyclopedia of American Ethnic Groups* (Cambridge: Harvard University Press, 1980), 478.

6. Thomas J. Archdeacon, *Becoming American: An Ethnic History* (New York: Free Press, 1983), 135–36, 139.

7. Calculated from U.S. figures for arrivals by national origin and ethnicity in Willcox and Ferenczi, *International Migrations.*

8. Anthony Leeds, "Women in the Migratory Process: A Reductionist Outlook," *Anthropological Quarterly* 49 (1976): 69–76.

9. See especially Mirjana Morokvasic, "Women in Migration: Beyond the Reductionist Outlook," in *One Way Ticket: Migration and Female Labour,* ed. Annie Phizacklea (London: Routledge and Kegan Paul, 1983), 13–31, and Morokvasic, "Birds of Passage are also Women," *International Migration Review* 28 (Winter 1984): 886–907.

10. Most concern Irish immigration. See Hasia R. Diner, *Erin's Daughters in America: Irish Immigrant Women in the Nineteenth Century* (Baltimore: Johns Hopkins University Press, 1983), chap. 2; Pauline Jackson, "Women in 19th Century Irish Emigration," *International Migration Review* 28 (Winter 1984): 1004–20; Janet A. Nolan, *Ourselves Alone: Women's Emigration from Ireland, 1885–1920* (Knoxville: University Press of Kentucky, 1989).

11. Archdeacon, *Becoming American,* 136–37; Diner, *Erin's Daughters,* chap. 2.

12. Besides Houstoun et al., "Female Predominance," and Tyree and Donato, "Demographic Overview," see Andrea Tyree and Katharine M. Donato, "The Sex Composition of Legal Immigrants to the United States," *Sociology and Social Research* 69 (July 1985): 577–84; Tyree and Donato, "Family Reunification, Health Professionals and the Sex Composition of Immigrants to the United States," *Sociology and Social Research* 70 (April 1986): 226–30.

13. Dirk Hoerder, "An Introduction to Labor Migration in the Atlantic Economies, 1815–1914," in *Labor Migration in the Atlantic Economies: The European and North American Working Classes during the Period of Industrialization,* ed. Dirk Hoerder (Westport, Conn.: Greenwood Press, 1985), 3–32; John Bodnar, *The Transplanted: A History of Immigrants in Urban America* (Bloomington: Indiana University Press, 1985), chaps. 1–2.

14. Houstoun et al., "Female Predominance," fig. 1.

15. For the years 1868–1902, Willcox and Ferenczi, *International Migrations,* table XIV, give figures for noncabin passengers departing from the United States; for 1908–30, information about departures is from U.S. Department of Labor, Bureau of Immigration, *Annual Report of the Commissioner of Immigration* (Washington: Government Printing Office, 1892–1930).

16. U.S. Bureau of Immigration, *Annual Report,* 1908–30.

17. Ibid., 1908–24.

18. On changing age, marital and family status among migrants, see Archdeacon, *Becoming American,* 135; Willcox and Ferenczi, *International Migrations,* 212–13. Information on age and marital status by sex is available for individual groups in U.S. Bureau of Immigration, *Annual Report,* 1908–29.

19. U.S. Bureau of Immigration, *Annual Report*, 1898–1901.

20. Ibid., 1892–1902.

21. Ibid., 1896; for this phenomenon among Finns, see Carl Ross, "Servant Girls, Community Leaders: Finnish American Women in Transition (1910–1920)," in *Women Who Dared: The History of Finnish American Women*, ed. Carl Ross and K. Marianne Wargelin Brown (St. Paul: Immigration History Research Center, University of Minnesota, 1986), 43–44.

22. U.S. Department of Labor, Bureau of the Census, *Special Reports, Supplementary Analysis and Derivative Tables, Twelfth Census, 1900* (Washington: Government Printing Office, 1906), tables 20–21.

23. U.S. Census Office, *Statistics of the Population of the United States, 1870* (Washington: Government Printing Office, 1872), vol. 1, also includes statewide data on the numbers of foreign-born men and women for 1850 and 1860; *Special Reports, 1900* gives data for 1890 and 1900. For the twentieth century, see U.S. Census Bureau, *Thirteenth Census, 1910, Population: Composition and Characteristics, Preliminary Reports* (Washington: Government Printing Office, 1913), and U.S. Department of Commerce, Bureau of the Census, *Immigrants and Their Children, 1920,* by Niles Carpenter, Census Monographs 7 (Washington: Government Printing Office, 1927), table 173.

24. U.S. Bureau of Immigration, *Annual Report*, 1896.

25. See ibid., 1892 and 1898–1930; data are available by ethnic group, but not by sex.

26. All domestic servants and seamstresses, and half of all teachers, weavers, and spinners enumerated in *Annual Report*, 1910, were assumed to be female.

27. Willcox and Ferenczi, *International Migrations*, vol. 2, includes some European occupational figures for emigrating British, Finnish, Italian, and Bulgarian women.

28. Donna Gabaccia, "In the Shadows of the Periphery: Italian Women in the Nineteenth Century," in *Connecting Spheres: Women in the Western World, 1500 to the Present*, ed. Jean Quataert and Marilyn Boxer (New York: Oxford University Press, 1987), 166–76.

29. Bernard Bailyn, *The Peopling of British North America: An Introduction* (New York: Alfred A. Knopf, 1986), 12–15, and *Voyagers to the West: A Passage in the Peopling of America on the Eve of the Revolution* (New York: Alfred A. Knopf, 1986); Robert P. Swierenga, "Dutch Immigrant Demography, 1820–1880," *Journal of Family History* 5 (Winter 1980): 397.

30. A common enough assumption among demographers who study migration: see Wolfgang Köllmann and Peter Marschalck, "German Emigration to the United States," *Perspectives in American History* 7 (1973): 499–544.

31. Walter D. Kamphoefner, *The Westfalians: From Germany to Missouri* (Princeton: Princeton University Press, 1987), 13; Leo Schelbert, "On Becoming an Emigrant: A Structural View of Eighteenth- and Nineteenth-Century Swiss Data," *Perspectives in American History* 7 (1973): 454–55; see also Bodnar, *The Transplanted,* 30–34.

32. J. S. MacDonald, "Italy's Rural Social Structure and Emigration," *Occidente* 12 (1956): 437–53, and "Some Socio-Economic Emigration Differentials in Rural Italy," *Economic Development and Cultural Change* 7 (1958): 55–72. For historians' use of MacDonald, see Bodnar, *The Transplanted,* chap. 1; Josef J. Barton, *Peasants and Strangers: Italians, Rumanians, and Slovaks in an American City, 1890–1950* (Cambridge, Mass.: Harvard University Press, 1975).

33. Hoerder, "An Introduction to Labor Migration," 13–16; Dino Cinel, "The Seasonal Emigration of Italians in the Nineteenth Century: From Internal to International Destinations," *Journal of Ethnic Studies* 10 (1982): 43–68; J. D. Gould, "European Inter-Continental Emigration, 1815–1914: Patterns and Causes," *Journal of European Economic History* 8 (Winter 1979): 658.

34. For Germany, see Kamphoefner, *The Westfalians,* 13; Köllmann and Marschalck, "German Emigration," 505. For Sweden, see Robert C. Ostergren, *A Community Transplanted: The Trans-Atlantic Experience of a Swedish Immigrant Settlement in the Upper Midwest, 1835–1915* (Madison: University of Wisconsin Press, 1988), 36–60.

35. Ronald Takaki, *Strangers from a Different Shore: A History of Asian Americans* (Boston: Little, Brown and Co., 1989), 15–30, 49.

36. Ewa Morawska, *For Bread with Butter: The Life-Worlds of East Central Europeans in Johnstown, Pennsylvania, 1890–1940* (New York: Cambridge University Press, 1985), 25. See also Bodnar, *The Transplanted,* 10; MacDonald, "Some Socio-Economic Emigration Differentials."

37. Eric Wolf, *Peasant Wars of the Twentieth Century* (New York: Harper Torchbooks, 1969), 111; Béla Gunda, "The Ethno-Sociological Structure of the Hungarian Extended Family," *Journal of Family History* 7 (Spring 1982): 40–51; Milovan Gavazzi, "The Extended Family in Southeastern Europe," in ibid., 89–102; Olga Supek and Jasna Capo, "Women in the Culture of Late 19th Century Croatia" (paper in possession of the author), 5–6.

38. Takaki, *Strangers from a Different Shore,* p. 37.

39. Gabaccia, "In the Shadows of the Periphery," 171; Mary Cygan, "Mothers and Managers: A Revolution in Polish Agriculture" (unpublished paper in possession of the author); Supek and Capo, "Women in the Culture of Late 19th Century Croatia," 6.

40. Jon Gjerde, *From Peasants to Farmers: The Migration from Balestrand, Norway, to the Upper Middle West* (New York: Cambridge University Press, 1985), chap. 2.

41. Ester Boserup, *Women's Role in Economic Development* (1970; London: Earthscan, 1989), 175–83.

42. Diner, *Erin's Daughters,* chap. 2; Gjerde, *From Peasants to Farmers,* 47; Malcolm Gray, "Scottish Emigration: The Social Impact of Agrarian Change in the Rural Lowlands, 1775–1885," in *Perspectives in American History* 7 (1973): 134. The pattern may have been typical of parts of Austria and Bohemia as well.

43. Takaki, *Strangers from a Different Shore,* 48.

44. Kamphoefner, *The Westfalians,* 13; Peter Marschalck, *Deutsche Überseewanderung im 19. Jahrhundert: Ein Beitrag zur soziologischen Theorie der Bevölkerung* (Stuttgart: Ernst Klett Verlag, 1973), 72–77; Dudley Baines, *Migration in a Mature Economy: Emigration and Internal Migration in England and Wales, 1861–1900* (New York: Cambridge University Press, 1985), 195.

45. Morawska, *For Bread with Butter,* 53.

46. Franco Ramella, *Terra and Telai: Sistemi di Parentela e Manifattura nel Biellese dell'Ottocento* (Turin: Einaudi, 1983), chap. 4; Takaki, *Strangers from a Different Shore,* 47–48.

47. Peter Schmidtbauer, "Households and Household Forms of Viennese Jews in 1857," *Journal of Family History* 5 (Winter 1980): 378; Sten Carlsson, "Unmarried Women in the Swedish Society of Estates," in *Chance and Change, Social and Economic Studies in Historical Demography in the Baltic Area,* ed. Sune Ackerman et al. (Odense: Odense University Press, 1978), 223; Anna Zarnowska, "Rural Immigrants and Their Adaptation to the Working Class Community in Warsaw at the Turn of the Century," (unpublished paper in possession of the author), 2, 5.

48. Emphasis mine; Theresa McBride, *The Domestic Revolution: The Modernization of Household Service in England and France 1820–1920* (New York: Holmes and Meier, 1976), 34.

49. This was certainly true of the Irish and Swedish cases. Besides Diner, *Erin's Daughters,* and Ross, "Servant Girls," see Joy Lintelman, " 'America is the Woman's Promised Land': Swedish Immigrant Women and American Domestic Service," *Journal of American Ethnic History* 8 (Spring 1989): 9–23.

50. John Hajnal, "European Marriage Patterns in Perspective," in *Population in History: Essays in Historical Demography,* ed. D. V. Glass and D.E.C. Eversley (Chicago: Aldine, 1965). The Caribbean is also noted for its distinctive marriage system (see Judith Blake, *Family Structure in Jamaica: The Social Context of Reproduction* [New York: Free Press of Glencoe, Inc., 1961]), and the relation between it and female migration from the region also requires further exploration.

51. Bo Kronborg and Thomas Nilsson, "Social Mobility, Migration and Family Building in Urban Environments," in Ackerman et al., *Chance and Change,* 233; Harald Runblom and Hans Norman, *From Sweden to America: A History of the Migration* (Minneapolis: University of Minnesota Press, 1976), 187–90.

52. Maxine Schwartz Seller, *To Seek America: A History of Ethnic Life in the United States* (Englewood, N.J.: Jerome S. Ozer, 1988), 65–68.

53. On the settlement patterns of Irish, Dutch, and Swedes, see James Stuart Olson, *The Ethnic Dimension in American History* (New York: St. Martin's, 1979), 79–80, 91, 115; on the Swedes, see Runblom and Norman, *From Sweden to America*; for the Dutch, see Robert P. Swierenga, *They Came to Stay: Essays on Dutch Immigration and Settlement in America* (New Brunswick: Rutgers University Press, 1988).

54. These numbers had to be estimated, as U.S. immigration data for the nineteenth century do not give information on age and marital status. U.S. Bureau of Immigration, *Annual Report,* 1892, summarizes data for the 1870s, providing total migrations by sex, as well as occupational information and a figure for those (women and children) without occupation. By subtracting migrants with female occupations from the total number of women arrivals, an estimate of nonworking women could be made; when subtracted from the figure for those without occupations, this gave an estimate of the number of children arriving in the U.S. For the 1850s, Willcox and Ferenczi, *International Migrations,* 740, note even higher representations of children among the Dutch (40 to 50 percent) and the Swedes (30 to 40 percent) in European emigration statistics.

55. See U.S. Census Office, *Statistics of the Population, 1870,* and *Special Reports, 1900.*

56. U.S. Census Office, *Population of the United States in 1860* (Washington: Government Printing Office, 1864), gives figures for male and female foreign-born for Boston, New York, Philadelphia, Baltimore, Cincinnati, Chicago, St. Louis, and New Orleans.

57. U.S. Bureau of the Census, *Immigrants and Their Children, 1920,* 162–65.

58. Morokvasic, "Birds of Passage are also Women"; Caroline B. Brettell and Rita James Simon, "Immigrant Women: An Introduction," in Simon and Brettell, *International Migration: The Female Experience,* 10–13.

59. Gould, "European Inter-Continental Emigration, 1815–1914," 642.

60. Alice Kessler-Harris, *Out to Work: A History of Wage-Earning Women in the United States* (New York: Oxford University Press, 1982), chap. 5; for a more quantitative analysis, see Valerie Kincaide Oppenheimer, *The Female Labor Force in the United States: Demographic and Economic Factors Governing Its Growth and Changing Composition,* Population Monograph 5 (Berkeley: University of California Press, 1970).

61. Joan Younger Dickinson, *The Role of the Immigrant Women in the U.S. Labor Force, 1890–1910* (New York: Arno Press, 1980).

62. U.S. Bureau of the Census, *Women in Gainful Occupations, 1870–1920,* by Joseph A. Hill, Census Monographs 9 (Washington: Government Printing Office, 1929), table 75; see also Dickinson, *The Role of the Immigrant Women,* table 15.

63. U.S. Bureau of the Census, *Women in Gainful Occupations,* 101.

64. U.S. Bureau of the Census, *Statistics of Women at Work* (Washington: Government Printing Office, 1907), table 2.

65. S. J. Kleinberg, *The Shadow of the Mills: Working-Class Families in Pittsburgh, 1870–1907* (Pittsburgh: University of Pittsburgh Press, 1989).

66. On Finns, contrast Ross, "Servant Girls," to Matti Kaups, "The Finns in the Copper and Iron Ore Mines of the Western Great Lakes Region, 1864–1905: Some Preliminary Observations," in *The Finnish Experience in the Western Great Lakes Region: New Perspectives,* ed. Michael Karni (Vammala: Institute for Migration of Turku, Finland, 1975), 58–88.

67. Virginia Yans-McLaughlin, *Family and Community: Italian Immigrants in Buffalo, 1880–1930* (Ithaca: Cornell University Press, 1977).

68. U.S. Bureau of Immigration, *Annual Reports,* 1900, 1910.

69. Easterlin, "Immigration," 483; see also U.S. Bureau of the Census, *Immigrants and Their Children,* 160.

70. David M. Katzman, *Seven Days a Week: Women and Domestic Service in Industrializing America* (New York: Oxford University Press, 1978), chap. 6.

71. Faye Dudden, "Experts and Servants: The National Council on Household Employment and the Decline of Domestic Service in the Twentieth Century," *Journal of Social History* 20 (Winter 1986): 269–90.

72. Dickinson, *The Role of the Immigrant Women,* 209–10; Kessler-Harris, *Out to Work,* 147–49.

73. Dickinson, *The Role of the Immigrant Women,* 22–23.

74. Christine E. Bose, "Household Resources and U.S. Women's Work: Factors Affecting Gainful Employment at the Turn of the Century," *American Sociological Review* 49 (1984): 474–90.

75. Elizabeth H. Pleck, "A Mother's Wages: Income Earning among Married Italian and Black Women, 1896–1911," in *The American Family in Social-Historical Perspective,* ed. Michael Gordon, 2d ed. (New York: St. Martin's Press, 1978), 490–510.

76. Kessler-Harris, *Out to Work,* 127–28; U.S. Bureau of the Census, *Immigrants and Their Children,* table 132. An important exception to this generalization may be the product of racial discrimination: both Japanese and Mexican women were likely to migrate as parts of families, but both nonetheless had high rates of employment in domestic service. See Evelyn N. Glenn, "Occupational Ghettoization: Japanese American Women and Domestic Service, 1905–1970," *Ethnicity* 8 (1981): 351–86, and "The Dialectics of Wage Work: Japanese American Women and Domestic Service, 1905–1940," in *Labor Immigration under Capitalism: Asian Workers in the United States before World War II,* ed. Lucie Cheng and Edna Bonacich (Berkeley: University of California Press, 1987), 470–514; Vicki L. Ruiz, "By the Day or Week: Mexican Domestic Workers in El Paso," in *"To Toil the Livelong Day": America's Women at Work, 1780–1980,* ed. Carol Groneman and Mary Beth Norton (Ithaca: Cornell University Press, 1987), 269–83.

77. Michael C. LeMay, *From Open Door to Dutch Door: An Analysis of U.S. Immigration Policy since 1820* (New York: Praeger, 1987).

78. U.S. Bureau of Immigration, *Annual Report,* 1919, 50–55; for the Gentlemen's Agreement, see *Annual Report,* 1908, 125–28; for a general discussion, see Takaki, *Strangers from a Different Shore,* 40–41, 46–47.

79. Calculated from U.S. figures in Willcox and Ferenczi, *International Migrations.*

80. Besides *Annual Report,* 1908, 126, and 1919, 57, see Evelyn Nakano Glenn, *Issei, Nisei, Warbride: Three Generations of Japanese American Women in Domestic Service* (Philadelphia: Temple University Press, 1986).

81. U.S. Bureau of Immigration, *Annual Report,* 1907, 100–101.

82. George A. Peffer, "Forbidden Families: Emigration Experiences of Chinese Women Under the Page Law, 1875–1882," *Journal of American Ethnic History* 6 (Fall 1986): 28–46.

83. U.S. Bureau of Immigration, *Annual Report,* 1917.

84. See ibid., 1918, 1921, 1928.

85. Ibid., 1921.

86. For descriptions of these laws, see *Annual Report,* 1921, 16–17, and 1924, 28.

87. U.S. Bureau of Immigration, *Annual Report,* 1925, 3.

88. Ibid., 1924, 27–28.

89. Figures were taken from the *Annual Reports* for 1912–1930.

90. Swierenga, "Dutch Immigrant Demography," 390.

91. Charlotte Erickson, "Emigration from the British Isles to the U.S.A. in 1841: Part I, Emigration from the British Isles," *Population Studies* 43 (1989): 347–67.

PART II

Leaving Home

The European Perspective: Changing Conditions and Multiple Migrations, 1750–1914

LESLIE PAGE MOCH

The migration of Europeans to the Americas is a crucial part of the global movement of the labor force in the nineteenth and early twentieth centuries to core industrial and commercial arenas.[1] This essay will place that migration of Europeans in the context of total European migration during the 1750–1914 period. Viewed from the distance of the Americas, and from the twentieth century, it is easy to imagine that European societies were sedentary before the mass migrations of the nineteenth century, but the reality of the European population is much more supple and complex. The migration systems that developed in the nineteenth century moved greater numbers of Europeans and moved them to destinations that were in many cases new, but they did not introduce migration to sedentary societies. In eighteenth-century Europe, rather, departures from home—whether systems of temporary migration or permanent relocation—were embedded in patterns of family, landholding, and production.

In this essay I will delineate (a) the workings of permanent and temporary migration in relation to early modern European population, family, and landholding, and (b) the relationship between migration and the most significant economic trend of the eighteenth century, the proliferation of rural industry. Taking the view that the movement of European peoples beyond their continent is part of the processes that took them to other nation-states within Europe and to other areas within their own countries, I then will sketch (c) the changes in European life that promoted an increase in emigration to the Americas. Following this will be a (d) survey of the transatlantic, continental, and internal migration in western Europe. Finally, (e) this essay will pinpoint the connections among migration systems and the dynamics that brought Europeans into one migration system or another. In short, I will attempt to answer these questions: How did the familial, landholding, and labor systems of western Europe shape eighteenth-century migration patterns? What large-scale changes underlay shifts in European migration in the 1750–1914 period? When Europeans left their homes in the nineteenth century, where did they go? What are the connections among migration systems to these various destinations?

Unfortunately, a precise measurement of eighteenth-century population movements is not possible, because there is very little hard or systematic evidence about migration patterns in early modern Europe. I can quantify neither the number of migrants, nor the proportion of people who moved overall. Because there are no national data on migration, I rely on regional and local studies to assess mobility. As a consequence, this essay draws on studies of particular regions, rural areas, and cities emphasizing the mobility trends in certain *kinds* of areas. But this approach has a singular strength: reliance on local studies brings into focus the relationship between particular economies and migration itineraries. This produces a more vivid understanding of mobility than do national-level data produced in the age of the census, when national counts disguise regional trends. Aside from questions of law and nationality, the village or region is a much more telling unit of study for migration than the nation-state. As a consequence, the localized migration studies for the eighteenth century possess a strength that national statistics for the nineteenth century do not.

In the period under review here, most Europeans moved in migration systems.[2] Farmhands and brides moved short distances within fairly *local* systems. Harvesters and sawyers traveled a *circular* route that in some cases covered long distances, returning home when their tasks were accomplished. As workers in industrial villages, cities, or other countries sent for their compatriots and loved ones, creating systems of *chain* migration, a small proportion struck out in *colonizing* movements to farms in the United States and Siberia.[3]

Population, Family, and Migration in the Eighteenth Century

In 1750, the vast majority of Europeans resided in small towns, villages, and hamlets; indeed, an estimated 93 percent of Europeans lived in burgs of under ten thousand. Ireland, Switzerland, and parts of Scandinavia were over 95 percent rural, and the Dutch, Belgians, and English were least so (only 70, 80, and 83 percent, respectively, lived in villages and small towns). There were few cities of over one hundred thousand in 1750—in northwestern Europe, only London, Amsterdam, Lyon, and Paris attained that size. Interestingly, Jan de Vries calculates that the growth of smaller cities was most important after 1750, when the number of small cities more than tripled, from 138 to 551. Although great cities were visible, then, the people of western Europe were primarily rurals, and the cities that attracted newcomers were most likely towns of about ten thousand people.[4]

This rural population was growing. After subsistence crises on the continent in the 1690s to 1730s, the population began to expand. The entire population of Europe nearly doubled between 1750 and 1850 as the number of people rose from about 62 million to 116 million. The number of Irish grew about three and one-half times, the population of England and Wales grew 2.9 times, and that of Germany nearly doubled; France, by contrast, increased by less than 50 percent.[5] The cause for the population increase is debated, and it clearly varied from place to place, but its level seems to have been rooted in the survival of an increasing number of infants, on the one hand, and in earlier and more widespread marriage, on the other.[6] The countryside grew more crowded in the period after 1750, and this fundamental fact of European life affected the propensity of people to leave home.

Who was likely to migrate in early modern Europe? This depended most fundamentally on gender, because most tasks were sex-specific. Consequently, migration systems responding to a need for harvesters, for example (like the Germans who mowed hay in seventeenth-century Holland), were overwhelmingly male. By contrast, the insatiable need for domestic servants in the cities increased the demand for female labor. Of course, men and women moved to every kind of destination, and women went to locations where men were in the majority, such as coal-mining towns, frontier farms, and metalworking cities because their domestic skills were prized. Women's ability to bear children also shaped their migrations. Families, communities, and church institutions attempted to protect female migrants because they were vulnerable to pregnancy. For this reason, women moved primarily short distances in the eighteenth century, sponsored more by private and familial arrangements than were men in harvest gangs or urban construction teams. Pregnancy out of wedlock motivated departures for some single women; for others it was a cost of living away from the social protection of home. Finally, women moved when they married.[7]

Short-range local migration was founded in European family, landholding, and inheritance systems. Family formation began with migration. Most marriage markets included several parishes or hamlets, partly because throughout Europe the taboo on incest prevented marriages of close relatives.[8] For example, in the northern French parish of Longuenesse, half the marriage partners came from outside the village, the vast majority of whom were from the region, but nonetheless were from beyond adjoining villages.[9] Where couples set up an independent household, as in England, husband and wife moved into a new household; where stem families prevailed, as in southwestern France, wives moved into the husband's household.[10]

Inheritance systems gave some children a privileged position from the first years of their lives and condemned their siblings to celibacy or departure. This was most true where systems of strict primogeniture prevailed; in such places, all children, except the eldest son, knew early on that they could not remain at home and marry. Those who would not inherit the family land could depart or remain on with a status like that of a servant. The inheriting child in systems that divided property among the children often worked to pay most of the children off in order to keep the holding intact.[11] Only systems of extended and multiple families like the southern French *frèrèches* could retain all family members in the household working together. Even in these cases, daughters who married would depart—for their husband's household.

The goal of landowning families in all inheritance systems was to preserve the patrimony. It cannot be overemphasized that everything peasants did to maintain their land was more *"for the household than for individuals."*[12] Peasant families would avoid dividing the land, even where inheritance was legally partible. Temporary migrations numbered among peasant strategies to maintain or expand landholdings; fathers and/or children would work away from home in order to earn cash for taxes or land. This was especially true of inhospitable regions that had few resources; the parents in the upland Auvergne in central France, for example, had good reason to fear that their sons would never return from their annual cash-earning trip to the lowlands.[13]

Families who owned no land—or so little land that they were de facto proletarians—were more likely to relocate than peasant families because they were not bound to a particular location by substantial ownership; they could find another cottage to rent or buy when taxes, fees, or relations with the landlord necessitated departure. In fact, in early modern Sweden the key demographic difference between proletarian and landowning families was not the numbers of children they bore, but rather how often they moved from parish to parish. Although 59 percent to 71 percent of men and women died in their parish of birth, where mining and hauling were combined with farming, only 24 percent to 32 percent died in their home parish, where farming was performed by estate workers. "Movement from village or farm of birth," writes David Gaunt, "was the predominant experience of men and women living in manor parishes."[14] Geographical stability, then, was a privilege.

The fact that Europeans with "dwarf holdings"—only a cottage and garden, or no land whatsoever—were more likely to move than more self-sufficient peasants is particularly crucial in an era when proletarians were on the increase. Local studies from southern France to Sweden record the parcelization of landholdings and the proletarianization of rural peoples in the eighteenth century. Albert Soboul estimated the proletarians and semiproletarians of France to be 40 percent of the rural population by 1790. In western Germany, at about the same time, an estimated 80 percent of rurals had to live from wage labor because their landholdings were inadequate or nonexistent.[15] Steve Hochstadt explicates the many ways in which this trend evolved in Germany in his essay in this volume. By the year 1800, the numbers of rural proletarians—or smallholders who were de facto proletarians—were expanding disproportionately; Europeans were becoming more mobile as a result of this shift in population composition.[16]

Leaving home was a normal part of the life cycle in the late eighteenth century, when the most mobile people were men and women aged fifteen to twenty-five. They most likely departed to work as farmhands, an occupation that was the backbone of training and employment in many agricultural regions. Farmhands were the children of cottagers, proletarians, and peasants alike. Although it is difficult to find records of this population (that neither married, left wills, nor wrote diaries), farm servants were clearly important to eighteenth-century Europe. For example, in the sixty-three available English parish listings dating from 1574 to 1821, servants accounted for about 60 percent of the male and female population aged fifteen to twenty-four.[17] And adolescent servants were more likely to move than people in any other stage of life; the majority moved annually, taking one-year contracts, then moving on—albeit usually within their home region. Of the male servants in their early twenties in the northern French village of Longuenesse, 70 percent moved in any given year in the 1780s; the figure for women was over 50 percent. At the same time, in the English Midlands village of Cardington, 78 percent of the boys and 29 percent of the girls were out in service between the ages of fifteen and nineteen.[18] Sharecroppers, on the other hand, had distinct patterns of family and migration: young men worked the land together with their siblings and remained at home after marriage; entire households moved together if relations with estate managers became strained or altered; only women were likely to leave home alone—to work as domestics and to marry.[19]

Thus, whether peasant, proletarian, or sharecropper, Europeans were likely to move—at least within their home region—in the period between 1750 and 1840; more important, perhaps, is the fact that migration was related in a systematic way to family economics, life cycle, and gender. David Gaunt's summary statement would stand for much of northwestern Europe: "Real stability in the sense of remaining in the village of birth was no general feature of early modern Swedish society. Such stability could be found in certain types of parishes primarily among males."[20] Between service and marriage, young women were probably more likely to leave their home parish than young men. Yet we associate migrant labor with men—perhaps because the most visible groups of migrants were males.

In addition to local and regional movements, European men engaged in temporary migrations that took them far from home, in many cases across national borders. Jan Lucassen has canvassed seven migration systems, each of which engaged at least twenty thousand men per year. Among the most important is the North Sea system that drew men every year from northern France, Belgium, and Germany into the Netherlands, where they would mow hay, harvest grain, cut peat, dig madder, manufacture bricks, maintain dikes, or work in construction. A long-standing system of migration brought men from France's central highlands into Spain, where they worked for a few months or a period of years as shepherds, harvesters, urban laborers, or retailers. Italians from many regions flooded into the Tiber plain to harvest grain each year; another system supplied Piedmont with rice workers. People from the French, Spanish, and Italian mountains cut grain, harvested grapes, and worked the olive and salt crops on the Mediterranean littoral of Provence, Languedoc, and Catalonia. Bands of harvest workers came from East Anglia to work the breadbasket of London, and from northern France to work that of Paris.[21] Although some women went along with harvest teams, it was to glean and to beg rather than to cut or sheave the grain, since men, in the main, staffed these long-distance systems.[22] These seven migration systems were not peripheral to the economies of western Europe, but rather they were central to the economies of the Netherlands and Spain, to the grain-producing areas of England, France, and Italy, and to the hungry rurals of Germany, France, England, Spain, and Italy whom they supported. In the nineteenth century, several of these systems would fade or be supplanted by new ones; nonetheless, they were very important migration itineraries on which rural families depended.

If migrants were crucial to the harvest teams of western Europe, they were equally crucial to the cities of the continent, where the high death rates meant that a sizable influx of newcomers was required for a city to maintain its population. The most accurate records of this precensus era—German *Bürgerbuch* and French marriage records—testify to the influx of outsiders who made their lives in the cities of Europe. For example, nearly half the citizens of Frankfurt, and over 70 percent of Berlin citizens, were migrants from the outside in the early eighteenth century. About half of those who married in French cities, from Rouen and Caen in the north to Bordeaux and Marseille in the south, were migrants as well.[23] Citizen registers and marriage records provide only a dim echo of actual movement to cities, because both marrying couples and citizens were less mobile than the scores of temporary migrants who arrived and departed. These migrants labored as construction workers, domestic servants, and transport workers such as longshoremen and carters, who spent the autumn, the summer months, or a few years of their youth in the city.[24]

Migrants entered and left the city as part of migration systems. The workings of migration systems and their evolution have been analyzed in an exemplary way for southwestern France and the city of Bordeaux. The poverty of the countryside deepened in southwestern France as its population increased during the eighteenth century; simultaneously, migration to Bordeaux intensified as this city grew to become a major Atlantic port and entrepôt where wine, grain, and colonial products were exchanged. Most migrants from the greater Southwest were men who hailed from the uplands of central France; others came from riverside villages that dotted the water routes to Bordeaux. Many of these men worked in construction to build this prosperous port; others worked in transport trades. A small, but significant, contingent of merchants and sailors came from other coastal cities of France. Finally, masses of young women came to the city from its surrounding communities to work as domestics in the homes and shops of the city.[25] Bordeaux is typical in that it drew male workers from farther afield than women and drew its elite from a relatively large, and urban, arena.

Migration and Early Industry

Perhaps the most important hallmark of the European economy in the century before 1850 was the expansion of rural industry.[26] Although rural production was very old, particularly in some industries such as nailmaking, the rural production of commercial goods expanded to unprecedented dimensions in the late seventeenth and the eighteenth centuries.[27] It thrived in western Europe's commercially active regions with export outlets. In Normandy, for example, the number of textile workers was estimated to be about 57,000 in 1732 and 188,200 fifty years later. In the Rhineland, the Wupper Valley produced silk, linen, and cotton that expanded to employ over 30,000 workers by 1800.[28] Rural production provided employment for hundreds of thousands of men, women, and children. Rural industry was fundamentally important in providing an important third sector for employment, in addition to agriculture and the urban sector.[29]

Population mobility was crucial to the establishment of successful cottage industries. In the West, the freedom to settle in industrial villages was at the core of successful rural industry; legal systems and landholding patterns made it possible to divide holdings, build new cottages, and occupy a variety of buildings. In eastern Europe, where feudalism restricted free movement, rural industry thrived only in regions like Silesia, where rural landlords gleaned enormous profit from industrial labor, which was incorporated into the feudal obligations of the serf.[30] English, French, and Belgian industrial villages attracted newcomers more than agricultural or pastoral villages. Most growth occurred early on in their village industrial history, before prolific marriages supplied the number of new workers that was adequate to the task. Sites like the knitting village of Shepshed in the English midlands and the Norman spinning village of Auffay attracted single people and families who set up new households.[31]

Once domestic production was established in villages, it anchored populations in place. Surveys of English, French, German, and Belgian villages show that they had relatively little turnover.[32] For those whose age and gender fit the tasks of village production, there was no need for seasonal migration in search of work. Consequently, the lowlands of northern France, the Netherlands, and present-day Belgium, where rural industry was especially vigorous, were areas without widespread massive currents of temporary migration. There was less movement than in the seventeenth century, when population and industrial work were more scarce, or than there would be in the late nineteenth century, when a surfeit of people and lack of work would force rurals from home.

Rural industry is central to the configuration of population and landholding that emerged in Europe before 1850. The population expanded most impressively in rural industrial areas (where high fertility rates prevailed). Expanding industry had a great impact on landholding. The availability of wages meant that less land was required to support a family and, as a consequence, more siblings could marry and stay at home while landholdings were divided. Families became more dependent on industry and less able to support themselves by agriculture alone, because their landholdings became very small; industrial areas like the Zurich highlands, Flanders, and the Rhineland became more crowded and more proletarian.[33] Rural industry enabled the countryside to hold many more people than before.

The expansion of rural industry was important to the city as well. Although the focus of early industry is properly on the countryside, the structural framework for rural industry is located in cities and towns: the markets, merchants, capital, and credit were all urban; decision making, exchange, and the flow of information about goods and markets were urban. For some industries, such as metalware and textiles, urban artisans processed, finished, and assembled village products. For example, nearly half the town of Verviers, Belgium, worked in the textile industry in 1800, primarily as weavers, but also as artisan fabric finishers (teaselers and shearmen), drapers, and merchants.[34]

People came and went from these centers of industry. Although there are no records from this period of the gross flows of migration, studies of urban areas suggest that industrial-node cities were short-term homes in particular for the young people who came to work as carters, domestics, or spinners. The industrial center Verviers is fairly typical of the growing cities of Europe in this age; it expanded from about 10,500 in 1700 to about 13,000 in 1785.[35] The distinction between urban area and industrial village blurred as a result of the movement of people, raw materials, and finished goods between industrial centers like Verviers and their hinterland. Village workers, like the spinners of Auffay, who marketed their own yarn every week, became familiar with the market town that they visited regularly. The physical distinction between town and country also was reduced in many regions as industrial suburbs grew outside city walls; these were newly settled, growing areas intimately related to the city economy. For example, the center city of the French industrial hub of Rouen grew little in the eighteenth century, but an estimated two thousand new households appeared in outlying, suburban villages.[36] Although virtually no research has been done on such areas, they obviously grew by immigration of new families, perhaps from nearby villages.

Changing Conditions in the Nineteenth Century

In the opening years of the nineteenth century, the long Napoleonic wars disrupted the migration patterns of a crowded countryside that was increasingly dependent on seasonal migration and rural industry. The wars themselves damaged most deeply the lives of young men, the very group that was most likely to leave home for harvest work and other seasonal migrations; as a consequence, the primary systems of harvest and temporary migrations were depressed between 1804 and 1815.[37] A postwar depression struck both England and the continent, exacerbated by the exposure of rural industries on the continent to English competition and the flooding of the English labor force with returned soldiers.

After 1815, shifts in British and continental life struck at the ability of rural folk—who were the vast majority of Europeans in 1815—to make a living at home. None of these changes is exclusive to the nineteenth century and none affected Europeans evenly from region to region, yet they all reduced life-chances in the countryside for a large proportion of rurals.

The most fundamental of these changes was unprecedented population growth, continuing on the trajectory established in the eighteenth century. Excluding the 52 million Europeans who departed the continent in the nineteenth century, the population increased from 187 million to 266 million between 1800 and 1850, then to 468 million by 1913, by 43 percent in the first half of the century, and by 50 percent in the second half. About one person in five on the globe lived in Europe in 1800; that proportion rose to one in four by 1900. Europe became far and away the most densely populated continent on earth. (As before, this population growth was by no means even. In Great Britain, Denmark, and Finland, the population more than tripled; it more than doubled in Germany, Sweden, Austria-Hungary, Belgium, and Holland; and it doubled in Italy. France grew by a mere 55 percent over the century, and as the population of Great Britain doubled for a second time in 1850–1910, that of France increased by only 14 percent.)[38] Population expansion produced a great squeeze on European resources, for the same land could not feed two and one-half times as many people as in 1800; the same occupational structure could not support twice the workers. This demographic shock was cushioned by the emigration of over fifty million Europeans.

Two trends, exacerbated by population growth, acted in concert to promote European migration. First, the consolidation of land ownership increased the proportion of proletarians in the countryside. In some regions, the land-poor were bought out; in others, the size of landholdings diminished below a tenable minimum, so that many country folk gradually became proletarian. Nineteenth-century proletarianization, like population growth, followed a previously established trend that was uneven in Europe; it had a long history with the enclosure acts beginning in the English midlands, followed population pressures in eighteenth-century France, for example, and came to the region east of the Elbe only after the emancipation of serfs in the mid-nineteenth century.[39]

Second, changes in the rural labor force altered the nineteenth-century countryside, making agricultural work less secure and reducing manufacturing altogether. With the increase in large-scale crop production in some regions came the increased use of harvest teams and other short-term seasonal workers at the expense of the long-lived year-round rural worker, the servant in husbandry or *domestique de ferme* who was hired by the year. Short-term harvest work had long been a part of European history, yet it became much more important with the proliferation of labor-intensive cash crops—grain for the growing cities, sugar beets, fresh vegetables and fruits, flowers, and grapes. This meant that those men and women who could find agricultural work in the countryside were less likely to find year-round work. Simultaneously, rural manufacturing waned. As prices for hand-produced goods—such as cloth, nails, lace, and stockings—collapsed in the face of competition from machine-produced goods between 1850 and World War I, the entire or partial livelihood of whole regions was destroyed. This collapse of rural livelihoods directly forced Europeans from home.[40]

Transoceanic Migrations in the Nineteenth Century

Along with these changes came unprecedented human movement. About 52 million emigrants left Europe between 1824 and 1924, of whom roughly 37 million (72 percent) traveled to North America, 11 million to South America (21 percent), and 3.5 million, primarily British, to Australia and New Zealand.[41]

Migration from Europe to the United States was not new in the nineteenth century, but rather greatly expanded on previous trends. An estimated 1.5 million emigrated from Britain in the eighteenth century; some 200,000 German settlers were increased by about 17,000 mercenaries who stayed on after the American Revolution.[42] This migration increased after the Napoleonic wars, then exploded in the "hungry forties," when crop failures exacerbated the suffering of underemployed and crowded Europeans. Although it is best understood in regional terms, I briefly review this history using national-level data.

Irish outnumbered any immigrant group in the 1840s, when over 780,000 arrived. In the 1850s, 914,000 Irish came to the United States. Thereafter, immigration was reduced to about 435,000 per decade until the 1880s, when it rose again to over 655,000. Fewer English than Irish came to the United States in the 1840–70 period (over 200,000 per decade); then English emigration rose in the 1870s and 1880s to nearly match the Irish at over 640,000 per decade. English immigration to the United States remained at this high level until World War I.

Like the Irish, Germans emigrated to the United States en masse in the 1840s and 1850s, when about 434,000 and then 951,000 arrived. After a falling off of emigration in the 1860s and 1870s, nearly a million and a half Germans arrived in the United States in the 1880s. This emigration fell sharply in the 1890s with the American Panic of 1893 and the simultaneous industrial boom in western Germany.[43]

Beginning in the 1880s, eastern and southern European immigrants joined the Irish, Germans, and English in the United States. Emigrants from Russia increased from 39,000 in the 1870s to over 213,000 in the 1880s. Some of these were Jews escaping czarist pogroms that increased in intensity with the twentieth century; others were part of the mass emigration of Poles from the regions of Russia, Austria-Hungary, and the German Empire, which had divided the Kingdom of Poland in 1772–95. An estimated 100,000 Poles arrived in the United States in the 1880s; this number would grow from 30,000 to 50,000 per year in the 1890s, to 130,000 to 175,000 per year before World War I.[44]

Italians were most visible among late-century migrants to the United States. Where nearly 56,000 immigrated in the 1870s, over 655,000 arrived in the 1880s—a number equal to that of the English or Irish. Even more Italians, however, went to Brazil and Argentina, where they were the vast majority of immigrants until the turn of the century. At this point, they were superseded by the growing migration of Spanish to Latin America.[45]

The vast majority of emigrants from Europe moved in systems of chain migration, maintained by letters and through word sent by kin and compatriots across the ocean. Case studies of migrant groups, such as those from Sicily who lived on Elizabeth Street in Manhattan, Italian harvesters in Argentina, or German farmers in Missouri, reveal rich, lively contacts among kin.[46] A study of Sweden's Langosjö parish and its emigrants specifies family relations and transatlantic moves; it diagrams kin and home contacts as the lifeblood of migration systems.[47] On the eve of World War I, nearly 80 percent of immigrants to the United States had a relative waiting for them; 15 percent were joining friends.[48] Similarly, moves on the continent worked through networks of kin, contact, and friendship.[49]

Shipping agents and labor recruiters played an important role in initiating migration streams. Recruiters sought out iron miners and industrial workers for North America, cane cutters for Louisiana, and agricultural laborers for Brazil and Argentina.[50] Because shipping companies were highly motivated to fill their increasingly large steerage and cabin quarters, shipping agents and transportation companies eagerly sought out passengers. Emigration agents were especially aggressive in eastern Europe, where agents like Friedrich Missler in Bremen, Germany, distributed advertising handkerchiefs, snuff boxes, change purses, and beer mugs as far as Hungary and Croatia. Some agents used unscrupulous means to get Russians from their country to German port cities, and shipping companies operated their own health inspections so that emigrants would not be sent back (at the shipper's expense).[51] But although advertising and recruiting helped to initiate migration streams, they did not cause emigration, which was rooted in social and economic conditions. Agent-sponsored emigration and personal networks mixed to promote departures. For example, when Italian government investigators interviewed laborers bound for South America, they found that single groups of emigrants had friendship, village, *and* agent relationships.[52] Migration networks, then, were not a mechanistic phenomenon, but rather operated on multiple contacts.

Migration among European Nations

For Europeans, transatlantic emigrations were far from the entire panorama of human movement in the period 1840–1914, especially because movements between the nations of Europe were increasingly visible. The Irish, for example, came in droves to England and Scotland. Before the great potato famine in 1841, the British census recorded over 126,000 in Scotland and nearly 290,000 in England. During the worst years of the famine, the Irish arrived in England by the thousands every month, so that the 1851 census recorded a half million in England and Wales. The Irish were a most visible addition on this small island, although there were fewer in England than in the United States. Because most Irish immigrants lived in cities, the English, who had had no large-scale immigration since the Norman Conquest of 1066, experienced this influx of Irish as "an urban invasion."[53]

Belgian immigration to France was nearly as significant. "In a situation only slightly less awful than that of Ireland," the Flemish fled a region simultaneously devastated by the collapse of rural industry, the potato blight, poor grain harvests, and high mortality in the 1840s. For the Belgians of Flanders, as for the Irish, the disasters of the 1840s marked a new, voluminous phase of a long-lived migration pattern. By 1871, 375,000 Belgians lived in France, where they were easily the largest group of foreigners.

Fifteen years later, 489,000 Belgians lived in France, the great majority in the industrial north.[54]

Later in the century, Italian migration to other European nations reached a peak. Indeed, some studies show that in the 1876–1976 period, more Italians worked in other European countries than in the Western Hemisphere. Before World War I, the greatest number worked first in southern France (where today's border between the two countries was set only in 1860), then in Germany, Austria-Hungary, and Switzerland. For example, between 1876 and 1915, the number of Italians emigrating annually averaged nearly 43,000 to France, over 33,000 to Switzerland, over 30,000 to Germany, and over 28,000 to Austria-Hungary. (A large but unspecifiable proportion of these moves was temporary.) Each province has its own history of migration to specific destinations, with Venetians, Piedmontese, and Lombards among the first and most important migrants to their northern neighbors.[55]

Beginning a bit later, Poles living in the portion of today's Poland that was the eastern German empire (1871–1918) moved into western Germany to work. Although these ethnic Poles were not counted as foreigners, they were certainly a distinct, segregated ethnic minority in the Ruhr valley of western Germany, where the vast majority worked as miners; it is estimated that they numbered 300,000 to 400,000 on the eve of World War I. In response to the labor vacuum created by the departures of natives from the eastern German provinces, estate owners and mine foremen hired some 400,000 Polish women, men, and children from Austrian Galacia and Russian Poland annually for seasonal labor. By 1910, men, women, and children came annually to eastern Germany where they worked in agriculture and industry.[56]

Between 1880 and 1914, then, international migration in Europe developed dramatically with new industrial cities, coal and steel producing regions, and the expansion of capitalist agriculture. The most important node of international labor migration was centered on the Rhine-Ruhr zone, which recruited and attracted unprecedented numbers of workers; this stretched south into Switzerland, where an uncommonly high proportion of foreigners labored in factory, shop, and construction site. The international army of agricultural field laborers worked to the west and east of this central core.

Most foreign labor in western Europe worked in Germany, France, and Switzerland, where Poles, Italians, Belgians, and Germans were the mainstay of the foreign populations. Of the over one million foreign workers in Germany, 580,000 were Poles and 150,000 were Italians in 1910; foreigners were about 1.7 percent of the total population of the country. France, too, included over a million foreigners, of whom Italians were 419,000 and Belgians 287,000 in 1911, when foreigners were 2.9 percent of the population. Foreign populations played a much more important role in Switzerland, where there were over 552,000 foreign born, including 219,000 Germans and 203,000 Italians; indeed, in 1910, 14.7 percent of the Swiss population was foreign born, and 16.7 percent of its labor force were foreigners. England, by contrast, needed relatively few foreign workers by 1900.[57]

Internal Migration

In addition to these movements of population across the borders of Europe, Europeans moved within their own nations. Many men and women relocated in the countryside, but the movement that fascinated (and horrified) contemporaries was the movement that expanded cities at the expense of the countryside. The cities of the continent grew to unheard-of size; where there were only twenty-three cities of 100,000 or more in 1800, there were one hundred thirty-five a century later. Capital cities became spectacular metropolises: London grew by 340 percent, Paris by 345 percent, Vienna by 490 percent, and Berlin by 872 percent. The suburbs of large cities grew at an even greater pace.[58] And, for the first time since the Middle Ages, many new towns appeared, most of them industrial towns. For example, the textile town dubbed the "French Manchester," Roubaix, started the century as a textile-processing center of 8,000 and finished it as an industrial giant of 125,000 people. The most prodigious development of such centers occurred in the Ruhr zone, where villages and small towns like Essen, Düsseldorf, Dortmund, and Duisberg became cities of 200,000 to 350,000. By 1910, the German Empire included forty-five cities of over 100,000 where there had been only Hamburg and Berlin in 1800.[59]

This urbanized population gathered in small cities also. By the 1890s, small towns dotted the landscape and a good proportion of Europeans lived in cities of 20,000 or more. In England and Wales, over half the population lived in such cities; over a quarter of Belgians and Dutch did so. In Germany, France, and Denmark, over one-fifth of the population lived in cities of over 20,000; this was true of about one in seven Italians, Norwegians, Swiss, and Austro-Hungarians.[60] In every case, the gain in proportion of people in cities and small towns came at the expense of the countryside.[61]

Migration was at the heart of European urbanization. In most countries, migrants made up the lion's share of capital-city and large-city populations. For example, by the late nineteenth century, censuses recorded that 68 percent of the residents of Paris were migrants, 59 percent in Berlin, 65 percent in Vienna, 69 percent in Stockholm; in Saxony, 61 percent of Dresden and 64 percent of Leipzig residents were migrants. Generally, the larger the city, the larger the proportion of people who had been born elsewhere, because large cities had a stronger and broader appeal than smaller towns. For example, although 69 percent of Stockholm residents were migrants, only 32 percent of other Swedish urbanites had migrated to their towns; although

57 percent of residents of Bavarian cities of over 30,000 were migrants, only 46 percent of residents in Bavarian towns of under 10,000 had been born elsewhere.[62] Provincial towns drew on nearby villages, larger cities had a regional draw, and the capital cities and world cities like London and Paris drew people nationwide and beyond.[63]

Migration was particularly important to growth in the city, where urban death rates were high. It was especially crucial to the growth of French and Italian large cities (over 200,000), and then to German and Scandinavian cities. Because the English had an exceptionally low urban death rate and a higher birth rate, natural increase was more important to British cities than migration. By contrast, migration was essential to the population of a city like Marseille, where the birth rate was low and mortality was high.[64] Generally, however, the importance of migration to urban growth diminished in the late nineteenth century as urban death rates dropped throughout Europe and a greater proportion of urban infants survived to adulthood.[65]

Temporary Movement

Europeans clearly moved in unprecedented numbers as the nineteenth century progressed.[66] Walking, and riding in carts, railroad trains, sailing ships, and steamships, they left home for rural work, for the cities, for neighboring countries, and for the western hemisphere. Our understanding of these migrants—of those who stayed relatively close to home as well as of those who traveled thousands of miles—is fundamentally distorted when we attempt to order their movements by envisioning a single move only, by imagining that men and women left home for one destination and remained there. This is clearly not the case. Rather, a large proportion of migrants remained only a matter of months or a few years before their itinerary carried them to a new destination or home again. Many movements were "step migrations" to larger villages, towns, and cities.

Transatlantic migration was increasingly a temporary move, after about 1860, when the steamship rendered the ocean crossing easier and cheaper. Thousands of Italian and Spanish workers—named *golondrinas* after the swallows' seasonal movements—harvested grain and fruit in Argentina beginning in October; some then worked in Brazilian coffee plantations and then returned home in May. They may have numbered from 25,000 to nearly 100,000 annually in the 1880–1914 period.[67] Portuguese worked in Brazil with every intention of returning home. An obscure and extreme, but illuminating, example is that of the English interior decorators who spent a season in London, another in the English countryside, and a third in New York; more common were the "some hundreds" of English masons and stonecutters who worked in the United States from spring until fall.[68]

As immigrants in the United States were increasingly urban proletarian workers rather than farmers in the late nineteenth century, those who returned home were primarily men who worked in construction gangs or factories for a few years. In the years before World War I (1907–14), the most recently formed migration streams included the most temporary migrants: people from the Baltic states, Greece, Italy, Austria, and Hungary. Return migration was primarily the movement of working-age people (ages fifteen to forty-five) who could use their income at home. And although women's patterns echoed men's in any one migrant group, men were more likely to return to Europe. For example, in the 1909–28 period, when Italian male immigrants outnumbered females by over two to one, returnees outnumbered their female counterparts by over seven to one.[69]

Within Europe, most international migration was temporary. It was linked to centuries-old patterns of harvest migration that had moved harvesters across borders to gather English wheat and Dutch hay. In the nineteenth century, however, two kinds of labor demands generated a new need for large numbers of foreigners. The first was the harvest migrations for large-scale capitalist farms. This intensified earlier trends, resulting in the new importation of Galician Poles and Belgians to the sugar beet fields of East Prussia and northern France. The second is the construction of the massive trade and transport infrastructure that laid roads, dug canals, built railroad systems, and pierced tunnels. These projects required teams of temporary workers: the Irish navvies in England, the Galician Poles in eastern Germany, and the Italians in Switzerland, France, and southern Germany. Work was temporary, but nowhere more explicitly so than in the eastern provinces of the German empire, where hundreds of thousands of Austrian Poles were required by law to be out of the country from mid-December to February.[70]

Although most international migration was temporary and male, women figured more prominently than in past centuries. Over half the Poles in eastern Germany were women, favored by employers because they were skilled at working root crops, accepted low wages, and were perceived as docile workers. Italian women cut flowers, harvested vegetables, and picked olives in southern France. They were also a quarter of the embroidery workers in the mechanized Swiss embroidery industry of 1911; recruited and housed by their employers, most were single women aged fourteen to twenty. A quarter of Swiss domestics were foreign women, most of whom had moved south from Germany.[71]

Much of the internal migration within the nations of Europe was temporary as well, because indigenous labor also worked on the railroad gangs of Britain and the continent, dug the canals, and blasted out tunnels. Mountain folk, flatland villagers, and underemployed urban workers joined harvest teams. Among them were women who worked as hop pickers, gleaners, and diggers of beets and potatoes.[72]

Likewise, and less well understood, is the fact that movements to the city in the nineteenth century were often temporary. Urbanization was less a vast permanent movement of rural people to the city than a respiration and expulsion of several kinds of migration systems from which some people would settle in the city.[73] For the poorest of Europeans, migration to the city was part of the itinerary of the dispossessed and insecure; for many country folk it was one side of a vacillation between the rural life of a semiproletarian and urban proletarian life. For a third group, temporary residence in one town was part of movement to progressively larger cities (step migration), often as part of a bureaucratic career.[74] In all three cases, men and women entered the city, then departed, perhaps to enter again.

Recent research on cityward migration has emphasized that arrivals and departures far outnumbered the net volume of urban population gain. For example, while the industrial city of Duisburg in the Ruhr valley grew by 97,836 people between 1848 and 1904, it temporarily hosted 719,903 individuals who moved to, then exited, the town.[75] (Unfortunately, these temporary movements appear only in the population registers and statistics of Belgian, Italian, and some German cities.) For most people, migration was intensely age-specific: a Rhineland male may have moved fifteen times in his life, but ten of those moves would have been between the ages of fifteen and thirty.[76]

Links among Migration Systems

What are the links between the temporary migrations described above and patterns of permanent relocation that shifted populations to the Western Hemisphere and to European cities in the years before 1914? What are the links among movements to the many destinations of Europeans: the rural area, the town, the foreign nation on the continent, and the New World? Were these destinations part of the same migration itinerary in a serial way; did people move from town to city or from city to the New World in systems of step migration? Or, alternatively, did men and women move to one kind of destination or another?

These are important questions because migration systems proliferated and changed in the nineteenth century, as men and women left more remote rural areas for village and town, as burgeoning cities drew from farther afield than before, and as new migration streams formed between countries on the continent and with the New World. Men and women who had moved in local circuits to marry and work went farther afield after 1850. Those from many obscure mountain valleys joined movements to lowland cities. Women joined long-distance migration streams that previously had been all-male. People whose ancestors had previously stayed in their home region—be it the provinces of southern Italy, East Elbia, Poland, or central Germany—traveled as far as the New World to work. Those whose ancestors had migrated to the New World in the eighteenth century (the English, the Portuguese, the Germans) did so in far greater numbers than before.

On the other hand, the proliferation of migration streams and choices of destination was not a difference in kind from past movement; it was rather a difference in distance traveled. Generations of men and women had left home to harvest and to work in the urban shop or bourgeois kitchen, respectively. The way migration systems had worked in the past, drawing people from particular locations to areas that had work to offer—specific kinds of work for men and women—continued to work in the nineteenth century, as new industrial regions and the New World offered employment on an unprecedented scale.

Powerful sociodemographic and economic elements shaped the migration stream into which a man or woman might enter; nonetheless, migrants were by no means without choices. Paul Hohenberg and Lynn Lees note:

> [the] metaphors for migration—the "drift" into a city or the "flow" of people from place to place—fail to capture the purposeful element in the process. Individual moves were directed by many constraints: stage in the life cycle, kin, occupation, place of origin, the business cycle. Together they created a nexus for choice. . . .[77]

How did Europeans operate at this "nexus for choice"? Research on a broad range of migration systems in rural areas, to cities, and abroad confirms that people move to locations about which they have prior information and where they have personal contacts. Knowledge and acquaintance shape destination; the past behavior of one's family and acquaintances shapes one's own possibilities. Migrants travel along established paths. As Dudley Baines succinctly concluded after building and surveying fifty years of county-level data on emigration from Britain: the best predictor of emigration is previous emigration from the same locale.[78] Indeed, this is the sole unanimous finding of the broad range of econometric studies of immigration to the United States surveyed by J. D. Gould.[79]

Among the European migrants at every distance from home were those who became permanent settlers rather than temporary workers. Systems of circular migration evolved into systems of chain migration. Young women, who in other times might have returned to their villages after a stint as an urban domestic servant, become urban workers and wives.[80] Men in long-distance teams of seasonal migrants who stayed on as workers settled and sent for sweethearts, wives, and children. On the continent, this included construction workers like the masons from central France in Paris who had traveled to the capital for seasonal work since the early eighteenth century. In the nineteenth century, they began to settle in Paris and send for their wives. By 1900, the Auvergnat "colony" in Paris included over 69,000 people—equal numbers of men and women.[81] Likewise, as some temporary workers from southern and eastern Europe chose to stay in the United States, they sent for family members and produced settlements like those of the Italians in New York and the Poles in Detroit.[82]

As this essay has contended from the beginning, migrants to every sort of destination—from the regional capital to the mines of Missouri—were pushed by the same kinds of forces. Destinations varied, but they depended on opportunity and information, so people from the same village traveled locally, then extended their journey as they learned about more distant opportunities. For example, Polish ethnographer Franciszek Bujak related that his home village of Maszkienice sent out 40 percent of its young adults in 1899, most of whom traveled for seasonal work to Austrian coal mines in Ostrava (eighty), to Denmark (seventeen), or to cities in the region. People from neighboring villages had been traveling to the United States for some time, and their earnings were known in the area, but until 1898, most Maszkienicans had stayed in Austria. Migration to America had begun when a miner was persuaded by a neighboring villager to dig coal in Pennsylvania rather than Ostrava. When Bujak returned in 1911, sixty-three villagers were at work in the mines of Ostrava, fifty in Denmark, and between fifteen and thirty in the United States.[83]

As this example suggests, overseas migration systems were intimately linked with those on the continent. People who also moved abroad could, and did, move within their region or in agricultural circuits. Movements within Europe to earn money were used to finance transoceanic moves, or were discontinued in favor of an overseas move when it appeared feasible and profitable. This is what happened to the men of Maszkienice, who left off more local migrations to travel to the United States. Men from Piedmont in northern Italy worked in the fields, and they worked in Switzerland, and they also traveled to South America for grain harvests.[84] Swedish emigrants from Stockholm also came from regions with strong migration traditions. In particular, Swedish women who went to the United States would first follow the long-standing trip to the city for a stint of work as a domestic servant (partly to finance their journey, no doubt).[85] These Swedish "stage emigrants" were more likely to be women than men. Irish "stage emigrants"—most likely to be skilled workers departing from cities than unskilled laborers—also had worked in a city before leaving for North America. These findings about step migration are incomplete, but they strongly suggest that migration to the New World was intimately linked with cityward movements. Small towns were relay stations, in many cases, for Europeans who moved on either to a major city or abroad.[86]

In the long run, the intense temporary migrations of the 1880–1914 period gave way to more permanent moves and less mobility. U.S. legislation placing restrictive quotas on southern and eastern Europeans in the 1920s, the international economic depression of the 1930s, and the increasingly year-round nature of work favored permanent migration, or staying home altogether. In Germany, urban migration rates fell from an all-time high of 15 to 20 percent in 1912 to a rate of 10 percent and below after 1924.[87]

Conclusion

This survey of the varieties of European migration in the eighteenth and nineteenth centuries has emphasized the context of the European exodus to the New World—both in terms of the root causes of emigration and the important simultaneous movements on the continent. In past centuries as well as today, migrations within and emigrations from the European continent are part of the redistribution of the labor force. What sets the nineteenth century aside in Europe is the dramatic decrease of resources available to an increased rural population and the equally dramatic reordering of employment in urban areas and North America, particularly between 1840 and World War I.

Although the composition of migration systems and their proliferation in the nineteenth century are products of economic and demographic change, migration streams themselves are a manifestation of social connections. Shifts in capital and employment were mediated by socially transmitted information. Moreover, as the century drew to a close, as a more literate population wrote letters home and the railroad and steamship eased travel, information about destinations improved.[88] Europeans had much more exact information about their chances in a faraway city or in the United States than they had in the initial stages of mass migration. This information, transmitted by kin and compatriots, shaped the migration systems that drastically shifted the distribution of Europeans over the globe. A perspective on migration systems places human relations at the core of migration processes. Likewise, a focus on migration connects the common folk of Europe with the large-scale economic and social changes that transformed both Europe and America in the nineteenth century.

Notes

I would like to thank Walter Kamphoefner for comments on an earlier version of this paper.

1. The migration of Europeans was only part of a global movement of the labor force that included many Asians; see Lucie Cheng and Edna Bonacich, eds., *Labor Migration under Capitalism: Asian Workers in the United States before World War II* (Berkeley: University of California Press, 1984); Philip Curtin, "Migration in the Tropical World," in *Immi-*

gration Reconsidered: History, Sociology, and Politics, ed. Virginia Yans-McLaughlin (New York: Oxford University Press, 1990), 21–36.

2. See James Jackson, Jr., and Leslie Page Moch, "Migration and the Social History of Modern Europe," essay in this volume.

3. Charles Tilly, "Transplanted Networks," in Yans-McLaughlin, *Immigration Reconsidered*, 79–90.

4. Michael Anderson, *Population Change in North-Western Europe, 1750–1850* (London: Macmillan Education, Ltd., 1988), 26; Jan de Vries, *European Urbanization, 1500–1800* (Cambridge, Mass.: Harvard University Press, 1984), 70–73.

5. Anderson, *Population Change in North-Western Europe*, 21–23.

6. For example, the French population increased relatively little because French peasants had begun controlling fertility within marriage by the end of the eighteenth century; a decrease in infant and child mortality enabled that population to grow as much as it did. The English, who had a much greater population increase, did not experience such a drop in mortality as the French, but rather became more likely to marry, and to do so earlier, which put more women at risk of pregnancy during more of their fertile years (ibid., 51–52).

7. Caroline Brettell, *Men Who Migrate, Women Who Wait* (Princeton: Princeton University Press, 1987); Rachel Fuchs and Leslie Page Moch, "Pregnant, Single, and Far from Home: Migrant Women in Nineteenth-Century Paris," *American Historical Review* 95 (1990): 1007–35.

8. For a broad perspective on family formation, see Emmanuel Todd, *The Explanation of Ideology: Family Structures and Social Systems* (London: Basil Blackwell, 1985), 19–20.

9. Idem, "Mobilité géographique et cycle de vie en Artois et en Toscane au XVIIIe siècle," *Annales: Economies, Sociétés, Civilisations* 30 (1975): 739.

10. For the setting up of a new household in England, see Peter Laslett, *The World We Have Lost* (New York: Scribner's, 1983); for management of small properties and households without sons and migration, see Abel Poitrineau, *Remues d'hommes: Essai sur les migrations montagnardes en France aux XVIIe et XVIIIe siècles* (Paris: Aubier Montaigne, 1983).

11. In the vast literature on inheritance, this essay is very useful: Lutz Berkner and Franklin Mendels, "Inheritance Systems, Family Structure, and Demographic Patterns in Western Europe, 1700–1900," in *Historical Studies of Changing Fertility*, ed. Charles Tilly (Princeton: Princeton University Press, 1978), 209–23.

12. Goubert, "Family and Province: A Contribution to the Knowledge of Family Structures in Early Modern France," *Journal of Family History* 2 (1977): 190; emphasis in the original. For the family economy, see Louise Tilly and Joan Scott, *Women, Work and Family* (New York: Holt, Rinehart and Winston, 1978).

13. See, for example, Poitrineau, *Remues d'hommes*.

14. David Gaunt, "Pre-Industrial Economy and Population Structure," *Scandinavian Journal of History* 2 (1977): 195–97.

15. Studies cited in Catarina Lis and Hugo Soly, *Poverty and Capitalism in Pre-Industrial Europe* (Atlantic Highlands, N.J.: Humanities Press, 1979), 171, 173.

16. For the proletarianization of early modern Europeans, see Charles Tilly, "Demographic Origins of the European Proletariat," in *Proletarianization and Family History*, ed. D. Levine (Orlando, Fla.: Academic Press, 1984), 1–85; for the relation of this trend to migration, see Steve Hochstadt, "The Socioeconomic Determinants of Increasing Mobility in Nineteenth-Century Germany," essay in this volume.

17. Ann Kussmaul, *Servants in Husbandry in Early Modern England* (Cambridge: Cambridge University Press, 1981), 5.

18. Todd, "Mobilité géographique," 729–30; Roger Schofield, "Age-Specific Mobility in an Eighteenth-Century Rural English Parish," *Annales de démographie historique* (1970):

265–66; the most complete study of this group is Kussmaul, *Servants in Husbandry in Early Modern England.*

19. Todd, "Mobilité géographique," 732–34. For the evocative biography of a nineteenth-century sharecropper and his family, see Emile Guillaumin, *Life of a Simple Man* (Hanover, N.H.: University Press of New England, 1983).

20. Gaunt, "Pre-Industrial Economy and Population Structure," 198.

21. See Jan Lucassen for a summary of these migration systems, *Migrant Labour in Europe, 1600–1900: The Drift to the North Sea* (London: Croom Helm, 1987), chap. 6.

22. Olwen Hufton, *The Poor of Eighteenth-Century France* (Oxford: Clarendon Press, 1974), 76–77. There were exceptions; Lucassen points out that women worked at some jobs reserved for migrants, such as bleachers (*Migrant Labour in Europe*, 83–88).

23. The findings for these cities are summarized in the pathbreaking article by Steve Hochstadt, "Migration in Preindustrial Germany," *Central European History* 16 (1983): 195–224; Jean-Pierre Bardet, *Rouen aux XVIIe et XVIIIe siècles*, 2 vols. (Paris: Société d'Edition d'Enseignement Supérieur, 1983), 1:211.

24. Bardet, *Rouen aux XVIIe et XVIIIe siècles*, 1:217; see also Hochstadt, "Migration in Preindustrial Germany," 204–6.

25. Jean-Pierre Poussou, *Bordeaux et le sud-ouest au XVIIIe siècle* (Paris: Ecole des Hautes Etudes en Sciences Sociales, 1983).

26. Paul M. Hohenberg and Lynn Hollen Lees, *The Making of Urban Europe, 1000–1950* (Cambridge, Mass.: Harvard University Press, 1985).

27. Unfortunately, there is no centralized information about the extent of rural production; this is only now being revealed painstakingly by individual researchers. Even available information may undercount rural workers because neither the urban merchant who put out raw materials nor the village worker—both taxpayers—had an interest in the full disclosure of their volume of work. See, for example, Gay Gullickson, *Spinners and Weavers of Auffay: Rural Industry and Sexual Division of Labor in a French Village, 1750–1850* (Cambridge: Cambridge University Press, 1986), 68–70.

28. Ibid., 69; Herbert Kisch, "The Textile Industries in Silesia and the Rhineland: A Comparative Study in Industrialization," in *Industrialization before Industrialization*, ed. P. Kriedtke, H. Medick, and J. Schlumbohm (Cambridge: Cambridge University Press, 1981), 188–90. For a survey of the various types of rural production, see Myron Gutmann, *Toward the Modern Economy: Early Industry in Europe, 1500–1800* (New York: Knopf, 1988).

29. de Vries, *European Urbanization*, 221–40.

30. Lutz Berkner, "Family, Social Structure, and Rural Industry: A Comparative Study of the Waldviertel and the Pays de Caux in the Eighteenth Century" (Ph.D. diss., Harvard University, 1973), 139–40; Kisch, "The Textile Industries in Silesia and the Rhineland," 179–82.

31. David Levine, *Family Formation in an Age of Nascent Capitalism* (New York: Academic Press, 1977), 36–41; Gullickson, *Spinners and Weavers of Auffay*, 134, 146; see also Gutmann, *Toward the Modern Economy*, 140–42.

32. Gullickson, *Spinners and Weavers of Auffay*, 16, 134, 136, 153–54; Gutmann, *Toward the Modern Economy*, 138–42; Steve Hochstadt, "Migration and Industrialization in Germany, 1815–1977," *Social Science History* 5 (1981): 445–68; Levine, *Family Formation in an Age of Nascent Capitalism*, 4–6, 36–41; David Souden, "Movers and Stayers in Family Reconstitution Populations, 1660–1780," *Local Population Studies* 33 (1984): 20–21, 24.

33. In the Flemish villages of Schorisse and Sint-Kornelis-Horebeke, for example, the proportion of very small farms (less than one hectare, or 2.47 acres) increased from 44 and 49 percent to 66 and 58 percent in the 1711–90 period (Lis and Soly, *Poverty and Capitalism in Pre-Industrial Europe*).

34. de Vries, *European Urbanization*, 206–7; Gutmann, *Toward the Modern Economy*, 135; Gullickson, *Spinners and Weavers of Auffay*, 45–46, 65–67; Hohenberg and Lees, *The Making of Urban Europe*, 130–31; Hufton, *The Poor of Eighteenth-Century France*, 16–18.

35. Gutmann, *Toward the Modern Economy,* 136–40.

36. Bardet, *Rouen aux XVIIe et XVIIIe siècles,* 1:209; Michel Mollat, *Histoire de Rouen* (Toulouse: Privat, 1979), 209, 219, 221.

37. This has also had a deleterious effect on the study of migrations, because the sole international study of temporary migration, a Napoleonic inquiry that covered the French empire from present-day Italy north through the Netherlands and east to the Rhineland, was carried out in 1810–11, when seasonal migrations were at a low ebb; see Lucassen, *Migrant Labour in Europe.*

38. André Armengaud, "Population in Europe, 1700–1914," in *The Fontana Economic History of Europe,* vol. 3, *The Industrial Revolution, 1700–1914,* ed. C. Cipolla (New York: Barnes and Noble, 1976), 28–30. Early French fertility decline is primarily responsible for the relatively small population growth in that country; see E. Anthony Wrigley, "The Growth of Population in Eighteenth-Century England: A Conundrum Resolved," *Past and Present,* no. 98 (1983): 121–50.

39. See Eugene Rice, Jr., *The Foundations of Early Modern Europe, 1460–1559* (New York: Norton, 1970), chap. 2; Poussou, *Bordeaux et le sud-ouest au XVIIIe siècle,* pt. 2, chap. 3; Abel Poitrineau, *La vie rurale en Basse-Auvergne au XVIIIe siècle* (Aurillac: Imprimerie Moderne, 1966); Hochstadt, "Socioeconomic Determinants of Increasing Mobility."

40. For an important general argument about the links between the decline of rural industry and emigration, see Walter Kamphoefner, *The Westfalians: From Germany to Missouri* (Princeton: Princeton University Press, 1987), 16–38.

41. Magnus Mörner, *Adventurers and Proletarians: The Story of Migrants in Latin America,* trans. Harold Sims (Paris: United Nations Educational, Scientific, and Cultural Organization, 1985), 47.

42. Armengaud, "Population in Europe, 1700–1914," 70.

43. For an overview of immigration to the United States, see Leonard Dinnerstein, Roger Nichols, and David Reimers, *Natives and Strangers: Ethnic Groups and the Building of America* (New York: Oxford University Press, 1979), 87, 101. Klaus Bade, "German Emigration to the United States and Continental Immigration to Germany," *Central European History* 13 (1980): 365.

44. Eva Morawska, "Labor Migrations of Poles in the Atlantic World Economy, 1880–1914," essay in this volume.

45. See Samuel Baily, "The Adjustment of Italian Immigrants in Buenos Aires and New York, 1870–1914," essay in this volume. Mörner, *Adventurers and Proletarians,* 39–43.

46. Among the numerous and excellent studies of the origins and workings of migrant groups are Donna Gabaccia, *From Sicily to Elizabeth Street: Housing and Social Change among Italian Immigrants, 1880–1930* (Albany: SUNY Press, 1984); Kamphoefner, *The Westfalians.*

47. Sune Åkerman, "Towards an Understanding of Emigrational Processes," in *Human Migration: Patterns and Policies,* ed. William McNeill and Ruth Adams (Bloomington: Indiana University Press, 1978), 296–301.

48. U.S. Congress, Senate, *Reports of the Immigration Commission* (Washington, D.C.: Government Printing Office, 1911), 360–65; reported in Kamphoefner, *The Westfalians,* 188.

49. Leslie Page Moch, *Paths to the City: Regional Migration in Nineteenth-Century France* (Beverly Hills: Sage Publications, 1983).

50. J. D. Gould, "European Inter-Continental Emigration: The Role of 'Diffusion' and 'Feedback,' " *Journal of European Economic History* 9 (1980): 272–82.

51. Agnes Bretting, "From the Old World to the New," in *Fame, Fortune, and Sweet Liberty: The Great European Emigration,* ed. D. Hoerder and D. Knauf (Bremen: Ed. Temmon, 1992), 87–95.

52. Emilio Franzina, "The Commerce of Migration: Aspects of Recruitment of Italian

Workers for Argentina and Brazil in the Nineteenth Century (1867–1887)" (Universita degli studi di Verona, 1986, photocopy).

53. Lynn Hollen Lees, *Exiles of Erin: Irish Migrants in Victorian London* (Ithaca: Cornell University Press, 1979), 15, 42.

54. Carl Strikwerda, "France and the Belgian Immigration of the Nineteenth Century," in *The Politics of Immigrant Workers*, ed. C. Guerin-Gonzales and C. Strikwerda (New York: Holmes and Meier, 1991).

55. Gianfausto Rosoli, "Italian Migration to European Countries from Political Unification to World War I," in *Labor Migration in the Atlantic Economies: The European and North American Working Classes during the Period of Industrialization*, ed. D. Hoerder (Westport: Greenwood Press, 1985), 99–104.

56. Klaus Bade, "Labour, Migration, and the State: Germany from the Late Nineteenth Century to the Onset of the Great Depression," 66–67, and Christoph Klessmann, "Long-Distance Migration, Integration and Segregation of an Ethnic Minority in Industrial Germany: The Case of the 'Ruhr Poles,' " in *Population, Labour and Migration in 19th and 20th Century Germany*, ed. Klaus Bade (New York, 1987), 103; Morawska, "Labor Migrations of Poles."

57. Gary Cross, *Immigrant Workers in Industrial France: The Making of a New Laboring Class* (Philadelphia: Temple University Press, 1983), 21–22; Madelyn Holmes, *Forgotten Migrants: Foreign Workers in Switzerland before World War I* (Rutherford: Farleigh Dickinson University Press, 1988), 14; Lucassen, *Migrant Labour in Europe*, 189, 199–200.

58. Armengaud, "Population in Europe, 1700–1914," 32–33; Maurice Garden, "Le bilan démographique des villes: Un système complexe," *Annales de démographie historique* (1982): 267–75.

59. Armengaud, "Population in Europe, 1700–1914," 33–34; Michel Raman, "Mésure de la croissance d'un centre textile: Roubaix de 1789 à 1913," *Revue d'histoire économique et sociale* 51 (1973): 473.

60. Adna Weber, *The Growth of Cities in the Nineteenth Century* (Ithaca: Cornell University Press, 1899, 1965), frontispiece.

61. Rural populations were reduced in proportion to the total, but not in numbers; only in France, where natural increase was exceptionally low, did the growth of cities significantly detract from rural areas in absolute numbers; see Paul E. White, "Migration in Later Nineteenth- and Twentieth-Century France: The Social and Economic Context," in *Migrants in Modern France: Population Mobility in the Later Nineteenth and Twentieth Centuries*, ed. P. E. White and P. E. Ogden (London: Unwin Hyman, 1989), 17–22.

62. Weber, *The Growth of Cities in the Nineteenth Century*, 262–64.

63. For an excellent study, see David Kertzer and Dennis Hogan, "On the Move: Migration in an Italian Community, 1865–1921," *Social Science History* 9 (1985): 1–23; see also Leslie Page Moch, "The Importance of Mundane Movements: Small Towns, Nearby Places, and Individual Itineraries in the History of Migration," in White and Ogden, *Migrants in Modern France*, 97–117.

64. Weber, *The Growth of Cities in the Nineteenth Century*, 239–40.

65. de Vries, *European Urbanization, 1500–1800*, 233–34.

66. Among the most thorough studies underlying this common assertion is Hochstadt, "Migration and Industrialization in Germany," 445–68; idem, "Urban Mobility in Germany, 1850–1914" (Bates College, 1987). For nineteenth-century migration rates, see also James Jackson, Jr., "Migration in Duisburg, 1867–1890: Occupational and Familial Contexts," *Journal of Urban History* 8 (1982): 235–70.

67. Mörner and Sims, *Adventurers and Proletarians*, 43, chap. 4.

68. Raphael Samuel, "Comers and Goers," in *The Victorian City: Images and Realities*, ed. H. J. Dyos and M. Wolff (London: Routledge and Kegan Paul, 1973), 1:124.

69. Donna Gabaccia, "Women of the Mass Migrations: From Minority to Majority,

1820–1930," essay in this volume. See also J. D. Gould, "European Inter-Continental Emigration—The Road Home: Return Migration from the U.S.A.," *Journal of European Economic History* 9 (1980): 50–63; Gould draws on Massimo Livi-Bacci, *L'Immigrazione e l'Assimilazione degli Italiani negli Stati Uniti secondo le Statistiche Demografiche Americane* (Milano: Guiffrè, 1961), 41. See also Lars-Göran Tedebrand, "Remigration from America to Sweden," in Hoerder, *Labor Migration in the Atlantic Economies*, 374.

70. Klaus Bade, "Labour, Migration, and the State," 66–77.

71. Holmes, *Forgotten Migrants*, 30, 93, 118; J. A. Perkins, "The Agricultural Revolution in Germany, 1850–1914," *Journal of European Economic History* 10 (1981): 106–8; Rosoli, "Italian Migration to European Countries," 106.

72. See, for example, Samuel, "Comers and Goers," 135–37; Nancy Green, " 'Filling the Void': Immigration to France before World War I," in Hoerder, *Labor Migration in the Atlantic Economies*, 149–56; Gould, "European Inter-Continental Emigration: The Role of 'Diffusion' and 'Feedback,' " 312–13; Hans Norman and Harald Runblom, "Migration Patterns in the Nordic Countries," in Hoerder, *Labor Migration in the Atlantic Economies*, 41.

73. For example, see Michael Hanagan, "Agriculture and Industry in the Nineteenth-Century Stéphanois: Household Employment Patterns and the Rise of a Permanent Proletariat," in *Proletarians and Protest: The Roots of Class Formation in an Industrializing World* (Westport: Greenwood Press, 1986), 77–106; Hochstadt, "Migration and Industrialization"; Jackson, "Migration in Duisburg."

74. Hanagan, "Agriculture and Industry"; Walter Kamphoefner, "The Social Consequences of Rural-Urban Migration in Imperial Germany: The 'Floating Proletariat' Thesis Reconsidered," Social Science Working Paper 414 (California Institute of Technology, 1982); Moch, "The Importance of Mundane Movements," 97–117; Heilwig Schomerus, "The Family Life-Cycle: A Study of Factory Workers in Nineteenth-Century Württemberg," in *The German Family: Essays on the Social History of the Family in Nineteenth- and Twentieth-Century Germany*, ed. R. J. Evans and W. R. Lee (London: Croom Helm, 1981), 178–83; Weber, *The Growth of Cities in the Nineteenth Century*, 267–68.

75. Jackson, "Migration in Duisburg," 248.

76. James Jackson, Jr., "Migration and Urbanization in the Ruhr Valley, 1850–1900" (Ph.D. diss., University of Minnesota, 1980), 169; see also Kamphoefner, "The Social Consequences of Rural-Urban Migration," 7.

77. Hohenberg and Lees, *The Making of Urban Europe*, 257.

78. Dudley Baines, *Migration in a Mature Economy: Emigration and Internal Migration in England and Wales, 1861–1900* (New York, 1985), 175–77, 279–80.

79. J. D. Gould, "European Inter-Continental Emigration, 1815–1914: Patterns and Causes," *Journal of European Economic History* 8 (Winter 1979): 658.

80. See, for example, the life stories of Jeanne Bouvier, *Mes mémoires: Ou 59 années d'activité industrielle, sociale et intellectuelle d'une ouvrière, 1876–1935* (Paris: Maspéro, 1985), and Juliette Sauget, "Un exemple de migration rurale: De la Somme dans la capitale: Domestique de la Belle Epoque à Paris," *Etudes de la région parisienne* 44 (1970): 1–9; Fuchs and Moch, "Pregnant, Single, and Far from Home."

81. Fuchs and Moch, "Pregnant, Single, and Far from Home," 1024–25; Françoise Raison-Jourde, *La colonie auvergnate de Paris au XIXe siècle* (Paris: Ville de Paris: 1976).

82. See, for example, Gabaccia, *From Sicily to Elizabeth Street*; John Bukowczyk, *And My Children Did Not Know Me: A History of the Polish Americans* (Bloomington: Indiana University Press, 1987).

83. Morawska, "Labor Migrations of Poles."

84. Maurizio Gribaudi, *Itinéraires ouvriers: Espaces et groupes sociaux à Turin au début du XXe siècle* (Paris: Ecole des Hautes Etudes en Sciences Sociales, 1987).

85. Reported in Norman and Runblom, "Migration Patterns in the Nordic Countries,"

50–51; Gabaccia, "Women of the Mass Migrations"; Ingrid Semmingsen, *Veien mot Vest: Utvandringen fra Norge til Amerika, 1865–1915* (Oslo, 1941), 80; idem, *Veien mot Vest* (Oslo, 1950), 2:233 ff., cited in Sten Carlsson, "Chronology and Composition of Swedish Emigration to America," in *From Sweden to America: A History of the Migration*, ed. Harald Runblom and Hans Norman (Minneapolis: University of Minnesota Press, 1976), 138.

86. Kamphoefner, "The Social Consequences of Rural-Urban Migration"; Moch, "The Importance of Mundane Movements."

87. Hochstadt, "Migration and Industrialization in Germany, 1815–1977," 455.

88. Gould, "European Inter-Continental Migration, 1815–1914: The Role of 'Diffusion' and 'Feedback,' " 267–304.

The Socioeconomic Determinants of Increasing Mobility in Nineteenth-Century Germany

STEVE HOCHSTADT

The increase in mobility of the German population during the nineteenth century has been recognized for over one hundred years. Both demographers and social critics at the end of the nineteenth century were fascinated by the high levels of geographic mobility and the resulting redistribution of population, especially toward the cities. Recent interest in demographic history and quantitative techniques has revived the discussion of historical changes in German mobility rates. As in most migration research, this discussion has taken place mainly within the confines of modernization theory, which locates increasing mobility at the center of the broader transformation of society and economy.

Two key empirical findings about Germany cast doubt on the modernization consensus on the nature and causes of changing mobility. As has been found for other European nations, much, probably most, of the migration during the nineteenth and early twentieth centuries was temporary.[1] The second finding is an extension of the first: the unprecedented bulge in migration rates was itself a temporary phenomenon, ending with a sharp fall in mobility after World War I and a continued decline since then.[2] Thus, the unusually high rates of geographic mobility in Germany during the period of rapid industrialization were not the result of fundamental shifts in behavior toward "modern" mobile society. High rates of temporary mobility were a specific reaction to the particular circumstances of early and rapid industrialization in Germany; when those circumstances disappeared, so did high levels of migration.

The economic descriptions of nineteenth-century industrialization which are currently accepted do not explain why so much temporary migration would occur. The explosive growth of cities, the replacement of rural cottage industry with urban factories, and the general rationalization of production in agriculture and industry would all appear to favor permanent rural-to-urban migration. Perhaps the logic of this connection has led to the stress on this form of migration, when the empirical evidence on forms of movement points toward the importance of temporary migration. In fact, the broad evolution of the German economy during the nineteenth century was certainly responsible for changes in migration patterns. In the conjuncture of rapid population increase, agricultural revolution, and industrialization over more than a century, the structure of German migration was transformed. The causal patterns driving this transformation are logical, but they are not the logic of modernization. This essay will describe those socioeconomic trends which caused the unique growth in temporary mobility during the nineteenth century. Stress will be placed on those changes which reduced the ability of substantial segments of the population to earn their living where they lived, thus increasing their need to migrate to seek work. None of these trends represents a new discovery. It is their relation to migration patterns which has not previously been treated in detail.

Population Growth and Social Structure before 1800

The nineteenth-century changes had their roots in social and economic processes that began long before 1800. These roots must be laid bare before those changes can be described. Population growth was at the foundation of the sweeping transformation of German life in the past several centuries. Certainly population growth has been a constant factor in German history since the Middle Ages, with the important exception of those periodic disasters caused by plague and war. The migratory response to population pressure is just as ancient. The weight of increasing numbers on subsistence agriculture in Westphalia between the twelfth and fourteenth centuries caused streams of "pioneers" to move hundreds of miles eastward toward sparsely settled Saxony and the Baltic coast.[3] After the fourteenth century, the rural population increased faster than the number of families who could support themselves on their own land.[4] The overproportional growth of an agricultural underclass, an incipient rural proletariat, was thus already a problem in the late Middle Ages.

The Thirty Years' War was a catastrophe for the German people, but it temporarily reduced the pressure of numbers on the land. Not until about 1750 was the prewar population level reached again.[5] But after this point, the accelerated tempo of population growth could not be held within the bounds of traditional subsistence agriculture and locally self-sufficient secondary production.

During the late eighteenth century, population growth continued at a rapid rate: annual growth between 1750 and 1800 ranged from 0.7 to 0.9 percent for regions in western, central, and eastern Germany.[6] The population explosion in agricultural areas created unprecedented pressure on land and employment. The underclasses in peasant society, land-poor and landless peasants, servants, and hired laborers, already a majority in many areas, expanded precipitously, while the number of self-sufficient landholdings remained relatively constant. From Lippe and Kreis Tecklenburg in the northwest to the Mark Brandenburg in Prussia to northern Bavaria, population counts show the expansion of the agricultural poor in the eighteenth and early nineteenth centuries.[7] A series of censuses in the area around Magdeburg (called the *Börde*) delineate this process clearly: between 1756 and 1805, farmers with sufficient land to support a family (*Bauern* and *Kossaten*) decreased 9 percent, and those with insufficient holdings increased 81 percent, while servants grew by 64 percent and landless *Einlieger* by 167 percent.[8]

Population growth was universal in Germany, but the specific social consequences depended upon locally differentiated inheritance customs, political systems, and peasant community reactions. Where self-sufficient peasants protected their holdings through undivided inheritances and control over commons usage, population growth could be funneled into the propertyless class of *Tagelöhner* (day laborers) or *Einlieger*.[9] In some places, though, especially in the northwest, the community used control over land to create new dependent classes of peasants with tiny parcels. In the Delbrücker area near Paderborn, so-called *Zulagererstätten* were created in the eighteenth century with about one hectare of land per family. The owners of these plots were dependent on the better-off peasants for supplementary employment.[10] In southwestern Germany, where inheritances were divided, population growth meant relatively equalized pressure on all peasants, whose poverty had already caused widespread emigration in the seventeenth century. Population growth was less quickly translated into population pressure east of the Elbe, where new land could be brought under cultivation, notably through the colonization policies of Frederick the Great. Yet there, too, population growth meant disproportionate increases of land-poor peasants. Many of the colonists were placed on plots small enough to insure available labor to their wealthier neighbors: in Mecklenburg-Schwerin, the settlers after 1750, called *Büdner*, were given about two hectares.[11] *Tagelöhner* and *Einlieger* began the eighteenth century as a small proportion of the population in Pomerania, but easily surpassed the self-sufficient *Bauern* by 1800. Landless laborers also grew strongly.[12] In the most general terms, rural population growth meant the increase of those who did not control enough property to provide for their own subsistence.[13]

As the possibilities of agricultural income declined, a major new source of employment was developing, through the expansion of rural industrial production, the process now commonly termed protoindustrialization. Population growth and especially the existence of surplus labor in rural communities were in fact the prerequisites for the recruitment of the rural poor for industrial labor in their own homes.[14] Traditional skills based on local self-sufficiency were reorganized into a dispersed manufacturing system, which created a flexible source of income for the underemployed. In Osnabrück, for example, linen weaving served as a seasonal supplement for a farming population, while in Bielefeld, linen production was a year-round occupation for landless rural families.[15] Cottage industrial labor had many advantages: it could involve the entire family; it could be used to even out the rhythms of the agricultural year; it allowed the foundation of new households without waiting for the previous generation to give up control over landed property.

Protoindustrialization was not simply a result of population pressure and agricultural underemployment; rather these processes were mutually reinforcing mechanisms in the transformation of traditional German agricultural society. Rudolf Braun emphasizes this two-way causality for the highly protoindustrialized areas of Switzerland: not only was cottage industry encouraged by the existence of tiny agricultural holdings, its expansion brought partible inheritance into new areas, whose growing population could then only be supported by industrial labor.[16] The contribution of protoindustrialization to social and demographic change and its functional equivalence to migration as a response to population pressure are demonstrated by the growth of the class of *Heuerleute*, semidependent peasant-proletarians, in northwestern Germany in the eighteenth century.[17]

The origins of the *Heuerleute* lie both in the growth of population beyond the ability of available arable and common land to support more families and in the increased need of the self-supporting peasants for cash to pay taxes and dues in a developing market economy. Peasants began to allow noninheriting sons and other landless families to settle on tiny parcels of their land in exchange for occasional labor. At the same time, the bigger peasants became middlemen for urban manufacturers seeking rural producers; by providing industrial work for the *Heuerleute*, the peasants could gather the cash they needed while supplementing the inadequate agricultural income from the tiny plots of their new dependents. They also assured themselves of available labor at planting and harvest. In Minden-Ravensberg and the regions around Osnabrück and Münster, this class provided the foundation for protoindustrial linen production. Flax cultivation expanded with the increase in *Heuerleute*. But the calculations of the peasants also depended on the existence of another source of income for their new tenants: migratory labor. With the growth of *Heuerleute* came an expansion of the migration to Holland in the summer for hay harvests or herring fishing. By the end of the eighteenth century, these people made up the majority of the population in parts of the northwest.

The *Heuerleute* represented an adaptation of the traditional rural economy to population growth and economic change. They personified the integration of expanded industrial production into peasant agriculture, the essential feature of protoindustrialization. Textile production and migratory labor were supplements to local farm work, on their own or their landlords' land. Although *Heuerleute* lived on the social outskirts of the community, their existence also depended on the use of the commons for their animals, and on the three-field system to provide a relatively even distribution of labor during the year.

Protoindustrialization was one of the mechanisms which allowed rural German society to absorb population growth in the eighteenth century without reaching a crisis. In the northwest, the Rhineland, Silesia, and the area around Berlin, it provided the income supplements needed by the new and growing classes of rural poor who were becoming less and less like peasants. In other regions, the adaptations also remained within traditional confines. East of the Elbe, the paternalism of feudal relationships could still provide for a larger population, especially as new land was brought under cultivation. Only in the unindustrialized and densely populated southwest did population growth reach a critical stage.

When population density outstrips the capacity of the local economy to provide work and income, migration is the universal demographic response. In some regions, increased mobility was an important mechanism in maintaining the traditional agricultural system under this pressure. In the parcelized southwest, poor peasants exploited the traditional German escape valve of eastward migration, but added new destinations as well. Attracted by Frederick II's colonization policies, thousands migrated to eastern Prussia and the Kurmark.[18] While the southwest provided the majority of eighteenth-century emigrants, other areas added to the flow. Perhaps 350,000 Germans emigrated to Hapsburg lands in the Balkans, and 40,000 traveled more than fifteen hundred miles to the Black Sea and Volga regions of Russia. Over 100,000 Germans, mostly from the southwest, landed in America in the eighteenth century. But permanent emigration over large distances could not fully release the demographic pressure. While half a million left Germany in the eighteenth century, the population increased from about sixteen million in 1740 to twenty-three million in 1800.[19] For those who struggled with insufficient land and employment at home, temporary migration was also a traditional answer. The *Hollandsgehen*, a seasonal oscillation between summer work in Holland and grain production in northwestern Germany, reached its peak in the eighteenth century, including over half of the adult males in some districts.[20]

On the national level, eighteenth-century demographic and economic change provided opposing and possibly balancing pressures on mobility. While population growth without new employment might have led to increased migration, protoindustrialization served to anchor a potentially migratory population.[21] Although the evidence is scattered, available migration statistics for the eighteenth century fit comfortably within older patterns.[22] The anchoring effects of rural industry can be seen in the migration statistics for the Regierungsbezirk Düsseldorf as late as 1821. Annual migration rates were about 50 percent lower in cottage industrial communities than in either agricultural villages or cities.[23] In the eighteenth century, increased mobility remained a secondary means of creating the income supplements required by growing numbers of rural poor. But rural society had limited elasticity, and these limits were reached soon after 1800. Population growth spiraled upwards, multiplying the numbers of the land-poor. Worse, the protoindustrial balloon expanded and then burst in the nineteenth century, removing this crucial source of local income for the rural poor. German agricultural organization was at the same time transformed from self-sufficiency to a market orientation. Mobility then became the primary response to the nineteenth-century crisis of employment for the rural underclasses.

Population Growth and the Transformation of Agriculture in the Nineteenth Century

The growth of the German population continued in the nineteenth century, affecting all regions of Germany. The yearly growth rate averaged just under 1 percent until 1871, then grew to nearly 1.5 percent between 1895 and 1914.[24] Although most demographers stress urbanization as the major characteristic of the nineteenth century, the rural population kept pace with urban growth well into the nineteenth century. The *proportion* of the population that was rural did not decline at all until after 1850. In the first half of the century the *number* of rural Germans increased by about 50 percent, and there was no significant decline until after World War I.[25] Thus, only in the twentieth century did the pressure on the land diminish.

For most of the nineteenth century, the majority of Germans were dependent on agriculture for their livelihood. Population growth at the bottom of the rural social pyramid thus tended to imbalance the social-economic system, which distributed employment to different social classes. Where inheritances were divided, the majority of peasants already had insufficient land. Those regions that became known early in the nineteenth century as sources of migratory laborers tended to be geographically isolated with highly parcelized poor soil. The Eichsfeld was an island of *Realteilung* in Saxony. Lippe in Westphalia and the Westerwald in Hessen were also covered with dwarf holdings, as was the entire southwest and Oppeln in Silesia.[26] Statistics for the village of Halsdorf in Oberhessen demonstrate how an eighteenth-century problem became a nineteenth-century crisis. In 1785, 27 percent of all farms were under one hectare, and another 23 percent were one to five hectares. By 1894, 58 percent were less than one hectare, with 19 percent one to five hectares. At the same time, the proportion of the population that was landless grew from one-fifth to one-half. Put another way, in Halsdorf during the nineteenth century, the proportion of families who could support themselves on their property fell from about half to one-sixth.[27]

The peasants in fertile areas with undivided inheritances were also mainly smallholders. Already by 1840 in the Magdeburger Börde, 55 percent of landowners were *Häusler* with only garden plots, and a further 29 percent *Kossaten*, barely able to support themselves.[28] Multiplication of small farms continued to weaken the self-sufficiency of German peasants until 1914. By 1882 only 11 percent of landowners in the Börde had over five hectares.[29] In the period of most rapid population growth, between the agricultural censuses of 1882 and 1907, the total number of agricultural holdings in Germany grew by 9 percent, while the number of peasants who considered themselves self-supporting (*selbständig*) fell 4 percent.[30] By the beginning of the twentieth century, peasants with plots under two hectares were the majority among landholders. This division is crucial for determining whether a family needed to look outside their own farm for income supplements. For the nineteenth century, five hectares were generally considered as the normal minimum to support a family, although regional variations in soil character and crops were a significant influence.[31]

The 1907 census provides evidence that every region of Germany had a majority of smallholders; the frequently cited division of Germany by inheritance patterns or by the dominance of large farms had only a secondary effect on the proportion of the rural landholding population with insufficient property. Certainly the regions of *Realteilung* had among the highest proportions of tiny holdings under two hectares: Lippe 79 percent, Hessen 61 percent, Baden 55 percent. But even in the provinces where most of the land was held by *Großgrundbesitzer*, such as East Prussia and Pomerania, two-thirds of the landowners held under five hectares. In the two Mecklenburgs, where estates over one hundred hectares comprised 58 percent of the land (the German average was 22 percent), 75 percent of peasant owners worked less than two hectares. An unusual structure was to be found only in Bavaria east of the Rhine, a region dominated by middle-sized farms. Bavaria had exceptionally low proportions of farms under two and over one hundred hectares. Only 29 percent of Bavarian landholdings were smaller than two hectares, with 26 percent between two and five. Furthermore, Bavarian peasants owned the highest percentage of the land they used, over 95 percent.[32] If we roughly estimate that all of those with under two hectares and half with two to five hectares were not self-sufficient, then 42 percent of all Bavarian landowning peasants needed income supplements, but it was 68 percent of all other German landowners in 1907.[33]

The most explosive growth was experienced by the landless rural population. While the total number of *Tagelöhner* in German agriculture changed insignificantly between the 1882 and 1907 censuses, the proportion without land rose from 27 to 46 percent of this occupational category.[34]

Thus population growth in the nineteenth century further tipped the balance of the rural population toward those classes of people dependent upon earnings outside their own property for subsistence. In the nineteenth century, rapid population increase was, however, only one component of a more fundamental transformation of the social and technical basis of agriculture. This restructuring involved changes in the relationship of people to land, in relations among the rural classes, and finally in the kind and timing of work done. Liberal agrarian reforms accelerated this process through support of the propertied classes. One of the most significant general results was a vast increase in the number of rural Germans who needed to supplement their agricultural income.

The most notable set of government reforms in agriculture was the Prussian legislation, in the early nineteenth century, freeing the peasants east of the Elbe from feudal dependence upon landowners. Similar reforms had occurred earlier in western and southern Germany and came somewhat later in Mecklenburg. Despite the original motivation of creating a numerous and loyal self-supporting peasantry, the Prussian monarchy stopped short of depriving large landowners of their dependent labor force without compensation. Peasants had to give up one-third to one-half of the land they worked or pay compensation in exchange for their freedom. The East Elbian peasants lost about one million hectares, perhaps 8 percent of the total arable land, to landlords.[35] Many who could no longer subsist on reduced plots or could not pay their debts in the years of low agricultural prices that followed the reforms had to sell their properties. Especially hard hit were small owners who could not harness their own team (*nicht spannfähig*). It is estimated that in eastern Prussia over one hundred thousand peasants (about 15 percent of total landowners) lost their property.[36] The social results can be seen in the further growth of the class of landless laborers: in the province of Posen, for example, the proportion of all heads of household who were without land jumped from 71 percent in 1810 to 79 percent in 1861.[37]

A further blow to small peasant landholders, in both East and West Prussia, was the more gradual division and enclosure of common land, encouraged by the governments of various German states in the interest of more productive farming. This process began in the eighteenth century, accelerated through 1850, and was essentially completed by 1900. The area of collectively owned land is hard to estimate, but certainly sizable: in Westphalia and parts of East Prussia, it comprised about 50 percent of total agricultural land. Perhaps 20 to 40 percent of agricultural land in Germany was collectively used before the reforms.[38] Those with weak legal rights to the commons, who had nevertheless been allowed to use this land, such as the *Heuerleute* in the northwest, received nothing. Throughout Germany, the division of common land resulted in a significant reduction in the ability of the rural underclasses to keep animals, get wood for fuel and building, and fertilize their fields.[39] In the villages, the poor said, "Through the division of the commons, the *Bauern* have become noblemen and we have become beggars."[40]

The liberal reforms did serve to free many German peasants from the legal inequalities that had ensured their hereditary dependence, but in their tendency to support the interests of the larger landowners in all regions of Germany, the reforms also increased the gap between agrarian classes. Combined with population growth, governmental reforms resulted in an overproportional increase in the numbers of land-poor and landless. The number of peasants who were thus thrown onto the rural labor market was greatly increasing at the same time that local opportunities for paid labor were changing drastically, both inside and outside agriculture. One of the most significant new conditions that this agricultural labor force had to face was the increasing seasonality of the labor market. As an effect of evolving agricultural techniques and a cause of further social disruption, the seasonalization of the rural labor market played a major role in shaping migration patterns in the nineteenth century.

Agriculture is inherently a seasonal labor process determined by soil, crops, and climate. But seasonal fluctuations in labor input are also significantly affected by the social and technological organization of farming. Traditional three-field farming was organized to spread work throughout the year as evenly as possible in order to minimize the seasonal unemployment that plagued peasant producers on the edge of subsistence. The work of planting, tending, and harvesting in the warm half of the year was at least partially balanced by the tedious process of hand threshing, which extended through the winter. According to tabulations made at the end of the nineteenth century, a three-field system required about 40 percent more labor in the six months from spring planting to fall harvest than in the colder half of the year. This extra labor was nearly all concentrated in July and August, while the work in the other ten months was evenly distributed.[41]

The nineteenth century brought several forces of change into agrarian production. The most fundamental was the changeover from extensive to intensive cultivation through new crop rotations designed to feed the growing population. After sustaining German agriculture for nearly a millennium, the three-field system was rapidly replaced by the planting of forage crops, such as clover, on the formerly fallow field (improved three-field system), and then by new rotations involving root crops. The popular Norfolk rotation alternated winter and summer grains with clover, legumes, and potatoes. The most intensive rotation, the so-called *Rübenwirtschaft*, included sugar beets on one-third of the acreage.[42] These rotations greatly improved the productivity of the land. The acreage in root crops grew from about 1 percent of planted land in 1800 to about 20 percent in 1914, with the fastest growth late in the nineteenth century.[43] The potato and the sugar beet radically changed the intensity and distribution of work during the year. These *Hackfrüchte* needed frequent hoeing before finally being dug up. On a given plot, potatoes required three times as much labor as grain, while sugar beets further doubled the work. Each step up the ladder of intensification increased the total labor input per acre, but also further imbalanced the seasons, since virtually all of the new work had to be done in the warm months. While the relation of summer to winter work in the three-field system was 1.4:1, it changed to 1.9:1 when potatoes were introduced, and reached 2.6:1 for the *Rübenwirtschaft*. In the more intensive rotations, every month from April through September required extra labor over the needs of the winter months; the late summer peak could require nearly four times the labor input of the quietest winter month.[44] Continued technical progress in plant selection and farming methods after 1850 further concentrated the workload by shortening the sugar beet season from about 150 days in 1850 to 110 in the 1870s and down to 70 after 1900.[45]

While the new work was added in the summer, the onset of mechanization began to replace the major winter work of hand threshing. In traditional grain agriculture, hand threshing represented over 80 percent of the total work between October and March. Machines could clean the harvest up to three times as fast. Furthermore, it was common on the most intensive large farms at the end of the century to use these machines at the end of summer.[46] The amount of winter work might thus be reduced to under 15 percent of summer work. While machines for planting and harvesting were well known, these processes were only minimally mechanized before 1914. The thresher was the most common labor-saving machine through the early twentieth century, by which time nearly all farms of over five hectares could eliminate hand threshing.[47]

This combination of forces destroyed the seasonal balance of agricultural labor and thereby encouraged significant changes in the labor market. During the nineteenth century, the rural labor market became seasonalized to an unprecedented extent as a result of the intensification of agricultural production. Seasonal specialists were used on large farms for each separate job: one large farm in West Prussia employed distinct groups of temporary workers for general summer work between April and October, for the hay harvest in July and August, and for the October potato harvest.[48] Regional differences in the timing of technical progress and the distribution of crops remained important. Sugar beets first became a major crop in the Prussian province of Saxony in the 1830s, and this district produced half of the beets in Germany until the 1870s; then Silesia, Braunschweig, Hannover, and the Rhineland began to specialize also.[49] In such areas agriculture was dominated by the need for summer labor in the beet fields. East of the Elbe, intensification of production altered the labor market only after the 1880s. There, too, seasonalization resulted from the encouragement of sugar beets through national tax policies and the mechanization of large estates.[50]

This seasonalization of the agricultural labor market could not have occurred within the social system that dominated rural Germany before 1800, in which the labor force consisted mainly of dependent workers with long-term obligations. In the East, unfree feudal subjects inherited their dependence on the *Gutsherr*; their geographical mobility was legally limited. West of the Elbe, single servants (*Gesinde*) and married day laborers typically contracted for at least one year, from harvest to harvest.[51] Thus, employers reciprocated for the labor of their dependents by providing an income throughout the year. While population growth and the growth of the market economy by the eighteenth century were already tending to replace this "moral economy" with a freer, more money-oriented system, the agricultural reforms destroyed the legal basis of mutual obligations. The growing supply of underemployed landless and land-poor peasants helped to accelerate the introduction of more intensive methods based on temporary hired labor. These processes, in turn, further encouraged agricultural employers to replace their year-round labor force in peak seasons with short-term workers, who did not require support in slower times. This social evolution in the composition of the agricultural labor force can most clearly be seen in the simultaneous decline in servants and increase in day laborers. This process moved slowly in the years following the Prussian reforms and then accelerated after 1860.[52] In the Regierungsbezirk Magdeburg, heart of Saxon sugar beet production, the number of servants in agriculture fell 70 percent between 1882 and 1907.[53] This rapid decline took place in all German regions, although not in such exaggerated form: between the two occupational censuses in 1895 and 1907, the total servants in agriculture fell 29 percent.[54]

The transition to hired temporary labor meant the decline of those social groups that were created as permanent agricultural satellites of larger holdings. The socioeconomic evolution in northeastern Prussia provides the clearest example of this progressive replacement of social strata. The *Insten* (cottagers, elsewhere called *Drescher* or *Dreschgärtner*) were a basic part of the social structure of early nineteenth-century East Elbian agriculture; they received houses on small plots and payment in goods in exchange for services rendered to large landowners. In the wake of the reforms, cottagers were replaced by laborers paid in kind. As intensification and rationalization spread toward the end of the century, mostly in the form of increased sugar beet production, monetary rewards for temporary labor replaced payment in land or goods, and agricultural labor was provided by *Tagelöhner*.[55] A similar process occurred throughout Germany: in the northwest, for example, *Heuerleute* came to be replaced by hired laborers, while Silesian *Dreschgärtner* received money payments for labor instead of land after 1845.[56] The final step was to rely entirely on imported migratory labor at seasonal peaks, eliminating the need to provide any support in the off-seasons.

The 1907 agricultural census of June 12 provides a detailed picture of the agricultural labor force at the end of a century of change.[57] Farm workers consisted mostly of owners and their families, who made up 70 percent of all workers. Of the 5.7 million separate farms, the majority, 59 percent, were under two hectares, and were considered mainly to be secondary sources of income for their owners. One-fifth of these small holdings were not even being worked on census day, because their owners were otherwise occupied, while two-fifths were being tended by a single female, typically the wife of the absent owner. On only 25 percent of these farms was the owner actually in residence working the holding. Another 18 percent of all farms were between two and five hectares; these farms usually represented the main source of income for their owners, but here, too, 25 percent of the owners were working elsewhere. The self-sufficient holdings over five hectares included only 24 percent of all farms. Nearly half of all nonfamily labor was provided by temporary workers, among whom seasonal migrants were probably a majority. Another 20 percent of workers were hired labor (*Tagelöhner, Arbeiter, Instleute*). Servants had been reduced to one-third of the nonfamily labor force by 1907, and were concentrated on middle-sized farms of between five and fifty hectares. The June census counted 15.2 million people employed on farms in 1907, but this number did not cover the entire German agricultural labor force, because June was not a month of peak employment. The census also asked for the highest number employed over the previous twelve months and found that another several million people had done farm labor.[58] When these figures are considered in the light of the question of permanence, it becomes clear that socioeconomic changes in agriculture had resulted in a farm labor force dominated by part-time labor. Under half of all owners were self-sufficient farmers, while the majority of all nonfamily laborers who had done agricultural work during the twelve months preceding the census were temporary. Much of the German peasantry had been transformed into a mobile agricultural proletariat, although exactly how many of these were fully migrant laborers remains unknown.[59]

The processes sketched here could be amalgamated as the transition from a paternalist toward a capitalist agriculture, based on intensive methods and hired labor. Max Weber, in his first book in 1892, summarized the recent history of agricultural labor in eastern Germany as the general replacement of workers who participated in the fortunes of a particular estate by hired workers whose economic interests clashed with those of the landowners.[60] The same forces brought agricultural migrant labor into western Germany, as the considerable literature on turn-of-the-century rural labor shows.[61] The proportion of Germany's agricultural labor force which had to seek work outside agriculture each year rose in tandem with the sugar beet harvest and the use of threshing machines. The connection between the new capitalistic orientation and temporary labor could be brutally direct: in Mecklenburg, where laborers could establish a right to welfare payments after two years of residence, many estate owners kept firing their workers, forcing them to migrate, in order to keep the local tax burden down.[62] But the transformation of traditional German agriculture generally worked less directly to reduce the ability of the rural population to earn a living year-round in local farming, on their own or their neighbors' land. Throughout Germany, increasing numbers of peasants with insufficient plots and laborers with seasonal underemployment sought nonagricultural income. At this moment of greatest need, the familiar recourse of needy peasants—cottage industry—utterly failed. Farming was only altered, but rural industry practically disappeared. In this conjunction lay both the tragedy of rural pauperization in nineteenth-century Germany and the impetus toward unprecedented mobility.

Rural Deindustrialization

Friedrich Henning estimated that in the early nineteenth century about two-thirds of the rural population required a supplementary income.[63] The demographic, political, and economic processes sketched above combined to increase this rural need for *Nebenerwerb*. This enormous pressure intensified the dependence of the rural population on cottage and local industry, pushing protoindustrialization to its economic limits just when the mechanized urban competitor was appearing on the horizon. Even among signs of the upcoming crisis, cottage industry expanded still further after the return of peace in 1815. The waves of emigrants from the southwest, the increasingly public discussion of *Pauperismus*, and the revolutionary outbreaks of the 1840s clearly demonstrated that this form of rural industrialization alone could not solve the problem of rural underemployment. The dissolution of cottage industry after 1850 removed the last alternative to geographic mobility for rural Germans.

By the beginning of the nineteenth century, cottage industry had spread across Germany as a necessary supplement to agriculture for the rural population. Certain regions were so thickly settled with textile producers that they appeared as industrial islands in an agricultural sea: the lower Rhine, upper Silesia, and the area surrounding Berlin are major examples. But industrial employment was crucial in all parts of Germany: about one million people were employed in various forms of *Verlagswesen* (putting out),[64] representing perhaps 7 percent of the adult population. When all types of industrial employment are considered, this proportion grows significantly: over 20 percent of the rural population of southern Bavaria, for example, was nourished by secondary production in the early nineteenth century.[65]

The concept of protoindustrialization does not fully cover the crucial role that secondary production played in the rural economy. In certain regions the gradual historical development of industry on the land had created dense networks of full-time producers for the market. Yet perhaps more important for the German rural population as a whole was the existence of industrial and commercial secondary occupations, which could be blended with agriculture to provide a subsistence income. Even in the most agricultural regions of Germany, a wide variety of nonagricultural pursuits supported the growing population. In the Kurfürstentum of Hannover around 1800, the rural population supplemented farming income with mining, glassmaking, brickmaking, pottery, freight handling, and peat cutting for fuel. The great majority of forges and ironworks were in rural communities.[66] Flax and linen provided the most important secondary occupations throughout rural Germany. Poor peasants rented land for flax, paying in work at harvest time. Over half of the linen looms used as secondary employment in early nineteenth-century Prussia were located in the most agricultural provinces of East and West Prussia, Posen, and Pomerania, where official statisticians counted one loom for every fifteen to twenty adults in 1816.[67] As long as transportation was slow, power was derived from natural sources, and local trading dominated commerce, rural industrial production was an integral element of the agricultural landscape.

For the next several decades rural industry continued to expand, perhaps somewhat faster than the rural population itself.[68] The number of looms used in part-time linen weaving in Prussia nearly doubled between 1816 and 1858.[69] Home cotton weaving in Württemberg expanded strongly in the 1850s.[70] Other forms of local manufacture were encouraged by a growing demand. Rural nailmaking, typically located in hilly wooded areas with weak agriculture such as the Taunus and Harz regions, expanded production and employment into the 1860s.[71] But this general growth was spread unevenly, as signs of the weaknesses of rural industry mounted toward mid-century. While competition from overseas increased, especially from English textiles and from newly mechanized urban factories, population pressures were translated into falling wages in cottage industry. Linen production was the first to suffer.[72] Although part-time weaving for personal and local consumption grew, market-oriented full-time weaving in Silesia, Saxony, and the western provinces of Prussia suffered during the Napoleonic wars and declined thereafter. The same population growth that pushed the rural lower classes into greater dependence on flax and linen encouraged large landholders to intensify grain production through rising food prices. Land previously rented for flax to *Heuerleute* or *Häuslinge* in Lower Saxony was increasingly used for grain after the 1830s. By then, part-time weaving was beginning to disappear in Silesia. In the 1840s the crisis expanded in the cottage industrial regions of the northwest: Minden-Ravensberg, Osnabrück, the Münsterland. In Lippe the number of linen looms fell by half between 1836 and 1861.[73]

By 1850, rural industry had probably reached its peak, still expanding in some areas, already contracting in others. Mechanization had only begun to compete with cottage production. Despite the existence of mechanized spinning factories in the lower Rhineland since the 1780s, cotton and silk spinning were fully mechanized only by the 1840s in the Elberfeld-Barmen section of the Wupper valley, the most highly industrialized area of the Rhine.[74] Henning estimated that the number of people employed in *Verlagswesen* peaked around 1850 at 1.5 million.[75]

The second half of the nineteenth century, especially after the founding of the German empire in 1871, witnessed the collapse and dissolution of the traditional forms of rural industry. In textiles, mechanization meant the removal of work from the rural cottage to the urban factory, first in cotton, then in wool. The number of handlooms in the Kreis Gladbach near Düsseldorf fell by 80 percent between 1855 and 1875, while the power looms increased tenfold; cottage silkmaking there lasted a short while longer.[76] Hand weaving in the Wuppertal was only finally replaced by machines in the 1890s.[77] In some communities, like Rixdorf outside Berlin, cottage weaving could continue to expand late in the century due to the huge local demand. Even there, the crisis finally came in the 1880s.[78] The backbone of German rural industry, linen production, nearly disappeared in the late nineteenth century. Rising food and land prices and competition from cheaper Russian flax reduced the willingness of landowners to rent flax land to poor peasants, while mechanization and changing popular tastes in textiles cut the demand for linen, at home and overseas. In Württemberg and in Oberhessen, linen weavers declined rapidly after 1875 and were gone by 1900, as were the part-time looms throughout eastern Prussia.[79] The acreage in flax reached a high point in 1850 at 250,000 hectares, fell to 215,000 by 1872, and then collapsed to 17,000 by 1913.[80]

Textiles were, of course, the major "protoindustry" and the most important branch of rural industrial production in general, but urban industrialization after 1870 absorbed many varied types of rural work. A crucial factor was the expansion of the railroad network and the consequent reduction of transport costs. Small centers of manufacture could no longer depend on the barrier of high transport costs to protect their less efficient production methods. The scattered metalworking industry became concentrated around the major ore fields in the Ruhr or near Berlin. The railroad then took these better goods throughout Germany, putting traditional metal centers out of business. Mining and ironwork in the Eisenach region, in the Rhön mountains, in the Schwarzwald, in the Spessart in northern Bavaria, and in the Westerwald in Hesse-Nassau and nailmaking in the Taunus, Harz, and Erzgebirge regions all disappeared by the early twentieth century.[81] The railroad's ability to connect large urban factories with the coal fields removed the need for charcoal, thus eliminating a major forest industry.[82] Formerly decentralized glass production followed the drift toward the cities after 1870, switching from charcoal to coal.[83] Rural self-sufficiency in secondary goods was transformed into dependence on the cities through industrialization. In this process the relationship of rural to urban crafts dramatically shifted. While urban *Handwerk* was able to grow by adapting to new techniques, such as in the repair of industrial products or machine construction, traditional rural crafts were concentrated and mechanized. Rural shoemakers, carpet weavers, and soap, hat, and button manufacturers lost their livelihoods.[84] Local millers and beer brewers were pushed out of business.[85]

The transformation of Germany from a primarily agrarian to a primarily industrial nation during the nineteenth century not only represented an increase in total industrial employment, but also a considerable shift in the location of existing jobs. Expansion of production was accomplished by geographical concentration at the national and regional levels. The most obvious effects were felt by those areas where a formerly flourishing protoindustrial base could not make the transition to modern industrial methods, or made this transition only after a long crisis. The attendant social distress reached the public's attention through the weavers' revolt in Silesia or the mid-nineteenth-century emigration waves from Hessen and Württemberg. Other regions which suffered from new competition were the Grafschaft Tecklenburg, the surroundings of Osnabrück, Hessen, the Rhön, the Fichtelgebirge, and the Vogtland in Saxony. Even in regions which successfully made the transition to the factory system, the concentration process absorbed work from the countryside into a few urban centers, such as Bielefeld in eastern Westphalia.[86] Broader than the replacement of protoindustry by modern industry in particular regions was the general deindustrialization of the countryside. Even in predominantly agricultural communities, the scattered possibilities for by-employment in secondary production disappeared. The mechanization of secondary production broke the close geographical links between agricultural and industrial production and led to a "reagrarianization" of the land.[87] This slow process affected mainly the land-poor and landless rural population, whose existence had been predicated either on rural industry alone, as in the developed protoindustrial regions, or on a mixture of agricultural and industrial employment. The end of rural industry, especially after 1850, left migration as the only alternative for the growing rural underclasses.

Industrialization and Temporary Labor

Thus far I have examined how rural agricultural change and urban industrialization destroyed the balance of the rural labor market by contracting employment opportunities or removing them entirely. This process represented one side of the newly developing labor market equation, the process which brought millions of rural Germans out of their local markets in search of work. The other side was the creation of new jobs through industrialization and the expansion of demand for labor, especially after the 1870s. According to the censuses, the number of workers in the secondary sector grew from 6.4 million to 11.3 million between 1882 and 1907.[88] The great majority of these new jobs were in urban industry. Hermann Schäfer estimates that the employment in firms with more than five employees grew in this period from 1.6 to 5.8 million.[89] While the number of workers in secondary industry living in rural communities grew from 2.5 to 2.9 million, the expansion in cities was from 4.0 to 8.4 million. The textile industry was collapsing as a major employer on the land in these decades: the total rural employed fell by 20 percent.[90]

These consequences of nineteenth-century industrialization are well known and tend to overshadow other aspects of this economic process which had decisive effects on the structure of mobility. There is no need here to retrace the history of German industrialization. Rather I wish to examine two aspects of late nineteenth- and early twentieth-century economic change that had a direct impact on the enormous rural labor surplus described above, and which determined the way rural workers reacted to the new geographical distribution of employment. First, industrialization greatly increased the demand for seasonal and temporary labor in both the countryside and the city. Second, certain crucial structural characteristics of new urban industrial employment encouraged impermanence.

The process of German industrial development before World War I was strongly influenced by the growth of infrastructure, especially the railroad, which some see as a leading sector.[91] Virtually the entire current German railroad network was laid in the fifty years before the war: between 1860 and 1913 an average of nearly one thousand miles of track were added yearly. Since World War I, hardly any new track has been added.[92] The length of roads in Germany grew from only 25,000 kilometers in 1835 to 115,000 in 1873 to over 300,000 by 1913.[93] Most striking to contemporaries was the explosion of the urban population and thereby the rapid expansion of old cities and the building of new ones. These feats of construction occupied an increasing proportion of workers: while the percentage of the total labor force employed in the construction industry remained constant at slightly over 2 percent between 1800 and 1850, it climbed to 5.5 percent in the last years before World War I. Railroad building alone consistently employed over 300,000 people for the entire period of the *Kaiserreich*.[94]

More than any other sector, construction was based on seasonal migratory labor. The gangs of unskilled workers on rails and roads were necessarily mobile as their place of work slowly advanced through the countryside.[95] Railroad gangs drew from the rural underclasses of *Heuerleute*, whose incomes from spinning and weaving were disappearing.[96] An 1898 survey of the Zentralverband der Maurer showed that over half of its members lived away from their mainly urban place of work. Because the average worker experienced several months of unemployment due to the weather, the ownership of land provided a crucial supplementary income. The organization of work offered rich opportunities for temporary labor but poor prospects for those seeking year-round permanent income. Seasonal labor peaks varied by specific occupation, since the inside workers (*Zimmerer*) had to wait for the framers (*Maurer*) to finish.[97] Furthermore, the typical practice of employers was to hire workers for specific sites rather than to create a core of permanent employees, leading to short periods of employment and a highly fluctuating labor force.[98]

The urban building boom required vast amounts of materials, notably the ubiquitous brick. Brickmaking had long been a traditional migratory occupation for rural workers. After 1800 a new method of burning the bricks was developed in which layers of brick were alternated with coal on huge outdoor fields. Clay was mined in the fall and allowed to dry over the winter. Beginning about April, the clay was kneaded by trampling it underfoot before firing. The brickmaking season lasted until October, when the demand from construction dropped. The overwhelming majority of brickworkers (*Ziegler*) in the Düsseldorf region, one of the major sources of production, were migrants. Before 1860, Belgians had been a sizable contingent; later they were increasingly replaced by natives. In 1900, ten brick factories in Oberkassel (now part of Düsseldorf) employed 205 people, of whom 177 were migratory workers. Elsewhere in Germany, foreigners remained important: Czechs in Saxony, Poles in the East, Italians in the South.[99] The small area around Lippe sent streams of *Ziegler* throughout Germany, reaching 14,000 by the end of the nineteenth century. Between 1861 and 1907 the total number of brickmakers within the current province of Nordrhein-Westfalen grew from 3,850 to 32,800.[100]

The other materials required for construction, such as stone, cement, gypsum, and calcium, were also provided mainly by seasonal workers. With the *Ziegler*, these workers belonged to the official industrial category of *Steine und Erden*, which after 1900 included about 7 percent of the industrial labor force.[101] Together with construction, the growth of this industrial sector helped to absorb the rural workers who were pushed out of textiles. Between 1882 and 1907, *rural* employment in construction and construction materials grew by about 350,000 workers; the fall in rural cottage industry for this period was probably slightly higher.[102] This transition replaced work at home with labor based on migration, to both the city and the countryside.

Industrialization and population growth encouraged other forms of seasonal industrial labor, mainly in food production. Most important as an employer of migrant labor was the sugar beet industry. Beginning in the 1830s, the growing sugar beet harvest was processed in factories operating through the late fall and winter months, the so-called *Campagne*. Sugar production skyrocketed to over a half-million tons by the 1880s, when Germany produced nearly half of the world's beet sugar. By 1910, total output had multiplied another four times.[103] These factories were concentrated in the Prussian provinces of Saxony, Silesia, and in Braunschweig-Anhalt, and employed about one hundred thousand workers around 1900.[104] The *Campagne* lasted from the beet harvest in October through February during most of the nineteenth century, although technical improvements in production processes moved the end of the season back to January by 1900. For the rest of the year, the factories employed only skeleton crews.[105] A variety of other agricultural products were processed by seasonal factory labor. Distilleries dotted the landscape, especially in eastern Prussia. The city of Magdeburg was dominated by the food industry, with sugar, brandy, and chicory factories.[106] A plant-oil factory in Neuss, near Düsseldorf, operated from fall to spring, employing about six hundred people.[107]

It is impossible to ascertain the total number of seasonal workers in the above-mentioned sectors of German industry. Certainly there were permanent employees, especially among managerial staff or construction foremen, in all these trades. Noteworthy, however, is that the overwhelmingly seasonal jobs in construction, construction materials, and sugar production accounted for roughly 22 percent of the total employment in the secondary sector of the German economy between 1900 and 1914, representing about five times as many jobs as in 1850.[108]

A sizable proportion of other industrial workers experienced significant seasonal fluctuations in employment, especially in mines and factories. Coal production was strongly influenced by changing seasonal demand, which naturally peaked during the cold season. Around 1850, the number of Ruhr coal miners during the winter was double that of the summer. Although the seasonal fluctuations tended to smooth out somewhat during the course of industrialization, coal mining continued to provide seasonal work for peasants in the winter, with labor forces between October and December about 50 percent higher than in March through May.[109] Careful studies of labor fluctuation in selected factories also reveal seasonal patterns. In a Württemberg textile factory from 1858 to 1914, the labor force tended to grow between November and April, falling in the summer. About 18 percent of the workers during this period entered the factory three or more separate times, probably indicating the seasonal nature of their employment.[110] Similar seasonal changes were found for the Maschinenfabrik Augsburg-Nürnberg (MAN) in Nürnberg, with gains in the spring and losses around the fall harvest.[111]

Seasonal changes in the industrial labor force remain largely unexplored territory. We can assume that other industrial branches besides those mentioned were also affected by regular fluctuations in levels of employment, which offered opportunities for repeated short-term labor. The number of seasonal workers reached at least one-quarter and perhaps one-third of the entire industrial labor force at the end of the *Kaiserreich*.

Apart from periodic seasonal changes in the labor market, structural conditions in the industrial sector reduced the security and tenure of even more "permanent" workers. During the period of rapid industrial growth between the *Gründerjahre* and World War I, especially from the 1890s through 1914, when the total industrial labor force more than doubled, stark and sudden declines in the labor force of individual firms were common. For example, between 1827 and 1874 the Maschinenfabrik André Koechlin et Cie. in Mülhausen quintupled its size, but had as many years of reductions as additions.[112] The Maschinenfabrik Esslingen grew from 1,200 to 4,500 workers between 1870 and 1913, but extremely sporadically: in twenty-four years the workforce grew, but in nineteen years it fell, by an average of 8 percent each time.[113] The largest iron and steel firms in the Ruhr also experienced numerous force reductions in this period, despite a quintupling of total workers. The largest reductions there coincided with the frequent cyclical recessions in industrial activity, in the late 1870s, mid-1880s, 1891, 1901, and 1907–9.[114] These broad trends were exacerbated by management policies that stressed maximum production when demand was high and immediate workforce reductions as the primary method of cutting costs when demand fell.[115] To these recurring uncertainties must be added the general unwillingness of industrialists to employ workers after their fortieth and especially after their fiftieth birthdays.[116] Before World War I, industrial labor offered little hope for lengthy tenure at a particular firm; seasonal and short-term employment were encouraged by the structure of German industrialization.

Numerous local studies make clear that the migrant workers who filled the temporary jobs in German industry were drawn from those rural underclasses described above, increasingly underemployed in their home villages. Westphalian *Heuerleute* worked on the railroads; *Tagelöhner* from Oberhessen migrated seasonally to Ruhr cities; in Baden, rural women went to Karlsruhe into chemical factories, while men worked construction. Agricultural poverty led directly to temporary migration: in parcelized Lippe, the communities with the highest proportion of tiny plots also had the highest proportion of migratory laborers.[117] "Modern" industrial work was incorporated into the traditional seasonal patterns of rural life as a last resort for the underclasses of the German countryside.

Conclusion

All the socioeconomic factors promoting mobility that have been traced in this essay existed well before 1800. The rural land-poor and landless in

Germany had long sought and found temporary employment away from home, in both the countryside and the city. Mobility was an integral characteristic of preindustrial society throughout Europe, as recent research has stressed.[118] Yet, during the nineteenth century, mobility within Germany and emigration abroad reached possibly unprecedented heights, only to fall again in the twentieth century to levels which had been common before industrialization. This unique jump in societal mobility was a result of a particular set of socioeconomic processes which simultaneously expanded and transformed the rural and urban labor markets. As Braudel has masterfully shown, in 1800 capitalism had not yet thoroughly penetrated to the daily lives of most of Europe's laborers. A century later, local markets were no longer dominant in food or goods, large-scale manufacture had pushed aside traditional craftsmanship for items of daily consumption, and intensive farming had replaced the three-field system. The growth of population caused by the demographic transition fed nearly exclusively the class of wage workers, who came to dominate rural and urban populations. These workers were faced with a labor market in transition, or better, in formation, since the free market in labor had never before played such a crucial economic role.

In field and factory, on construction sites in town and country, this expanding market demanded vast quantities of temporary labor. The rural poor, who had lost or never possessed sufficient land or employment to subsist at home, were forced to migrate. Germans in increasing numbers were mobilized by abstract and impersonal economic forces to move to those sources of temporary employment, and then move again. The result was the astounding rates of migration that characterized German communities at the turn of the twentieth century.[119] The fluctuation within the industrial labor force, which has lately become an object of historical interest, was determined by the particular fit of urban employment with rural needs. Problems in urban housing, improved transportation systems, and the search of urban workers for higher wages added to this structural problem, but did not cause it. Only the further process of agricultural and industrial development during the twentieth century was able to relieve the elemental pressure of the rural underemployed and thereby reduce mobility to "normal" levels.

Notes

This essay is a revised version of "Socioeconomic Determinants of Mobility in Nineteenth-Century Germany," Arbeitspapier 1/85, Institut für Europäische Geschichte, Mainz (1985). I gratefully acknowledge the support of the Institut, where much of the research was done.

1. Steve Hochstadt, "Urban Migration in Imperial Germany: Towards a Quantitative

Model," *Historical Papers / Communications Historiques 1986* (1987): 200–204. Dieter Langewiesche discusses urban mobility at its peak in "Wanderungsbewegungen in der Hochindustrialisierungsperiode: Regionale, interstädtische und innerstädtische Mobilität in Deutschland 1880–1914," *Vierteljahrschrift für Sozial- und Wirtschaftsgeschichte* 64 (1977): 1–40.

2. For a broad survey of changing migration rates, see Steve Hochstadt, "Migration and Industrialization in Germany, 1815-1977," *Social Science History* 5 (Fall 1981): 445–68; for evidence that this decline actually began about 1900, see Steve Hochstadt, "Städtische Wanderungsbewegungen in Deutschland 1850–1914," in *Deutschland und Europa in der Neuzeit: Festschrift für Karl Otmar Freiherr von Aretin zum 65. Geburtstag*, ed. Ralph Melville et al. (Stuttgart, 1988), 575–98.

3. Theodor Penners has investigated this movement most thoroughly. See *Untersuchungen über die Herkunft der Stadtbewohner im Deutsch-Ordensland Preußen bis in die Zeit um 1400* (Leipzig, 1942), 138–51; idem, "Der Umfang der altdeutschen Nachwanderung des 14. Jahrhunderts in die Städte des Ostseegebiets," *Lüneburger Blätter*, no. 2 (1951): 39–41; and idem, "Fragen der Zuwanderung in den Hansestädten des späten Mittelalters," *Hansische Geschichtsblätter* 83 (1965): 39–40. See also Karlheinz Blaschke, *Bevölkerungsgeschichte von Sachsen bis zur industriellen Revolution* (Weimar, 1967), 76.

4. For a brief description of available data and references to literature, see Steve Hochstadt, "Migration in Preindustrial Germany," *Central European History* 16 (1983): 219–21.

5. Peter Marschalck, *Bevölkerungsgeschichte Deutschlands im 19. und 20. Jahrhundert* (Frankfurt am Main, 1984), 21.

6. The figure of 0.3 percent for all of Germany in the second half of the eighteenth century given by Marschalck (*Bevölkerungsgeschichte*, 21) is far too low; for regional data see Wolfgang Köllmann, "Bevölkerung und Raum in Neuerer und Neuester Zeit," in *Raum und Bevölkerung in der Weltgeschichte: Bevölkerungs-Ploetz*, ed. Ernst Kirsten, Ernst Wolfgang Buchholz, and Wolfgang Köllmann (Würzburg, 1955), 2:157; Johann Georg von Viebahn, *Statistik und Topographie des Regierungsbezirks Düsseldorf* (Düsseldorf, 1836), 116, 124; Wolfgang von Hippel, *Auswanderung aus Südwestdeutschland: Studien zur Württembergischen Auswanderung und Auswanderungspolitik im 18. und 19. Jahrhundert* (Stuttgart, 1984), 29; Hanna Haack, "Der Einfluß der Herrschaftsstrukturen auf die Siedlungsverhältnisse in Mecklenburg-Schwerin im 19. Jahrhundert," *Jahrbuch für Wirtschaftsgeschichte*, no. 2 (1984): 117.

7. Hans Hüls, "Das Lipperland als Ausgangsgebiet saisonaler Arbeiterwanderungen in den ersten Jahrzehnten des 20. Jahrhunderts," *Lippische Mitteilungen aus Geschichte und Landeskunde* 40 (1971): 8–9; Albin Gladen, *Der Kreis Tecklenburg an der Schwelle des Zeitalters der Industrialisierung* (Münster, 1970), 119–22; Hartmut Harnisch, *Die Herrschaft Boitzenburg: Untersuchungen zur Entwicklung der sozial-ökonomischen Struktur ländlicher Gebiete in der Mark Brandenburg von 14. bis zum 19. Jahrhundert* (Weimar, 1968), 100; Walter Hartinger, "Zur Bevölkerungs- und Sozialstruktur von Oberpfalz und Niederbayern in vorindustrieller Zeit," *Zeitschrift für bayerische Landesgeschichte* 39 (1976): 789–91. Werner Conze, "Vom 'Pöbel' zum 'Proletariat'," *Vierteljahrschrift für Sozial- und Wirtschaftsgeschichte* 41 (1954): 333–64, gives other examples, and claims this process was general in Germany.

8. Hartmut Harnisch, "Produktivkräfte und Produktionsverhältnisse in der Landwirtschaft der Magdeburger Börde von der Mitte des 18. Jahrhunderts bis zum Beginn des Zuckerrübenausbaus in der Mitte der dreißiger Jahre des 19. Jahrhunderts," in *Landwirtschaft und Kapitalismus: Zur Entwicklung der ökonomischen und sozialen Verhältnisse in der Magdeburger Börde vom Ausgang des 18. Jahrhunderts bis zum Ende des ersten Weltkrieges*, ed. Hans Jürgen Rach and Bernhard Weissel (Berlin, 1978), 1:111–14.

9. Alan Mayhew, *Rural Settlement and Farming in Germany* (New York, 1973), 124.

10. Friedrich-Wilhelm Henning, *Landwirtschaft und ländliche Gesellschaft in Deutschland, 800 bis 1750* (Paderborn, 1979), 1:101–2.

11. Hanna Haack, "Bäuerliche Betriebe und soziale Gruppen landarmer Produzenten in Mecklenburg-Schwerin im 19. Jahrhundert," *Jahrbuch für Wirtschaftgeschichte*, pt. 1 (1982): 82–83.

12. Jan Peters, "Ostelbische Landarmut—Statistisches über landlose und landarme Agrarproduzenten im Spätfeudalismus (Schwedisch-Pommern und Sachsen)," *Jahrbuch für Wirtschaftgeschichte*, pt. 1 (1970): 100–114.

13. Population growth produced similar consequences in areas of widely differing social structure. Jan Peters demonstrates this for Pomerania and Saxony, both east of the Elbe, one dominated by Junkers, the other with a stronger middle class and more urban influence. See "Ostelbische Landarmut," 97, 122–24.

14. Peter Kriedte, Hans Medick, and Jürgen Schlumbohm, *Industrialization before Industrialization* (Cambridge, 1981), 17, 46–47, 54–55, 84; David Levine, *Family Formation in an Age of Nascent Capitalism* (New York, 1977), 36–42.

15. Jürgen Schlumbohm, "Seasonal Fluctuations and Social Division of Labour: Rural Linen Production in the Osnabrück and Bielefeld Regions and the Urban Woolen Industry in the Niederlausitz (c. 1770–c. 1850)," in *Manufacture in Town and Country before the Factory*, ed. Maxine Berg, Pat Hudson, and Michael Sonenscher (Cambridge, England, 1983), 104–17.

16. Rudolf Braun, *Das ausgehende Ancien Régime in der Schweiz: Aufriß einer Sozial- und Wirtschaftsgeschichte des 18. Jahrhunderts* (Göttingen, 1984), 127–30.

17. The following description is based on Hans-Jürgen Seraphim, *Das Heuerlingswesen in Nordwestdeutschland* (Münster, 1984), 12–15; *Heuerlinge* is a regional variant of *Heuerleute.*

18. Köllmann, "Bevölkerung und Raum in Neuerer und Neuester Zeit," 157.

19. Hans Fenske estimates numbers of emigrants in "International Migration: Germany in the Eighteenth Century," *Central European History* 13 (1980): 332–47.

20. On the history of the *Hollandsgehen*, see Johannes Tack, *Die Hollandsgänger in Hannover und Oldenburg* (Leipzig, 1902), esp. 86–97, 142–43, on numbers of migrants; Seraphim, *Heuerlingswesen*; Hüls, "Das Lipperland."

21. Many historical demographers and economic historians have noted the functional equivalence of cottage industry and migration as adaptations to rural underemployment. A notable recent example is Braun, *Das ausgehende Ancien Régime*, 127–30.

22. Hochstadt, "Migration in Preindustrial Germany," 201, 208.

23. Calculated from data in Hauptstaatsarchiv Düsseldorf, Regierung Düsseldorf 414; the economic classification of communities is based on Helmut Hahn and Wolfgang Zorn, *Historische Wirtschaftskarte der Rheinlande um 1820*, Rheinisches Archiv, vol. 87 (Bonn, 1973); for a full description of these migration data, see Steve Hochstadt and James H. Jackson, Jr., " 'New' Sources for the Study of Migration in Early Nineteenth-Century Germany," *Historical Social Research–Historische Sozialforschung*, no. 31 (1984): 85–92.

24. For data on total German population, see John E. Knodel, *The Decline of Fertility in Germany, 1871–1939* (Princeton, 1974), 23–24, 32; Marschalck, *Bevölkerungsgeschichte*, 145–46. The apparently rapid population spurt between 1816 and 1825 was due in part to more accurate census methods.

25. If five thousand were taken as the upper limit of a rural community, rather than two thousand, as is used in German official sources, then the rural population continued to grow until 1914. Data on rural and agricultural populations from 1780 through 1970 can be found in Friedrich-Wilhelm Henning, *Die Industrialisierung in Deutschland 1800 bis 1914* (Paderborn, 1973), 20, 31; *Statistik des Deutschen Reichs* (Berlin, 1913), 211:85; Statistiches Bundesamt, *Bevölkerung und Wirtschaft, 1872–1972* (Stuttgart, 1972), 90–94.

26. Fritz Molle, *Das Eichsfeld als Ausgangsbezirk für Arbeiterwanderungen* (Halberstadt,

1925), 73–75; Lawrence Schofer, *The Formation of a Modern Labor Force: Upper Silesia, 1865–1914* (Berkeley, 1975), 55; Hüls, "Das Lipperland," 8–9; Johann Plenge, "Westerwälder Hausierer und Landgänger," *Schriften des Vereins für Sozialpolitik* 78 (Leipzig, 1898): 11.

27. Konrad Vanja, *Dörflicher Strukturwandel zwischen Übervölkerung und Auswanderung: Zur Sozialgeschichte des oberhessischen Postortes Halsdorf, 1785–1867* (Marburg, 1978), 90–95.

28. Hainer Plaul, "Grundzüge der Entwicklung der sozialökonomischen Verhältnisse in der Magdeburger Börde unter den Bedingungen der Durchsetzung und vollen Entfaltung des Kapitalismus der freien Konkurrenz in der Landwirtschaft (1830 bis 1880)," in Rach and Weissel, *Landwirtschaft und Kapitalismus*, 186.

29. Hainer Plaul, *Landarbeiterleben im 19. Jahrhundert* (Berlin, 1979), 85.

30. Friedrich-Wilhelm Henning, *Landwirtschaft und ländliche Gesellschaft in Deutschland, 1750 bis 1976* (Paderborn, 1978), 2:149, 153.

31. The secondary literature provides a variety of estimates of this minimum for self-sufficiency, depending on locality and agricultural methods. Rudolf Fuchs estimated three to four hectares near Karlsruhe; see his *Die Verhältnisse der Industriearbeiter in 17 Landgemeinden bei Karlsruhe* (Karlsruhe, 1904), 95. Hainer Plaul says six hectares were needed in the Magdeburger Börde; see his *Landarbeiterleben*, 44.

32. *Statistisches Jahrbuch für das Deutsche Reich* (1930), 56–57, leaving out those farms under 0.05 hectare.

33. In 1907 less than 10 percent of peasants with under two hectares and less than 50 percent of those with two to five hectares were listed in the census as self-sufficient without secondary occupation; see Sigrid Dillwitz, "Die Struktur der Bauernschaft von 1871 bis 1914. Dargestellt auf der Grundlage der deutschen Reichsstatistik," *Jahrbuch für Geschichte* 9 (1973): 108.

34. Ilona Buchsteiner, "Die Entwicklung der Arbeitskräftestruktur in der deutschen Landwirtschaft von 1882 bis 1907," *Jahrbuch für Wirtschaftgeschichte*, pt. 2 (1982): 43–45.

35. Robert A. Dickler, "Organization and Change in Productivity in Eastern Prussia," in *European Peasants and Their Markets: Essays in Agrarian Economic History*, ed. William N. Parker and Eric L. Jones (Princeton, 1975), 276–77.

36. Henning, *Landwirtschaft, 1750 bis 1976*, 58. This figure, frequently cited in the literature, is disputed as far too high by Hartmut Harnisch, *Kapitalistische Agrarreform und industrielle Revolution: Agrarhistorische Untersuchungen über das ostelbische Preußen zwischen Spätfeudalismus und bürgerlich-demokratischer Revolution von 1848/49 unter besonderer Berücksichtigung der Provinz Brandenburg* (Weimar, 1984), 280–84.

37. Calculated from data in Dickler, "Organization and Change," 282.

38. Hans-Jürgen Teuteberg, "Der Einfluß der Agrarreformen auf die Betriebsorganisation und Produktion der bäuerlichen Wirtschaft Westfalens im 19. Jahrhundert," in *Entwicklungsprobleme einer Region: Das Beispiel Rheinland und Westfalen im 19. Jahrhundert*, ed. Peter Borscheid et al. (Berlin, 1981), 193; Henning, *Landwirtschaft, 1750 bis 1976*, 58, 72–73.

39. Seraphim, *Heuerlingswesen*, 19; Mayhew, *Rural Settlement*, 178–80; Henning, *Landwirtschaft, 1750 bis 1976*, 21–28; Gladen, *Der Kreis Tecklenburg*, 21–29; Eugen Katz, *Landarbeiter und Landwirtschaft in Oberhessen* (Stuttgart, 1904), 37–38.

40. Friedrich Lütge, *Geschichte der deutschen Agrarverfassung vom frühen Mittelalter bis zum 19. Jahrhundert* (Stuttgart, 1963), 236.

41. Data for the work requirements of various agricultural rotations are from Georg Meyer, *Über die Schwankungen in dem Bedarf an Handarbeit in der deutschen Landwirtschaft und die Möglichkeit ihrer Ausgleichung* (Jena, 1893); somewhat divergent although similar figures are given by Franz Bensing, *Der Einfluß der landwirtschaftlichen Maschinen auf Volks- und Privatwirtschaft* (Breslau, 1897), 39–42, and Alan S. Milward and S. B. Saul, *The Economic Development of Continental Europe 1780–1850* (Totowa, N.J., 1973), 150.

42. A wide variety of rotation systems coexisted during the nineteenth century; several typical varieties are discussed in Meyer, *Schwankungen*, 34–47, and Bensing, *Einfluß*, 39–42.

43. Statistisches Bundesamt, *Bevölkerung und Wirtschaft 1872–1972*, 141; Henning, *Landwirtschaft, 1750 bis 1976*, 25. Germany was unique in this dependence on root crops; see J. A. Perkins, "The Agricultural Revolution in Germany 1850–1914," *Journal of European Economic History* 10 (1981): 80.

44. Meyer, *Schwankungen*, 4–17, 34–55. Contemporary sources provided varying quantitative comparisons between the labor costs of three-field systems in grains and intensive sugar beet cultivations; see Perkins, "Agricultural Revolution," 99–100.

45. Hans-Heinrich Müller, "Zur Geschichte und Bedeutung der Rübenzuckerindustrie in der Provinz Sachsen im 19. Jahrhundert unter besonderer Berücksichtigung der Magdeburger Börde," in Rach and Weissel, *Landwirtschaft und Kapitalismus*, 2:54.

46. Meyer, *Schwankungen*, 70–71.

47. Walter Achilles, "Die Wechselbeziehung zwischen Industrie und Landwirtschaft," in *Sozialgeschichtliche Probleme in der Zeit der Hochindustrialisierung (1870–1914)*, ed. Hans Pohl (Paderborn, 1979), 71–80; Henning, *Landwirtschaft, 1750 bis 1976*, 139.

48. Meyer, *Schwankungen*, 6–9.

49. Müller, "Rübenzuckerindustrie," 13–22; W. Wygodzinski, "Die rheinische Landwirtschaft," in *Die Rheinprovinz 1815–1915: Hundert Jahre preussischer Herrschaft am Rhein*, ed. Joseph Hansen (Bonn, 1917), 252.

50. Klaus J. Bade, "Massenwanderung und Arbeitsmarkt im deutschen Nordosten vom 1880 bis zum Ersten Weltkrieg: Überseeische Auswanderung, interne Abwanderung und kontinentale Zuwanderung," *Archiv für Sozialgeschichte* 20 (1980): 296–97; Johannes Nichtweiß, *Die ausländischen Saisonarbeiter in der Landwirtschaft der östlichen und mittleren Gebiete des Deutschen Reiches* (Berlin, 1959), 30–34; Peter Quante, "Die ostdeutsche Bevölkerung in beruflicher und sozialer Schau," in Hans Raupach and Peter Quante, *Die Bilanz des deutschen Ostens* (Kitzingen-Main, 1953), 55–66.

51. Klaus Tenfelde, "Ländliches Gesinde in Preußen: Gesinderecht und Gesindestatistik 1810 bis 1861," *Archiv für Sozialgeschichte* 19 (1979): 201.

52. Tenfelde, "Ländliches Gesinde," 214.

53. Sieglinde Bandoly, "Veränderungen der sozialökonomischen Struktur in der Magdeburger Börde vor dem ersten Weltkrieg," in Rach and Weissel, *Landwirtschaft und Kapitalismus*, 1:246; Plaul, *Landarbeiterleben*, 110.

54. This figure results from combining the category "Knechte und Mägde" in agriculture (Iac2), with the category domestic servants (G) with employers in agriculture from *Statistik des Deutschen Reichs*, 211:85, 251, 283. Frank B. Tipton, Jr., "Farm Labor and Power Politics: Germany, 1850–1914," *Journal of Economic History* 34 (1974): 974–75, exaggerates the decline by looking only at domestic servants.

55. A fine description of this process is provided by J. A. Perkins, "The German Agricultural Worker, 1815–1914," *Journal of Peasant Studies* 11 (1984): 3–27. See also Bade, "Massenwanderung," 299–300; Plaul, *Landarbeiterleben*, 111–18; Lutge, *Geschichte der deutschen Agrarverfassung*, 235.

56. Seraphim, *Heuerlingswesen*, 25; Katz, *Landarbeiter*, 43–44.

57. The following description is based on data in *Statistik des Deutschen Reichs* 212, pt. 1 (Berlin, 1909), 4–6, 455–59, 606–67, and in Dillwitz, "Struktur der Bauernschaft."

58. The precise figures given in the source cannot be used with confidence because of unreliable survey methods and possible multiple counting of the same workers on different farms.

59. Jens Flemming, *Landwirtschaftliche Interessen und Demokratie: Ländliche Gesellschaft, Agrarverbände und Staat 1890–1925* (Bonn, 1978), 59, notes that 16 percent of all agricultural workers in the major sugar beet areas of Sachsen, Braunschweig, and Anhalt were *Wanderarbeiter*.

60. Max Weber, "Die Verhältnisse der Landarbeiter in ostelbischen Deutschland," *Schriften des Vereins für Sozialpolitik* 55 (Leipzig, 1892), 15–38.

61. Particularly good examples are Julius Ludwig, *Die wirtschaftliche und soziale Lage der Wanderarbeiter im Großherzogtum Baden* (Karlsruhe, 1915), and Katz, *Landarbeiter.*

62. E. H. Dietzsch, *Die Bewegung der mecklenburgischen Bevölkerung von 1850 bis 1910* (Schwerin, 1918), 70–71.

63. Friedrich-Wilhelm Henning, "Industrialisierung und dörfliche Einkommensmöglichkeiten," in *Agrarisches Nebengewerbe und Formen der Reagrarisierung im Spätmittelalter und 19./20. Jahrhundert*, ed. Hermann Kellenbenz (Stuttgart, 1975), 157.

64. Ibid., 159.

65. Pankraz Fried, "Reagrarisierung in Südbayern seit dem 19. Jahrhundert," in Kellenbenz, *Agrarisches Nebengewerbe*, 184.

66. Karl Heinrich Kaufhold, "Gewerbe und ländliche Nebentätigkeiten im Gebiet des heutigen Niedersachsens um 1800," *Archiv für Sozialgeschichte* 23 (1983): 163–218. The subject of secondary occupations in the nineteenth century appears to be of increasing interest to German historians.

67. Gustav Schmoller, *Zur Geschichte der deutschen Kleingewerbe im 19. Jahrhundert. Statistische und nationalökonomische Untersuchungen* (Halle, 1870), 508, 516. Per capita calculations based on population data are in Antje Kraus, *Quellen zur Bevölkerungsstatistik Deutschlands 1815–1875* (Boppard am Rhein, 1980), 153–64.

68. For international comparisons and references to literature, see Kriedte, Medick, and Schlumbohm, *Industrialization before Industrialization*, 280.

69. Schmoller, *Zur Geschichte der deutschen Kleingewerbe*, 505–6.

70. Peter Borscheid, *Textilarbeiterschaft in der Industrialisierung: Soziale Lage und Mobilität in Württemberg (19. Jahrhundert)* (Stuttgart, 1978), 25–26.

71. Gottlieb Schnapper-Arndt, *Fünf Dorfgemeinden auf dem Hohen Taunus: Eine socialstatistische Untersuchung über Kleinbauerthum, Hausindustrie und Volksleben* (Leipzig, 1883), 64–65; Fritz Flechtner, "Das Hausiergewerbe in Benneckenstein i. Harz," *Schriften des Vereins für Sozialpolitik* 80 (Leipzig, 1899), 361.

72. On the problems of German linen production in general, see Kriedte, Medick, and Schlumbohm, *Industrialization before Industrialization*, 295–96.

73. Walter Achilles, "Die Bedeutung des Flachsanbaues im südlichen Niedersachsen für Bauern und Angehörige der unterbäuerlichen Schicht im 18. und 19. Jahrhundert," in Kellenbenz, *Agrarisches Nebengewerbe*, 121; Schmoller, *Zur Geschichte der deutschen Kleingewerbe*, 508, 549; Seraphim, *Heuerlingswesen*, 21; Paul Dieterle, "Städtische Industrien und Industriebevölkerung im Landkreis Bielefeld, insbesondere unter dem Gesichtspunkte der Abwanderung aus der Stadt aufs Land: Gleichzeitig ein Beitrag zur Lehre von Standort der Industrien" (Ph.D. diss., Münster, 1913), 22–28; Hüls, "Das Lipperland," 9–10.

74. Wolfgang Hoth, *Die Industrialisierung einer rheinischen Gewerbestadt—dargestellt am Beispiel Wuppertal* (Köln, 1975), 137, 149, 219; Joachim Kermann, *Die Manufakturen im Rheinland 1750–1833* (Bonn, 1972), 194.

75. Henning, "Industrialisierung," 194.

76. John Dillard Hunley, "Society and Politics in the Düsseldorf Area, 1867–1878" (Ph.D. diss., University of Virginia, 1973), 76–79.

77. Hoth, *Die Industrialisierung*, 159–60, 177, 200, 211.

78. Ingrid Thienel, *Städtewachstum im Industrialisierungsprozess des 19. Jahrhunderts: Das Berliner Beispiel* (Berlin, 1973), 258–61.

79. Borscheid, *Textilarbeiterschaft*, 25–26, 61–64, 129; Tipton, "Farm Labor," 958–59; Katz, *Landarbeiter*, 99.

80. Henning, *Landwirtschaft, 1750 bis 1976*, 130–31.

81. Renate Schwemer, "Die Auswanderung aus dem Großherzogtum Sachsen-Wei-

mar-Eisenach vom Anfang des 19. Jahrhunderts bis zur Reichsgründung" (Ph.D. diss., Hamburg, 1944), 87–88; Otto Klingele, "Der Bürsten-Hausierhandel der Bewohner der ehemaligen Thalvogtei Todtnau im badischen Schwarzwalde," *Schriften des Vereins für Sozialpolitik* 81 (Leipzig, 1899), 296–97; Hellmuth Wolff, *Der Spessart: Sein Wirtschaftsleben* (Aschaffenburg, 1905), 387–408; Plenge, "Westerwälder Hausierer," 41–42, 118–19; Schnapper-Arndt, *Fünf Dorfgemeinden*, 63–66; Flechtner, "Das Hausiergewerbe," 361, 369; Kurt Kuntze, "Der Hausierhandel der Satzunger (Sächsisches Erzgebirge)," *Schriften des Vereins für Sozialpolitik* 79 (Leipzig, 1899), 29.

82. Heinrich Rubner, "Waldgewerbe und Agrarlandschaft im Spätmittelalter und im 19./20. Jahrhundert," in Kellenbenz, *Agrarisches Nebengewerbe*, 97–102.

83. Richard Ehrenberg, "Schwäche und Stärkung neuzeitlicher Arbeitsgemeinschaften," *Archiv für exakte Wirtschaftsforschung* 3 (1911): 441.

84. Henning, *Die Industrialisierung*, 128–32.

85. Karl Friedrich Wernet, *Wettbewerbs- und Absatzverhältnisse des Handwerks in historischer Sicht* (Berlin, 1967), 143, 231–80, 424.

86. Kriedte, Medick, and Schlumbohm, *Industrialization before Industrialization*, 293, 306–7, 315; Henning, *Landwirtschaft, 1750 bis 1976*, 131.

87. On this rather new subject, see the articles in Kellenbenz, *Agrarisches Nebengewerbe*, especially Alfred Hoffmann, "Zur Problematik der agrarischen Nebengewerbe und der Reagrarisierung," 29–37; Tipton, "Farm Labor," 953–55, discusses the increasing regional differentiation of the German economy in the late nineteenth century.

88. *Statistik des Deutschen Reichs* 211:42*. (Asterisks hereafter refer to pages added to volume.)

89. Hermann Schäfer, "Die Industriearbeiter: Lage und Lebenslauf im Bezugsfeld vom Beruf und Betrieb," in Pohl, *Sozialgeschichtliche Probleme*, 145.

90. *Statistik des Deutschen Reichs* 211:32*–34*, 42*; textiles here include the categories *Textilindustrie* and *Bekleidungsgewerbe*.

91. Hermann Kellenbenz, *Deutsche Wirtschaftsgeschichte*, Volume II: *Vom Ausgang des 18. Jahrhunderts bis zum Ende des Zweiten Weltkriegs* (München, 1981), 78–79, 112–13; Rainer Fremdling, "Eisenbahnen und deutsches Wirtschaftswachstum: Führungssektoranalyse mit einem Vergleich zu den Vereinigten Staaten und Großbritannien," in *Deutsche Wirtschaftsgeschichte im Industriezeitalter: Konjunktur, Krise, Wachstum*, ed. Werner Abelshauser and Dietmar Petzina (Königstein/Ts., 1981), 192–217; Richard Tilly, "Verkehrs- und Nachrichtenwesen, Handel, Geld-, Kredit-, und Versicherungswesen 1850–1914," in *Handbuch der deutschen Wirtschafts- und Sozialgeschichte*, ed. Hermann Aubin and Wolfgang Zorn (Stuttgart, 1976), 2:564–69.

92. Calculated from data in Tilly, "Verkehrs- und Nachrichtenwesen," 571, and Statistisches Bundesamt, *Bevölkerung und Wirtschaft*, 203.

93. Henning, *Die Industrialisierung*, 165, 237.

94. Proportions calculated from data in Walther G. Hoffmann, *Das Wachstum der deutschen Wirtschaft seit der Mitte des 19. Jahrhunderts* (Berlin, 1965), 196–205; Henning, *Die Industrialisierung*, 20, 137. Much nominal detail about railroad and road builders in a rural section of Holstein is provided by Werner Lemke, "Saisonarbeiter aus dem Großh. Oldenburgischen älteren Fideikommiß beim Arbeitseinsatz im Großraum Schleswig-Holstein während des Revolutionsjahrzehnts 1840–1849," *Jahrbuch für Heimatkunde im Kreis Oldenburg-Holstein* 13 (1969): 73–95.

95. For details on migration to railroad work in the mid-nineteenth century, see Karl Obermann, "Die Arbeitermigrationen in Deutschland im Prozess der Industrialisierung und der Entstehung der Arbeiterklasse in der Zeit von der Gründung bis zur Auflösung des Deutschen Bundes (1815 bis 1867)," *Jahrbuch für Wirtschaftsgeschichte* 13 (1972): 150–60.

96. Wilhelm Wortmann, "Eisenbahnbauarbeiter im Vormärz: Sozialgeschichtliche Untersuchung der Bauarbeiter der Köln-Mindener Eisenbahn in Minden-Ravensberg

1844–1847" (Ph.D. diss., Philipps-Universität, Marburg, 1972), 78, 237; Josef A. Klocke, "Wirtschaftliche Entwicklung und soziale Lage der Unterschichten in Ostwestfalen von 1830 bis 1850" (Ph.D. diss., Ruhr-Universität Bochum, 1972), 96–99; Wortmann also provides detailed statistics on seasonal fluctuation in railroad work.

97. Data on seasonal variations in construction employment are found in Paul Voigt, "Die Lage des Handwerks in Eisleben," 312, and Theodor Kreuzkam, "Das Baugewerbe mit besonderer Rücksicht auf Leipzig," 548, both in *Schriften des Vereins für Sozialpolitik* 70 (Leipzig, 1897).

98. The secondary literature on construction workers is rather scarce; on Berlin in the 1870s see Wolfgang Renzsch, *Handwerker und Lohnarbeiter in der frühen Arbeiterbewegung: Zur sozialen Basis von Gewerkschaften und Sozialdemokratie im Reichsgründungsjahrzehnt* (Göttingen, 1980), 35–69; high annual rates of membership changes for construction unions are shown in Klaus Schönhoven, *Expansion und Konzentration: Studien zur Entwicklung der Freien Gewerkschaften im Wilhelminischen Deutschland 1890 bis 1914* (Stuttgart, 1980), 154–61, 177–79.

99. Hans Seeling, "Belgische Ziegel-Wallonen und Feldbrand Ziegelei am Niederrhein," *Düsseldorfer Jahrbuch* 51 (1963): 225–58.

100. Karl Eckart, "Die Ziegelindustrie in Nordrhein-Westfalen," *Westfälische Forschungen* 27 (1975): 146–48.

101. Hoffmann, *Wachstum*, 196–205; *Statistik des Deutschen Reichs* 211:130, 306, shows 6.3 percent for 1907.

102. *Statistik des Deutschen Reichs* 211:32*–34*; Henning, "Industrialisierung," 159.

103. Henning, *Landwirtschaft, 1750 bis 1976*, 78.

104. Gerhard B. Hagelberg and Hans-Heinrich Müller, "Kapitalgesellschaften für Anbau und Verarbeitung von Zuckerrüben in Deutschland im 19. Jahrhundert," *Jahrbuch für Wirtschaftsgeschichte* (1974), pt. 4, 114–18, 127–28; Müller, "Zur Geschichte der Rübenzuckerindustrie," 28.

105. Plaul, *Landarbeiterleben*, 169–75.

106. Helmut Asmus, "Grundzüge der ökonomischen Entwicklung der Stadt Magdeburg vom Ende des 18. Jahrhunderts bis 1917/18," in Rach and Weissel, *Landwirtschaft und Kapitalismus*, 211–22.

107. Hans Seeling, *Die Eisenhütten in Heerdt und Mülheim am Rhein* (Köln, 1972), 11.

108. This estimate is based on data in Hoffmann, *Wachstum*, 196–205; *Statistik des Deutschen Reichs* 211:130; Henning, *Die Industrialisierung*, 137; Hagelberg and Müller, "Kapitalgesellschaften," 118; the secondary sector includes *Industrie, Handwerk*, and *Bergbau*.

109. For the Ruhr see Diethelm Düsterloh, *Beiträge zur Kulturgeographie des Niederbergisch-Märkischen Hügellandes. Bergbau und Verhüttung vor 1850 als Elemente der Kulturlandschaft* (Göttingen, 1967), 149, and Klaus Tenfelde, *Sozialgeschichte der Bergarbeiterschaft an der Ruhr im 19. Jahrhundert* (Bonn–Bad Godesberg, 1977), 197, 231–32. Summer declines in coal mining in favor of agricultural work were noted for Oberschlesien by Otto Bosselmann, Theodor Bogelsten, and Felix Kuh, *Die Störungen im deutschen Wirtschaftsleben während der Jahre 1900 ff.*, vol. 2, *Schriften des Vereins für Sozialpolitik* 106 (Leipzig, 1903), 145.

110. Borscheid, *Textilarbeiterschaft*, 276–79.

111. Hermann-Josef Rupieper, "Regionale Herkunft, Fluktuation und innerbetriebliche Mobilität der Arbeiterschaft der Maschinenfabrik Augsburg-Nürnberg (MAN) 1844–1914," in *Arbeiter im Industrialisierungsprozess: Herkunft, Lage und Verhalten*, ed. Werner Conze and Ulrich Engelhardt (Stuttgart, 1979), 109. Seasonal workers used for internal plant reorganization formed a "relatively large proportion" of the labor force at the Gütehoffnungshütte in Oberhausen in the late nineteenth century; see Heinz Reif, "Soziale Lage und Erfahrungen des alternden Fabrikarbeiters in der Schwerindustrie des westlichen

Ruhrgebiets während der Hochindustrialisierung," *Archiv für Sozialgeschichte* 22 (1982): 28 n. 28.

112. Hermann Schäfer, "Arbeitslosigkeit im 19. Jahrhundert: Fallstudie am Beispiel der Maschinenfabrik André Koechlin & Cie., Mülhausen/Elsaß (1827–1875)," in *Arbeiterexistenz im 19. Jahrhundert: Lebensstandard und Lebensgestaltung deutscher Arbeiter und Handwerker*, ed. Werner Conze and Ulrich Engelhardt (Stuttgart, 1981), 341.

113. Calculated from data in Heilwig Schomerus, *Die Arbeiter der Maschinenfabrik Esslingen* (Stuttgart, 1977), 296–97.

114. Calculated from data in Wilfried Feldenkirchen, *Die Eisen- und Stahlindustrie des Ruhrgebiets 1879–1914* (Wiesbaden, 1982), table 105a; the economic cycles are shown graphically in Gerd Hohorst, Jürgen Kocka, and Gerhard A. Ritter, *Sozialgeschichtliches Arbeitsbuch*, Volume II: *Materialien zur Statistik des Kaiserreichs 1870–1914*, 2d ed. (München, 1978), 78, 92. Statistics on the fluctuating total number of employees (*Belegschaft*) of particular large firms hide even larger fluctuations within different divisions of these enterprises. Data from the Bochumer Verein, a major metals firm, show that between 1900 and 1913, as the *Belegschaft* grew from 10,500 to 14,500, there were overall declines in four years. But the steel-pouring factory had declines in five years, another steel division in seven years, and the coal mines in five years, as individual parts of the firm responded to specific market conditions. The workers in these divisions were not interchangeable. See Jürgen Kuczynski, *Die Geschichte der Lage der Arbeiter unter dem Kapitalismus: Darstellung der Lage der Arbeiter in Deutschland von 1900 bis 1917/18* (Berlin, 1967), 4:315.

115. Feldenkirchen, *Eisen- und Stahlindustrie*, 254–55; Tenfelde, *Bergarbeiterschaft*, 231.

116. Reif, "Soziale Lage," 1–94, handles this question in detail.

117. Wortmann, "Eisenbahnbauarbeiter im Vormärz," 78; Vanja, *Dörflicher Strukturwandel*, 187–91; Fuchs, *Industriearbeiter*, 22–23; Fritz Fleege-Althoff, *Die lippischen Wanderarbeiter* (Detmold, 1928), 204–9.

118. For example, Peter Clark, "Migration in England during the Late Seventeenth and Early Eighteenth Centuries," *Past and Present*, no. 83 (1979): 57–90; Emmanuel Todd, "Mobilité géographique et cycle de vie en Artois et en Toscane au XVIIIe siècle," *Annales: Economies, Sociétés, Civilisations* 30 (1975): 726–44; Jean-Pierre Poussou, "Les mouvements migratoires en France et à partir de la France de la fin du XVe siècle au début du XIXe siècle: Approches pour une synthèse," *Annales de Démographie Historique* (1970): 11–78; David Gaunt, "Pre-Industrial Economy and Population Structure," *Scandinavian Journal of History* 2 (1977): 195–98.

119. Small towns and rural communities also had high rates of migration; see Hochstadt, "Städtische Wanderungsbewegungen," 591–93. Further study is required on this question.

Labor Migrations of Poles in the Atlantic World Economy, 1880–1914

EWA MORAWSKA

The recent influx to the United States of a new large wave of immigrants from Hispanic America and Asia has reinvigorated immigration and ethnic studies, including those devoted to the analysis of the origins and process of international migrations. The accumulation of research in this field in the last fifteen years has brought about a shift in the theoretical paradigm designed to interpret these movements. The classical approach explains the mass flow into North America of immigrants (from southern and eastern Europe, in the period 1880 to 1914) as an international migration interpreted in terms of *push* and *pull* forces. Demographic and economic conditions prompted individuals to move from places with a surplus of population, little capital, and underemployment, to areas where labor was scarce and wages were higher.[1] This interpretation views individual decisions and actions as the outcome of a rational economic calculation of the costs and benefits of migration. Recent studies of international population movements have reconceptualized this problem, recasting the unit(s) of analysis from separate nation-states, linked by one-way transfer of migrants between two unequally developed economies, to a comprehensive economic system composed of a dominant *core* and a dependent *periphery*—a world system that forms a complex network of supranational exchanges of technology, capital, and labor.[2] In this conceptualization, the development of the core and the underdevelopment of the peripheral societies are seen not as two distinct phenomena, but as two aspects of the same process—the expanding capitalist world system, explained in terms of each other. Generated by the economic imbalances and social dislocations resulting from the incorporation of the peripheries into the orbit of the core, international labor migrations between the developing and industrialized regions are viewed as part of a global circulation of resources within a single system of world economy. This interpretation shifts the central emphasis from the individual (and his/her decisions) to the broad structural determinants of human migrations within a global economic system.

In the sociological literature of immigration, the global system and dependency theories have been applied predominantly to the analysis of current population flow from Third World countries. Most of the recent historical studies of the turn-of-the-century mass migrations from southern and eastern Europe are conducted within a refined push-and-pull conceptual framework that views individual and social group-embedded decisions and actions in generating and sustaining migrations as important, but as played out within the constraining context of structural forces from both sides of the process.[3] These studies acknowledge the impact on individual movements of capitalist transformations occurring within the economies and societies of the southern and eastern peripheries between 1870 and 1914, and of the volume of labor demand in the industrialized western European and American core, but they do not fully articulate the multiple reciprocal links connecting the two in a single Atlantic world economy.

This essay offers an interpretation of mass labor migrations of Poles to western Europe and the United States between 1880 and 1914, by extending the historical-comparative scope of sociological analysis of immigration and integrating the compelling macro- and micro-explanatory frameworks: first, in terms of the circular push-and-pull forces that operated within the expanding Atlantic economic system of reciprocal exchanges of goods, capital, and labor; and second, within this structural context, in terms of the local conditions from which millions of people from all corners of the Polish countryside were set in motion.

Thrice partitioned between 1772 and 1795 among Russia, Prussia, and Austria, Poland as a political entity disappeared from the map of eastern Europe for six generations until it regained state sovereignty in 1918. With western regions incorporated into Prussia (Germany since 1870/71), central and eastern portions into Russia, and the southern section into Austria (Austria-Hungary since 1867), the subjugated Polish territories were part of the state systems and the economies of these three powers. Between 1870 and 1914, over two million Poles had permanently left the country in continental and overseas emigration, while 100,000 to 200,000 per annum toward the end of the nineteenth century and 300,000 to 600,000 in the last decade prior to World War I participated in seasonal labor migrations to western Europe. The remainder of this essay outlines the process of incorporation of eastern Europe into the Atlantic capitalist economy during the last decades of the nineteenth and the beginning of the twentieth centuries. Then, it discusses a "double-dependent" economic development in Poland, resulting from her partition and political subordination. Within this context, it presents the mechanisms, general directions and volume of Polish labor migrations, with a major focus on movements that carried the greatest numbers of people to Germany and America. In the last part, the discussion moves to the migrants themselves: to the villages and the immediate sociocultural environment in which they made their decisions to go and seek wages in western Europe and across the Atlantic.

Incorporation of Eastern European Periphery into the Atlantic World Economy

Through the eighteenth century, European societies were largely self-sustaining. International trade played a supplementary, rather than determinative role in their economic growth.[4] In the nineteenth century, as the rapid urbanization and industrialization of western Europe generated increasing demand for foodstuffs and raw materials to supply the domestic economies, and for external markets to sell accumulating manufactured products and capital, the southern and eastern parts of the European continent, as well as more remote regions of the globe, were drawn into the orbit of the expanding capitalist economy. Gaining momentum since the beginning of the century, the process of globalization of the capitalist economy had greatly accelerated after 1860.[5] Between 1870 and 1910, the combined industrial output of Great Britain, France, and Germany nearly tripled (that of the United States increased sixfold). By the outbreak of World War I, it accounted for over 70 percent of the continental total.[6] Until the 1860s, western Europe was self-supporting in foodstuffs, but its per capita food imports grew by more than 40 percent between 1870 and 1913. At the turn of the century, the share of western European imports of foodstuffs and raw materials in the global world trade was 65 percent (74 percent including the United States). The increased need of the industrialized Western economy for outside supply of foodstuffs and raw materials was matched by its growing demand for new markets in which to sell manufactured goods and to invest capital. By 1910, manufactured products formed 60 percent of its combined exports, while the volume of foreign capital investments had increased nearly eightfold since 1850.[7]

Conveniently close, vast, and "underused" markets of Russia and Austria-Hungary in eastern Europe were a natural target for western penetration; they also opened the way toward the Ottoman empire and Asia. The Russian and Austro-Hungarian imperial states, with strong ambitions for political leadership and military prowess, but with backward, underdeveloped economies, welcomed this interest because it promised the stimulation of sluggish economic growth and the strengthening of their military standing. The eastern European periphery received about one-fifth of all the capital invested outside by the Western core during the four decades preceding World War I. The leading exporters were France, Belgium, and Germany, with U.S. capital playing an increasing (though much less forceful) role concentrating predominantly in the oil and electrical industry and in agricultural machinery production. British capital for the most part was committed in its colonies, and in North and South America. Thus, around 1910, 66 percent of the total French capital exports in Europe were invested in

Russia and Austria-Hungary, and 71 percent of the German foreign investments on the Continent went to the Austro-Hungarian monarchy.[8] By mutual desire of the investors and the receiver states, the greatest share—50 percent—of Western capital in eastern Europe was invested in railways (state-controlled in both Russia and Austria-Hungary), to facilitate the transport of goods and, if need be, of armies. Another 15 percent went into industries, mostly mining, iron and steel, oil, agricultural production, and machinery. This pronounced concentration of Western investments in the eastern European periphery was particularly spectacular in Russia, where, in the first decade of this century, foreign capital carried 75 percent of the costs of railway construction, 85 percent of the production of iron and steel and of mining, and 55 percent of all new industrial investments.[9] In addition to direct investments in transportation and industry, Western capital owned a substantial share of the assets in eastern European banks that were proliferating toward the end of the century. In 1900, 35 percent of the total shares and securities held by the banks in the Hapsburg monarchy were in Western hands, as were 45 percent of the capital assets of the ten largest banks in czarist Russia.[10]

Strong pull exerted on the eastern European economies by the increasing Western demand for foodstuffs and raw materials and massive local investment of foreign capital, pushed along by the energetic interventionist policies of the Russian and Austro-Hungarian states, had indeed stimulated the economic development of the region. The transportation network (in railway kilometers) expanded by 150 percent between 1880 and 1910. This, in turn, had greatly aided the movement of goods, so that by 1910 the eastern European periphery provided about one-fifth of the world exports of foodstuffs and raw materials (directed almost in toto to markets in western parts of the Continent). Between 1860 and 1910, the gross national product of the Hapsburg monarchy more than doubled, while that of the czarist empire grew threefold. Throughout this period, both countries showed respectable average annual gross national product (GNP) growth rates of 3.5 percent and 5 percent, respectively, as compared with the U.S. rate of 4.4 percent.[11] Western investments in eastern European industry contributed significantly to rapid growth in the number of factories and industrial manpower. During the last decade of the nineteenth century, they increased by 75 percent in Austria-Hungary and by 67 percent in Russia. By 1913, industrial production amounted to 28 percent of the national income of Russia, which had already replaced France as the fourth-ranking world producer of iron and the fifth in the manufacture of steel. In the same year in Austria-Hungary, primary and light industry's share in the national income was a high 60 percent.[12]

Chaperoned from above by the strong centralized states interested in the enhancement of their domestic and international position, the incorporation of eastern Europe into the orbit of the world capitalist economy through the expansion of transport, trade, and Western investments, produced some "spin-off" or "multiplier" effects in the form of diversification of local economic production and the development of native autonomous industries. These were most visible in the Hapsburg monarchy, with its more central location and long-established political and cultural ties with the Western core. The vastness of Russia and its more pronounced economic and social backwardness considerably hindered this process. However, the economic development that took place in eastern Europe at the turn of the century had a peripheral character substantially tied to, sustained by, and dependent on the needs of the Western core. The proportion of the population in eastern Europe employed in agriculture at the beginning of the century was much larger (65 percent in Austria-Hungary and 78 percent in Russia) than in the Western core countries, including Great Britain (9 percent), France (4.3 percent), Germany (34 percent), and the United State (37 percent). Foodstuffs, primary goods, and raw materials remained the dominant exports of both Russia and Austria-Hungary throughout the whole period of accelerated economic growth (1870 to 1914), accounting for about three-quarters of their international trade.[13] Starting from a low base, the value of the industrial output of these two eastern European empires increased an impressive fourfold in Austria-Hungary, and eightfold in Russia between 1880 and 1910. Still, at the beginning of this century, their average per capita industrial production was only about a third of that of the Western core, which had the advantages of an earlier start and largely independent development.[14] While at the beginning of the nineteenth century, the per capita GNP of eastern Europe was 65 percent of that produced in the West, by 1860 this proportion had dropped to 61 percent and by 1910 to 58 percent.[15] As the capitalist economy spread farther out from its center, absorbing new territories during the century before World War I, the dependent advance of the peripheral parts of the system was accompanied by the perpetuation and accentuation of disparities between them and the dominant core.

Double-Dependency of Poland's Economic Development

Divided among the three partitioner states that ruled eastern Europe, Poland shared the basic characteristics of the economic development of the region. Although there existed some significant differences in the situation of Prussian, Russian, and Austrian segments, resulting from the specific economic structures of the partitioner states and their particular policies toward the conquered Polish territories (see the discussion below), the underlying socioeconomic processes were similar in all three sections.

The abolition of serfdom and the alienation of noble estates and communal lands (1807 in Prussian, 1848 in Austrian, and 1864 in Russian sections of Poland) produced cumulative long-term effects on the Polish rural economy. On the one hand, within twenty-five to thirty years from the implementation of emancipation laws, it brought about an increase of 10 to 25 percent in the total acreage owned by the peasantry. On the other, it intensified the process of internal economic and social diversification of the peasantry. One effect of this was the gradual consolidation of land and the formation of a group of peasants owning medium-sized holdings. Another, much faster and more significant consequence was the systematic fragmentation of peasant landholdings as the land was divided and subdivided among their progeny. At the turn of the century, no less than 72 percent of landowning peasantry in the combined Polish territories were dwarf and smallholders (up to five hectares). The third long-term consequence of the enfranchisement of the peasantry was the creation of a large rural proletariat. The land reforms of 1807, 1848, and 1864 left thousands of peasants as landless as they had been previously, and the continuing fragmentation of landholdings among the landowning peasantry added new members to the landless each year. Between 1860 and 1910, the Polish population (in the three partitions combined) increased by 117 percent, as compared with a 70 percent average for all of Europe. This demographic boom, resulting from a decrease in death rates, combined with an explosion in births following the emancipation of the peasantry, greatly fostered the numerical increase of the agrarian proletariat. At the beginning of the century, the proportion of landless, wage-dependent peasants in the rural population of all Polish territories was 33 percent, or about 3.5 million people—an increase of more than 500 percent over the previous forty years.[16]

Although Poland remained predominantly an agrarian society, with about two-thirds of its population still employed in agriculture at the beginning of this century, it was subject to capitalist transformations, similar to those affecting the rest of eastern Europe during the four decades preceding World War I. A number of industries, heavily financed by Western investors, providing from 40 to 95 percent of the capital, were launched and developed. They were predominantly concentrated in the sectors of extracting (Russian and Austrian partitions, and Prussian Upper Silesia), textiles (Russian partition), and agricultural production (Prussian and Austrian partitions). With the development of industry, the combined labor force employed in mining and manufacturing in the three sections of Poland increased fourfold from 320,000 to 1,200,000 between 1870 and 1913. By World War I, the overall proportion of Poles occupied in industrial production had reached 18 percent. Concurrent with the growth of the factories and the industrial workforce, the urban population increased 75 percent between 1880/90 and 1910. The proportion of city dwellers in the total population grew from 19 percent to 32 percent.[17]

As capitalism expanded with eastern Europe at its periphery, the dependent nature of Poland's development was made even more pronounced by her lack of political sovereignty and by the deliberate economic and national policies of the partitioner states, which treated the annexed Polish territories as their "colonies" and the Poles as a "hostile element" and potential rebels. (In national uprisings in 1830 and 1861, the Poles twice tried, both times unsuccessfully, to regain independence.) Although it affected each sector, this double-dependence of Poland varied in degree and form in Prussian, Russian, and Austrian partitions.

Germany (Poland's western partitioner, politically unified in one centralist empire only in 1807/71 and a relative latecomer to capitalist development) quickly became the "wonder of Europe," as it transformed itself from a largely agrarian to an urban-industrial society and a world power within three and one-half decades. Characteristic of Germany's rapid capitalist expansion were the leading roles played by state interventionist policies and a regional split of the economy into a highly industrialized area located in the western and central regions of the country, and an agricultural hinterland—literally, *internal periphery*—in the east, consisting largely of the territories annexed from Poland by Prussia at the end of the eighteenth century. This eastern German hinterland, particularly its Polish part, was to serve (with the exception of the industrialized enclave in Upper Silesia) in the state program of economic development strongly supported by the politically influential Prussian *junkers* (landowners), mostly as the producer of primary and manufactured foodstuffs and as a huge granary for western parts of the country. The hinterland's population was to provide the reservoir of labor for local agriculture and, from the turn of the century, for the expanding German industries in the west. Systematic actions, paired with the policy of economic peripheralization of Polish territories, were aimed at the Germanization of the conquered land. These were carried out by specially organized bodies, like the Zentralstelle für Förderung industrieller Unternehmungen in den östlichen Provinzen (1900), whose function, supported by the German Ostbank (Eastern Bank for Commerce and Industry), was to take control of Polish enterprises and to initiate German ones; and the *Kulturkampf*—an unrelenting administrative campaign to eradicate "Polishness" from local institutions.[18]

The situation in the Russian section of Poland was different. It was a politically subordinate *semiperiphery of the periphery.* In comparison with the czarist empire, where the highly concentrated industrial enclaves were surrounded by vast agrarian tracts, the Polish part, most westward, was more advanced in the process of capitalist transformations. At the beginning of the century, 17 percent of its population (compared to less than 10 percent in Russia) was employed in industry, and 33 percent (13 percent in Russia) lived in the cities. Although it occupied only 3 percent of the empire's territory and made up about 9 percent of its population, the Polish part contributed 12 percent of Russia's gross national product. In 1913, the share of industrial output in the GNP of Russian Poland was 49 percent, as compared with 28 percent for the whole of Russia.[19] Textile manufacturing, selling predominantly on the Russian markets, accounted for almost half of Polish industrial production; mining and smelting of ore, mostly for domestic use, amounted to over one-fifth. As semiperiphery, rather than hinterland, of the czarist empire, the Russian section of Poland did profit from the closeness of the vast "hungry" markets of Russia, but the dependence of Polish industry on Western capital and Russian economic policies, and political powerlessness vis-à-vis the unfriendly partitioner state, did not permit her to take more substantial advantage of this relative superiority. At the beginning of the century, French, Belgian, and German banks and joint-stock companies investing in Russian Poland owned 40 percent of all industrial capital, 25 percent of all factories (employing over one-half of the total number of workers), and 60 percent of the value of gross industrial production and total assets of major Polish banks.[20] As its Western, capital-directed industry developed, the Polish economy needed increasing quantities of raw materials: cotton for textile factories, plus coke and iron ore, whose domestic supply was not sufficient. *Russian* Poland was increasingly eastern-dependent for these products, but suffered from unfavorable conditions of preferential railway and customs tariffs, introduced between 1877 and 1896 by the czarist government to protect the interests of the Russian industrial centers in the interior.[21] Significantly, in the allocation of huge government orders for railway construction, including the works conducted in Russian Poland (designed more for military than for economic purposes), the latter's interests were generally disregarded by the czarist partitioner state. As involved as it was in developing and protecting its own economy, the czarist partitioner had little interest in doing the same for the annexed Polish territories, especially if it meant competition for the Russian industry. From the perspective of the czarist state, Russian Poland was to serve primarily as an advanced strategic bulwark to delay foreign invasion (the czars' constant fear).

The double-dependence of *Austrian* Poland, at the easternmost flanks of the Hapsburg monarchy, was similar to that of the Prussian partition, but, owing to the profound socioeconomic backwardness of this region and to the way it was treated by the Austrian center, its adverse effects were much more pronounced. Like that of Germany, the economy of Austria-Hungary was regionally split into a western Austro-Bohemian part that was industrializing at a steady rate, and a vast eastern sector, covering the territories of southern Poland, Slovakia, Bukovina, and Transylvania. If the Polish part of Germany was a *periphery of the core*, and that of Russia was a *semiperiphery of the periphery*, the segment annexed by Austria could be called a *periphery of the periphery*. First, and most notably, it was very poor. With one-third of the monarchy's total population, it received only one-twelfth of its income, and its per capita production and consumption were both lower by nearly

40 percent than those in the Austrian part.[22] At the beginning of the century, 80 percent of the population in Austrian Poland, as compared with 40 percent in Austria, still lived in the countryside.[23] Further, while they lived in it, they could hardly live from it. Two-thirds of the rural population of Austrian Poland—the landless agrarian proletariat (nearly one-fifth of the total), and owners of minuscule holdings that could not provide livelihood (about one-half of all peasant holdings)—had to rely wholly or in part on wage labor. Industry in Austrian Poland, employing barely 10 percent of the population, could hardly provide a livelihood for them. Nearly 90 percent of the industrial establishments were of the handicraft type, employing fewer than five persons and selling their products from homes, or at the local markets and fairs.[24] Of the remaining 10 percent, a few large industrial enterprises (oil, coal, zinc, and salt extractors, and a smaller textile center) scarcely employed more than five to six thousand workers each. There were no signs of any substantial future expansion in labor demand, because the owners—practically all Austrian or Western core investors such as Standard Oil of the United States—preferred to transport extracted materials for processing outside the region.[25] Of the three parts of the divided Poland, the economic situation of the Austrian segment resembled most closely the classic colonial one, and it was described as such by contemporary observers.[26] The Hapsburg monarchy, itself a periphery in the world capitalist economy at the turn of the century, assumed a role of the core in relation to its eastern dependencies. Like a true core capitalist, it exploited and plundered the natural resources of the annexed Polish territories, using a variety of means: protective rail and customs tariffs, government banks, and joint-stock companies with or without government participation. All of these repeatedly annihilated local attempts to create autonomous industry.[27] As if concerned that the effects of its policies might be revealed in hard data, the Austrian government stubbornly refused the representatives of the local diet permission to conduct an independent economic census in the Polish part, a census that the Poles repeatedly requested.[28] But raw and primary materials (of which, besides some oil and much wood, grain and beets, Austrian Poland did not really possess very many) were not of greatest interest to the Austrian periphery-colonizer and its core partners. The Polish territories, like the surrounding areas in the eastern sector, served chiefly as a vast, easy market for Austrian industry to dump increasing quantities of the famed *Galizienwaren*: low-quality, cheap manufactured products found at all town markets and in the village stores throughout the region.[29] With her natural resources plundered by core Western investors and the internal colonizer, with almost no industry of her own, with agriculture fragmented into lilliputian holdings incapable of sustaining the majority of the rural population, and with her markets annually flooded with all kinds of *Galizienwaren*, it was not surprising that, according to the estimates of contemporary Polish observers, the imports of Austrian Poland were more than

double the amount of her exports. "Therefore it is not astonishing," concluded the authors, "that [the Polish part of the Hapsburg monarchy], poor and debt-encumbered, can only balance her accounts by the exportation on a large scale of her own labour."[30]

Polish Labor Migrations: Mechanisms, Directions, and Volume

Turn-of-the-century commentators on the mass labor migrations from Poland seem to have better grasped the underlying mechanisms of this movement than did developers of later classical theories of immigration at western universities. As the former saw it, the profound economic and social imbalances of the region, resulting from its *dependent* pull into the foreign economy (both directly, from alien domination, and indirectly, from economic forces penetrating from the outside), were pushing out the domestic labor to become part of this larger system. In the preceding pages, we have shown the incorporation of the eastern European periphery (and Polish periphery within it) into the Atlantic world system through the exchange of capital and products.

The mobilization and increasing internationalization of labor formed the next link in this process. At one pole of the system, the push mechanisms were the consolidation in the countryside of a middle group of capitalist farmers and the simultaneous rapid increase in numbers of the agrarian proletariat and semiproletariat. By the turn of the century, about two-thirds of the total rural population in both Prussian and Austrian divisions of Poland and over one-third in its Russian section had to seek outside wage labor as the sole basis, or the necessary supplement, of their livelihood. The proletarianization of the mass of the agrarian population in all three partitions of Poland was fostered by the destruction of traditional rural handicrafts. These were increasingly eliminated by the development of transportation and the penetration into Polish markets of manufactured goods produced by the Western core, or, in the case of the Austrian partition, mainly by the periphery-colonizer, and by the industries they created in the Polish cities.[31] At the other pole of the extended system of resource circulation, the pull mechanisms of the mobilization of the Polish workforce and its incorporation into the international labor market were the increased needs for manpower of the core economy in the industrial sectors within Poland, where it invested its capital, and most of all, in its Western centers, both in Europe and the United States. This issue will be developed shortly, in the discussion of Polish labor migrations to Germany and America.

Seasonal short- and middle-distance harvest migrations of Polish peasantry within the eastern European countryside were already commonplace during the 1860s and 1870s. From the 1880s on, the back-and-forth economic migrations of Poles (and of other eastern Europeans as well) assumed an unprecedented massive scale, as industrial employment was added to agricultural wage labor and greatly widened in distance, scope, and direction, extending into the growing cities in the region and farther into western Europe and across the Atlantic. Between 1860 and 1914, these multidirectional movements (within the Polish countryside and to the cities, to other regions of eastern Europe, to western parts of the Continent, and overseas to the United States, Canada, Brazil, and Argentina) involved a total of about 10 million people or roughly one-third of the population of 29 million.[32] In the first decade of this century, 25 percent of the combined Polish population (all three partitions) depended directly or indirectly on economic migrations.[33]

A significant proportion of this movement—between one-fifth and one-fourth of the total number of immigrants—was directed to growing Polish cities. (Unfortunately, data on the relative shares of migrants from particular partitions going to the cities, to western Europe, and to America are not available.) At the turn of the century, migrants ("unpermanent residents") constituted about one-half of the population of the largest urban conglomerates on Polish territories. In the fastest growing centers of coal and iron production, such as Upper Silesia and the Dąbrowa Basin, they reached 60 to 70 percent. On the average, between 1890 and 1914, about 30 percent of the population of Polish cities was "migrant." Peasants who came to work in the cities usually spent six to eight months a year there. In the spring and summer, they abandoned their factory jobs and returned home to work in the fields.[34]

Although Poland's industries grew as capitalism penetrated deeper into the region, they were latecomers and, to a considerable degree, dependent on foreign capital and economic priorities and not developing at a rate sufficient to absorb all the superfluous rural population seeking wages. In increasing volume toward the end of the century, Polish labor migrants were flowing toward the core. Their movement was greatly facilitated by the network of railways linking eastern Europe to the western parts of the Continent and by the improved and relatively cheap ocean transportation connecting Poland to the United States on the other side of the Atlantic.

The central and western parts of Germany received 85 to 90 percent of Polish laborers migrating to western Europe, and the United States absorbed the same proportion overseas.[35] Customary interpretations in American ethnic literature emphasize the uniqueness of the United States in attracting the largest proportion of turn-of-the-century emigrants from eastern Europe. In fact, the number of Poles migrating into the western part of the Continent in the three-and-a-half decades preceding World War I was several times larger than the number emigrating to America. Of the estimated total numerical volume of all kinds of multidirectional migrations of Poles between 1880 and 1914, the United States received no more than 20 percent. If we compare only the two destinations that attracted the largest proportions of migrants, Germany and the United States, it turns out that, in numerical volume, Polish migrations to America were only one-third of those to Germany[36] (see table 1). While it was indeed only America that had a Great Legend of the unmatched riches awaiting immigrants, the common expression (still used idiomatically in present-day Poland) was *chodzić na saksy* ("going to Saxony"), referring to customary seasonal employment in Germany to earn money that was needed to supplement chronically insufficient domestic incomes.

The remainder of this section offers a closer inspection of these two largest migratory labor flows from Polish territories to the core during the last decades of the nineteenth and the beginning of the twentieth centuries, leaving aside minor streams to other countries in western Europe, Canada, and South America. They occurred simultaneously, and their underlying push-and-pull mechanisms were the same, but there were also differences between these two migrations.

In the period of rapid transportation into urban-industrial society between 1850 and 1900, Germany lost 4.5 million of her population in emigration to the United States. Within the two decades after the unification of the country in 1870/71, nearly 2.5 million left for America, and only after 1895 did this massive outflow eventually abate.[37] Concomitant with this movement, and gaining momentum since the 1870s, was an equally massive internal migration from the northern and eastern agricultural regions of the country to the industrializing west, the *Ostflucht* (flight from the East) and *Landflucht* (flight from agriculture), that involved over four million people from the eastern provinces alone. By the 1900s, one-half of the labor force in the industrial centers of Rhineland-Westphalia in western Germany was migrants from the eastern parts of the country.[38] Together, American emigration and the flight from agriculture resulted, by the 1880s, in an acute shortage of agricultural labor in the northeastern regions of Germany. In the west, the quickly growing industries were also in need of more manpower, especially unskilled labor for the coal mines and steel factories in the Ruhr region, into which it was difficult to attract the native German *Ostfluchters*. Toward the turn of the century, Germany herself had become an importer of immigrant workers drawn from the southern and eastern European peripheries, while still supplying her own emigrant laborers to the expanding American economy.

To secure much-needed labor, agents were sent to different regions of southern and eastern Europe to recruit workers for German industry and agriculture.[39] In the first decade of this century, there were over one million foreign migrant workers in Germany, with an approximately equal proportion employed in industry and in agriculture. Of these, Poles from Russia

Table 1
Polish Migration Flows to Germany and the United States, 1886–1913(N)

	Seasonal Migrations to Germany from Russian and Austrian Poland[a]	To the United States (from all 3 partitions)	U.S. Unemployment Rate (percent)
1886		20,839	
1887		27,428	
1888		27,626	
1889		24,822	
1890	} 20,000 annually (est.)	29,573	4
1891		44,497	5
1892		58,436	3
1893		27,428	12
1894		20,041	18
1895	60,230	9,422	14
1896	67,405	14,676	14
1897		12,132	14
1898		18,846	12
1899		28,466	7
1900	154,284	46,938	5
1901	174,664	43,617	4
1902	177,389	69,620	4
1903	183,875	82,343	4
1904	196,601	67,757	5
1905[b]	306,000	102,437	4
1906	315,876	95,835	2
1907	347,876	138,033	3
1908	393,074	68,105	8
1909	525,702	77,500	5
1910	525,441	128,300	5
1911	556,561	71,450	7
1912	607,838	85,000	5
1913	643,415	174,300	4

[a]The figures include only seasonal migrant workers from the Russian and Austrian partitions. For Prussian Poles, not evidenced in the German statistics, the existing Polish data are only fragmentary, indicating 67,000 seasonal migrants in 1889, 90,000 in 1891, 97,000 in 1892, and 43,000 in 1902. By 1910, there resided also in the western industrial region of the Ruhr 400,000–500,000 Poles from the Prussian partition.

[b]The surge in the volume of migrations to Germany and the United States in 1905, a relatively good period in terms of labor market conditions in both countries, was most likely the effect of the political upheaval and the resulting economic disturbances that took place that year in Russia and Poland.

SOURCES: Compiled from Zanna Kormanowa et al., Historia Polski, Vol. 3:1850/1864–1918 (Warsaw: Państwowe Wydawnictwo Naukowe, 1963), pt. 2, 777–78; Andrzej Brożek, *Polonia Amerykańska, 1854–1939* (Warsaw: Interpress, 1977), 227; Andrzej Pilch, "Emigracja z Ziem Zaboru Austriackiego (od połowy XIXw do 1918)," in Andrzej Pilch, ed., *Emigracja z Ziem Polskich w Czasach Nowożytnich i Najnowszych* (Warsaw: Państwowe Wydawnictwo Naukowe, 1940), 282; Krzysztof Groniowski, "Emigracja z Ziem Zaboru Rosyjskiego," in Pilch, *Emigracja z Ziem Polskich,* 213–19; Willcox and Ferenczi, *International Migrations,* I: 423, 477–78, 480, 488–89, 496; Klaus Bade, "Migration and Foreign Labour in Imperial Germany and Weimar Germany," paper delivered at the conference, "A Century of European Migrations, 1830–1930: Comparative Perspectives," Immigration History Research Center, St. Paul, Minn., November 6–9, 1986; *Historical Statistics of the United States: Colonial Times to 1970* (Washington: U.S. Government Printing Office, 1971).

and Austria-Hungary were the largest group (about 40 percent), followed by the Italians and other eastern Europeans. In addition, over 400,000 Poles from the Prussian partition resided in western Germany, not counted as foreigners in German statistics.[40] As needed as the *willig und billig* (eager and cheap) Polish migrant laborers were for the German economy, the prospect of their eventual permanent settlement was definitely against the declared political interests and national policy of the German state that intended to eradicate Polishness or, in any case, to prevent the mingling of Poles from Russia and Austria-Hungary with those from the Prussian partition. The German authorities feared such contact could easily lead to a renewed upsurge of *Polonismus* (Polish national agitation and a possible rebellion). As a result, special regulations (issued in 1886, 1891, and 1907) prohibited the employment of foreign (that is, Russian- and Austrian-partition) Polish migrant laborers in western German industries in the Ruhr region, where there existed a large colony of Prussian Poles, and required that migrants arrive without families, register in the *Deutsche Arbeiterzentrale* (German Workers Agency), and, most of all, return each year to their countries for the *Karenzzeit* (the "waiting period" from December until March). Thus restricted, Polish labor migrations to Germany, although they grew steadily from about 60,000 in 1895 to 150,000 in 1900 to over 600,000 in 1913, and had an enforced seasonal character, peaking during the summer season and dropping sharply in the winter months.[41]

In the decade before World War I, each year over 800,000 Poles worked in Germany, including those from its eastern territories laboring in western German industries. Among Polish migrants from Austria-Hungary and Russia, the overwhelming majority (80 to 90 percent) were employed on the farms and estates in the northeastern and central parts of Germany, where they constituted two-thirds of all agricultural workers. Clearly, by the turn of the century the agricultural capacity of these German provinces had become directly dependent on Polish migrant labor. As the German administration reluctantly admitted, its elimination "would almost mean the death knell for agriculture."[42] To a lesser but significant degree, the same was also true for the German mining industry in the Rhenish-Westphalian (Ruhr) region, where Prussian Poles, constituting one-tenth of all workers employed, made up nearly 40 percent of all miners, and their proportion reached 75 percent in some factories.[43]

The dependence of the American economy on immigrant manpower is well known and does not require belaboring. Briefly, between 1860 and 1914, Europe sent nearly one-fourth of its labor force to the United States, and, during the last four decades preceding World War I, about one-third of the increase in the American labor force came from immigration.[44] By 1910, immigrants represented one-fifth of the U.S. workforce: two-thirds of nonfarm laborers, and one-third of industrial operatives.[45] As the nineteenth century was coming to a close, southern and eastern Europeans provided increasingly large proportions of immigrants to America: from 5 percent in the decade 1870 to 1880, to 33 percent between 1891 and 1900. By 1914, they made up 66 percent of all arrivals.[46] Among them, Poles constituted 20 percent and 40 percent of all Slavic arrivals. Between 1870 and 1914, 1.8 to 2.0 million of them came to the United States.[47]

The arrival of southern and eastern Europeans at the turn of the century coincided with the restructuring of the American economy that shifted to heavy industry and construction requiring large quantities of low-skilled manpower. With the decrease in the supply of immigrants from western Europe, resulting from the rapid industrialization there, the United States, like Germany, drew the necessary labor resources from the peripheries at the southern and eastern corners of the Continent. Before 1885, when contracting labor became officially outlawed by the U.S. government, agents of American employers regularly traveled to Europe to recruit workers.[48] According to the local authorities in Lvov (Austrian Poland), in the spring of 1884, "through the agents' mediation there arrived weekly in Hamburg [one of the main ports of departure for the United States] 200 to 300 Polish emigrants, as well as Hungarians."[49] After 1885, the agents of steamship companies in Hamburg, Antwerp, and Bremen took over the solicitation of potential migrants.[50]

This advertising and solicitation of transportation agencies performed a function, in the words of a contemporary observer, of "opening up new regions [of eastern Europe] which are ripe for emigration [due to the local conditions] and in setting the ball rolling. [They hasten] the starting and make smooth the avalanche."[51] As in case of seasonal migrations to Germany, once initiated by the interaction of pull-and-push impulses, travels from the Polish countryside to America in search of wages soon became self-sustaining: the more people migrated, the larger the flow grew.[52] During the 1880s, about 100,000 Poles arrived in America, but the annual total grew from 30,000 in 1890, to 50,000 in 1900, to 130,000 in 1910, and to 175,000 in 1913. Altogether, considering that country dwellers constituted over 80 percent of the arrivals, migration to America between 1880 and 1914 involved about 7 to 8 percent of the rural population of the three Polish partitions combined.[53] The majority of emigrants, approximately two-thirds, were landless peasants and the agrarian proletariat; the remaining third were owners of small- and medium-size holdings.[54]

Unlike Poles who earned wages in Germany, 60 percent of whom worked in agriculture and only 40 percent were in industry, those in America were predominantly (95 percent) employed in the factories as low-skilled labor, with three-quarters of (male) immigrants concentrated in three major branches of industry: coal, steel and metal, and slaughtering and meat packing. Also, unlike the migrants to Germany, who, with the exception of Prussian Poles in the industrial region of Ruhr, worked in small groups dispersed across German provinces, the Poles in America formed large residential clusters in the cities where they found employment. Thus, at the beginning of the century, over one-half of the Polish-American immigrants resided in seven industrial cities: Chicago, Detroit, Pittsburgh, Cleveland, Milwaukee, New York, and Buffalo, with another one-fifth in the coal-mining towns in eastern and western Pennsylvania.[55]

The majority of Poles migrating to the United States at the turn of the century went there as laborers, not as permanent settlers. Their intended stay in America was to be temporary. Although longer than a six- to eight-month seasonal sojourn into Germany, it was, however, not to exceed a few years. According to the report of the Warsaw Statistical Committee compiled at the beginning of the century, only 30 to 40 percent of Polish emigrants from the Russian partition who left for America in 1904, and 1909 to 1913 (the data for other years are not available) declared their departure as permanent.[56] The U.S. figures for reemigration are available only from 1908 on, but fragmentary Polish sources indicate that, in the first phase of labor migrations to America (the 1880s and 1890s), 60 to 70 percent of emigrants did indeed return after two or three years.[57] As more immigrants arrived, and their social embeddedness in the Polish colonies in American cities increased, the return flow gradually abated. Still, estimates show a considerable proportion of about 30 to 35 percent returnees in the total number of Poles who went to the United States prior to World War I.[58] In further support of the interpretation of these labor migrations as circular rather than unidirectional, the data on the overseas travels of Poles at the turn of the century indicate that many made several trips. According to the U.S. immigration statistics, in 1906 alone, 6 percent of the Polish arrivals admitted to previous visits in America, and the contemporary Polish sources reported that up to 40 percent of returnees in different parts of the country made such repeat journeys.[59]

American labor market conditions significantly affected the volume and direction of the migration flows. Calculated for the period 1890 to 1916, the correlation between the contemporary rates of unemployment in the United States and the total annual volume of immigration shows a strong inverse relationship of −.61: the higher the unemployment in a given year, the lower the immigration.[60] Not surprisingly, the pattern of Polish immigration reflected this relationship. Table 1 shows the strongly depressing effects of the economic crises in the United States in 1893 to 1898 and 1908 and the impact of industrial recession in 1911 on the inflow of immigrants from Poland. The average volume decreased 70 percent for the years 1893 to 1898, as compared to 1892, and was about 50 percent in 1908 and 1911, as compared with 1907 and 1910, respectively. The same table shows the volume of seasonal migrations to Germany from the combined Russian and Austrian partitions, indicating, as noted earlier, much larger numerical flows than those directed to the United States. As the figures show, Polish seasonal migrations to Germany increased systematically each year, as well as during the periods of economic crises in Europe in the 1890s (only the figures for 1895 and 1896 are available), 1900 to 1903, and 1908. A particularly sharp increase (34 percent) in the number of migrant laborers in 1909, in comparison with the preceding year, corresponds to a substantial drop in the immigration to America during 1908 and 1909. Seasonal migration to Germany, where most Russian and Austrian Poles worked in agriculture—a sector not directly affected by the industrial depression—could have served as a safety valve for some of those laid off from American factories, as well as for those who were planning to go to the United States, but, hearing about widespread unemployment, went instead to seek wages closer by. (Unfortunately, no data is available on the origins and numbers of Polish migrants who shifted in their wage-seeking travels between Germany and the United States.) This multidirectional international migratory flow reinforces the argument for the treatment of labor migrations as part of the global economic system extending across the Atlantic, rather than as an exchange between separate pairs of countries.

Village Communities as Senders and Receivers in the Labor Migration Process

We have been moving down what Fernand Braudel called multistoried historical structures: from the top levels of the operation of world capitalism, traversing the globe in "seven-league boots," to the intermediate levels of trade in products and labor, and now to the lowest local "structures of everyday life" of the people.[61] While the configuration and pressure of forces at the upper structural layers set the limits of the possible and the impossible within which people moved, it was at the level of their close, immediate surroundings that individuals made decisions, defined purposes, and undertook actions. This last part of this essay looks at the local social environment from which Polish migrant laborers ventured out at the turn of the century.

While the conventional interpretation of modern migrations posits a direct correlation between the demographic and economic pressure and mass population movement, global system/dependency theories view this relationship as mediated by the incorporation of the regions in question into the orbit of the expanding capitalist economy. Earlier in this essay, we have shown the structural ramifications of this process, as it took place at the turn of the century, on the territories of partitioned Poland. For the inhabitants of the Polish countryside, this incorporation meant, first, large-scale railway construction in the area, then the trains coming and going, and with them, swarms of labor recruitment agents from afar. "The ocean [ships] and railways are [for the peasants] the bridge linking the two worlds," wrote F. Bujak, a Polish ethnographer and student of emig[illegible] from Maszkienice, a village in the central part of Austrian Poland. [illegible] 1900, Maszkienice, like other villages in this region, was ripe for emigration. Unable to sustain themselves from the soil, over one-half of its landowning peasant households were forced to seek supplementary wages elsewhere. A quarter of the total number of inhabitants was landless, relying completely on wage labor. Since the 1870s, the local rural population had participated en masse in the construction of railways to link Vienna, Kraków, and Lvov and in the building of cement factories in Przemyśl, a town in the southeast.[63] From the 1880s on, this region was also regularly visited by the recruitment agents, first from the coal mines in the Austrian Ostrava-Karvin district and then from the transatlantic steamship companies and the agricultural estates in Germany. The latter sent hundreds of such deputies every year to the villages in all three sections of Poland. A contemporary observer described a typical recruiting campaign in the 1890s: "As early as January, 'recruiting Sergeants' come to hire labour for the western [German] provinces. . . . The agent hands out cigars, beer, schnapps to the workers, and each recruit receives one Mark in earnest money, and after contracts are signed the manager organizes a general dance."[64] Indeed, when Bujak came to Maszkienice in 1899, no less than 40 percent of all young adults were temporarily absent from the village, employed mostly in Austria and Germany, with a few in America.[65] When he visited Maszkienice again in 1911, Bujak found the number of seasonal labor migrants had increased by more than half and that to the United States had grown fourteenfold.[66] In comparison, villages in the Polesie region in the remote eastern part of Russian Poland, and in the Horodło county in even more southeastern Podolia—demographically and economically similar, if not more emigration-prone—had continued to rely on traditional short- and middle-distance harvest migrations within their respective regions, and did not send laborers to the Western core until World War I. Both these geographically isolated regions were located at a considerable distance from the railroads and "about [recruitment] agents no one heard" anything there.[67] Without the experience of direct contact with the messengers from the outside capitalist economy (i.e., transportation, employment, and steamship agents, and earlier local migrants to serve as mobilizers), "unincorporated" Polesie and Horodło peasants had remained in place.

The classical push-and-pull model of labor migrations predicts the movement of people from places where wages are lower, to those offering higher remuneration, as the aggregate outcome of individual rational, cost-and-benefit economic calculations. Table 2 shows the average wage earnings and typical seasonal/annual savings in agricultural and industrial sectors for the three partitions of Poland, the rest of eastern Europe, Germany, and the United States at the beginning of the century. As the figures indicate,

Table 2

Approximate Average Wages and Seasonal Savings of Farm Laborers and Industrial Workers in Poland, Eastern Europe, Germany, and the United States at the Beginning of the Century (U.S. dollars in 1900)

Poland[a]						Elsewhere in Eastern Europe		Germany		United States		
Prussian		Russian		Austrian								
M[b]	W	M	W	M	W	M	W	M	W	M	W	
												Agriculture
38c[c]	—	32c	21c	25c	—	28–37c	20–23c	50–60c	28–40c			Daily wages (seasonal labor)
						$20–30	$15–25	$50–60	$25–40			Seasonal savings
												Industry
												Average annual earnings:
$200		$217		$100–170				$340		$500–700		Mining
		$160										Textiles
		$180										Metal
								$200–260		$370–500 ($1.30–2.00/day)		Low-skilled factory labor
											$240–300	Light industry
											$95–120	Domestic (with board)
						$40		$100 (factory labor)				Seasonal savings
										$200	$120	Annual savings

[a]Poland is divided into the three regions discussed: Prussian Poland, Russian Poland, Austrian Poland.

[b]Each of the categories is subdivided into columns for men and women in each area.

[c]Amounts less than $1 are shown as "c" (cents).

SOURCES: Compiled from Elzbieta Kaczyńska, *Spoteczeństwo i Gospodarka Ziem Pótnocno-Wschodnich Królestwa Polskiego w Okresie Rozkwitu Kapitalizmu* (Warsaw: Wydawnictwa Uniwersytetu Warszawskiego, 1974), 109; Jósef Okotowicz, *Wychodźstwo i Osadnictwo Polskie przed Wojną Światową* (Warsaw: Nakt. Urzędu Emigracyjnego, 1920), chap. 21; Maria Misińska, "Podhale Dawne i Wspótczesne," *Prace i Materiaty Muzeum Archeologii i Etnografii w Łodzi* 13 (1971): 20; Irena Lechowa, "Tradycje Emigracyjne w Klonowej," *Prace i Materiaty Muzeum Archeologii i Etnografii w Łodzi* 3 (1961): 51; Pilch, "Emigracja z Ziem Polskich Zaboru Austriackiego," 282; Ewa Morawska, *For Bread with Butter: Lifeworlds of East Central Europeans in Johnstown, Pennsylvania, 1890–1940* (Cambridge: Cambridge University Press, 1985), 45–47; *Abstracts of the Reports of the Immigration Commission* (Washington: U.S. Government Printing Office, 1911), I:367; *Polish Encyclopaedia* (Geneva: Atar Ltd., 1922), III:95, 217, 220, 537–43; Kormanowa, *Historia Polski,* III, pt. 1, 225, 564–66, 643.

agricultural wages (for men) in Poland were on the average 40 to 50 percent lower than those obtained in Germany. Although about 50 percent higher than local agricultural wages, Polish industrial wages were nevertheless 35 to 40 percent lower than those in Germany, and 65 to 70 percent lower than in the United States. German industrial wages, in turn, were, on the average, only 60 percent of those received in the United States. The disproportion in wage-derived savings showed a similar pattern as one moved from the east to the west of the Continent and across the Atlantic. If purely economic advantage were indeed the sole consideration in the decisions of Polish rural migrants at the turn of the century, once they had become incorporated into the Atlantic world economy and learned about its wage conditions, there would have been no continuing labor migrations within the Polish countryside and into Polish cities, Germany would also have been abandoned as a destination, and the immense volume would have flowed to the United States. However, instead of "rationally" following higher wages and abandoning places that offered lower remuneration, labor migrants from Polish villages had moved in several different directions, at the turn of the century and until World War I. Thus, in 1890, from a small county of Rypin in Russian Poland, 593 migrants traveled to America, 858 went north into West Prussia to work on agricultural estates, and an unspecified number moved in the opposite southern direction to the factories in Warsaw.[68] In 1899, 70 percent of the 116 Maszkienicans who left the village for the season, went to work in the coal mines in the Austrian Ostrava-Karvin district, while 25 percent found employment in different cities in the region. Even though people from nearby villages had already been traveling to America for quite some time, and their earnings there were known in the area, most Maszkienicans repeated each year their journeys within Austria.[69] In 1911, already 20 percent of all labor emigrants from Maszkienice were in the United States, another 20 percent (including many young women) worked in the fields in Germany, and 28 percent were in the Austrian Ostrava coal mines, with the remainder dispersed in small groups in different cities within Austrian Poland. From ten surrounding hamlets, 27 percent of all migrants went that year to America, 38 percent worked on the estates and in the cities within the region, 10 percent dug coal in Ostrava, 15 percent dug beets in the fields of Prussia, and another 10 percent (mostly young women) went to Denmark as agricultural laborers.[70] From southernmost Podhale on the Carpathian slopes, migrant laborers went in about equal proportion to Hungary (some to work on the farms and some to the Budapest factories), to Germany, and to America.[71]

The basic economic need of the majority of Polish rural households was survival. Beyond this, farm animals were needed. At the beginning of the century, a cow cost $24–30, depending on the region; a pig, $12–15; a pair of oxen, $50–70. A hectare of land could be purchased for $200–$500, the prices varying with the region and the quality of soil. The average cost of a house and farm buildings needed by newly married couples varied between $120–200, depending again on the size and the region. Young girls needed dowries. A customary dowry for a girl from a well-off peasant family did not fall far below $400 (landless peasants and dwarf holders gave their daughters approximately $25–30). The oldest sons, first in line to inherit land, needed money to buy out their siblings; the average amount per family varied from a few hundred dollars for large farms to $25–30 for dwarf holdings. There were also debts to be paid that, in all three sections of Poland at the beginning of the century, commonly amounted to $60–100 per peasant household. Finally, if one or more members of the family were planning a voyage to America, money had to be earned for a steamship ticket (about $25 one way at the beginning of the century) and for related travel expenditures (about $15–20).[72]

Several sociocultural factors mediated between the economic needs of wage-dependent rural households and the directions of migratory movement of their members. Village custom and local public opinion played an important role in their decisions regarding where to go in search of wages. So, for instance, peasants with a long-established tradition of agricultural migrations to Prussia dating back to the middle of the nineteenth century, from the counties of Kolno, Lipno, Mława, and Ostrołęka in the northern part of the Russian partition along the border with East Prussia and from the counties of Wieluń and Sieradz in its western region along the border with the Poznan district of the Prussian section of Poland, continued to go there until World War I, rather than to America. It was a well-tried and socially approved route, and the geographic proximity allowed several trips home during the season, including a return trip to bring additional family members to work or if new household needs unexpectedly appeared.[73] In Maszkienice (Austrian Poland), it took the villagers well over a decade to begin migrations to America, because, as Bujak observed in 1899, "Maszkienicans are fearful of alien unknown places and they do not like adventure . . . so every spring they return to familiar Ostrava [in Austria], content with mediocre wages that they find there and do not thirst for much higher earnings in America.[74] In the nearby hamlets of Dębny and Wola Dembieńska, German agricultural estates, rather than Ostrava coal mines, were the most preferred foreign destination, attracting until World War I the majority of annual migrants.[75] Not far away, in Zmiąca, where the village opinion accepted travels to Germany and to America, but strongly condemned those to Ostrava because of their supposedly demoralizing effects on the migrants, only about 10 percent of all Zmiącan laborers had gone there during the decade 1890 to 1901; the rest headed to more socially acceptable destinations.[76]

Migrations of Polish rural workers at the turn of the century were not an individual, but a collective movement. The social networks created in this process played a very significant role in channeling, building up, and then sustaining these ventures of the villages. Particularly important were networks of information about prospective employment. "[Rural] laborers working in the country, and in Austria and Germany," remarked Bujak on the basis of his studies of the migration movement in several villages in Austrian Poland at the beginning of the century, "constitute among themselves a kind of employment agency, remaining in constant contact with each other either personally or through correspondence. . . . From one or a few [who had gone earlier] they receive . . . information about the [employment] prospects in a given area, so that most often they leave with a conviction that even though they do not have work contracts, they will find jobs in the course of a few days. Returning from work in the fall they learn in advance [from their employers] whether they will need them in the following year."[77] Having thus established contact, at the beginning of each season migrant laborers set off from their villages in groups: the Maszkienice women to Denmark (the original group of seventeen in 1899 had increased to about fifty by 1911), the men (at the turn of the century a contingent of eighty, and a decade later sixty-three) to Ostrava, the Podhalans to Hungary in groups of twenty to forty men and a similar number of women. They boarded and worked together through the season, and then returned home together in the fall, to leave again the following spring. The majority of men migrated thus *za zarobkiem* (after wages) for 15 to 20 years in a row, and young women usually for two to five years, until they got married.[78]

Migrations across the Atlantic followed a similar pattern of network-building. In Babica, another village in the Austrian section of Poland, the first emigrant (not a native Babican and a socially peripheral member of the community) left in 1883 because he lost the court suit against his neighbor about a cow. He settled in Detroit. After three years he returned, then went back to Detroit in 1888, taking with him a group of five relatives and neighbors. After that, more Babicans followed, so that by 1900, there were seventeen of them together in Detroit.[79] Transatlantic migrations from Maszkienice developed only after a seed-group of the local people had formed in America. In 1898, the first pioneer, persuaded by an acquaintance from the neighboring village, gave up his accustomed travels to Ostrava and accompanied him instead to dig coal in Pennsylvania. After a year, he brought over two of his relatives; more Maszkienicans followed, "always going, men as well as women, to relatives and friends, and, if possible, journeying in the company of the local people."[80] Intense circulation of international mail—over five million letters were sent between 1900 and 1906 from the United States to Europe, and three million arrived—greatly supported the operation of personal networks in bringing laborers to America. "The most effective method of distributing immigrant labor in the United States . . . is the [international and domestic] mail service," concluded a report, prepared for the U.S. Bureau of Labor at the beginning of the century, on southern and eastern European unskilled workers in American factories.[81] As social networks of information, as well as travel and employment assistance, directed the increasing flow of immigrants to places where the original colonies of settlers had formed, the village communities were partially reestablished in American cities. "We have here now the second Babica," wrote an immigrant from Detroit in his letter home several years after the first Babican arrived there in 1883.[82] Maszkienicans concentrated in four places: Chicago, and Pleasant, Somerset, and Pittsburgh, Pennsylvania. In Pittsburgh, 150 emigrants from nearby Moczarka had also settled and worked together in the same factory.[83] Over 80 percent of the 174 migrants from Kurzyny, who left for America between 1890 and 1914, lived in St. Louis, Missouri; Oil City, Pennsylvania; and Youngstown, Ohio; but most migrants from the village Skrzypne landed in Chicago. Podgaje, split by a long-standing feud between two groups over the local pasture, transplanted this division across the Atlantic: the left side of the village, following its own social network, migrated to Elizabeth, New Jersey, and the right side followed a different one, to Detroit.[84]

The partial transplantation of village communities from Europe to American cities, and a continuous back-and-forth flow of migrants, via social networks linking the two worlds, created an extended transatlantic system of social control and long-distance management of family and local public affairs. Letters to and from the United States, compiled and analyzed by Thomas and Znaniecki, in the five-volume *The Polish Peasant in Europe and America* (1918–20), and other similar collections,[85] plus contemporary studies of Polish migrations in the period 1880–1914 quoted elsewhere in this essay, provide ample documentation of this two-way social process. "You went with piglets to Rzeszów and Niebylec," wrote an immigrant in Detroit to his wife in Babica, "but you did not sell them, did you? Because I know every movement in the village." In a follow-up letter, commenting on some unpleasant gossip he heard about his wife, from someone who just arrived: "Every movement in Babica I know, because I live here among the Babicans, and I hope it is not all true [what I have been told about you]."[86] A wife in Poland wrote to her husband in America, "Now, dear husband, I write to you for advice [about] what to do with this house which is for sale. . . . Now people give for it 500 *renski* [$200]. It seems to me too expensive, but if you order so, I will buy."[87] Another Babican wrote to his family home: "Wojtek wants to return [to Poland], but he does not have much [to come] with. When we get work [i.e., save some money] we'll both come back in the fall. [So now] tell me whether you left clover in the fields and whether you plowed. . . . Buy rye how[ever] much you need. . . . And those plum trees that were planted in the spring [tell me] whether they all have taken root or some withered. Nothing more of interest I have to say. . . ."[88] A son from Massachusetts, to his mother in Poland: "Tell me how is the weather, the crops, and how big the harvest. . . . Buy potatoes and you may also buy a pig."[89] Similar messages, sent in letters and carried in person by traveling migrants, crossed the Atlantic by the thousands. Evidence of these complex networks of communication, travel, and employment assistance, social control and household management—extending both *forward* from the immigrants' place of origin in Europe into the United States, and *backwards* from America in a home-bound direction, and paralleling the two-way population flow that they partly serviced and partly created—provides an additional, sociological argument for the interpretation of overseas migrations within the framework of the global system of interrelated parts.

We have been concerned thus far with the village communities as the senders of migrant laborers into the extended socioeconomic system of capital and labor circulation. Let us now, before closing, briefly look at them as the receivers of the returnees and their wage-savings.

If they moved within the region, migrant laborers returned to their villages every few weeks or months during the season. Those who went farther away, to western Europe, came back after six to eight months for the winter, but they stayed longer in America. Those who came back before World War I—as indicated earlier, about one-third of the total number of Poles who went to the United States during the period of mass labor migration—had usually spent two to five years there. Of the number who had gone to America from Broniszów (in the Austrian section of Poland), 35 percent had returned by 1914; in Żmiąca, in the same region, the proportion was 42 percent. Even more American migrants, 53 percent, returned to Babica in the same period, and no less than one-third of them had crossed the Atlantic several times before the final trip home.[90]

While away, migrant laborers sent home remittances in money orders and letters. When they returned, they brought material goods and savings with them. Returning from seasonal labor in western parts of the Continent, they usually carried supplies of bacon, sausages, and sugar (rarities on the peasant tables in the Polish countryside, where the staples of daily diet were gruel, cabbage, and potatoes). In addition, they also brought hand tools, irons, pieces of city furniture and clothing, watches with chains, brimmed hats, rubber gaiters, and other material objects of Western civilization.

Most important, they brought their savings. The internationalization of labor, paralleling the operations of "grand capitalism" at the upper levels of the Atlantic world economy, generated its own transmission circuit of wage-derived capital. This capital circulation at the base can be construed as yet another dimension of the incorporation of the periphery into the extended economic system—an aspect to which macrostructural global system/dependency theories have not paid very much attention.[91] Taken together, the amount of money flowing into the Polish countryside during the period of mass labor migrations was huge. For instance, in the five years between 1902 and 1906, money orders alone amounted to $70 million, from the United States to Austria-Hungary and Russia.[92] Using just one year of 1902 as an illustration, Polish emigrants sent American money orders in the sum of about $3.5 million (not counting small bills enclosed in correspondence, a common practice), to the Austrian section, and in that same year, an additional sum of $4 million was brought in by the returnees.[93] In that same year (1902), 42,000 Poles from the Austrian section traveled to Germany in seasonal migration. The figures for their remittances are not available, but, assuming that they amassed capital similar to the amount of savings of their compatriots from the Russian partition (for which data exist), an additional sum of over $1 million also came (in 1902) to this part of Poland. In that same year (1902), seasonal migrants brought back from Germany $4.2 million to the Russian section, and sent money orders for about $3.5 million from America.[94] Adding the sums brought home by workers returning from the United States to those arriving in letters, the figure reaches about $12 million. In one year, Polish rural households (in the Russian and Austrian partitions) accrued a sum of no less than $20 million from the export of labor to these two most popular destinations—Germany and America—equaling or adding slightly over 5 percent of the value of the combined export revenues of these two sections ($373 million in 1910). In particular *gubernyas* (provinces) of the Russian section, the wage-derived capital transmitted home by the migrants employed in the Western core ranged from $0.5 to $2.3 million. In the *powiaty* (counties) of Austrian Poland, whose rural population participated in international labor migrations, the amount of money that came in during 1902 ranged from $70,000 to $200,000.[95]

Even at the county level, these were staggering sums of money, never previously handled by local Polish post offices; but they became much smaller when divided among individual households. And so, for instance, from their season's earnings in Germany and Austria in 1899, the Maszkienicans had saved, on average, 60 to 70 percent, bringing a total of $5,600, exceeding the total net income from village farm production in that year by one-fifth. It was about $50 per "migrant capita" (seven persons or 6 percent of the 116 who went out to work came back with no savings). A decade later, in 1911, about 200 continental seasonal laborers (men and women) brought savings of approximately $100 per capita to Maszkienice.[96] It was a significant sum, considering that the value of the farms of more than a half of the landowning households in the area averaged $200–250. It would carry the family through the winter and suffice for the purchase of clothing or a pair of animals for the farm, for paying off current debts or for a steamship ticket to America and related travel expenses. Yet it was not enough to buy an additional hectare of land or build a new house with farm buildings, needs particularly pressing for young newlyweds setting up households. A series of annual migrations was needed to save for these; even this was not always sufficient, if other needs took away earnings. In Klonowa, a village in Russian Poland (near the Prussian border), with a long tradition of seasonal labor in the fields of the *Bauers* on the other side, the savings of fifty-two such seasonal repeaters prior to World War I (not counting expenditures on household operations, clothing, and recreation) permitted 56 percent to purchase or build a new house; 27 percent spent them to pay off family and other debts and on dowries for daughters. The remaining 17 percent used up their money to survive and on other unspecified needs.[97]

Savings from work in America were more substantial. In the county of Ropczyce in the central part of Austrian Poland, the average sum sent by money orders (to seven villages between 1902 and 1907) was $140 per household per year, ranging from $70 to $300. In Broniszów in that same period, it was $119.[98] In Maszkienice for 1911, the combined postal remittances and personal savings of thirteen returnees from America averaged $850 per capita, ranging from $180 to $2,200. The average number of years spent in the United States was 3.5.[99] Greater savings permitted more considerable investments and improvements in lifestyle. Thus, one-half of the forty-six returnees to Babica before World War I bought land (usually sections of 1 to 4 hectares) and built or purchased brick houses and farming equipment. Still, the savings of 13 percent had to be dispensed for debts and needs of daily living. Thirty-seven percent of the returnees brought back no savings at all, except for city clothing and various American gadgets for household use.[100] Clearly, with all its great promise, America was not evenly generous, and those who went there perceived this quite acutely. "America is not the same for everyone," an immigrant advised his cousins in Poland, who intended to join him for a few years. "For one person it is better; for another, worse. I am here almost two years, and I have only saved $150 [plus] I sent 50 rubles to the old country. And one person who came with me from the district of Rypin . . . sent home almost 500 rubles [$250]."[101] America indeed meant a fortune if their laboring sojourn was lucky, that is, if they found a good job—paying $2.00 to $2.50 a day for unskilled foreigners (prior to World War I), instead of a customary $1.00–1.50—and if they worked without interruption or lay-off from slumps in industrial activity. "When . . . after a few years in America, Walenty Podlasek returned [to southern Poland] and with the dollars he brought with him purchased a dozen or so hectares and started to build one house in Wierzchosławice and one in Tarnów, the people went wild from envy and desire."[102] But if their stay in America was plagued by recurrent unemployment, sickness, or other adverse events, it was a bitter disappointment and shame as they returned empty-handed from the Golden Land. "No, no more America for me . . . I am going back a beggar." The immigrant-returnees traveling on a ship from New York to Hamburg with Edward Steiner, a U.S. immigration specialist on his way to investigate the emigration conditions in eastern Europe, ranged from failures to successes—perhaps in almost equal distribution.[103]

Polish migrations prior to World War I issued from and returned to a socioeconomic environment still heavily encumbered by remnants of the feudal past, and articulated into the world system largely by exogenous forces. All in all, international labor migrations of Poles had not become a foundation for self-sustained capitalist development of the Polish countryside. Besides the inflow of consumer goods produced by the urban-industrial economy, these migrations made for the increased monetization of rural households as a rapidly growing proportion was becoming dependent on incomes derived from outside. However considerable in global amounts, the international capital brought annually to the villages by thousands of migrant laborers was fragmented among individual households, their shares predominantly sufficient to subsidize subsistence production, to carry the family through the year, until the next wage-seeking journey. At best, when larger amounts were acquired from longer successful work in America, they were used to enlarge diminishing landholdings and to accumulate private material possessions. Of crucial importance to the individual households and their daily existence—the reward for their incorporation into the world-economic system—this lower circuit of international capital investment by Polish migrant laborers did not transform the structure of their peripheral society, but rather repaired it somewhat at the base, perpetuating the status quo.

Conclusion

The massive flow to the United States of immigrants from southern and eastern Europe in the period 1880–1914 has traditionally been interpreted in American historiography within a conventional push-and-pull theoretical model that views the movement of people between two unequally developed economies as an aggregate outcome of individual decisions and actions. More recent historical studies of this immigration are conducted within a modified push-and-pull framework that acknowledges the impact of structural forces, from both the push and the pull side of the process, but does not fully articulate the multiple reciprocal links connecting the two into a single system of world economy. The aim of this essay has been twofold. First, it tries out a newer, global system/dependency theoretical model (applied thus far mostly to the analyses of the post–World War II international population movement originating from the third world) in the interpretation of mass labor migrations of Poles from the eastern European periphery to the core Western countries between 1880 and 1914, as part of the circular exchange of capital and labor within the expanding Atlantic world-economic system. Second, it integrates the competing macro- and microexplanatory frameworks of international migrations, by presenting the mediating role of local conditions and sociocultural environment from which Polish migrant laborers ventured into the outside world.

The interpretation of turn-of-the-century Polish labor migrations, within the model of core-periphery interdependence, seems indeed to expand our understanding considerably of both the global ramifications and the macrostructural factors (economic as well as political) acting as the inducements for this mass movement from all parts of Poland. Unavoidably, the discussion presented has left unanswered a number of relevant and more specific questions. A few interesting ones can be mentioned. Lack of reliable comparative data does not permit, for instance, an assessment of the relative proportions of migrants who traveled to growing Polish urban-industrial centers, to western Europe, and to America from particular partitions and their subregions with differing demographic and economic characteristics; nor does it allow us to ascertain to what extent, for which particular groups, and under what circumstances, these wage-seeking journeys were interchangeable or took a sequential pattern. One other issue has remained underinterpreted for the same reason. Existing evidence on effects of capital inflow into the Polish countryside from international labor migrations of its inhabitants supports the general conclusion presented here: that in structural terms this capital played a predominantly preserving, rather than transforming role. Yet there exist some data, unfortunately very little and fragmentary, indicating that such transforming initiatives were occasionally undertaken by the more enterprising returnees with larger amounts of capital, and it would be interesting to know more about these actions: whether and how they affected the behavior of others in a similar situation, and why and how these attempts eventually failed (as most of them seemed to have). Given the absence of systematic contemporary evidence, the only way to pursue this investigation would be through interviews with the surviving returnees and their families, and, as a matter of fact, such research is presently being conducted in Poland in certain areas in southern parts of the country that had high reemigration from America.

The last section of this essay is aimed at demonstrating not only that it is possible to integrate the macro- and microexplanatory frameworks in the interpretation of international labor migrations (traditionally applied as alternatives), but also that social-historical analysis at the lowest, community/individual level can significantly contribute to our knowledge of the directions and mechanisms of labor migration movement. These purposes, I believe, this essay has also been able to accomplish, if only in a preliminary fashion, by demonstrating how the local conditions—the situation in particular villages, with their customs and public opinion, social networks built by the migrants, and the concrete results of their ventures (as seen by the residents)—played an important mediating role in shaping the patterns of these migrations induced by higher-level structural forces.

Notes

1. Harry Jerome, *Migration and Business Cycles* (New York: National Bureau of Economic Research, 1926); Brinley Thomas, *Migration and Economic Growth* (New York: Cambridge University Press, 1973); Michael Piore, *Birds of Passage: Migrant Labor and Industrial Societies* (New York: Cambridge University Press, 1979); J. D. Gould, "European Inter-Continental Immigration, 1815–1914: Patterns and Causes," *Journal of European Economic History* 8, no. 3 (Winter 1979): 593–681.

2. M. Castells, "Immigrant Workers and Class Struggles in Advanced Capitalism: The Western European Experience," *Politics and Society* 5, no. 1 (1975): 33–66; F. H. Cardoso and E. Faletto, eds., "Preface to the English Edition," in *Dependency and Development in Latin America* (Berkeley: University of California Press, 1979); Mary Kritz et al., eds., *Global Trends in Migration: Theory and Research on International Population Movements* (New York: Center for Migration Studies, 1983); Saskia Sassen-Koob, "The Internalization of the Labor Force," *Studies in Comparative International Development* 15, no. 4 (Winter 1980): 3–26; Alejandro Portes, "Migration and Underdevelopment," *Politics and Society* 8, no. 1 (1978): 1–48; Alejandro Portes and John Walton, *Labor, Class and International System* (New York: Academic Press, 1981); Charles Wood, "Equilibrium and Historical-Structural Perspectives on Migration," *International Migration Review* 16, no. 2 (Summer 1982): 298–319.

3. Klaus Bade, "German Emigration to the U.S. and Continental Immigration to Germany in the Late 19th and Early 20th Centuries," in *Labor Migration in the Atlantic Economies: The European and North American Working Classes during the Period of Industrialization*, ed. Dirk Hoerder (Westport: Greenwood Press, 1985), 117–43; John Bodnar, *The Transplanted: A History of Immigrants in Urban America* (Bloomington: Indiana University Press, 1985); Celina Bobińska and Andrzej Pilch, eds., *Employment-Seeking Emigrations of the Poles World Wide, XIXc and XXc* (Kraków: Państwowe Wydawnictwo Naukowe, 1975); Milorad Ekmečić, "The International and Intercontinental Migrational Movements from the Yugoslav Lands from the End of the XVIIIth Century till 1941," in *Les Migrations internationales de la fin du XVIIIe siècle à nos jours* (Paris: Editions du Centre National de la Recherche Scientifique, 1980), 564–94; Dirk Hoerder, ed., *Labor Migration in the Atlantic Economies: The European and North American Working Classes during the Period of Industrialization* (Westport: Greenwood Press, 1985); Julianna Puskás, *From Hungary to the United States, 1880–1914* (Budapest: Akademiai Kiado, 1982); Gianfausto Rosoli, ed., *Un secolo di emigrazione italiana, 1876–1976* (Rome: Centro Studi Emigrazione, 1978).

4. Immanuel Wallerstein, "Periphery in the Era of Slow Growth," and "Semiperipheries at the Crossroads," in *The Modern World-System II* (New York: Academic Press, 1980); T. Ivan Berend and Gÿorgi Ranki, *Economic Development in East Central Europe in the 19th and 20th Centuries* (New York: Columbia University Press, 1974).

5. Sidney Pollard, "Industrialization and the European Economy," *The Economic History Review*, 2d series, 26, no. 4 (1973): 636–49.

6. Berend and Ranki, *Economic Development*, 130–31; Daniel Chirot, *Social Change in the Modern Era* (San Diego: Harcourt Brace Jovanovich, 1986), 90.

7. Ivan T. Berend and Gÿorgi Ranki, *The European Periphery and Industrialization, 1780–1914* (New York: Cambridge University Press, 1982).

8. Ibid., 72–88.

9. Ibid., 79–86; Clive Trebilcock, *The Industrialization of the Continental Powers, 1780–1914* (New York: Longman, 1981), 233, 244–46; cf. Boris Filipovich Brandt, *Inostrannye Kapitaly, Ikh Vlijanie na Ekonomicheskoe Razvite Stravy*, 2 vols. (St. Petersburg: V. Kirpbayma, 1901); M. R. Gefter, "Iz Istorri Proniknovenia Amerikanskogo Kapitala v Carskuiu Rossiu do Pervoi Mirovoi Voiny," *Istoricheskie Zapiski* 35 (1950): 62–86; Alexander Ger-

schenkron, *Economic Backwardness in Historical Perspective* (Cambridge: Belknap Press of Harvard University Press, 1962).

10. Berend and Ranki, *Economic Development*, 97; Trebilcock, *The Industrialization of the Continental Powers*, 278–80.

11. Berend and Ranki, *Economic Development*, 136; idem, *The European Periphery*, 25; Chirot, *Social Change*, 87; Trebilcock, *The Industrialization of the Continental Powers*, 235, 300–301, 351.

12. Berend and Ranki, *Economic Development*, 118–20, 128–35; Trebilcock, *The Industrialization of the Continental Powers*, 233, 358–59.

13. Berend and Ranki, *Economic Development*, 135–37; idem, *The European Periphery*, 25; Chirot, *Social Change*, 102–3; *Historical Statistics of the United States: From Colonial Times to the Present* (Washington, D.C.: U.S. Department of Commerce, Bureau of the Census, 1962), 74.

14. Berend and Ranki, *Economic Development*, 119, 128, 132; idem, *The European Periphery*, 144.

15. Calculated from Berend and Ranki, *The European Periphery*, 15–16, 158.

16. *Polish Encyclopaedia*, 3 vols. (Geneva: Atar Ltd., 1922), 2:128–46; 3:52–53, 55–57, 250, 404. Also Stefan Kieniewicz, *The Emancipation of Polish Peasantry* (Chicago: University of Chicago Press, 1969), 180–89; Zanna Kormanowa et al., eds., *Historia Polski* (Warsaw: Państwowe Wydawnictwo Naukowe, 1963), vol. 3, pt. 1, 108–9, 193–95, 377, 494, 502, 531–34, 562–67, 601; Irena Kostrowicka et al., *Historia Gospodarcza Polski XIX i XX Wieku* (Warsaw: Książka i Wiedza, 1978), 175, 237; Ewa Morawska, *For Bread with Butter: Lifeworlds of East Central Europeans in Johnstown, Pennsylvania, 1890–1940* (New York: Cambridge University Press, 1985), 26–27.

17. Kormanowa et al., *Historia Polski*, vol. 3, pt. 1, 217–21, 406, 641–52; *Polish Encyclopaedia*, 3:108, 114–15, 263, 377, 418–19, 539; Anna Zarnowska, *Klasa Robotnicza Królestwa Polskiego, 1870–1914* (Warsaw: Państwowe Wydawnictwo Naukowe, 1974), 17–20, 33, 48; Ireneusz Ihnatowicz et al., *Społeczeństwo Polskie od X do XX Wieku* (Warsaw: Książka i Wiedza, 1979), 459–60; Morawska, *For Bread with Butter*, 32–34; Stanisław Jasiczek, "Kapitał Francuski w Przemyśle Górniczo-Hutniczym Zagłębia Dąbrowskiego, 1870–1914," *Zeszyty Naukowe SGPiS* 15 (1959): 77–93; idem, "Kapitat Niemiecki w Przemyśle Górniczo-Hutniczym Zagłębia Dąbrowskiego, *1880–1914*," *Zeszyty Naukowe SGPiS* 19 (1960): 91–113.

18. *Polish Encyclopaedia*, 3:107, 126, 130–39, 201–4; Kormanowa et al., *Historia Polski*, vol. 2, pt. 1, 207–9, 213, 227; Trebilcock, *The Industrialization of the Continental Powers*, 50, 251.

19. Berend and Ranki, *Economic Development*, 137; Brandt, *Inostrannye Kapitaly*, 3:144; Kormanowa et al., *Historia Polski*, vol. 3, pt. 1, 551; *Polish Encyclopaedia*, 3:398.

20. Berend and Ranki, *Economic Development*, 133; Kormanowa et al., *Historia Polski*, vol. 3, pt. 2, 53, 91–92, 118; Kostrowicka et al., *Historia Gospodarcza Polski*, 194, 238.

21. Brandt, *Inostrannye Kapitaly*, 3:73–74, 227–28; *Polish Encyclopaedia*, 3:390–91, 437–38, 555–71.

22. Berend and Ranki, *Fconomic Development*, 121–22; Franciszek Bujak, *Galicja*, 2 vols. (Lvov: H. Altenberg, 1902), 1:392; Herman Diamand, *Położenie Gospodarcze Galicji Przed Wojną* (Leipzig: N.n., 1915), 20.

23. Berend and Ranki, *Economic Development*, 115.

24. Bujak, *Galicja*, 2:239–62, 392; *Polish Encyclopaedia*, 3:267, 294, 343.

25. Diamand, *Położenie Gospodarcze*, 58–61; *Polish Encyclopaedia*, 3:258–59; Yitzhak Schiper, *Dzieje Handlu Żydowskiego na Ziemiach Polskich* (Warsaw: Nakład Centrali Związku Kupców, 1937), 446; Kormanowa et al., *Historia Polski*, vol. 3, pt. 1, 631–38, 543–47, and pt. 2, 168; Kostrowicka et al., *Historia Gospodarcza Polski*, 195.

26. *Polish Encyclopaedia*, 3:263, 258–59, 286–87, 289–91.

27. Ibid., 3:258–59, 263; Kormanowa et al., *Historia Polski*, vol. 3, pt. 2, 164.

28. *Polish Encyclopaedia,* 3:289–91.

29. Ibid., 3:263, 281; cf. Berend and Ranki, *Economic Development,* 130.

30. *Polish Encyclopaedia,* 3:293; see Diamand, *Położenie Gospodarcze,* 101, for an estimation of a triple excess of trade liabilities over assets.

31. Franciszek Bujak, *Maszkienice: Wieś Powiatu Brzeskiego: Rozwój od R. 1900 do R. 1911* (Lvov: G. Gebethner, 1914), 68–73; Elżbieta Kaczyńska, *Społeczeństwo i Gospodarka Północno-Wschodnich Ziem Królestwa Polskiego w Okresie Rozkwitu Kapitalizmu* (Warsaw: Wydawnictwa Uniwersytetu Warszawskiego, 1974), 127–29; Jan Słomka, *From Serfdom to Self-Government: Memoirs of a Polish Village Mayor, 1842–1927* (London: Minerva Publishing Co., 1941), 64. On similar processes in other parts of eastern Europe, see Josef Barton, "Migration as Transition: An Illustration from the Experience of Migrant Miners to North America" (paper delivered at the annual conference of the American Historical Association, Washington, D.C., 28–30 December 1982); Bodnar, *The Transplanted,* 31–33.

32. According to contemporary (unverified) estimates, continental and permanent emigration from all Polish territories before World War I took away nearly 50 percent of the natural population growth (Władysław Grabski, *Materyały w Sprawie Włościańskiej,* 3 vols. [Warsaw: Nakład Gebethnera i Wolffa, 1907], 1:85–87). More recently, eastern European historians have estimated the loss of natural population growth due to emigration for the whole Austro-Hungarian empire at the beginning of the century at 25 percent (Berend and Ranki, *Economic Development,* 20–21).

33. Estimated from Kormanowa et al., *Historia Polski,* vol. 3, pt. 1, 95–98, 102–8; Ihnatowicz et al., *Społeczeństwo Polskie,* 466; Andrzej Pilch, ed., *Emigracja z Ziem Polskich w Czasach Nowożytnich i Najnowszych* (Warsaw: Państwowe Wydawnictwo Naukowe, 1984), 9–11; *Polish Encyclopaedia,* 3:241.

34. Kaczyńska, *Społeczeństwo i Gospodarka,* 31–33, 119–21; Kormanowa et al., *Historia Polski,* vol. 3, pt. 1, 221, 409; Zarnowska, *Klasa Robotnicza,* 111–14, 131; Franciszek Bujak, *Zmiąca: Wieś Powiatu Limanowskiego: Stosunki Gospodarcze i Społeczne* (Kraków: G. Gebethner, 1903), 2:65; Stanisław Pawłowski, *Ludność Rzymsko-Katolicka w Polsko-Ruskiej Części Galicji* (Lvov: Książnica Polska Tow. Naucz. Szkół Wyższych, 1919), 33; Lawrence Schofer, *The Formation of a Modern Labor Force: Upper Silesia, 1865–1914* (Berkeley: University of California Press, 1975), 123–27; Ryszard Turski, *Między Miastem a Wsią: Struktura SpołecznoZawodowa ChłopówRobotników w Polsce* (Warsaw: Państwowe Wydawnictwo Naukowe, 1965), chap. 2.

35. Pilch, *Emigracja z Ziem Polskich.*

36. The numerical volume of migration should be distinguished from its "composition": a third went to the United States in terms of *numbers,* compared to seasonal migrations to nearby Germany that actually involved a large proportion of *the same people* going there year after year.

For comparison, of approximately 14 million emigrants from Italy from 1876 to 1915, only 30 percent went to the United States, while 44 percent migrated to the European countries, and 27 percent to other overseas destinations in Canada, South America, and Africa (Luigi Favero and Graziano Tassello, "Cent'anni di Emigrazione Italiana, 1876–1976," in *Un secolo di emigrazione italiana, 1876–1976,* ed. Gianfausto Rosoli [Rome: Centro Studi Emigrazione, 1980], 19).

37. Wolfgang Köllmann and Peter Marschalck, "German Emigration to the United States," *Perspectives in American History* 7, *Dislocation and Emigration: The Social Background of American Immigration* (1973): 518; Walter Willcox and Imre Ferenczi, *International Migrations,* 2 vols. (New York: National Bureau of Economic Research, 1929), 2:316–36.

38. Bade, "German Emigration to the U.S.," 123–25; Trebilcock, *The Industrialization of the Continental Powers,* 54.

39. On the role of employment agents in the recruitment of Polish labor to Germany from all three partitions, see Christoph Klessmann, "Long Distance Migration, Integra-

tion and Segregation of an Ethnic Minority in Industrial Germany: The Case of the Ruhr-Poles," in *Population, Labour and Migration in 19th and 20th Century Germany*, ed. Klaus Bade (New York: St. Martin's Press, 1986), 101; Schofer, *The Formation of a Modern Labor Force*, 73; Elaine Spencer, *Management and Labor in Imperial Germany: Ruhr Industrialists as Employers, 1896–1914* (New Brunswick: Rutgers University Press, 1984), 40–43; Krzysztof Groniowski, "Emigracja z Ziem Zaboru Rosyjskiego, 1864–1918," in *Emigracja z Ziem Polskich w Czasach Nowożytnich i Najnowszych*, ed. Andrzej Pilch (Warsaw: Państwowe Wydawnictwo Naukowe, 1984), 216; Klaus Bade, "Massenwanderung und Arbeitsmarkt im Deutschen Nordosten von 1880 bis zum Ersten Weltkrieg," *Archiv für Sozialgeschichte* 20 (1980): 265–323, 313–20; Andrzej Pilch, "Emigracja z Ziem Zaboru Austriackiego (od połowy XIXw do 1918)," in *Emigracja z Ziem Polskich w Czasach Nowożytnich i Najnowszych*, ed. Andrzej Pilch (Warsaw: Państwowe Wydawnictwo Naukowe, 1984[a]), 286; Witold Nowosz, "Tradycyjne Gospodarstwo Chłopskie i Jego Przemiany," *Prace i Materiały Muzeum Archeologicznego i Etnograficznego w Łodzi* 18 (1976): 110; Leopold Caro, *Emigracja i Polityka Emigracyjna* (Poznań: Św. Wojciech, 1914), 262–71.

40. Klaus Bade, " 'Preußengänger' und 'Abwehrpolitik': Ausländerbeschäftigung, Ausländerpolitik und Ausländerkontrolle auf dem Arbeitsmarkt in Preußen vor dem Ersten Weltkrieg," *Archiv für Sozialgeschichte* 24 (1984): 140–43; Schofer, *The Formation of a Modern Labor Force*, 60; Willcox and Ferenczi, *International Migrations*, 2:378–79.

41. Bade, " 'Preußengänger' und 'Abwehrpolitik'," 140–46; Kormanowa et al., *Historia Polski*, pt. 1, 107, and pt. 2, 777–78; Willcox and Ferenczi, *International Migrations*, 1:789, and 2:380; Groniowski, "Emigracja z Ziem Zaboru Rosyjskiego," 214–19.

42. Cited after Bade, "German Emigration to the U.S.," 133. See also Klaus Bade, "Migration and Foreign Labour in Imperial Germany and Weimar Germany" (paper delivered at the conference, "A Century of European Migrations, 1830–1930: Comparative Perspectives," Immigration History Research Center, St. Paul, Minnesota, 6–9 November 1986), 8; Caro, *Emigracja i Polityka Emigracyjna*, 260; *Polish Encyclopaedia*, 2:96–97, 220; Kormanowa et al., *Historia Polski*, vol. 3, pt. 2, 764.

43. Christoph Klessmann, *Polnische Bergarbeiter in Ruhrgebiet, 1870–1945* (Göttingen: Vandenhoek and Rupprecht, 1978), 262, 265; idem, "Polish Miners in the Ruhr District: Their Social Situation and Trade Union Activity," in *Labor Migration in the Atlantic Economies*, ed. Dirk Hoerder (Westport: Greenwood Press, 1985), 259; Spencer, *Management and Labor in Imperial Germany*, 44.

44. Gould, "European Inter-Continental Immigration," 633; Jeffrey Williamson, "Migration to the New World: Long Term Influences and Impact," *Explorations in Economic History* 11, no. 4 (Summer 1974), 331.

45. Harold Wool and Bruce Phillips, *The Labor Supply for Lower Level Occupations* (New York: Praeger, 1976), 45–54.

46. Berend and Ranki, *Economic Development*, 20–21.

47. Emily Balch, *Our Slavic Fellow Citizens* (New York: Charities Publication Committee, 1910; reprint, New York: Arno Press, 1969), 265, 460–61; Willcox and Ferenczi, *International Migrations*, 1:418–39; Pilch, *Emigracja z Ziem Polskich*, 9–11. Polish estimates are considerably higher—up to 3–3.5 million, but they often include Rusyns (Ukrainians) and Jews. For a discussion of these, see Andrzej Brożek, *Polonia Amerykańska, 1854–1939* (Warsaw: Interpress, 1977), 35.

48. Piore, *Birds of Passage*, 23–25, 152–53.

49. Cited after Pilch, "Emigracja z Ziem Zaboru Austriackiego," 260.

50. On the role of transportation agents in instigating emigration to America from the Polish countryside, see Caro, *Emigracja i Polityka Emigracyjna*, 82–95.

51. Balch, *Our Slavic Fellow Citizens*, 52–53.

52. On the precipitating function of "previous migration" as a variable in the economic models of immigration to the United States, see Gould, "European Inter-Continental Immigration," 654–62.

53. Balch, *Our Slavic Fellow Citizens*, 133; Brożek, *Polonia Amerykańska*, 224; Groniowski, "Emigracja z Ziem Zaboru Rosyjskiego," 203; Mieczysław Szawleski, *Wychodźstwo Polski w Stanach Zjednoczonych* (Lvov: Wydawnictwo Zakładu Narodowego im. Ossolińskich, 1924), 15–17; Willcox and Ferenczi, *International Migrations*, 1:480–83. The estimated proportions for the Russian, Prussian, and Austrian partitions are 8 percent, 5 percent, and 7 percent, respectively.

54. *Abstracts of the Reports of the Immigration Commission*, 2 vols. (Washington, D.C.: U.S. Government Printing Office, 1911), 1:358; Grabski, *Materyały w Sprawie Włościańskiej*, 3:83–84; Kaczyńska, *Społeczeństwo i Gospodarka*, 145; *Polish Encyclopaedia*, 2:150; Józef Okołowicz, *Wychodźstwo i Osadnictwo Polskie przed Wojną Światową* (Warsaw: Nakł. Urzędu Emigracyjnego, 1920), 25; Pilch, "Emigracja z Ziem Zaboru Austriackiego," 271.

55. Balch, *Our Slavic Fellow Citizens*, 263–64; Brożek, *Polonia Amerykańska*, 38–40; *Abstracts of the Reports of the Immigration Commission*, 1:364.

56. Calculated from Willcox and Ferenczi, *International Migrations*, 1:787–88.

57. Groniowski, "Emigracja z Ziem Zaboru Rosyjskiego," 202; *Polish Encyclopaedia*, 3:241. M. Simon estimates the proportion of all immigrant departures from the United States in that period as 45 percent (M. Simon, "The U.S. Balance of Payments, 1861–1900," in *Trends in the American Economy in the Nineteenth Century*, National Bureau of Economic Research Studies in Income and Wealth, no. 24 [New York: Ballinger, 1960], 664–66, 690).

58. Grabski, *Materyały w Sprawie Włościańskiej*, 1:87–88; J. D. Gould, "European Inter-Continental Emigration: The Road Home: Return Migration from the U.S.A.," *Journal of European Economic History* 9, no. 1 (Spring 1980): 41–113; Charles Price, "Methods of Estimating Size of Groups," *Harvard Encyclopedia of American Ethnic Groups* (Cambridge, Mass.: Belknap Press, 1980); Dirk Hoerder, "Immigration and the Working Class: The Reemigration Factor," *International Labor and Working Class History* 21 (Spring 1982): 28–41. Interestingly, returns to the much poorer Austrian section of Poland were considerably more frequent (40 percent) than to the more economically developed Russian partition (25 percent). (See Grabski, *Materyały w Sprawie Włościańskiej*, 1:87–88; Willcox and Ferenczi, *International Migrations*, 1:423, 477, 483, 488.) This might have been because in Russian Poland there were more wholly landless peasants who did not have anything to return to, whereas in the Austrian section dwarf and smallholders predominated, still strongly attached to the land that the migrants returning with savings wanted to keep and enlarge. It could also have been that peasants from the more economically backward Austrian Poland were more strongly traditional in their outlooks, and that their adaptation to America was therefore more difficult than for the immigrants from the Russian and Prussian sections. Unfortunately, there are no studies in the Polish-American literature that investigate this interesting problem. There exists, however, some information (John Bodnar, Michael Weber, and Roger Simon, *Lives of Their Own* [Urbana: University of Illinois Press, 1982]) indicating that immigrants from Prussian Poland adapted more successfully than others. They also had the lowest return rates as reported in American statistics from 1908 on, but then, since they were the first to arrive (most of the Prussian Poles came to the United States during the 1870s and 1880s in the wave of mass German immigration), they had already been in this country for several years.

59. Balch, *Our Slavic Fellow Citizens*, 464; Morawska, *For Bread with Butter*, 39.

60. Alejandro Portes and Robert Bach, *Latin Journey: Cuban and Mexican Immigrants in the United States* (Berkeley: University of California Press, 1985), 32–34.

61. Fernand Braudel, *Civilization and Capitalism, 15th–18th Centuries*, 3 vols. (New York: Harper and Row, 1981).

62. Bujak, *Maszkienice: Wieś Powiatu Brzeskiego: Rozwój . . .*, 106. On the role of the railways in bringing Polish villages "into the world," see also Krystyna Duda-Dziewierz, *Wieś Małopolska a Emigracja Amerykańska: Studium Wsi Babica Pow. Rzeszowskiego* (Warsaw: Polski Instytut Socjologiczny, 1938), 27.

63. Franciszek Bujak, *Maszkienice: Wieś Powiatu Brzeskiego: Stosunki Gospodarcze i Społeczne* (Kraków: G. Gebethner, 1901), 17–25, 45–47; idem, *Zmiąca*, 62–63.

64. Cited after Klessmann, "Long Distance Migration," 101.

65. Bujak, *Maszkienice: Wieś Powiatu Brzeskiego: Stosunki . . .*, 46–54.

66. Bujak, *Maszkienice: Wieś Powiatu Brzeskiego: Rozwój . . .*, 76–77, 86.

67. Władysław Przybysławski, *Uniż: Wieś Powiatu Horodelskiego* (Warsaw: Państwowy Instytut Naukowy Gospodarstwa Wiejskiego w Puławach, 1933), 1–12, 60–67; Józef Obrębski, *The Changing Peasantry of Eastern Europe* (Cambridge, Mass.: Schenkman, 1976), 29–30, 39–40, 50–56.

68. Groniowski, "Emigracja z Ziem Zaboru Rosyjskiego," 199–202, 213–14.

69. Bujak, *Maszkienice: Wieś Powiatu Brzeskiego: Stosunki . . .*, 46, 54.

70. Bujak, *Maszkienice: Wieś Powiatu Brzeskiego: Rozwój . . .*, 86, 88–91.

71. Maria Misińska, "Podhale Dawne i Współczesne," *Prace i Materiały Muzeum Archeologicznego i Etnograficznego w Łodzi* 13 (1971): 33–40, 44–45.

72. Ibid., 36; Morawska, *For Bread with Butter*, 65; Pilch, "Emigracja z Ziem Zaboru Austriackiego," 286.

73. Jan Milczarek, "Emigracja Zarobkowa z Wieluńskiego," *Łodzkie Studia Etnograficzne* 19 (1977): 141–44; Irena Lechowa, "Tradycje Emigracyjne w Klonowej," *Prace i Materiały Muzeum Archeologicznego i Etnograficznego w Łodzi* 3 (1961): 44–47; Kaczyńska, *Społeczeństwo i Gospodarka*, 140.

74. Bujak, *Maszkienice: Wieś Powiatu Brzeskiego: Stosunki . . .*, 54.

75. Ibid., 89.

76. Bujak, *Zmiąca*, 99–100.

77. Bujak, *Maszkienice: Wieś Powiatu Brzeskiego: Rozwój . . .*, 93–94.

78. Bujak, *Maszkienice: Wieś Powiatu Brzeskiego: Stosunki . . .*, 50–55; idem, *Maszkienice: Wieś Powiatu Brzeskiego: Rozwój . . .*, 93, 96–98; Misińska, "Podhale Dawne i Współczesne," 30–37.

79. Duda-Dziewierz, *Wieś Małopolska a Emigracja Amerykańska*, 23–28.

80. Bujak, *Maszkienice: Wieś Powiatu Brzeskiego: Stosunki . . .*, 54; idem, *Maszkienice: Wieś Powiatu Brzeskiego: Rozwój . . .*, 94.

81. Frank Sheridan, "Italian, Slavic and Hungarian Unskilled Immigrant Laborers in the United States," in U.S. Department of Commerce and Labor, *Bulletin of the Bureau of Labor* 72 (Washington, D.C.: U.S. Government Printing Office, September 1907): 407–8.

82. Duda-Dziewierz, *Wieś Małopolska a Emigracja Amerykańska*, 57.

83. Bujak, *Maszkienice: Wieś Powiatu Brzeskiego: Rozwój . . .*, 87–88; idem, *Zmiąca*, 100.

84. Franciszek Guściora, *Trzy Kurzyny: Wsie Powiatu Niskiego* (Warsaw: Państwowy Instytut Naukowy Gospodarstwa Wiejskiego w Puławach, 1929), 74; Maria Gliwicówna, *Drogi Emigracji* (Warsaw: Polski Instytut Socjologiczny, 1937), 507–9.

85. Witold Kula, Nina Assorodobraj-Kula, and Marcin Kula, eds., *Listy Emigrantów z Brazylii i Stanów Zjednoczonych* (Warsaw: Ludowa Spółdzielnia Wydawnicza, 1973; English translation, without authors' introduction, by Josephine Wtulich, ed. and trans., *Writing Home: Immigrants in Brazil and the United States* [Boulder, Colo.: East European Monographs; New York: distributed by Columbia University Press, 1986]); Marek M. Drozdowski, ed., *Pamiętniki Emigrantów ze Stanów Zjednoczonych*, 2 vols. (Warsaw: Książka i Wiedza, 1977).

86. Duda-Dziewierz, *Wieś Małopolska a Emigracja Amerykańska*, 61.

87. William I. Thomas and Florian Znaniecki, *The Polish Peasant in Europe and America*, 5 vols. (Boston: Richard G. Badger, 1918–20), 2:300.

88. Duda-Dziewierz, *Wieś Małopolska a Emigracja Amerykańska*, 95.

89. Kula et al., *Listy Emigrantów z Brazylii i Stanów Zjednoczonych*, Introduction, 57.

90. Duda-Dziewierz, *Wieś Małopolska a Emigracja Amerykańska*, 27–28, 69; Jerzy Fierich, *Broniszów: Wieś Powiatu Ropczyckiego* (Warsaw: Państwowy Instytut Naukowy Gos-

podarstwa Wiejskiego w Puławach, 1929), 53–57; Zdzisław Wierzbicki, *Żmiąca Pół Wieku Później* (Warsaw: Zakład Narodowy im. Ossolińskich, 1963), 67.

91. On this issue, see Kritz et al., *Global Trends in Migration*, Introduction.

92. Balch, *Our Slavic Fellow Citizens*, 471–72.

93. Grabski, *Materyały w Sprawie Włościańskiej*, 3:91.

94. Okołowicz, *Wychodźstwo i Osadnictwo Polskie przed Wojną Światową*, 280; Balch, *Our Slavic Fellow Citizens*, 471–72.

95. Caro, *Emigracja i Polityka Emigracyjna*, 77; Stanislaw Hupka, *Über die Entwicklung der westgalizischen Dorfzustände in der 2. Hälfte des XIX Jahrhunderts* (Teschen: Buchdr. P. Mitrega, 1911), 192–225; Okołowicz *Wychodźstwo i Osadnictwo Polskie przed Wojną Światową*, 280. Of course, labor-migration capital also flew in the opposite direction—out of the sending societies, as the emigrants purchased tickets to travel and took money with them for their journeys. Generally, however, the balance was positive on the incoming side. For instance, in that same year, 1902, the total amount of money that came from labor migrations to the Austrian part of the Hapsburg monarchy equaled $28 million, and the capital exported by emigrants was $13 million, leaving a balance of $15 million (Caro, *Emigracja i Polityka Emigracyjna*, 69–72; Grabski, *Materyały w Sprawie Włościańskiej*, 3:91). Similarly, in 1903, emigrants from the Austrian part of Poland took out $2.5 million, but sent or brought back $7.5 million (Pilch, "Emigracja z Ziem Zaboru Austriackiego," 276–77).

96. Bujak, *Maszkienice: Wieś Powiatu Brzeskiego: Stosunki . . .*, 49–50; idem, *Maszkienice: Wieś Powiatu Brzeskiego: Rozwój . . .*, 102–5.

97. Lechowa, "Tradycje Emigracyjne w Klonowej," 65.

98. Hupka, *Über die Entwicklung der westgalizischen Dorfzustände*, 210; Fierich, *Broniszów: Wieś Powiatu Ropczyckiego*, 55–56.

99. Bujak, *Maszkienice: Wieś Powiatu Brzeskiego: Rozwój . . .*, 101–5.

100. Duda-Dziewierz, *Wieś Małopolska a Emigracja Amerykańska*, 79–86.

101. Kula et al./Wtulich, *Listy Emigrantów z Brazylii i Stanów Zjednoczonych*, 350.

102. Wincenty Witos, *Moje Wspomnienia*, 2 vols. (Paris: Instytut Literacki, 1964), 1:188.

103. Edward Steiner, *On the Trail of the Immigrant* (New York: Revell, 1906; reprint, New York: Arno Press, 1969), 340.

References

Abstracts of the Reports of the Immigration Commission. 2 vols. Washington, D.C.: U.S. Government Printing Office, 1911.

Bade, Klaus. "Massenwanderung und Arbeitsmarkt im Deutschen Nordosten von 1880 bis zum Ersten Weltkrieg." *Archiv für Sozialgeschichte* 20 (1980): 265–323.

———. " 'Preußengänger' und 'Abwehrpolitik': Ausländerbeschäftigung. Ausländerpolitik und Ausländerkontrolle auf dem Arbeitsmarkt in Preußen vor dem Ersten Weltkrieg." *Archiv für Sozialgeschichte* 24 (1984): 91–273.

———. "German Emigration to the U.S. and Continental Immigration to Germany in the Late 19th and Early 20th Centuries." In *Labor Migration in the Atlantic Economies*, ed. Dirk Hoerder, 117–43. Westport, Conn.: Greenwood Press, 1985.

———. "Migration and Foreign Labour in Imperial Germany and Weimar Germany." Paper delivered at the conference, "A Century of European Migrations, 1830–1930: Comparative Perspectives," Immigration History Research Center, St. Paul, Minn., 6–9 November 1986.

Balch, Emily. *Our Slavic Fellow Citizens*. New York: Charities Publication Committee, 1910. Reprint, New York: Arno Press, 1969.

Barton, Josef. "Migration as Transition: An Illustration from the Experience of Migrant Miners to North America." Paper delivered at the annual conference of the American Historical Association, Washington, D.C., 28–30 December 1982.

Berend, T. Ivan, and György Ranki. *Economic Development in East Central Europe in the 19th and 20th Centuries*. New York: Columbia University Press, 1974.

———. *The European Periphery and Industrialization, 1780–1914*. New York: Cambridge University Press, 1982.

Bobińska, Celina, and Andrzej Pilch, eds. *Employment-Seeking Emigrations of the Poles World Wide, XIXc and XXc*. Kraków: Państwowe Wydawnictwo Naukowe, 1975.

Bodnar, John. *The Transplanted: A History of Immigrants in Urban America*. Bloomington: Indiana University Press, 1985.

Bodnar, John, Michael Weber, and Roger Simon. *Lives of their Own*. Urbana: University of Illinois Press, 1982.

Brandt, Boris Filipovich. *Inostrannye Kapitaly, lkh Vlijanie na Ekonomicheskoe Razvite Stravy*. 2 vols. St. Petersburg: V. Kirpbayma, 1901.

Braudel, Fernand. *Civilization and Capitalism, 15th–18th Centuries*. 3 vols. New York: Harper and Row, 1981.

Brożek, Andrzej. *Polonia Amerykańska, 1854–1939*. Warsaw: Interpress, 1977.

———. "Ruchy Migracyjne z Ziem Polskich pod Panowaniem Pruskim w Latach 1850–1918." In *Emigracja z Ziem Polskich w Czasach Nowożytnich i Najnowszych*, ed. A. Pilch, 141–96. Warsaw: Państwowe Wydawnictwo Naukowe, 1984.

———. "Partitioned Poland as a Land of Migrations." Paper delivered at the conference, "A Century of European Migrations, 1830–1930: Comparative Perspectives," Immigration History Research Center, St. Paul, Minn., 6–9 November 1986.

Bujak, Franciszek. *Maszkienice: Wieś Powiatu Brzeskiego: Stosunki Gospodarcze i Społeczne*. Kraków: G. Gebethner, 1901.

———. *Galicja*. 2 vols. Lvov: H. Altenberg, 1902.

———. *Zmiąca. Wieś Powiatu Limanowskiego: Stosunki Gospodarcze i Społeczne*. Kraków: G. Gebethner, 1903.

———. *Maskienice: Wieś Powiatu Brzeskiego: Rozwój od R. 1900 do R. 1911*. Lvov: G. Gebethner, 1914.

Cardoso, F. H., and E. Faletto, eds. "Preface to the English Edition." In *Dependency and Development in Latin America*, vii–xxv. Berkeley: University of California Press, 1979.

Caro, Leopold. *Emigracja i Polityka Emigracyjna*. Poznań: Św. Wojciech, 1914.

Castells, M. "Immigrant Workers and Class Struggles in Advanced Capitalism: The Western European Experience." *Politics and Society* 5, no. 1 (1975): 33–66.

Chirot, Daniel. *Social Change in the Modern Era*. San Diego: Harcourt Brace Jovanovich, 1986.

Diamand, Herman. *Położenie Gospodarcze Galicji Przed Wojną*. Leipzig: N.n., 1915.

Drozdowski, Marek M., ed. *Pamiętniki Emigrantów ze Stanów Zjednoczonych*. 2 vols. Warsaw: Książka i Wiedza, 1977.

Duda-Dziewierz, Krystyna. *Wieś Małopolska a Emigracja Amerykańska. Studium Wsi Babica Pow. Rzeszowskiego*. Warsaw: Polski Instytut Socjologiczny, 1938.

Ekmečić, Milorad. "The International and Intercontinental Migrational Movements from the Yugoslav Lands from the End of the XVIIIth Century till 1941." In *Les Migrations internationales de la fin du XVIIIe siècle à nos jours*, 564–94. Paris: Editions du Centre National de la Recherche Scientifique, 1980.

Favero, Luigi, and Graziano Tassello. "Cent'anni de Emigrazione Italiana, 1876–1976." In *Un secolo di emigrazione italiana, 1876–1976*, ed. Gianfausto Rosoli, 9–64. Rome: Centro Studi Emigrazione, 1980.

Fierich, Jerzy. *Broniszów: Wieś Powiatu Ropczyckiego*. Warsaw: Państwowy Instytut Naukowy Gospodarstwa Wiejskiego w Puławach, 1929.

Gefter, M. R. "Iz Istorri Proniknovenia Amerikanskogo Kapitala v Carskuiu Rossiu do Pervoi Mirovoi Voiny." *Istoricheskie Zapiski* 35 (1950): 62–86.

Gerschenkron, Alexander. *Economic Backwardness in Historical Perspective*. Cambridge: Belknap Press of Harvard University Press, 1962.

Gliwicówna, Maria. *Drogi Emigracji*. Warsaw: Polski Instytut Socjologiczny, 1937.

Gould, J. D. "European Inter-Continental Emigration, 1815–1914: Patterns and Causes." *Journal of European Economic History* 8, no. 3 (Winter 1979): 593–681.

———. "European Inter-Continental Emigration: The Road Home: Return Migration from the U.S.A." *Journal of European Economic History* 9, no. 1 (Spring 1980): 41–113.

Grabski, Władysław. *Materyały w Sprawie Włościańskiej*. 3 vols. Warsaw: Nakład Gebethnera i Wolffa, 1907.

Groniowski, Krzysztof. "Emigracja z Ziem Zaboru Rosyjskiego, 1864–1918." In *Emigracja z Ziem Polskich w Czasach Nowożytnich i Najnowszych*, ed. Andrzej Pilch, 196–252. Warsaw: Państwowe Wydawnictwo Naukowe, 1984.

Guściora, Franciszek. *Trzy Kurzyny. Wsie Powiatu Niskiego*. Warsaw: Państwowy Instytut Naukowy Gospodarstwa Wiejskiego w Puławach, 1929.

Historical Statistics of the United States: From Colonial Times to the Present. Washington, D.C.: U.S. Department of Commerce, Bureau of the Census, 1962.

Hoerder, Dirk. "Immigration and the Working Class: The Reemigration Factor." *International Labor and Working Class History* 21 (Spring 1982): 28–41.

———, ed. *Labor Migration in the Atlantic Economies: The European and North American Working Classes during the Period of Industrialization*. Westport, Conn.: Greenwood Press, 1985.

Hupka, Stanisław. *Über die Entwicklung der westgalizischen Dorfzustände in der 2. Hälfte des XIX Jahrhunderts*. Teschen: Buchdr. P. Mitrega, 1911.

Ihnatowicz, Ireneusz. "Z Badań nad Kapitałem Obcym w Przemyśle Lódzkim w Latach 1860–1880." *Kwartalnik Historyczny* 63, nos. 4–5 (1956): 245–54.

Ihnatowicz, Ireneusz, et al. *Społeczeństwo Polskie od X do XX Wieku*. Warsaw: Książka i Wiedza, 1979.

Jasiczek, Stanisław. "Kapitał Francuski w Przemyśle Górniczo-Hutniczym Zagłębia Dąbrowskiego, 1870–1914." *Zeszyty Naukowe SGPiS* 15 (1959): 77–93.

———. "Kapitał Niemiecki w Przemyśle Górniczo-Hutniczym Zagłębia Dąbrowskiego, 1880–1914." *Zeszyty Naukowe SGPiS* 19 (1960): 91–118.

Jerome, Harry. *Migration and Business Cycles*. New York: National Bureau of Economic Research, 1926.

Kaczyńska, Elżbieta. *Dzieje Robotników Przemysłowych w Polsce pod Zaborami*. Warsaw: Państwowe Wydawnictwo Naukowe, 1970.

———. *Społeczeństwo i Gospodarka Północno-Wschodnich Ziem Królestwa Polskiego w Okresie Rozkwitu Kapitalizmu*. Warsaw: Wydawnictwa Uniwersytetu Warszawskiego, 1974.

Kieniewicz, Stefan. *The Emancipation of Polish Peasantry*. Chicago: University of Chicago Press, 1969.

Klessmann, Christoph. *Polnische Bergarbeiter in Ruhrgebiet, 1870–1945*. Göttingen: Vandenhoek and Rupprecht, 1978.

———. "Polish Miners in the Ruhr District: Their Social Situation and Trade Union Activity." In *Labor Migration in the Atlantic Economies*, ed. Dirk Hoerder, 253–75. Westport, Conn.: Greenwood Press, 1985.

———. "Long Distance Migration, Integration and Segregation of an Ethnic Minority in Industrial Germany: The Case of the Ruhr-Poles." In *Population, Labour and Migration in 19th and 20th Century Germany*, ed. Klaus Bade, 101–14. New York: St. Martin's Press, 1986.

Köllmann, Wolfgang, and Peter Marschalck. "German Emigration to the United States." In

Perspectives in American History 7, *Dislocation and Emigration: The Social Background of American Immigration* (1973): 499–544.

Kormanowa, Zanna, et al., eds. *Historia Polski.* pts. 1 and 2, 1850/1864–1918. Warsaw: Państwowe Wydawnictwo Naukowe, 1963.

Kostrowicka, Irena, et al. *Historia Gospodarcza Polski XIX i XX Wieku.* Warsaw: Książka i Wiedza, 1978.

Kritz, Mary, et al., eds. *Global Trends in Migration: Theory and Research on International Population Movements.* New York: Center for Migration Studies, 1983.

Kula, Witold, Nina Assorodobraj-Kula, and Marcin Kula, eds. *Listy Emigrantów z Brazylii i Stanów Zjednoczonych.* Warsaw: Ludowa Spółdzielnia Wydawnicza, 1973. English translation without authors' introduction: Josephine Wtulich, ed. and trans. *Writing Home: Immigrants in Brazil and the United States.* Boulder, Colo.: East European Monographs; New York: Dist. by Columbia University Press, 1986.

Lechowa, Irena. "Tradycje Emigracyjne w Klonowej." *Prace i Materiały Muzeum Archeologicznego i Etnograficznego w Łodzi* 3 (1961): 43–73.

Milczarek, Jan. "Emigracja Zarobkowa z Wieluńskiego." *Łodzkie Studia Etnograficzne* 19 (1977): 5–29.

Milward, Alan, and S. B. Saul. *The Economic Development of Continental Europe, 1780–1870.* London: Allen and Unwin, 1973.

Misińska, Maria. "Podhale Dawne i Współczesne." *Prace i Materiały Muzeum Archeologicznego i Etnograficznego w Łodzi* 13 (1971): 33–70.

Morawska, Ewa. *For Bread with Butter: Lifeworlds of East Central Europeans in Johnstown, Pennsylvania, 1890–1940.* New York: Cambridge University Press, 1985.

Nowosz, Witold. "Tradycyjne Gospodarstwo Chłopskie i Jego Przemiany." *Prace i Materiały Muzeum Archeologicznego i Etnograficznego w Łodzi* 18 (1976): 85–177.

Obręski, Józef. *The Changing Peasantry of Eastern Europe.* Cambridge, Mass.: Schenkman, 1976.

Okołowicz, Józef. *Wychodźstwo i Osadnictwo Polskie przed Wojną Światową.* Warsaw: Nakł. Urzędu Emigracyjnego, 1920.

Pawłowski, Stanisław. *Ludność Rzymsko-Katolicka w Polsko-Ruskiej Cząści Galicji.* Lvov: Książnica Polska Tow. Naucz. Szkół Wyższych, 1919.

Pietrzak-Pawłowska, Irena. "Z Dziejów Monopolizacji Górnictwa i Hutnictwa w Królestwie Polskim." *Kwartalnik Historyczny* 83, no. 2 (1956): 341–67.

Pilch, Andrzej, ed. *Emigracja z Ziem Polskich w Czasach Nowożytnich i Najnowszych.* Warsaw: Państwowe Wydawnictwo Naukowe, 1984.

———. "Emigracja z Ziem Zaboru Austriackiego (od połowy XIXw do 1918)." In *Emigracja z Ziem Polskich w Czasach Nowożytnich,* ed. Andrzej Pilch, 252–326. Warsaw: Państwowe Wydawnictwo Naukowe, 1984a.

Piore, Michael. *Birds of Passage: Migrant Labor and Industrial Societies.* New York and Cambridge: Cambridge University Press, 1979.

Polish Encyclopaedia. 3 vols. Geneva: Atar Ltd., 1922.

Pollard, Sidney. "Industrialization and the European Economy." *The Economic History Review,* 2d series, 26, no. 4 (1973): 636–49.

Portes, Alejandro. "Migration and Underdevelopment." *Politics and Society* 8, no. 1 (1978): 1–48.

Portes, Alejandro, and Robert Bach. *Latin Journey: Cuban and Mexican Immigrants in the United States.* Berkeley: University of California Press, 1985.

Portes, Alejandro, and John Walton. *Labor, Class and International System.* New York: Academic Press, 1981.

Price, Charles. "Methods of Estimating Size of Groups." *Harvard Encyclopedia of American Ethnic Groups,* app. 1, 1033–44. Cambridge, Mass.: Belknap Press, 1980.

Przybysławski, Władysław. *Uniż: Wieś Powiatu Horodelskiego.* Warsaw: Państwowy Instytut Naukowy Gospodarstwa Wiejskiego w Puławach, 1933.

Puskás, Julianna. *From Hungary to the United States, 1880–1914.* Budapest: Akademiai Kiado, 1982.

Rosoli, Gianfausto, ed. *Un secolo di emigrazione italiana, 1876–1976.* Rome: Centro Studi Emigrazione, 1980.

Sassen-Koob, Saskia. "The Internalization of the Labor Force." *Studies in Comparative International Development* 15, no. 4 (Winter 1980): 3–26.

Schiper, Yitzhak. *Dzieje Handlu Żydowskiego na Ziemiach Polskich.* Warsaw: Nakład Centrali Związku Kupców, 1937.

Schofer, Lawrence. *The Formation of a Modern Labor Force: Upper Silesia, 1865–1914.* Berkeley: University of California Press, 1975.

Sheridan, Frank. "Italian, Slavic and Hungarian Unskilled Immigrant Laborers in the United States," 403–86. U.S. Department of Commerce and Labor, *Bulletin of the Bureau of Labor* 72. Washington, D.C.: U.S. Government Printing Office, September 1907.

Simon, M. "The U.S. Balance of Payments, 1861–1900." *Trends in the American Economy in the Nineteenth Century,* 629–715. National Bureau of Economic Research Studies in Income and Wealth, no. 24. New York: Ballinger, 1960.

Słomka, Jan. *From Serfdom to Self-Government: Memoirs of a Polish Village Mayor, 1842–1927.* London: Minerva Publishing Co., 1941.

Spencer, Elaine. *Management and Labor in Imperial Germany: Ruhr Industrialists as Employers, 1896–1914.* New Brunswick, N.J.: Rutgers University Press, 1984.

Steiner, Edward. *On the Trail of the Immigrant.* New York: Revell, 1906. Reprint, New York: Arno Press, 1969.

Szawleski, Mieczysław. *Wychodźstwo Polski w Stanach Zjednoczonych.* Lvov: Wydawnictwo Zakładu Narodowego im. Ossolińskich, 1924.

Thomas, Brinley. *Migration and Economic Growth.* New York and Cambridge: Cambridge University Press, 1973.

Thomas, William I., and Florian Znaniecki. *The Polish Peasant in Europe and America.* 5 vols. Boston: Richard G. Badger, 1918–20.

Trebilcock, Clive. *The Industrialization of the Continental Powers, 1780–1914.* New York: Longman, 1981.

Turski, Ryszard. *Między Miastem a Wsią: Struktura SpołecznoZawodowa ChłopówRobotników w Polsce.* Warsaw: Państwowe Wydawnictwo Naukowe, 1965.

Wallerstein, Immanuel. "Periphery in the Era of Slow Growth," and "Semiperipheries at the Crossroads." *The Modern World-System II.* New York: Academic Press, 1980.

Wierzbicki, Zdzisław. *Żmiąca Pół Wieku Później.* Warsaw: Zakład Narodowy im. Ossolińskich, 1963.

Willcox, Walter, and Imre Ferenczi. *International Migrations.* 2 vols. New York: National Bureau of Economic Research, 1929.

Williamson, Jeffrey. "Migration to the New World: Long Term Influences and Impact." *Explorations in Economic History* 11, no. 4 (Summer 1974), 357–89.

Witos, Wincenty. *Moje Wspomnienia.* 2 vols. Paris: Instytut Literacki, 1964.

Wood, Charles. "Equilibrium and Historical-Structural Perspectives on Migration." *International Migration Review* 16, no. 2 (Summer 1982): 298–319.

Wool, Harold, and Bruce Phillips. *The Labor Supply for Lower Level Occupations.* New York: Praeger, 1976.

Zarnowska, Anna. *Klasa Robotnicza Królestwa Polskiego, 1870–1914.* Warsaw: Państwowe Wydawnictwo Naukowe, 1974.

Zientara, Benedykt, et al. *Dzieje Gospodarcze Polski do 1939.* Warsaw: Wiedza Powszechna, 1965.

PART III

Approaches to Acculturation: Comparative Perspectives

From Migrants to Ethnics:

Acculturation in a Societal Framework

DIRK HOERDER

Prior to their interface with the new society, migrants will have experienced two formative phases in their lives. The first, socialization in the home culture, provides them with the cultural baggage which they carry with them. The second, the transition or voyage, comprises the slow mental weaning from their particular "old-world" village, town, or city; the decision to leave and the actual departure; the travel itself; and, finally, the sometimes jarring procedures of admission. Only then does acculturation begin.

In his classic study of the entry of migrants into the United States, Milton Gordon argued that "assimilation" proceeds in seven stages, from cultural or behavioral assimilation to civic assimilation.[1] As was customary at the time of his writing, he paid little attention to the culture of origin but took prior cultural formation for granted. Concerning terminology and concepts, Gordon quoted the mid-1930s definition of the Social Science Research Council: "[Acculturation] comprehends those phenomena which result when groups of individuals having different cultures come into continuous first-hand contact, with subsequent changes in the original cultural patterns of either or both groups."[2] For his own usage, Gordon reverted to the definition of "assimilation" by Park and Burgess.[3]

In an equally important discussion of immigrant "adaptation" published ten years after Gordon and based on a study of in-migration into metropolitan Toronto, Canadian sociologists Anthony Richmond and John Goldlust developed a more complex "multivariate model" in which they included premigration characteristics, discussed the objective and subjective aspects of the process, and differentiated between groups of migrants by length of residence. They defined "adaptation" as "the mutual interaction of individuals and collectives and their response to particular physical and social environments."[4] John Bodnar, in his study of Steelton, Pennsylvania, immigrants over seven decades (1870–1940), found "accommodation" between old customs or values and the new culture rather than a simple "change of cultural patterns to those of the host society."[5] Referring to Oscar Handlin's notion of immigrant uprootedness, Bodnar argued:

> Transition from preindustrial to industrial society involved a process of accommodation rather than of uprooting. After several decades in the industrial environment, the displaced peasants of southern Europe [and elsewhere] were neither wandering adrift, embracing traditional American middle-class values [or those of other receiving societies], nor living European life-styles. They were creating a new milieu which was a blend of their cultural heritage and emerging working-class status. At the confluence of ethnicity and class [as well as gender and demographic factors], this new milieu included a way of life which allowed them to adjust to the routine of the work week, the uncertainties of the economy, the paternalism of the higher classes, and the confinement of their socioeconomic status.[6]

In this study, acculturation is defined as a process of migrants' coming to terms with a new culture after having developed a full personality in the culture of origin (part 1). It implies a gradual withering of old roots while sinking new ones at the same time, a process that often takes place unconsciously. We do not use the term "assimilation" since in everyday usage it implies the unconditional acceptance of the values and forms of behavior of the new society. *Integrative measures* are what we call those opportunities provided to in-migrants by private or public agencies to facilitate movement toward the new society (language classes, access to citizenship, civics courses). Before leaving the old society, migrants have developed a personal identity within the existing structures and value systems—have experienced a first socialization (part 2). The transition during their voyage influences attitudes and behavior (part 3). In a second socialization, the process of acculturation, migrants have to deal with the "objective" conditions, the structures of the receiving society, that is, the economic (part 4), the social (part 5), and the political spheres (part 6). The "subjective" side comprises the experiences and the coping of men and women with the new environment via the ethnic communities and reconstituted personal relationships (part 7). This interaction changes the receiving society to a certain degree.

We should replace the terms *emigration* and *immigration* by *migration*, since many, perhaps most, moves were not intended to be permanent. Multidirectional moves, migration in stages, and return migration illustrate the openness of the migration processes, the fact that men and women on the move had to make choices and actively determined or tried to determine their life-courses.

1. A Model of Migration and Acculturation

Since Vecoli's critique of the "uprooted" and perhaps earlier, it is well known that migrants moved purposefully. Studies of migration and acculturation from the bottom up, using letters and autobiographical accounts as sources, provide ample evidence.[7] All temporary disorientation notwithstanding, migrants experienced a process of being transplanted (Bodnar) by economic forces. This imagery still underestimates the active component in the structuring of one's life, the decision to migrate.

In the model which we are using, the culture of origin and the receiving culture receive equal attention (see graph).[8] The structures of the former determine the objective premigration characteristics and conditions that shape prospective migrants. On the subjective side, a motivation that is derived from particular family situations has to be taken into account as well as a migrant's personal characteristics. During the process of migration, intervening obstacles or inducements include access to, as well as the quality and quantity of information about, the culture(s) of destination. If, as has been argued, information was extremely limited, migrants were not necessarily poorly prepared. Rather they knew of one mine, construction site, or factory only, where they had relatives/acquaintances, which at that time promised a job that seemed to be relatively better than the one in the village, town, or city of origin. The situation found upon arrival was sometimes so disappointing or the migrants' capacities so unsuited that immediate return migration occurred.[9]

In all other cases, a process of acculturation began. This interaction changed the receiving society, if only in limited aspects, so that subsequent immigrants found a modified receiving society. The modification is toward a pluralist or multicultural society unless strict homogeneity or demands for conformity are imposed by the hegemonial culture. A few groups, however, have opted for separation from the new society, for example the Mennonites. Separation may also be imposed by the receiving society, for example in the case of Asian in-migrants. In an extreme form, social exclusion may lead to the emergence of separate societies—the two societies which Myrdal and the Kerner Report found for Whites and Blacks in the United States—or to a process of secondary minority group formation when partly acculturated groups are pushed back into minority status, as was the experience of Polish labor migrants in Germany, from 1885 to 1914.[10]

Acculturation depends on economic status. Farmers (settlement migrants), artisans and skilled workers, unskilled laborers, and maids (labor migrants), and persons with urban middle-class status (professional migrants) enter the receiving society at different levels. Acculturation also depends on migrants' intentions: staying close to the land, helping families in the society of origin, or improving their personal status in the receiving society. Their "resources," often only a few dollars, determine their first steps upon arrival; the intended duration of their stay influences later life-course decisions in the receiving society.

The options and constraints faced by the migrants may be illustrated by the example of prospective farmers with no possessions to sell before departure and who thus arrived without the necessary starting capital. They ended up in factories, in canal and road construction—at least for a few

A Model of Migration and Acculturation

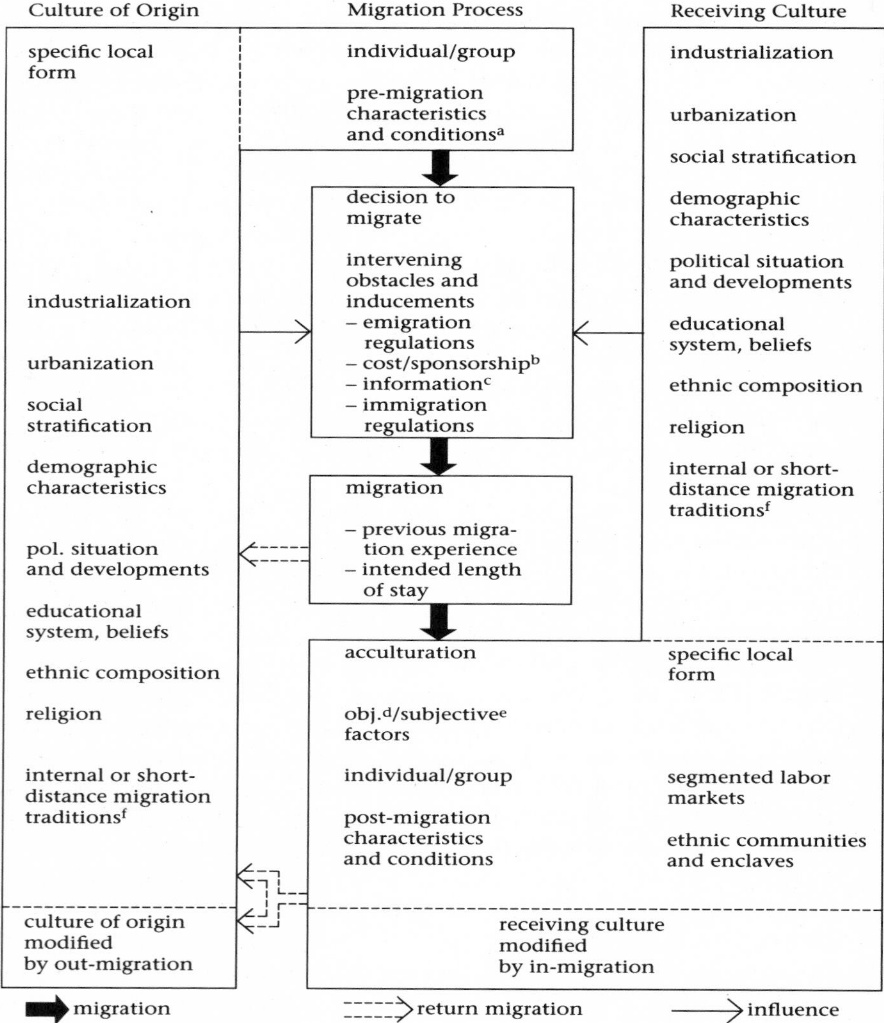

[a] Especially educational and technical training, demographic characteristics, prior migration and acculturation experience, individual social ties, and expectations.

[b] This includes psychic "costs," support by relatives or friends emotionally, by prepaid tickets, upon arrival.

[c] Information may come from the society of origin ("realist" version when sent by prior migrants) or from myths or printed guides in the society of origin (indirect "non-realist" variant).

[d] The specific political, social, cultural, and economic conditions into which a migrant (group) moves.

[e] The personal and/or collective satisfaction or disappointment and resulting identification or rejection as well as readiness for internalization.

[f] These categories are overlapping.

years—to save money for a return to the land. Some did establish marginal farms but worked in lumber camps or other seasonal employments as wage workers each winter. Others became agricultural wage laborers and set up independent farming only after several years, if at all. Similarly, labor migrants often did not cut their connections to the land. After spring sowing they moved within Europe in summer and returned for the harvest. A small number of artisans, skilled workers, and miners—separated from rural life by only one or two generations—moved back or attempted to move back to the land and to peasant lifestyles. Impoverished rural smallholders and laborers migrated with the intention to earn money to add to their landholding in the society of origin sufficient to make agriculture a viable lifestyle again. They thus chose a voluntary temporary proletarianization by migration to avoid sliding permanently into working-class status in the society of origin. Living in rural areas, as was the case for miners, or in small towns like the emerging steel centers in the Ruhr District or in Pennsylvania, permitted a continuation of semi-peasant lifestyles: in addition to wage work, pigs or goats were raised, vegetables grown, and the diet supplemented by hunting.

Compared to the migration of agrarian settlers, labor migration involved different parameters of acculturation. Most of this migration was by individuals who could reconstitute existing families from the society of origin through a long process of sequential family migration. Much of the migration was intended to be temporary and thus resulted in a sojourner status. The incidence of return migration was comparatively high. Living in urban areas and working in factories demanded immediate forms of acculturation even from sojourners. Most of the intra-European migration was labor migration. The migration of skilled workers and artisans was often undertaken for conservative reasons: to remain in a craft or to avoid the effects of industrial concentration in the society of origin. It could involve a change to factory work at the level of foreman or to the position of instructor of an unskilled labor force. It could also be a conscious move to new production methods and a new organization of production. Acculturation varied accordingly.

Unskilled workers came with a variety of motives—and different attitudes to acculturation. This "proletarian mass migration" was a move into the labor force of the receiving society but not necessarily into a class consciousness. Large numbers of migrant workers were not far removed from rural pursuits and often hoped to be able to return to them.

Professional migrants (journalists, priests, entrepreneurs, etc.), because of their educational standing, often mediated between working-class migrants of their own ethnicity and the new society and thus moved faster toward the new institutions and norms than men and women with low incomes. Journalists and priests, whose standing depended on the lower-class members of their ethnic group, had to move slowly in the acculturation process so as to remain sufficiently close to their own people in order to hold on to their economic base. Among lower-class persons, maids with close contacts to employers in the new society had the chance to observe (and join) the new forms of fast living, if they so chose.

Acculturation thus has ethnic, class, gender, and rural-urban components. Migrants with peasant backgrounds became seasonal agrarian or construction laborers. They moved through a sequence of peasant to peasant-worker to worker-peasant to worker, and attempted to influence the speed of this process or even to backtrack if possible. The first moves in the receiving society depended on the "starting capital." Labor migrants to the United States between 1899 and 1910 carried an average of $21.50 per person. Thus they had to find a job quickly unless friends or relatives were willing to pay for their living expenses. In other words, the choice of jobs according to preference or prior skill was very limited. A foothold had to be established in the labor market before a conscious selection of jobs and an adaptation to the conditions in the new society could take place. Acculturation was not yet self-determined.[11]

Economic migrants left with the intent to improve their personal or their family fortunes. They wanted to change neither the new nor the old society. Their interest in the political system of the new culture was secondary to the economic motive.[12] While those who decided to remain in the culture of birth and to struggle for better living and working conditions there expected reprisals and sacrifice for the sake of the ethnic group, of the class, or at least of fellow workers or villagers, migrants expected to make sacrifices for the sake of the families or children who remained behind. To turn to trade unions, socialist parties, or reform movements implied that they would have to change the expectations of their reference group, the family—or change the reference group itself. The latter occurred when sacrifices became too great and distance from new standards of living too large. The former occurred when workers turned from mutual aid associations to organizing for higher wages and better working conditions. Thus, the intention to improve one's personal fortune shaped attitudes toward the labor movement in the receiving culture, and the demands of the family at home could slow down the move toward the new society.

Social involvement in the area of arrival also depends on the intended duration of stay. Seasonal migrants will show little interest in the ways of the receiving society. The propensity to acculturate and—for workers—to organize will grow as the intended length of stay increases, the qualitative jump coming with a decision for long-term (return after retirement) or permanent settlement. This qualitative change will probably not occur when permanent migration was not originally intended but has happened involuntarily or inadvertently, under the pressure of circumstances. Many of the lifestyles and perspectives on life held by migrants can be explained by their "sojourner" status as temporary residents, who have migrated for economic reasons with no intention of dealing with the new culture in terms of a life-course strategy.[13]

Out-migration as a consequence of cultural oppression will also lead to an assertion of ethnic traits rather than toward acculturation in the new society. On the other hand, prior migration experience or a cosmopolitan or internationalist stance will ease the transition into the new society. Educational background and linguistic ability facilitate acculturation, which also depends on economic status, starting capital, the intended length of stay, the expectations of the reference group, and the skills that a migrant brings to the new society. This is not merely the baggage of old-world customs, but the individualized version of social practices and norms, along with individual motivations and expectations.

2. Premigration Mentalities: Push, Self-Selection, and Expectations

The mental disposition of migrants is shaped by three sets of factors that influence the move out of their particular home society. (1) The first set comprises the objective economic, social, and political conditions of the society of origin *and* the particular personal way of experiencing them. In the prospective migrant's mentality, the "objective" push factors become "subjective" ones.[14] (2) The specific aspects of a potential migrant's network of relations, including kinship and friendship ties as well as personality traits further or impede the weaning from this home world or microenvironment. (3) Information about migration patterns and the expectations of prospective migrants for their own future lives and achievements, as well as information, images, and myths about the receiving society, constitute the subjective pull factors.

Societal push factors have been well researched and will not be treated here. Rather, we will first deal with kinship relations and personality factors, then discuss the secularization of hope, and, finally, analyze individual expectations.

Social Relationships and Individual Self-Selection. The microenvironment of migrants—the (extended) family and neighborhood networks, especially friendship and kinship groups—determines sequential migration patterns, or "chain migration." One member of a family or neighborhood group leaves first, and upon his or—somewhat less often—her information, money remittances, or prepaid tickets, others follow to the same destination. Thus old-world relationships are partially reconstituted in new-world urban communities or agrarian settlements. The selection of who will receive money or advice to follow to the new social environment seems to be influenced, at least in the first years, by earning capacities more than by affectionate ties.[15] Additionally, gender plays a role: men establish predominantly male migration chains, while women tend to send for their sisters and female friends.[16]

What remains largely unexplored is the question of how, from a pool of potential migrants, male or female, the particular persons who actually leave select themselves. Inheritance and dowry-giving patterns and impending military service, especially in the armies of a dominating national group from among the European multinational empires, are more closely related to individual decision-making processes than the general shortage of land, absence of jobs and below-subsistence food levels. Second, norm-breaking and problematic personal relationships increase an individual's propensity to leave: a courtship not approved by family and kin, an unsuccessful love affair, childbirth out of wedlock, and disobedience toward a master, as well as minor offenses against customs and laws.[17]

Third, the migrant's personality itself has to be evaluated, using a psychological approach.[18] Some authors have argued that certain predispositions ("attachment behaviors") or types of character can help to explain why one "type" will not leave while another with weak relations to the home surroundings is looking for a "thrill" in distant "friendly expanses."[19] Other factors to be considered include sibling sequence and migratory behavior among the siblings as well as rites of passage from childhood dependence to adolescent independence, from the family as one moves into the larger world.

The fourth approach to self-selection relies more on the timing of departures within the development of family and friendship relations. A number of autobiographical accounts and case studies suggest that a comparatively high percentage of male and female migrants actually left when a death, usually of a parent, or the remarriage of a widowed parent imposed on the family a restructuring of established relationships. In particular, the death of a mother or the arrival of a stepmother seems to have influenced departures, or—in the case of return migration—the timing of reentry into the old family circle.[20]

Furthermore, young persons, who account for the majority of labor migrants, experience several changes in family relationships which exert a cumulative influence on the timing of departures: the passage from youth to adulthood, the capability of supporting oneself and founding a family of one's own, impending military service for males, and domestic service outside the family for females. In some areas of Europe, out-migration for this age group was a customary or even compulsory way of life.[21] Wherever such migration traditions existed, societal ways of thinking accepted the migration of individuals as "normal."[22]

The Secularization of Hope. The motivation to leave family and home—the notion of intentional active improvement of personal economic status and social standing—was a relatively new concept for the lower classes. Religion had relegated a better life to another world after death. There were social memories or, rather, myths about a distant golden past, as well as vague beliefs in the existence of a distant good ruler or a deceased benevolent landlord. Hope was but a memory of the past, beyond death, or in the unreachable realm of an emperor.[23] Enlightenment, the Age of Revolution, and Romanticism brought forth a new view of human activity. Romanticism, often interpreted as a countermovement to enlightened rationalism, served in some respects as a support, by embedding new, rationalist ideas in people's minds. Commoners were assigned new roles in literature, and popular sovereignty became an established part of political thought. Folk languages assumed importance when the new middle classes established national languages in opposition to the hegemonial ones of a ruling ethnic group. The position of women changed.[24]

Common people began to realize that a better, if distant, life was in this world, in a city or in a far-off country, reachable in their own or their children's lifetimes. This secularization of hope induced increasing numbers of men and women to take the initiative, to move out of stagnant social orders and oppressive norms. While earlier migrations, like the eighteenth-century movements of land-seeking German peasants to the plains of southern Russia or the relocating of persecuted religious groups, were undertaken in an effort to maintain a way of life, most nineteenth-century migrations aimed for something new. Bourgeois-democratic institutions and capitalist economies offered hope. By 1900, Jews in Polotzk no longer greeted each other at Passah with the age-old "Next year in Jerusalem" but with "Next year in America."[25] The notion that life-courses were predetermined by the will of a god, by fairies, or by demons evolved into the concept that by changing one's place of residence a person could influence the direction of his or her life. The active component in human existence—the planning, not of a whole life, but of certain crucial moves—became increasingly important.

Given the strong faith in the opportunities offered by new (urban) worlds, it may be argued that from the secularization of hope a secular religion developed. A few examples will explain the relation between hope and reality. People in Europe moved to the glittering capital of Vienna, or Paris, the city of enlightenment and liberty, and to industrializing regions that provided jobs. Others looked to "America," a construct of freedom and boundless offerings. In any event, migrants would arrive in an immigrant neighborhood in a European town or in a particular city or village of the United States or Canada. From afar, the new societies impressed the hopeful through their Potemkian facades.[26] Even those who had gleaned realistic information from the letters of previous migrants or from the labor press held on to unrealistic hopes for their areas of destination.[27] Some of these expectations point to the simple, credulous minds of backward peasants.

Trains in "America" were said to run over the roofs of houses. Absurd? No, this was actually a reference to the elevated streetcars of New York or Chicago. In the minds of those who were impressed by the mere sight of trains, such reports encouraged a belief that anything was possible. Another dimension was transcended by the report that in "America" everyone, even migrants from one's own village, used shoe polish. A modest advance, indeed, in modern terms. But at home only the lords of the manors could afford both shoes and polish. Within the stratified social setup of the Old World, where people were either in the manor or in the cottage, with no social "ladder" between the two, the logical conclusion was that if in America a person could blacken his boots like a lord then he actually lived like a lord.[28] Thus, specific, undistorted bits of information were received into minds developed in a different world. There, men or women could not understand the information received in terms relevant to the societies in the new worlds. Their hopes turned the limited possibilities for personal improvement via migration into a secular religion, into an unfounded belief in unlimited opportunity.

The largest single receiving area, the United States, thus became a complex myth, called "America," larger and more impressive than all others, even though migrations toward the other centers of attraction continued. Italian migrants, constrained only by local migration traditions, could choose between major destinations like France, Germany, and Switzerland or minor ones like Glasgow or Moscow. They could choose between South or North America, or Africa, or even other places. However, only the North American myth became the yardstick of comparison. When a quarter of Naples was constructed rapidly, it was called "Chicago." When, in the German Ruhr District, a mine shaft was brought down unusually fast, it was drilled "the American way."[29] Even though European cities grew rapidly, even though upward and downward social mobility had become relatively similar in comparable cities, and even though social differentiation and the distance between the top and the bottom layers of society was about equal, the image persisted.[30] Turn-of-the-century labor newspapers pointed to the glaring similarities between the aristocracy of the dollar and aristocracy by birth, but migrants came to North America anyway in ever larger numbers.[31] When they did not find what they had hoped to find, some continued to search for the "real" America. The dream had become more real than reality.[32]

Information and Independence. Considering the unlimited optimism of migrants to America, even clear and factually correct information stood in need of specification.[33] "Servant girls in America get from eight to sixteen dollars a month," stated one report.[34] Women did receive that much, but only if they found a job, if they were healthy, if they worked to the satisfaction of their employers. The author of this information attempted to draw cautious conclusions. If servant girls would "save half of that amount every year, and place it at interest" they could acquire "in the course of twenty or thirty years . . . from three to five thousand dollars." However, servant women would probably support their aging parents in the society of origin, or bring over siblings. Such sums, sufficient to buy a farm in the old world, assumed acquisitive individuals devoted to saving at interest, eschewing both old family obligations and new patterns of consumption. Middle-class authors were trying to inform peasants, laborers, and maids.

If savings were difficult to accumulate, at least jobs were easier to find in North America. Measured by population growth and the expansion of cities, American development was happening faster than in Europe.[35] In addition to finding a wage-paying occupation, migrants could construct their own social setting in North America. Men and women moving within their own countries to centers of investment and industrialization remained within the established structures. Moves into other stratified and bureaucratized countries implied (petrified) institutions and norms. Moves to North America, or to Siberia in the 1920s, or to other societies where new institutions and social structures on the local level were still being created provided the challenge of building a new community. The opportunities to recreate relationships and networks would never have occurred at home. The possibility that immigrant children might eventually select a spouse by themselves would have been impossible at home, where the older generation held sway. "Opportunity" thus meant the small, active influence on one's own life-course; it meant fewer norms and broader limits than at home.

A vignette may illustrate what "opportunity" meant in comparison to Europe. An Italian traveler, Carlo Gardini, visited Chicago when the city had about one hundred thousand inhabitants. At that time, the terrain was considered too low and too wet to build on. An engineer named Brown suggested that it might be possible to raise all the buildings by three meters and fill in the land underneath them. Gardini noted that rather than "leaving this task to later generations," the engineers solved the problem in "a very short time," and he concluded, "In Europe a scheming promoter like Brown . . . would have been declared 'fit for the insane asylum'."[36] This would have happened to many: the smallholder couple who wanted a sizable farm, the harvest laborer or dairymaid who wanted a money wage, the journeyman carpenter who wanted to connect two beams in an unusual way—all those who held "insane" proposals and dreams that in the Old World would have made those who dared utter them outsiders, to be marginalized and humiliated for forgetting their place.

Individualization in the structuring of life-courses had a further, unforeseen consequence. A negative outcome—the fact that the new order could break a person—never entered into the calculations of those intent on migrating.[37] Industrial accidents killed and maimed more Jews in Paris, London, and New York than pogroms did in imperial Russia.[38] Striking eastern European miners in Ludlow or elsewhere were shot down more easily by company thugs than were rural laborers by henchmen of the magnates at home.[39] Those who attempted to decide their own life-courses themselves never intended to end up in Ludlow tent colonies or in the Triangle Shirtwaist Co. building. In their minds, the miserable existence of many in the old society turned into the bad luck of some in the new.

Self-determined migration provided the modest but attractive prospect of escaping what were often paralyzing norms and customs, of finding jobs at comparatively higher wages, of facing fewer social barriers and wearing fewer badges of inferiority. Men did not have to doff their caps when asking for a job,[40] and women in domestic service could wear elaborate bonnets, reserved back at home for middle- and upper-class women.[41] There were taxes, but not the multitude of preying officials, tithe-sucking men of the church, and haughty princelings and their courts living off the people.[42] Bosses would not just sit down in their offices, they would actually work alongside their laborers.[43] A store clerk could become president and still be addressed with nothing more than "Mister."[44] For immigrants, "success" meant an income that permitted living according to one's tastes rather than becoming rich.[45]

Migration often was not to a mythical "America," but "to wages" in Polish usage, "to work" in Italian usage, "to bread" in several eastern European languages. Bread was sacred in agrarian societies where hunger was still a constant companion during the preharvest phase of the annual cycle of agriculture. Wages meant independence from family or employers paying in kind. Within the constraints of limited resources, money could be spent according to one's own preferences. The search for income and independence meant, for migrating artisans and skilled workers, the exertion of control over the hours and pace of work. For a few, independence meant becoming a self-made person. Immigrant women took note of their less subservient position. For the great mass of the lower classes, the unskilled workers from rural surplus populations, independence simply meant being no longer dependent on and a burden for their struggling families. From being supernumerary eaters, men and women, through migration, turned themselves into workers able to feed themselves. Even "girls" could earn a living in the mills and the needle trades. Rather than sleep in the corner of a hut at home, a hut that housed too many men, women, and children anyway, migrants moved into their own tenement rooms or even wooden-frame houses. The term "independence" was used by migrating New England mill girls in the 1830s, by English potters in the 1840s, by migrating textile workers in North Carolina in the 1900s, and by Finnish women in Canada in the 1910s.[46]

3. Transition

The actual experience of the voyage and admission into the new society came once the steps of mental weaning from the old society, of separation from friends, kin, and closest family, had been taken, and once the myths and news about the new society had been formed into a set of personal hopes and expectations.

The Voyage. The trip itself confirmed and increased hopes—or undermined them.[47] By paying for their voyage the migrants were transformed from subjects of monarchs into customers of merchants. In Bremen, the major continental port of emigration, food was better than at home, thus confirming expectations. Few took into consideration that at the end of their journey they would no longer be customers but common laborers. Others extrapolated from what they saw: if the Bremen main station was bigger than their home village, if it was illuminated by electric lights all night, how would New York shine? After all, Bremen was only a way station.[48] Turn-of-the-century steamers accommodated more migrants than did two or three villages back in the old country. How immense America must be!

Others felt that the pace was getting ever faster, that on the way people were hurried along, skinned by runners, shouted at by railroad conductors and border guards. Experiences in disinfection stations at the borders and in the port towns were like nightmares since migrants were not told in their own language what to do or what was to be done to them and why. Were they being treated like the cattle at home, some asked themselves?[49]

The complicated journey was relatively easy to complete for migrants who found guides or had contracted with a reliable migration agency. They met persons who were making the trip for the second or third time. Others went with men who had come back to recruit fellow villagers for a specific factory or mine.[50] Changing trains and embarkation were done under the supervision of emigration agency personnel. The numerous return migrants provided information about their journey. Twelve percent of all Europeans arriving from 1899 to 1910 had been in the United States before: every eighth traveler had prior experience and could act as a guide for others. In addition, between 1908 and 1910, ninety-four out of every one hundred persons arriving at U.S. ports declared that they were going to stay with relatives (79 percent) or with friends (15 percent).[51] These, too, were sources of information.

To gauge the mental distance traveled, it has to be remembered that many of the migrants had never seen a train before they stepped aboard one. In the early 1890s, a Polish migrant writing home on stationery provided by a Bremen emigrant agent had to explain the logo, a simplified rendering of a sailing ship, with the note "this is a ship." Accounts of the trip vary from bewilderment to easygoing confidence.[52]

Labor migration within Europe followed a somewhat different pattern with regard to travel and admission. Since distances were shorter and since agricultural and construction jobs were seasonal, return was regular for many, and thus departure was a less emotionally wrenching experience. Migration was a way of life rather than a break with the past. Traveling may have been more costly (from northern Italy, train tickets to the plains of the eastern Elbe were more expensive than ship fares to Argentina). Because of the seasonal character of much of the migration, because of the organization of work gangs of men and women, and because of the traditional routes from a specific village into a specific town or city, group or guided travel was the rule.

Admission or Exclusion. Admission procedures into the receiving societies were fraught with the possibility of one's being rejected, and—perhaps to a lesser degree if immigrant letters are a reliable source—of not being able to recognize waiting family members or get along with brothers or sisters or with husbands or wives that one had not seen for years. Germany's rigorous entry restrictions may be contrasted with the liberal policies of the United States at the turn of the century. From the point of view of migrants in general, and of illiterate peasant people in particular, even U.S. rules were difficult to cope with because of administrative changes, lack of precise information, and—sometimes unintentionally—the abusive treatment of migrants.

In the United States, criminals, prostitutes, the insane, and anarchists were successively excluded.[53] These restrictions applied only to a very small number of persons. Their ramifications, however, reached larger numbers in disconcerting ways, as when single women were readily suspected of being or becoming prostitutes. Regulations about health, jobs, and money at the time of entry caused more concern. These provisions led to the dreaded inspection at Ellis Island and other U.S. ports, which were hurtful and degrading. Migrants usually had no clear information about which diseases were grounds for exclusion, nor would they know whether or not an itch in one eye or a lame leg would fall under the regulations. The 1893 provision that passenger lists had to note whether each incoming migrant possessed thirty dollars (fifty dollars after 1903)—and if less, how much—caused much consternation: did people have to have that much money? Sometimes not only the migrants but the inspectors, too, seem to have had no clear notion of the meaning of this declaration.

Problems were also caused by the act of 1885, which prohibited the entry of contract labor. Professional, skilled, and domestic labor were excluded from the meaning of the law. Or, from the migrants' point of view, one person could have a contracted job and get in and the next one was kept out for the same reason. Since newcomers had to show that they could support themselves, what better proof could there be than having a job lined up? If the prospective job was not contracted but merely promised in a letter from a relative, what was the incoming migrant to tell the inspector, and how was the latter to distinguish between contract and promise?

Those who had to go through the admission process felt themselves to be at the mercy of arbitrary officials, the more so since they had to undergo inspection two or three times: at the German border, at the port of embarkation, and finally at the port of entry.[54] The rejection rate was one in one hundred at the ports of entry in 1907 and four in one hundred at the prior inspection stations, which adds up to a rate of 5 percent.[55] This meant that at Ellis Island, where hundreds of passengers, sometimes thousands, were waiting to be processed (and were processed at a rate of several hundred an hour), there was hardly anyone who did not see others being rejected. However, once in-migrants had passed through the gates, they were free to do what they wanted—within the limits of the law and the economic possibilities; there was no registering with the police, and no questions as to how soon they would leave.

In the German Reich, second in rank among labor-importing countries, in-migration was regulated by the individual states, though most followed the lead of Prussia. Because of late industrialization, in-migration was of little concern up to the 1880s. From the 1880s onward, Russian and Austrian Poles entered the eastern Prussian provinces as migrant agricultural laborers, while Italian workers went to the southern and central parts of Germany, mainly to construction jobs. Workers from other ethnic groups came in smaller numbers, a total of 433,000 in 1890, which increased to 1.26 million in 1910, among them 543,000 women (43 percent).[56]

While the northern, western, and southern borders were relatively open, the eastern ones were strictly controlled. To enter the Reich, workers had to have a job, and after 1903, they had to be registered with the Deutsche Arbeiterzentrale.[57] If found without the DAZ "legitimizing card," they could be expelled immediately. By accepting the hated card they agreed not to change jobs and that they were to behave submissively.[58] For northern and western European and Swiss workers these rules were loosely applied. Some of these groups were able to form ethnic communities. Italian workers could found few communities since, as construction workers, they were out of employment in winter and had to return to Italy. The opportunity for, or, from the German point of view, the "danger" of, acculturation was hardly present. The rules were strictly applied to eastern workers, who had to wait at the border—at their own expense—until their contract was signed and all formalities were completed. In most German states, foreign Poles had to be out of the country in winter to prevent their establishing permanent residence and becoming acculturated. An economic side-effect of this political measure was that agrarian employers did not have to pay wages in winter. Most states accepted only foreign Polish workers who were single. With the exception of the forewomen of female harvest gangs, they could bring no children under fourteen years of age. Special restrictions applied to Lithuanian and Czech migrants in ethnically mixed border provinces, and Russian Jews were subjected to restrictions after the 1905 uprising in Russia.[59] Attempts by the Austrian, Hungarian, and Russian governments to improve the status of their migrating citizens—if only modestly—were rebuffed by German authorities.[60] German policy was to admit a rotating labor force only and to prevent any acculturation.

Admission policies thus influenced attitudes toward the new society and determined chances for successful acculturation. Wherever migrant men and women arrived, in the Ruhr District, London, Buenos Aires, or New York, the sociogeographic landscape was full of "signs" almost inevitably leading them to the quarters where their fellow countrymen and women lived. Like modern freeways with their road signs, the streets in turn-of-the-century cities were full of information on where to go.

4. The Framework of the Receiving Society: The Economic Sphere

While politics provides the framework for acculturation, economic migrants move toward perceived opportunities, and labor migrants, in particular, move into a particular segment of the labor market of the receiving society. Usually they do not at first consciously move into a state, nation, or political system. Only subsequently do they experience the social system, and they usually turn to politics last.

Better economic opportunity was the distant magnet that seemed to draw the newcomers, whether to Silesian mines, bustling port cities, or factories. "America" reportedly provided good opportunities for anyone, man or woman, who was willing to work hard. The letters of earlier migrants provided realistic information about the availability of jobs, as well as about discrimination.[61] Since migrants came with little or no capital, they had to enter the labor market immediately. No time could be spent on acculturation. Thus the economic framework first and foremost determined the experiences of migrants.

Even in countries that encouraged immigration, newcomers had to realize that their fellow workers considered them to be strikebreakers or dumb aliens ready to undercut wages. Labor organizations often tried to keep migrants out or prevent acculturation. Their views received support from classical labor-market theory, which assumed the existence of one single labor pool within a state out of which employers selected workers according to "rational" criteria: productivity, skills, cost, and marginal profitability.

However, letters from migrants indicate that they did not go into a vast, anonymous labor pool. They went to New York City, to the Pennsylvania coal fields, or to the Montana mining industry. In England, Irish agricultural workers knew their destination, the particular farms where work would be waiting. In France, Belgian harvest workers or Spanish grape pickers also knew where to go. Migrants arriving in the United States went to friends who would have jobs waiting or would know how to find a job. The migrating men and women thus went into one particular local labor market with their particular capabilities—or lack of them—with specific access to a limited range of jobs.

In the Atlantic economies a dual labor market emerged. The native-born workers of a given country received (and defended) the more stable jobs demanding higher qualifications. In-migrating foreign workers entered the labor markets on the internationalized lower-skill levels of employment: manual labor, outdoor labor, unskilled and semi-skilled work at piecework rates, or domestic service, especially in the case of women. Men from one particular Hungarian village went to Holden, West Virginia, to work in the mines, while the women went to the cigar factories in New Brunswick, New Jersey. When they wanted to form families, the men went to New Brunswick and selected a spouse, and often the new couple moved on to an ethnic community elsewhere, for example in Hamilton, Ontario, where the labor market provided openings for both.[62]

This ability to move between different occupations and even different countries was caused by a homogenization of labor markets at the turn of the century, according to a recent study by Gordon, Edwards, and Reich.[63] This homogenization occurred, to a degree, through a process of de-skilling, and through the introduction of the disassembly line in the Chicago stockyards in the 1890s and of the assembly line in the automobile factories from 1913 onwards. Industrial jobs became available for unskilled men and women leaving the agricultural sector. But the levels of skill and regional and local differentiation of labor markets remained high. The homogenization did not reduce the multitude of separate labor markets; it merely evened out entrance requirements.

For skilled occupations, a degree of internationalization of the labor markets occurred as well. The eastern and southeastern European industrializing cities and mining areas attracted experts from central Europe, particularly the German states. Similarly, many factories and mines in the United States attracted skilled and experienced migrants for foreman positions. Welsh miners, German furniture makers, and Swedish ironworkers are but a few examples. Women's occupations, such as cooking and sewing, also depended on prior training. Thus the migration of Prague women into Vienna households as cooks or of Jewish seamstresses to New York is a migration of skilled workers, whether domestic, sweatshop, or factory. The deskilling of household work began only in the era of prefabricated foods and clothes. The keeping of boardinghouses by immigrant women assumed skills and entrepreneurial talents. In general, the migration of skilled personnel often led to supervisory positions, for example the training of local unskilled labor in southeastern Europe or the directing of unskilled in-migrants from other ethnic backgrounds in North America.

While the theory of a dual labor market (based on the theory of a dual economy) was an advance on classical labor-market theory, it fell short of explaining the complexities of job availability or underemployment in the Atlantic economies through which the labor migrants moved. Since the 1960s, theories of tertiary, segmented, and internal/external labor markets have been developed, the latter referring to hiring within a firm.[64] These concepts have important ramifications for the study of labor migration.

Economic systems in labor-importing countries consist of a growing, capital-intensive, and often highly concentrated or monopolistic primary sector, and a stagnating secondary sector where competition is particularly severe. Jobs in the primary sector (the core economy or center) offer relatively high pay and good working conditions, stable employment, and opportunities for promotion. Jobs in the secondary sector (the periphery) are characterized, in contrast, by irregular employment, low pay, and unpleasant or dangerous working conditions. The tertiary, marginal, or ghetto economy provides an even more insecure but also very flexible labor market. The letters of labor migrants, reporting long periods of unemployment, bad working conditions, and low promotion opportunities, show that they held jobs in the secondary sector, or that they were pushed into the tertiary sector or into return migration, particularly in times of economic crisis.[65]

Further differentiation shows that parts of the primary sector, too, are prone to cyclical developments and offer low-level jobs. Unskilled immigrant women find employment in the modern computer industry, for example. Around 1900, the U.S. steel industry offered irregular employment because of the frequent breakdown of machinery, the lowering of qualifications, a crisis-ridden development process, and dangerous working conditions. Here are found the typical jobs for migrants. The initial transfer of labor from the external markets into a company, and within a company to better jobs (the internal labor market), does not correspond to the classical model of rational hiring. Decisions are rather much more likely to be based on such factors as personal relationships, customary rights and procedures, the climate at work, and group dynamics.

The organizational behavior of migrant laborers is related to these aspects of hiring preferences. Laborers benefited little from trade unions whenever these restricted access to jobs in favor of their members, who usually belonged to the dominant culture. A foreman or small businessman from the same ethnic group, however arbitrary his conduct might be, could ensure access to jobs, or promotion to better positions, much more easily than could a trade union linked to the dominant ethnicity. Recent research on the particularly unstable tertiary sector shows that those employed there, because they are forced to adopt a high degree of flexibility, are capable of reacting more quickly to job loss or changes at the place of work than those employed in other sectors.

On the microeconomic level, labor markets are segmented, segregated, and stratified. Segmentation divides economic sectors into numerous separate labor markets. Segregation prevents particular groups, for example women, Blacks, and migrants, from gaining access to certain labor markets even if they do have the required qualifications. Stratification means horizontal barriers to advancement based on knowledge or skills (for example linguistic or technical knowledge), on age thresholds (seniority), or on other selection mechanisms.

The hypothesis of class fragmentation along ethnic lines, and the resulting concept of the incapacity for class solidarity and consistent class consciousness, is brought into question by this differentiated model of the labor market. Workers do not compete with all others for all available jobs independently of gender, skin color, ethnicity, or age. Rather, specific workers compete only for jobs within one segment. Miners do not compete with foundry workers, or masons with tailors. Migrant workers, be they in Milan, Berlin, or New York, never assumed that all jobs were open to them. Instead, they sought employment suitable to their premigration experience, jobs which ideally permitted contact with fellow ethnics.

Fragmentation does not arise until two or more groups of workers with the same qualifications within one segment (men/women, Whites/Blacks, native-born/migrant) compete for the same jobs but must sell their labor for different rates of pay in a split labor market. In such cases, ethnic stereotypes, racism, and sexism may develop, and latent prejudices may be exacerbated. In fast-growing branches of industry, a substratification may develop in boom years in which immigrant workers do not threaten to move into higher-ranking jobs. Labor migrants in segmented and segregated labor markets may be played off by employers against each other or against native-born workers. But labor migrants also have shown militancy and the ability to organize. Victor Greene has analyzed the militancy of Polish and Lithuanian miners in the Pennsylvania mining industry, using the same sources that a generation of earlier, biased historians had read as proving the rate-cutting maneuvers of eastern European migrant miners.[66]

Employment in the unstable sectors of the economy has often been considered particularly suited to the work habits of migrants coming from rural areas. Herbert Gutman, among others, has argued that migrant workers had to adjust or were forced to adjust to industrial time and work routines. Indeed, migrants often complained about the inexorable clock, about the tyranny of the factory whistle.[67] While immigrant men and women had to become used to the rigorous observance of time, whether they were in a European or a North American industrial setting, a look at agricultural work patterns shows that peasants did not arrive with unsteady work habits. The seasonal character of field work was regularized by additional tasks. A break in the fieldwork, be it for a day, due to rain, or for a season, was filled with activity: the repair of implements, inside chores, or the production of goods at home. Rural men, women, and children had regular work habits that ran according to natural time. Only those harvest workers for whom no off-season jobs were available worked irregularly.

The commercialization of agriculture and the change from raising crops that demanded more regular attention to highly seasonal crops like sugar beets resulted in unsteady work patterns. Large landowners like the Junkers of the eastern Elbe drove out their steady labor force, which then migrated into German and U.S. industry, and replaced it with seasonal migrants from farther east.[68] As labor migrants, the peasants, tenants, and laborers were likely workers for the primary sector, and the seasonal workers for the secondary sector. At the time of the proletarian mass migrations, even leading industries like steel could not (or would not) offer regular employment to the newly arriving peasant workers. For former peasants and rural laborers, industrial time with all its irregularities involved an adaptation to unsteady work patterns. The result was a "spoiled identity" that was less oriented to achievement over a longer period of time.[69]

Employer-imposed routines or irregularities may also have been experienced as more arbitrary than those of the natural harvest and other work cycles. The rigorous enforcement of factory time by employers and the frequent layoffs due to broken machinery or other reasons were often contradictory and irrational. It has also been said that the opposition by immigrant workers to the arbitrary actions of an employer were related to cultural practices, leading to a high turnover. But even some of the proverbially stable German unions experienced turnover rates of above 100 percent annually. Union activity continued unabated nonetheless, because there was a stable core of functionaries and a bond that came from having a common craft or class identity among all the members. Sewall has shown for Marseille how a native-born and an in-migrating labor force complemented each other during both strikes and organizational work.[70]

Acculturation in the economic sphere was propelled by the common wish of migrants to earn money wages. These might be low at the time of a migrant's entrance into a new labor market (unless unions demanded and secured union wages for newcomers[71]). Migrants sometimes accepted low wages in order to be able to gain a foothold and survive during the first days and months in a new location. German masons were bitter toward Italian migrant construction workers, and American-born steelworkers viewed eastern European fellow workers with distrust.[72] Once a foothold had been established, migrants had no reason to accept low wages and consider themselves inferior. They, too, struggled for better living and working conditions.[73] To achieve these, they had to come to terms with the existing labor organizations, or, if rejected by them, they had to build their own parallel organizations.

The spasmodic production patterns in many industries forced male and female workers, migrant or native-born, to weather long periods of unemployment or strikes. In this situation, the nonunion flexibility and militancy of the peasant-workers may have been as important as the skills and craft-based union membership of highly trained native-born workers. An unskilled migrant, accustomed to doing whatever chores had been necessary on a farm, could substitute one kind of work for another in periods when there were layoffs, strikes, and so on. The typical resident of a boardinghouse, in addition to doing wage labor, raised pigs or goats, tended gardens, and chopped wood. Skilled workers, who in the factories often hired their own help, did not accept such odd jobs; they went to other skilled persons, butchers and bakers, to get their food. High income achieved through identification with a craft and through organizational activity replaced flexibility. To oversimplify: by living a semipeasant lifestyle, peasant-workers could live through long periods of unemployment or strikes by relying on other income, but they could not afford an inflexible identification with a craft. Skilled workers, on the other hand, could not afford to compromise craft identity by being too flexible. The differences between the two ways of dealing with wages and working conditions are thus not differences of class consciousness or ethnicity but of lifestyle and bargaining position.

Acculturation in the economic sphere was as complex as in the other two spheres. But it was here that the interests of the receiving society and the newcomers met. The former wanted functioning persons suitable for the demands of the economy, while the latter wanted to earn a living. This conjuncture of interests caused a readiness, if not a complete willingness, among migrants to come to terms with the new society, at least to the degree that they would be able to achieve their goals. Whatever the way into the new society, whether full of obstacles or easy to travel, the first station was an ethnic niche in the labor market.

5. *The Social Sphere*

In the productive or economic sphere of a society, goods for sale are produced by paid labor. In the social or "reproductive" sphere, a worker's capability is reproduced usually by the unpaid housework of women. This social sphere consists of the structures of society as a complex interacting whole.

A restriction of this sphere to the daily reconstitution of a person's ability to work places too much emphasis on production by relegating life outside the workplace to a subsidiary function. Recreation, leisure, housework, child-rearing, and communication networks have to be included in this sphere. Its borders are fluid. Wage work in the home, unpaid agricultural work by family members, and families working in units in a small business are better understood by seeing them in terms of family economy, life perspectives, and the larger world of everyday life. Here, four aspects of immigrant expectations and experiences as related to social structures will be addressed: the standard of living, social barriers/social mobility, social republicanism, and, finally, gender roles.

The question of whether migrants achieved a higher standard of living once seemed easy to answer. There was plenty of land, whether in the plains of southern Russia, North America, or Australia. Immigrant workers, because of high earnings, lost interest in basic issues of class and societal change: "all Socialist utopias [in the U.S.] come to nothing on the reefs of roast beef and apple pie," as Werner Sombart expressed it in 1905.[74] A reading of the letters from German immigrant farmers up to the 1870s seems to corroborate such interpretations. Immigrant labor newspapers, on the other hand, contradict them. Much of the "evidence" for higher standards of living is an assumption on the part of contemporaries and historians that it must have been higher since otherwise neither men nor women would have migrated.

Settlement migrants usually did find cultivable land in sufficient quantity. Its annual yield was generally superior to that of the subsistence economies at home, whether on Swabian or Galician smallholdings, or on the rocky soil of Sweden, which had to be scratched by horizontal ploughs so as not to hit solid rock.[75] The fertility of the soil in Illinois and Wisconsin seems to explain, beyond the slightest doubt, why peasants left Europe.[76] Excepting those migrants who were cheated, who selected unproductive land, or who succumbed to diseases in areas infested with malaria, the change, measured in material terms, was for the better. Since, in some of the areas of destination, game was plentiful and could be hunted with no concern for state or feudal restrictions, the balance of total material benefits was even better. Migrant peasant families frequently ate meat and, sometimes, white bread.

Nonmaterial changes also have to be taken into consideration, however. In the case of immigrant farmers, working long hours was necessary to establish a freehold or to clear the forest cover. This was not necessarily experienced as an emotional burden since the work was done for one's own advancement rather than to pay taxes or tithes. Second, since new land had to be cultivated, standards of living declined sharply in the first years. Peasant migrants from the Scandinavian countries going to the American Midwest exchanged log cabins for holes in the earth or sod huts. Only later did they reach the previous level of log huts. But after additional years of toil they might build a large house, which would have been impossible at home. Third, for many the move implied a sharp curtailment of social activity. Migrants in North America, Russia, and elsewhere certainly did not miss the arrogant tax collectors, but they did miss neighbors wherever the "homestead" was on isolated plots of land. Women, in particular, suffered from this isolation, as letters attest and as novels graphically describe.[77]

Fourth, emigration often meant a break with familial obligations. This might engender deep and lifelong feelings of guilt among children and mean the loss of support for parents who remained at home. In a generational social-security system, where each working-age generation within a family supported the elderly as well as the children, out-migration implied a reallocation of resources from the support of one's aging parents to providing for one's own and one's children's future. Those left behind had to labor for their own support until death, or they had to depend on parish charity like the village poor. Money remittances back to the old culture could begin only when crops could be sold for surplus cash.[78] The net balance of payments of funds brought into the country by immigrants or sent to them from the "old world," in the case of the United States, was higher than those funds sent back to the family at home into the 1870s.[79]

If the standard of living is not measured merely as the amount of meat on the table years after migration—that is, if the deprivation of the first years, the excessive toil, the loss of social contacts, and the shifting of the cost of social security to the parent generation are taken into account—the question of whether the quality of life improved remains an open one. Achievement was perceived by migrants according to personal and gender-specific preferences. These did change. The quest for a better future, conceived as a search for a whole new way of life, sometimes (especially among men) turned into a quest for more acres and better food and thus was judged to be successful only after the yardstick had been changed. Sadness and loneliness are left out of this method of reckoning.

As to labor migrants, Peter Shergold, in a detailed analysis of Birmingham and Pittsburgh, has calculated comparable standards of living on the basis of hourly money wage, cost of living, and consumption preference.[80] His conclusions are worth quoting at length.

> The American manual worker's standard of living was not as much in advance of the English worker's as most contemporary comment suggested. The skilled Pittsburgh tradesman, it is true, received an income which, judged by the composite unit of consumables it could buy, was 50–100% greater than that received by an equivalent occupation in Birmingham. But, in stark contrast, the unskilled Pittsburgh worker gained a real wage that was the same as, or very little better than, that paid to the laborer in Birmingham.

Shergold continues: "if the definition of standard of living were extended, one might make a forceful argument" that Birmingham laborers were "decidedly better off, experienced a significantly higher quality of life," than did laborers in Pittsburgh. The "extent of annual unemployment" was probably similar on both sides.[81] In mining camps, two hundred workdays a year was considered normal; one third of each year was spent unemployed. This meant additional responsibility on the consumer side, since women spent the wages to sustain the family. Buying cheap, taking on odd jobs, or working for boarders were necessary measures to manage the family economy.[82]

Shergold concludes:

> . . . in nearly all other respects evidence—both quantitative and qualitative—indicates that the British worker experienced more substantial benefits. He generally had longer leisure time, enjoying (as did few Pittsburgh workers) a half-day on Saturday; he was far less likely to be killed or maimed while at the workplace; he labored under less pressure: and he was provided with superior social services and facilities—hospital accommodation, city-based unemployment benefits, garbage collection, park space, and so on.[83]

Shergold's analysis cannot be generalized for immigrants from other ethnic backgrounds. Men and women from the eastern Elbian latifundia, southern Italy, Galicia, or the Slovakian mountains had as their point of reference a standard of living that was low in comparison to that of Birmingham workers. But living in bunkhouses or shacks along railroad tracks, exploited in noisy factories, maimed by machinery, many felt that at home only draft animals were worked and fed in the same way. "America for the oxen, Europe for the men."[84] Elsewhere, migrant agricultural workers were housed worse than cattle. For these men and women, migration meant a lower standard of living—and they knew it—but they needed the wages to survive at home during the winter.[85] On the other hand, Polish miners in the Ruhr District might even live in comparatively comfortable company housing, or Pennsylvania miners might own a small piece of land.[86] Furthermore, for single women, wages were in many cases starvation wages, and this implied both a lower standard of living and higher sexual exploitation than life as a supernumerary old maid on a relatives' subsistence farm. Girls and women migrating as workers into Austrian factories or as nurses into Viennese families described in bitter words their low standard of living, both material and emotional.[87]

Further research is needed to determine where and how the notions of higher wages and better opportunities were derived. Were workers who achieved good wages more articulate in their letters or in the labor press? Were those who had to move to wherever jobs were available underrepresented in the statistics? Did common laborers write less because of a higher rate of illiteracy?[88] In industrializing areas the possibilities of finding work were better, but not necessarily the standard of living.

As for social mobility, European societies presented barriers within as well as between classes. In areas of comparable industrialization, whether in Europe or in America, intergenerational upward social mobility was similar and similarly limited, and by 1900, the differences between the top and bottom strata were as large in the United States as in Europe.[89] In the United States, however, the gradation was a sliding one, with some grades being impossible to scale. As mentioned above, migrants associated a more open social hierarchy with signs; for example, they could wear a hat or a bonnet instead of being restricted to a cap or a shawl. They did not have to doff their caps when asking for work or when greeting someone from a socially superior position. Everyone was "Mister"—no one was regarded as a superior being.

Social mobility in European towns and cities was similar to that in the United States and Canada, as studies of British, Danish, Dutch, French, German, and Swedish towns show. Concerning intergenerational mobility, Kaelble has argued: "There is no indication from the dozen studies of mobility rates between various social classes that the proportion of inhabitants who left the social class of their fathers was larger in America than in Europe."

A distinct difference did exist for downward mobility: the move "from white collar family background to the working class was much more frequent in European cities than in American cities." However, as for intragenerational (career) mobility, "the chances of social ascent of workers were clearly higher in American cities than in European cities," where "ten per cent or less of the workers reached lower middle class . . . positions within ten years time," while in most American cities the rate was 10 percent or more. Rates of downward career mobility, on the other hand, were about the same for both sides. The chances of upward mobility were particularly high for unskilled workers. Kaelble summarizes: "the bulk of evidence does not support the view of distinctly superior opportunities in nineteenth-century American cities."[90]

More rapid occupational change in America offered opportunities but did not necessarily include upward mobility. A comparatively large tertiary sector provided jobs (for women). Immigrants could move into shopkeeper and other lower-middle-class positions within their ethnic group. Did they need services on a commercial basis since the number of women was lower? The more rapid transition to highly mechanized mass production offered positions for un- and semiskilled labor. In the life cycle, higher upward mobility in America occurred up to the age of about fifty, with higher downward mobility after that. However, the perception may differ from the measurable data. The move from, for example, a Croatian village to a Cleveland slum did not necessarily imply upward mobility, but cash wages and the availability of jobs provided the opportunity to choose between different jobs and allocation of income.[91]

If the difference between the western European societies of origin and the North American receiving areas was not in social mobility, it may be found in the relative strength of social barriers. A rigid class system and a rigid ethnic stratification provide a high conflict potential. The barriers erected against Czech workers in Vienna and against Polish in-migrants in the Ruhr District led to struggles for linguistic and cultural survival. Swedish workers moved to the United States because class barriers were lower.[92] To discuss the question of the impact of social stratification on acculturation on an aggregate level raises the danger of bypassing the many microlevels, the experiences reported back home. The two forms of social organization, closed and highly stratified (the "European model") and stratified but comparatively open (the "American model") are the extreme ends of a continuum of a multiplicity of forms of social organization found on both sides of the Atlantic. Paternalist employers in Europe could mitigate the appearance of class barriers, while some mine owners in the American West crushed their workers with an iron heel.[93]

The migrant mass workers at the turn of the century and after fought as hard for better wages and working conditions as skilled native-born (or earlier immigrant) workers. Sometimes they were more radical.[94] The reportedly unorganizable migrant women struggled and struck, too. The letters of migrants and their press suggest that they considered barriers in the society of origin to be permanent, while in the United States it was individual employers who prevented them from living decent lives. Though labor newspapers by 1900 referred to the principles of the Declaration of Independence, more and more newcomers viewed the "new," reportedly open, system as class-based. The immigrant labor press and contemporary German diplomats both considered America a "plutocracy," a country where money ruled absolute. The personal "independence" which migrants sought could no longer be achieved.[95]

Working conditions in American cities were similar to those in European cities. U.S. monopolies were more oppressive to workers than policemen's clubs in Germany. Corruption was judged worse than in Russia, and the pace of work, because of the advanced machinery, higher than in England. The New York police were deeply involved in criminal rackets and were as one-sided as an instrument of employers as the Berlin police.[96] Italian-American radicals summarized their view: "Are we or are we not in free America? Unfortunately the word 'Liberty' has become a myth." America, "alleged land of liberty and bread," had been "dishonored."[97] A Swedish social democrat concurred.[98] Stratification increased dramatically from the 1870s on, and the societies of the two continents in the North Atlantic economies became socially almost identical, characterized by paupers and millionaires, starvation and extreme luxury, a growing class of speculators and idlers living off dividends rather than by honest work. Among immigrants, only healthy and physically robust people had a chance. They, through the "almighty dollar," could achieve a status that class position by birth would deny them in Europe.[99]

This experience of stratification had to be cast in the context of a worldview shared by both migrant and native-born workers. In the United States, a kind of social republicanism prevailed into the 1870s. It drew its inspiration from the rights of men and the unfulfilled founding principles of the republic. People did not receive "the fruits of their labor," had no time for family life and recreation, and lacked the "education to participate as active and intelligent citizens in the affairs of state." The position of "citizen," independent of want and social pressure, involved a notion of individual property: owning land, possessing lower-middle-class status, and receiving living wages that represented the value of labor.[100] Immigrant workers could tie into this tradition. The European revolutions of 1848–49 and before had raised similar issues.[101] Many of the migrants were still very close to the land.[102] Workers in Europe had been striving for a position that gave their class an accepted place in the social and political system.[103]

From the 1870s to the 1910s, the increasing concentration of production in factories, the spread of ever-larger urban agglomerates, and the replacement of skilled workers by unskilled or semiskilled masses of workers brought about a shift in worldview. The social-republican emphasis on the independent citizen changed into a labor view based on class. In Europe, social democratic parties emerged, while in North America a series of strikes brought the issues to public attention. The societal framework in which acculturation had to occur changed decisively. Migrants were involved in bringing about these changes, and later migrants would benefit from and build on the earlier achievements.

The new consciousness combined republicanism, self-organization, and militancy with ethnic, class, local, or regional variants of solidarity. The ideal of the independent citizen was turned into the ideal of the respected wage earner who was paid according to a labor theory of value and who participated in the political system. This new consciousness reached a high level during World War I, when immigrant workers-turned-soldiers fought to make *their* world safe for democracy. In 1919 the steel strike in the United States demonstrated this new consciousness, and it was evidenced in Germany in the postwar workers' councils, as many class and community studies illustrate. After the Paris Commune of 1871 and the nationwide U.S. railroad strike of 1877, class positions were in the open: "The mob is a wild beast and needs to be shot down" noted a *New York Herald* writer, while Ira Steward, of the Machinists' and Blacksmiths' Union, argued, "When the working classes are denied everything but the barest necessities of life, they have no decent use for liberty."[104]

In response to the new militancy, reforms were initiated from above: social security laws in Bismarckian/Wilhelmine Germany and the limited concessions of President Wilson, as well as moves by progressive capital to secure orderly production procedures rather than maximum exploitation. The reforms were coupled with harsh, repressive measures against the more radical parts of the labor movement, the "fellows with no fatherland," that is, social democrats in Germany, or the "seditious aliens," the Industrial Workers of the World in the United States.

Throughout the fifty years preceding World War I, acculturation depended on whether migrants were viewed by the receiving society economically as temporary workers, politically as aliens with no sociocultural identity, or presumably permanent workers, politically integratable persons with a sociocultural base that expressed itself first in an ethnic lower-class culture and later in an ethnic multiclass community. The process involved a double acculturation: from peasant or rural laborer to first-generation proletarian, and from immigrant to ethnic denizen to citizen.

Gender-specific analyses of acculturation argue that men went out into the new environment to work and earn money while women stayed at home in the ethnic neighborhood, having no contact with the new society. Such reasoning begs the question of how the consumption side of the family economy was organized. How was shopping done? How was information exchanged on street corners, after church, or in the tenement yards? Did migrant women talk only to people of their own ethnicity? Segregation indices show that different groups lived on the same street. Interaction occurred, but in some letters of migrant women only the dateline indicates from where they were written. The text does not refer to life in a different society. However, a son's measles and a daughter's birthday were important regardless of place of sojourn—considerably more important than Washington's birthday or the Fourth of July. The recipients of such letters—parents, relatives, and, above all, prospective migrants who would rejoin the family—also were more interested in these private aspects of life than in who had won the last elections.[105]

Women had different migration patterns and different expectations. But since they had less access to money, they often had to depend on (male) family members to send tickets. Being dependent, women often migrated within an international but ethnically segregated marriage market just as men migrated within international labor markets.[106] Letters by men show that they often inquired about marriage partners in their old village or town of origin, or that brothers brought over their sisters because friends were looking for brides. Many women followed such calls, some because of love, others because this was the only way to migrate across the Atlantic. This placed a double strain on them: they were being selected as partners (as "helpmeets") to ensure the continuity of old-culture living patterns. At the same time they were not to look or act like "greenhorns" and expose their husbands to ridicule. Men's letters about marriage partners sounded like help-wanted ads. Women were almost as necessary as bread, since washing, repairing, and sewing were too expensive to be given out. On the other hand, women were no longer judged by the size of the dowry they would bring into the family economy.[107]

Women also migrated on their own and created their separate migration chains. They left Europe because they disliked the negotiations between fathers and future husbands about dowry payments, as if the women were being "sold off."[108] The independence that came with wage work, as in the case of New England mill girls, was valued highly. A Swedish immigrant woman offered prepaid tickets to her girlfriends: their wages as maids would enable them to repay the passage money quickly. Women's wages in Swedish agrarian labor were forty to fifty öre a day, and less for crofter women. This ensured subsistence just above starvation. At that rate the crossing of the Atlantic, not counting the railroad trip, would have been the equivalent of 250 days of labor. In Swedish literature, the earning of fifty öre (fourteen cents) was considered the almost unachievable dream of children.[109]

Women established living patterns according to their specific interests. Swedish women migrating into Stockholm often deliberately did not marry, though they lived together with a partner and started a family. As single women, they kept their rights to property, wages, and children. Marriage would have transferred all of these rights to the male. Thus the stigma of concubinage, unbearable in a village society, was considerably less of an obstacle in an anonymous urban society. It was definitely less of a burden than a lawful husband might become.[110]

Autobiographical texts of women migrating within the German states present a different picture. Employers viewed women as sexually exploitable. Domestics had no rights and often were dismissed for the slightest of illnesses so as not to infect the employer's children. The experience of immigrant women in the needle trades in the United States was similarly degrading.

Women migrating to the United States sometimes emphasized the better position held by women in America.[111] After migration, women could go on their own to festive events, and they could dance without being chaperoned.[112] Maria Förschler suggested to her sister to join her in the United States: she would not have to work in the fields. Women could dress like the better sort at home. Women could make good money in America and marry well. Immigrant males definitely did gripe about this new position of women. One man wrote home that American women spend their days in the rocking chair, sewing a little and reading a little to pass the time.[113]

Once again, however, the evidence presents a complex picture. The different role of women is described mainly in letters from farming areas and by single women in domestic service. From life in the New York tenements, Anzia Yezierska narrated how her semiautobiographical heroine "Sara" was dealt out less meat in a soup kitchen then the men behind her.[114] "Rosa," an Italian woman, had to follow her husband to America and let herself be beaten up by him—and was expected to serve him when he opened a brothel.[115] German male socialists in America stubbornly argued that the best place for their wives and for women in general was in the home.[116] Women moved into gender relations which were more favorable to them—or at least made them less like beasts of burden.

6. *The Political System*

While the economic sphere provides the means for survival and the social sphere shapes attitudes and lifestyles, the political system determines admission standards, if any, and the exercise of citizens' rights. In immigration countries, the political sphere frequently is marginal to the short-term interests of migrants; in closed societies the system prevents entry into the economic sphere, or places restrictions on migrants.

Some political systems, in addition, act as pull factors. Western European states attracted Jewish migrants from the Russian empire because emancipation legislation came comparatively early. France, Great Britain, and Switzerland were attractive for political refugees from the Germanies, Austria, Italy, and Russia throughout much of the nineteenth century. On the other hand, Irish migrants going to England and Polish migrants going to Germany did move to destinations that were the imperial centers that contributed to or even caused the economic backwardness of the migrants' native areas. By contrast, the political system of the United States exerted a powerful hold over the minds of many prospective European migrants, from its Declaration of Independence to the demise of the European revolutions of 1848–49. The disenchanted reports of the Forty-eighters and, from the 1870s, the increasingly critical reports about the new American "plutocracy" partly offset the image.[117]

The political guidelines for the admission of migrants provided opportunities for acculturation or foreclosed them once and forever. The admission process, even in comparatively open countries, left a deep, often scarring impression upon the migrants' minds, as has been outlined above.

Everyday lives after admission were influenced by integrationist or exclusionist policies. In Germany, labor migrants had little or no chance to conduct a life unsupervised by the police. Once in the country, workers could not strike, move about, or change employers. They had to register with the police upon arrival and deregister before leaving. Male and female skilled workers from "racial and ethnic stock" acceptable to the authorities, for example Danish, Dutch, and Swiss migrants, had some security of status and freedom of movement provided they went to the cities. Polish migrants had practically no rights: "20,000 Galicians for offer" read a typical advertisement in 1909—men, girls, and boys for fieldwork, brickyards, and factories at hourly, daily, or monthly wages or piece rates. "If necessary I guarantee that the workers will not run away before the end of the work [not "contract"] through my own overseers."[118] Labor migrants could gain no political rights, and citizenship was impossible.

Poles from the annexed territories faced harassment and Germanization policies, although they were citizens with voting rights within the graded three-class system. Most were bilingual, and, once a conquered minority, they had become (reluctantly) partially acculturated individuals. The movement into the non-Polish environment of the Ruhr District, which about half a million men and women undertook (net figure) accelerated this move toward the hegemonial culture. The migrants formed ethnic organizations, married, and sent their children to German schools. However, social-democratic industrial unions and especially the Christian Miners' Union were reluctant to treat Polish miners on an equal basis. Since the 1890s, zealous anti-Polish German officials and the Law of Associations of 1908 decreed that the Polish language could no longer be used in public meetings. As a result, Polish-German organizations had to restrict membership and could meet in closed session under police supervision only. This discrimination forced them into a "secondary minority formation." Czechs in Vienna and Irish in New York had similar experiences.[119] The policies of the German Reich—and other states—were designed to make the stay for workers as disagreeable as possible.[120]

In immigration countries, the political framework was different, all discrimination notwithstanding. One important integrative aspect was the relative ease with which citizenship and voting rights could be acquired. Newcomers were reluctant to renounce old allegiances, and refugees fled governments, not cultures. Temporary labor migrants had to keep their citizenship. The possibility of receiving "first papers" in the United States by a declaration of intention to petition for citizenship later, and by merely renouncing allegiance to "foreign potentates" rather than to a culture, was as important a path of entry as dual citizenship is today in the 1990s. First papers conferred voting rights for local elections, that is, on the level which had the most influence on immigrant lives and which was certainly more important than what was going on in a distant national government.

While the psychological dimension of this integrative measure can hardly be overestimated, the question remains how many migrants actually participated in the political process. Of the total male population twenty-one years old and over, one-quarter was foreign-born in 1890. Of these, 2.5 million (58.6 percent) were naturalized, and another 236,000 had first papers (5.4 percent). Both groups together amounted to 16.4 percent of the voting-age population. Thus, on average, their influence—if they did vote—was low.[121]

For the second generation of immigrants, citizenship was conferred by birth and acculturation furthered by education in a public school system. The impact of schooling does merit further attention since immigrant children had language problems and were often required to earn money for their families; moreover, immigrant parents sometimes held a hostile view of teachers who caused the children to become estranged from the old ways and thus from their parents.[122] Attendance requirements as well were often low. For adults, educational opportunities were few: the settlement house activities and courses organized by well-meaning social workers met with indifference and hostility, as did many of the evening classes of later Americanization programs. Social workers usually could not see beyond their middle-class values and thus unconsciously clashed head-on with lower-class experiences and expectations.[123]

The often-raised question of why enfranchised labor migrants never turned to radical or socialist parties in large numbers cannot be discussed in detail here.[124] Political refugees among the newcomers, whether German, Czech, or Magyar Forty-eighters, or Russian Jewish workers after 1905, quickly realized that the republican system was far from perfect. The flexibility of the Democratic Party to take up issues concerning migrants and immigrant workers, or the temporary emergence of local labor parties, defused friction.[125] City machines provided access to the system for immigrants (whatever the bitter and usually justified complaints about corruption by native-born middle classes, to whom the system delivered the goods). The Democratic Party's ward heelers were able to solve numerous problems for their immigrant clientele, even to provide some of them with patronage jobs (compared to socialist parties, which had nothing to offer but a program). The boss system operated on business principles: pay for the votes and profit from the transaction. The struggle for voting rights was both a class and a women's affair in Europe; it concerned women only in the United States.[126] The notion that an open system and ethnic fragmentation prevent the emergence of or even the need for socialist alternatives and feelings of class identity cannot be sustained. (In Australia, class feeling and labor politics did emerge.) Another feature of U.S. society reportedly unique to the United States prior to industrialization, a "broad middle class of independent producers," also characterized Swedish and Norwegian societies. The latter produced a radical, the former a social-democratic, movement.[127]

While the participatory features of the U.S. system may have slowed down the emergence of organized opposition, any political stance outside the politically accepted ideological boundaries was repressed as rigidly as in Europe. The show trials against immigrant radicals, whether German workers, a Swedish bard or Italian fishpeddlers, served as a warning. Policing agencies were well developed in the United States but different from what existed in Europe. The state governors, the national executive, and the higher courts were the nerve centers for repressive measures during the "industrial wars." By 1895, corporation lawyers could impress the justices of the Supreme Court by pointing to the threat which the "communistic march of the 60 million," including more than eleven million first- and second-generation immigrants, posed to the other, property-owning, 9.6 million inhabitants.[128] The change from the unreliable militia system, an enforcement agency manned by peers (provided for by the Second Amendment), to a (middle-)class-based National Guard, to the use of the army during strikes, and to the role of the Attorney General in securing antilabor injunctions or, later, in destroying radical movements (as exemplified by the Palmer Raids) all point to the concentration of anti-immigrant labor activity at the level of government furthest removed from local pressures.[129] The local police, on the other hand, were less well armed and trained than in Europe. In fact, they could even become the domain of an ethnic group and were, to a degree, flexible and responsive to local needs. In Europe, the local policeman was inflexible, while the national government passed social security laws.

Repression in the United States reached unprecedented levels with the conjunction of a strong labor movement of native-born workers that included the radicalization of miners and seamstresses and the high tide of immigration. The inflexible, often brutal instruments of repression like the Pinkertons and the coal and iron police were privately owned by companies. The notorious deputies sworn in during strikes also were no permanent agents of the government but temporary auxiliaries sworn in by local sheriffs, with and for the support of private companies. Thus, the hatred of immigrant workers was not necessarily turned against the political system as a whole, but against some individual capitalists and those politicians and law-inforcement officials who supported them.

On the other hand, the state also provided symbols with which immigrants could identify. What Washington had been to native-born Anglo-Americans into the 1840s, Lincoln became for the recently arrived Euro-Americans from the 1860s: the simple store clerk with his down-to-earth way of speaking, the man who liberated slaves just as serfs had been liberated in Europe. Some of his immigrant admirers had known serfdom or were still paying off the indemnity imposed on them in return for their "freedom."[130] There was an irony in these two emancipation processes that was probably not noticed by contemporaries. European peasants did not get forty acres and a mule, either, and this was one important reason why so many of them had to migrate to the United States or elsewhere to work.

This kind of symbol was supplemented by shared elements of the respective political and social ideologies that permitted migrants and immigrants to join forces with native-born white Americans. A Slovak appeared, for example, in the 1886 Fourth of July parade in Homestead, Pennsylvania, in the uniform of the European revolutions of 1848–49. The immigrant women who attacked the Pinkertons in Homestead bitterly accused them of taking the bread out of honest workers' mouths. One hundred and fifty years earlier, Anglo-American women in the colonies had chased off British customs collectors with exactly the same words. This common ground may best be termed "social republicanism."[131]

The interaction of politics and ethnicity has been summarized by Linda Goldstein Schneider in a study of three industrial crises between 1873 and 1919, involving large numbers of immigrant workers:

> Workers' ideas about nationality are . . . neither exclusively the product of a national society, nor of a class subculture. . . . Insofar as they were derived from a system of nationally shared values, such ideas served to integrate workers in the national culture, restricting the bases of class opposition. Yet, at the same time, workers modified and reinterpreted the meaning of nationality, using such ideas to articulate class experience and express class consciousness.[132]

Two examples illustrate this. Homestead strikers, who organized their own town government during the strike, never considered their acts unlawful, to the amazement of the reporter who covered the event, who noted that every one of their acts was in violation of law and the constitution. And during World War I, the war "to make the world safe for democracy," a Polish American worker bought Liberty Bonds to help achieve the eight-hour-day, and immigrant miners in Alberta either enlisted to fight the Kaiser in Europe or struck for better working conditions to fight the other Kaisers at home.[133]

---

7. Ethnic Communities, Family Economy, and Private Lives

Migrants, particularly the pioneers who first came to a city, town, mining camp, or agricultural area, had to organize their everyday lives in the new neighborhood to form an ethnically and socially defined community. This community-building process repeated itself once a neighborhood could no longer expand and members of the group had to begin to settle in a new neighborhood and create a new community in another quarter of the same town, in a suburb, or elsewhere. It involved the recreation—under the conditions of the new society—of the old cultural values while discarding their restrictive and oppressive aspects. Ethnic clustering also came about because of discrimination by the native-born and because of poverty and the need for the cheapest accommodations. But the search for culturally similar persons was equally important.

In view of their extremely limited financial means, migrants had to find a job (or land) quickly and spend as little money as possible. Finding a place to sleep for the first few nights depended on *Landsleute, landslayt,* and *paesani* from the same ethnic background. National culture counted less than the aggregate statistics about Germans or Italians may suggest. Support preferably came from people from the same region or village—in Sicily, Tuscany, Swabia, or Mecklenburg. The same village level, the same dialect, the same living conditions, and the same work experience were what counted when decisions about where to settle were made. The search for a job depended on interpreters from the ethnic community. Arranging a household meant to learn—with the help of the community—where to shop, how to cook new kinds of food, and what was dispensable and what was indispensable in the new surroundings. Hardly a step was made without the help of the community members or the paid services of the immigrant entrepreneur, the padrone, the runner, and a whole set of petty trafficers who, under the guise of help and ethnic sympathy, preyed on their fellow countrymen.

This "clustering" of migrants from the same background occurred everywhere. In Paris, newcomers from other French provinces lived together. In the United States, Germans organized by regional affiliation as Swabians, Hessians, or people from Bremen. In everyday ways of living, loyalty was to the local culture rather than to nationality. The same holds true for Italians in France, Germany, Argentina, or the United States. Czechs in Vienna concentrated overproportionally in certain quarters, as did Silesians in Berlin and Jews in London. If numbers were small, several groups might join together: Scandinavian identity united the Swedes, Norwegians, and Danes in the north-central areas of the United States, and Slavic immigrants all cooperated, old-world tensions notwithstanding.[134] However, such broader affinities lost importance once a group, by size and duration of stay, became self-sufficient.

While jobs secured the daily material subsistence, the community secured the emotional, intellectual, and social needs. If not "bread and roses, too," at least bread and someone to talk to. The patterns of everyday life were formed by the community. It took years to establish a community with associations, a parish, and informal networks. Without it there was no basis for the ethnic self-confidence which permitted steps toward accommodation with the new society on terms acceptable to the migrants.[135]

Does residential segregation imply that ethnic groups could not join forces cross-culturally to approach the new, dominant culture, to force it to be responsive to migrant demands? Conflict as well as cooperation occurred among the diverse ethnic groups. In areas with established multicultural traditions and class identities, labor organizations and strikes transcended ethnic borderlines. In turn-of-the-century Budapest, labor newspapers appeared customarily in more than one language, and calls for meetings were issued in four languages: German, Magyar (later: Magyar and German), Slovak, and Rumanian. Second, immigrant "ghettos" were not closed quarters. Rather, in Vienna as in Chicago, segregation was by street, sometimes by house. One group dominated a street or several streets, but other groups intermingled particularly on the fringes. This means that private spaces with public access (shops and saloons) had to be shared to some degree and that public spaces (streets, parks, courtyards, schools, and sometimes churches) had to be used jointly. Women had to buy food in a nearby store—even if the owner was of a different ethnicity. Strikes as well as public festivities with symbolic content—Labor Day or the Fourth of July, and memorials to the Paris Commune or the Haymarket riots—were celebrated together and members of one ethnicity planning a picnic or other outing sometimes invited neighboring groups. Thus, if not cooperation, at least numerous points of contact existed.

In addition to the informal communal networks of women, men, and children, formal associations were founded. In an era without social security legislation, the first ones were usually mutual aid societies, often combined with craft, union, or cultural activities. Others had primarily recreational functions, for example singing societies and Turnvereine or sokols. They could be used for educational purposes (as lyceums and reading rooms); they could be gender-specific, like saloons, women's aid societies, or women's clubs. Such organizations were often transplanted from the culture of origin. Since the French Revolution, the emergence of the middle class and of national consciousness in Europe had brought forth a multipurpose associational life. Migrants coming from agrarian areas had less experience with formal organization but much experience with informal ways of working together: spinning bees, harvest work, and the frolicking of rural laborers and maids. In such associations class and ethnicity merged into a shared community.

Once ethnic communities grew, shops, saloons, and ticket agencies were established by small entrepreneurs. When parishes began to function, clerics joined the group. Services which demanded little or no initial capital were provided. Women took in boarders, men established barber shops. The families could thus eat and worship as they used to do, and they could use their own language when shopping. At the same time, the community began to undergo a process of social differentiation. A lower middle class and later a class of larger merchants and factory owners came into being. Subjectively, the notion of community remained strong. The massive intervention of big business was necessary, as Herbert Gutman and others have shown, to divide small town communities along class lines, to drive a wedge between small businessmen and (striking) workers. Grocers and their wives knew their prices and thus what was meant by a "living wage." Barbers, shoemakers, and laundresses participated in the daily problems of their clients. They knew that a decline in wages meant a decline of business for them. Internal social conflict within a group emerged when ascending group members became the employers of others, as is illustrated, for example, by the tensions between German master and journeyman bakers in Chicago.[136]

The community, within its means, also provided social security. In the old culture, people relied on family and kin, or perhaps on neighbors or occasionally on the paternalism of the landlord. In the new society, substitutes were needed since family resources had not yet been reestablished, while crises came aplenty: unemployment, illness, and wage cuts. With the help of the ethnic community, such crises could be weathered without returning to the security of the old society—though many did return. Thus, ethnic community-building was, in fact, a step toward establishing a permanent position in the wider new society. Migrants with longer experience and (rudimentary) knowledge of the new language mediated the contact with the larger world of foremen, employers, doctors, and lawyers. They also mediated some of the contacts with transatlantic relatives by writing letters and transferring money (usually getting rich along the way).

Ethnic communities also had an "international" function. Peoples dominated at home by the old empires received aid for cultural survival. Emigrants, not subject to national repression, printed newspapers and books in their own language to be smuggled home. Plans for independence were laid at the time of World War I. More Slovak papers were printed in the United States than in Slovakia (subject to Magyarization). Similarly, but on an ethnic and class level, German social democracy survived the repression from 1878 to 1890 only with considerable financial aid from comrades in the United States and print shops elsewhere in Europe. In these struggles, an intelligentsia and a group of political activists emerged in the migrant communities. Often these were priests, journalists, and entrepreneurs. The famous P. V. Rovnianek among the Pittsburgh Slovaks and Michael P. Kniola among the Poles in Cleveland may serve as examples. Priests founded newspapers that addressed a working-class audience, but since the readers could not live by the word alone, these papers had to address questions of wages and working conditions. The *Wiarus Polski* in the Ruhr District is as good an example of an ethnic paper founded by a Catholic priest who became labor-oriented as is the *Colorado Catholic.*[137]

Finally, the community secured the survival of the ethnic group in a biological sense. Since intermarriage was unusual, whether with members of the dominant culture or of other ethnic groups, the community had to ensure the possibility of marriage and child-raising. Given that in most migrant communities men outnumbered women—by large margins at first, and by a three-to-two ratio or two-to-one ratio later—women had to be invited in as marriage partners. Also, few men ever operated a boardinghouse without having sent for a woman to do the "domestic" labor—and probably marrying her in the process (which neatly solved the problem of wages). Since more men returned home than women, the sex ratio became somewhat more balanced over the years.

Within the community, the church played a particularly important role. While the spiritual role was similar to what it was in the old culture, the organizational setting and social meaning were different. Ethnic communities had to demand services in their own language from the church hierarchy, and they had to form their own parishes and build their own churches.

Sunday services and parish meetings became centers for the social activities of both sexes, but predominantly of women, just as the saloon was the male communication center. The rituals of the church were indispensable for the structuring of individual and familial life-courses. At birth, marriage, the baptism of children, and death, the religious culture provided the ritual to deal with these events. Czech freethinkers remained members of the church since they needed the clerics' services in these rituals. When one of the latter tried to insert religious meaning into the rituals, thereby interrupting the peaceful, culturally mediated coexistence, the freethinkers separated and developed lay rituals. Ethnic priests also had an important role in cementing community cohesion when ethnic interests had to be articulated in the face of an ethnically different church hierarchy. Sometimes magnificent churches were built to show the pride of the group in its achievements, the "peacock-effect" of religion.

If community life was based on multiple informal networks and relationships, so were the segments of the labor market.[138] Friends, relatives, and fellow villagers acted as transmitters. The letters from America were addressed to kin and read to friends. Even direct recruiting through agents or gang bosses, in the case of intra-European migration, relied on family networks and village relationships. Only in rare cases did trade unions provide the network among workers.[139] Such networks were often gender-specific.

In ethnic organizations, males dominated; even church councils were predominantly or exclusively male. Women, on the other hand, moved in informal networks. An important study of in-migration to Paris, based on interviews, described how men and women talked about their roles using very different frames of reference. Men talked about jobs, perhaps their activity in ethnic organizations, and they did so in the first-person singular: "I did." Women, on the other hand, connected specific events to relationships and used the plural, "we," or the neutral "one did." The perception of personal experiences was thus extremely different for males and females: it was individual activity versus collective network experiences.[140] A similar distinction emerged in a recent study of present-day North African migrants in France. In the case of customary parental authority over the choice of marriage partners for daughters, while fathers, after migration, would still decide that "she shall marry X," mothers questioned—in a circle of women—"should she not marry X?" Fathers thus staked their authority and identity and had to defend it in the event of a daughter's opposition, while the women's way of dealing with such conflicts between old and new norms suggests that customary behavior was considered worth continuing but that other possibilities were not ruled out. Other options, new norms, could enter into the discussion; the changing of traditions, that is, acculturation, became possible.[141] Both studies suggest that it is primarily women who build, adapt, and change the informal networks.

Migration in many cases was a migration of family members, with one person establishing the foothold and brothers, sisters, spouses, children, and sometimes parents following. Family relations had to be reconstituted, often after long years of separation. Each succeeding family member or friend was inserted into the labor market and integrated into the community. This was true for New England mill girls, eastern European men and women, and Italian families.[142] The informal relations left direct traces only in letters by women (and by single [!] male migrants) and in oral histories.[143]

Women reported in their letters in detail about other family members and thus kept open the option of either bringing over later migrants from the same family or friendship network or of returning and reacculturating into the old family after a long separation. They reported about kin and fellow or sister villagers who had migrated to another community and job, about marriages or separations, about illness and good fortune, about help from other network-related migrants, or about the cutting off of network ties. Some historians have considered such information trivial, since it supposedly tells us nothing about acculturation to the institutions of the new society. In such letters there was no mention of the new political system, little reference to the different social norms, few words about wages. However, it is just this personal information that permits the continuity of networks. In these private communications the objects of societal push and pull showed how they remained conscious and well-informed agents of their own futures.[144] If women had the role of establishing and maintaining the informal networks, while men, more marginal to their functioning, moved more easily into and out of them, then women also had more to lose when leaving the old society. Their whole network was left behind. This might explain the reportedly higher incidence of homesickness (network sickness, more precisely) among women.

Women's work and family relationships, of course, involved more than just emotional aspects and the aim of establishing networks the sum of which we call "community."[145] The economic status of families was determined as much by earning as by spending, the latter done primarily by women. Women also contributed to family income through their own wage work, which, again, depended upon networks: children had to be cared for by other women at least until the oldest child could be entrusted with the younger ones. Income for the family economy could also be increased by adding to the load of women's housework by taking boarders. Donna Gabaccia has demonstrated in her study of the acculturation of Sicilian migrants in New York how the flexible use of the labor power of women and children under given outer circumstances could either keep intact or change old social norms.[146]

In view of the research on the family economy and the wage work of women outside the home, the hypothesis that women retarded acculturation by staying at home and not getting in touch with the new society seems untenable.[147] Whether wages were earned by unskilled male workers stacking steel wire onto railroad cars or by a semiskilled female worker sewing shirtwaists, whether labor and skill were substituted for wages by male boarders tending vegetable gardens, raising pigs, or shooting venison or by women shopping judiciously, all contributed to the family economy. This family economy within a community was the basis for acculturation. All of these activities were done while in contact with the new society.

Individual migrants would have to approach a new society with little or no standing, but community members could look down from the heights—or the modest levels—of their achievements, survey the social landscape, and search for the easiest way, even if it was still a rocky one, to enter the dominant society's organizations. These institutions, whether political or educational, had to take note of community demands and adapt to the new population, to the new citizens.

In conclusion, the experience of one woman will illustrate the complexities of the acculturation process.[148] Rosa, a young Italian woman from the village of Bugiarno in Lombardy, worked in the silk factories and helped in her foster mother's small restaurant. She was married, as was the custom, by her foster mother to an older man (definitely not of her own choice). A few months later, the husband, having been thrown out of the house for being violent to his wife, joined a gang of workers recruited for an iron mine in Missouri. More than a year later, some of the gang returned carrying the news that the men in the "mines in Missouri need women to do the cooking and washing. . . . Three men have sent for their wives and two for some girls to marry." An international labor market, through the economics of love and reproductive work, became an international marriage market. Within two weeks, a new gang left for Missouri, and Rosa, about fifteen or sixteen years old, had to go with them, her baby staying with the foster mother—a family in transition. The parting words of kin and friends combined cliché with the reality of the new society. They suggested to Rosa, "you will get smart in America. And in America you will not be so poor," and to the men that they were on the way "to be millionaires." Three other women came along, one to marry a man who had left the home village when she was seven, the second "to marry a man I've never seen in my life. And he's not Lombardo—he's Toscano." She "didn't care who the man was" as long as she could go to America and marry, according to Rosa's report. A third woman with her child was to join her husband in Missouri.

In New York, Emilia (the first) found her husband-to-be, who gave her a kiss—a new custom—and told her he would buy her new clothes; she could not go to a wedding in the old-country ones.[149] The others of the group—after having been tricked by a runner posing as a friendly fellow countryman—went on to Union, Missouri, where the *paesani* "grew silent—as if they had expected something else." The shacks were poor accommodation compared to their stone houses at home. Rosa lived next door to a family from her village. The men for whom she was to cook and clean introduced her to the new habits the morning after her arrival, told her how to prepare coffee in a way they had learned from nearby German farmers. They sent her to a German woman to get chickens. Communication? "You just make her understand, that's all." Another Italian woman taught her how to cook, including southern Italian foods. There was less stratification than at home. The American store owner, his daughter, and the postmaster "were treating me like I was as good as them."[150] Within a short time she had undergone a process of acculturation into an Italian American community, made contact with a new society, and found the equality with a postmaster agreeable, but took note of the differences between the rich and the poor. The rich, whom she met later in Chicago, were those who could pay the fare for the streetcar.

After she had given birth to a second son, she returned unchaperoned to Italy to get her firstborn, guiding along an Italian man who hardly spoke any English. In her village she was greeted with awe: she was coming from America, she wore a hat and she had new shoes. She had to talk about America until late in the evening: meat every day, streetcars, and many other things. She showed that she no longer shared the superstitions of her listeners. In between she had to get acquainted with her firstborn, now a small boy who did not remember her. When she went to the bank and dared to sit down while waiting, this breach of norms brought forth a volley of invectives from the janitor. She dared to talk back. She wanted to eat a little better than before—just rice in the soup every day—and to turn the oil lamp a little higher, and was considered extravagant.

After returning to Missouri, she changed money for the men, since only she knew how to read and calculate. When her husband used her accumulated income from working for the boarders to buy a brothel, she fled to Chicago with her children. Lost in the city she met a Toscano, who, with the help of a network of Toscanos, sent her to the relatives of a friend that she was looking for. After divorce—another new opportunity—she married a cousin of a woman from her village and contributed to the family income by working as a cleaning woman. During the 1893 depression her unemployed husband had to migrate to Wisconsin to work as a lumberjack. When her children were starving, she joined a soupline but fled when a policeman clubbed the woman in front of her. She wished herself back in Italy but did not go—she would not have had the return fare anyway. Later she enjoyed the security of a cleaning job, on which she could remain for years.[151]

Moving within networks, moving from job to job and to a new continent while keeping networks intact, and living in a society where people could be desperately poor and be fed soup by some and clubbed by others, a society where "opportunity" for her husband-entrepreneur meant a brothel but where divorce was possible, Rosa became a very strong woman. In all those years of migration, Rosa lived more of a life of her own than she ever would have done at home.

Notes

I am grateful for comments by Donna Gabaccia, Christiane Harzig, Walter Kamphoefner, Leslie Page Moch, and Walter Nugent.

1. Milton Gordon, *Assimilation in American Life: The Role of Race, Religion, and National Origins* (New York, 1964), 70–71.

2. Robert Redfield, Ralph Linton, and Melville J. Hershkovits, "Memorandum for the Study of Acculturation," *American Anthropologist* 38 (1936): 149, quoted in Gordon, *Assimilation*, 61.

3. Robert E. Park and Ernest W. Burgess, *Introduction to the Science of Sociology* (Chicago, 1921), 735, quoted in Gordon, *Assimilation*, 62.

4. John Goldlust and Anthony H. Richmond, "A Multivariate Model of Immigrant Adaptation," *International Migration Review* 8 (1974): 193–225. Concerning the receiving society, the authors postulate a "pluralist" society. Following John Porter's argument in *Vertical Mosaic: An Analysis of Social Class and Power in Canada* (Toronto, 1965), our model follows a stratification approach. See Thomas J. Anton, "Power, Pluralism and Local Communities," *Administration Science Quarterly* 7 (1962–63): 425–57.

5. John Bodnar, *Immigration and Industrialization: Ethnicity in an American Mill Town, 1870–1940* (Pittsburgh, 1977), and "Immigration, Kinship and the Rise of Working-Class Realism in Industrial America," *Journal of Social History* 14 (1980): 45–65.

6. Bodnar, *Immigration and Industrialization*, xv, additions by D. H.

7. Rudolph J. Vecoli, "*Contadini* in Chicago: A Critique of *The Uprooted*," *Journal of American History* 51 (1964–65): 404–17; John Bodnar, *The Transplanted: A History of Immigrants in Urban America* (Bloomington, 1985).

8. This model assumes a process of acculturation but does not cover "extreme" cases: those who returned mentally ill, those who perished in dark and airless tenements, contract workers transported with little or no knowledge of either the route or the area of destination. On the other end, some migrants seem not to have experienced any transition at all, moving from one job to the next, and remaining within their ethnic community.

9. In the case of return migration after more than a brief stay, a further process of acculturation takes place (third socialization) because, during the intervening time period, both the culture of origin and the migrant have changed.

10. Christoph Klessmann, "Polish Miners in the Ruhr District: Their Social Situation and Trade Union Activity," in *Labor Migration in the Atlantic Economies: The European and North American Working Classes during the Period of Industrialization*, ed. Dirk Hoerder (Westport, Conn., 1985), 253–76.

11. *Reports of the Immigration Commission* (Dillingham Commission), 41 vols. (Washington, D.C., 1911), 3:349–54.

12. The debate about migrant workers as strikebreakers and "cheap" labor hinges on this attitude. For the specific case of the United States this involves parts of the "why is there no socialism" debate (see below).

13. Paul C. P. Siu, "The Sojourner," *American Journal of Sociology* 58 (1953): 34–44.

14. Migration novels, like those of Moberg and Rölvaag, provide a better guide to subjective factors than the analyses of most historians.

15. In migrants' letters, strong and healthy network members were usually asked to follow first. Only later were wives and children invited to come. Parents received affectionate remarks—and often financial support. "Clearly they loved their parents and their birthplace, but these loves apparently were secondary to the pursuit of the social and economic success for which they had emigrated," Samuel L. Baily and Franco Ramella noted about two Italian emigrant brothers in Buenos Aires; see their *One Family, Two Worlds: An Italian Family's Correspondence across the Atlantic, 1901–1922* (New Brunswick, N.J., 1988), 16–17. See also Herbert G. Gutman, *Work, Culture, and Society in Industrializing America* (New York, 1976), 30; William I. Thomas and Florian Znaniecki, *The Polish Peasant in Europe and America*, 5 vols. (Chicago and Boston, 1918–1920; reprinted in several different editions).

16. Hasia R. Diner, *Erin's Daughters in America: Irish Immigrant Women in the Nineteenth Century* (Baltimore, 1983), 34 passim.

17. Criminal behavior was a further cause for departure but never reached statistically significant proportions.

18. Most authors agree that this approach is neglected. See Paul R. Shaw, *Migration Theory and Fact: A Review and Bibliography of Current Literature* (Philadelphia, 1975), 115; see also the debate over "rational choice theory" in *International Migration Review* 18 (1984): 165–73, 377–81, 381–88.

19. Gerd Raeithel, *"Go West": Ein psychohistorischer Versuch über die Amerikaner* (Frankfurt am Main, 1981); Michael Balint, *Thrills and Regressions* (London, 1959).

20. Donna R. Gabaccia, *Militants and Migrants: Rural Sicilians Become American Workers* (New Brunswick, N.J., 1988), 80; autobiographical account of Antanas Kaztauskis, *Independent* 57 (4 August 1904): 241–48. Hasia Diner argues that the postfamine "rearrangement of family life" caused out-migration (*Erin's Daughters*, 31–32). See also Karen Schniedewind, *Begrenzter Aufenthalt im Land der unbegrenzten Möglichkeiten: Bremer Rückwanderer aus Amerika, 1850–1914* (Stuttgart, 1994); Louise A. Tilly and Joan W. Scott, *Women, Work and Family* (New York, 1978). Research on gender roles in the family suggest that mothers develop and determine relationships while fathers' influences remain marginal.

21. Michael John and Albert Lichtblau, "Vienna around 1900: Images and Expectations," in *Distant Magnets: Expectations and Realities in the Immigrant Experience*, ed. Dirk Hoerder and Horst Rössler (New York, 1993); Abel Chatelain, *Les migrants temporaires en France de 1800 à 1914*, 2 vols. (Lille, 1976).

22. Under different conditions, migration was considered a sign of failure. Those who broke norms and the ne'er-do-wells escaped. Occupations held in low esteem were the domain of migrants—and often of a different ethnic group; these occupations included peddlars, sellers of glass or wire, and itinerant shoemakers.

23. See, for example, Daniel Field, *Rebels in the Name of the Tsar* (Boston, 1989).

24. For a more detailed account of these changes, see Dirk Hoerder and Inge Blank, "Ethnic and National Consciousness from the Enlightenment to the 1800s," in *Roots of the Transplanted*, ed. Dirk Hoerder, Inge Blank, and Horst Rössler, 2 vols. (New York, 1994).

25. Mary Antin, *The Promsied Land* (New York, 1912), 141–42.

26. See the essays by Nancy Green on Paris and by John and Lichtblau on Vienna in Hoerder and Rössler, *Distant Magnets*; for the concept of Potemkian facades, see the introductory essay by Dirk Hoerder in *Distant Magnets.*

27. See immigrant autobiographies, for example, Josef N. Jodlbauer, "13 Jahre in Amerika [1910–1923]" (unpublished manuscript, copy in possession of the author).

28. Marcus E. Ravage, *An American in the Making* (New York, 1917), 30; Pascal D'Angelo, *Son of Italy* (New York, 1927), 60; Louis Adamic, *Laughing in the Jungle* (New York, 1932), 5. See also Matjaz Klemencic, "The Image of America among Yugoslav, Especially Slovene Migrants: Promised Land or Bad Jobs," in Hoerder and Rössler, *Distant Magnets.*

29. Dirk Hoerder, "German Immigrant Workers' Views of 'America' in the 1880s," in *In the Shadow of the Statue of Liberty: Immigrants, Workers and Citizens in the American Republic, 1880–1920*, ed. Marianne Debouzy (Paris, 1988), 17–33. Later the rapidly developing Siberia was called "the other America" (ibid.).

30. Paul M. Hohenberg and Lynn Hollen Lees, *The Making of Urban Europe, 1000–1950* (Cambridge, Mass., 1985), 179–330; Hartmut Kaelble, *Historical Research on Social Mobility: Western Europe and the USA in the Nineteenth and Twentieth Centuries* (New York, 1981), esp. 34–57; Peter R. Shergold, *Working-Class Life: The "American Standard" in Comparative Perspective 1899–1913* (Pittsburgh, 1982); Jeffrey Williamson and Peter Lindert, *American Inequality: A Macroeconomic History* (New York, 1980), 51–53.

31. See *New Yorker Volkszeitung* and Budapest *Volksstimme* (1900–1902).

32. Both Constantine M. Panunzio (*The Soul of an Immigrant* [New York, 1928], 139, 177–78, 208, 220 passim) and Anzia Yezierska (*Breadgivers* [New York, 1925; reprint, 1975], 210, 233) vividly described the desperate search for a "real" America when the one they lived in did not square with their dreams.

33. For the flow of information across the Atlantic see Philip Taylor, *The Distant Magnet: European Emigration to the U.S.A.* (New York, 1971), chaps. 4 and 5.

34. Stephen Byrne's report quoted in Diner, *Erin's Daughters*, 89–90.

35. The average growth rate of German cities was hardly over 30 percent per decade for the last part of the nineteenth century, with Dortmund reaching a high of nearly 60 percent. In the United States, many cities still doubled their population each decade; the average urban population growth per decade was well over 60 percent.

36. Carlo Gardini, *In der Sternenbanner-Republik: Reiseerinnerungen*, German edition (Oldenburg, 1900), 198–99, 207–9, 212–13.

37. Immigrant letters sometimes explicitly stated that earlier unemployment, deprivation, or illness had not been mentioned at the time so as not to trouble old-world parents and kin. Migrants killed in accidents or who had died of unsanitary living conditions could obviously no longer report back home. Thus much of the disagreeable information was screened out of the letters. Some of those who never wrote and who moved downwards are captured in the photos of Jacob Riis and Lewis W. Hine.

38. In the April 1903 Kishinev pogrom, more than fifty persons were killed and over five hundred injured, while in the March 1911 Triangle Shirtwaist Co. fire in New York, 146 women perished.

39. Oral communication of Julianna Puskás, Budapest, to author.

40. This particular fact was emphasized by a German immigrant in 1861 (Wolfgang Helbich, ed., *"Amerika ist ein freies Land . . ." Auswanderer schreiben nach Deutschland* [Darmstadt, 1985], 116); by a Swedish immigrant in 1903 (David M. Katzmann and William M. Tuttle, Jr., eds., *Plain Folk: The Life Stories of Undistinguished Americans* [Urbana, Ill., 1982], 33); by a Swiss technician (Hannes Siegrist, "Images of Host Countries: The U.S. and Germany in the Press of Swiss Technicians [1904–1935]," in *The Press of Labor Migrants in Europe and North America, 1880s to 1930s*, ed. Christiane Harzig and Dirk Hoerder, Labor Migration Project, University of Bremen [Bremen, 1985], 565).

41. Helbich, *Auswanderer schreiben*, 142.

42. This aspect of life in America is repeated again and again in the letters of German migrants (ibid., 32, 33, 35 passim).

43. Both in German and eastern European labor publications, the separation between worker and employer—the latter never stooping down to do manual work—is decried.

44. This was said about President Lincoln, who, in immigrant letters, held a position similar to that of George Washington in the imagination of native-born Americans. No systematic study of Lincoln as a symbol has come to the author's attention.

45. Jerre Mangione, *Mount Allegro: A Memoir of Italian American Life* (1942; reprint, New York, 1981).

46. See Varpu Lindstrom-Best and Allen Seager, "*Toveritar* and the Finnish Canadian Women, 1900–1930," in Harzig and Hoerder, *The Press of Labor Migrants*, 243–64; Thomas Dublin, *Women at Work: The Transformation of Work and Community in Lowell, Mass., 1826–1860* (New York, 1979), 36–39; Jacqueline Hall et al., "Cotton Mill People: Work, Community, and Protest in the Textile South, 1880–1940," *American Historical Review* 91 (1986): 246–86; Horst Rössler, "The Dream of Independence: The North Staffordshire Potters' America in the 1840s," in Hoerder and Rössler, *Distant Magnets*, 46.

47. Philip Taylor in his *The Distant Magnet* has first pointed to the impact of the trip.

48. In the ports of Bremen and Bremerhaven, emigration agents, merchants, and shipping companies successfully attempted to enlarge their share of the traffic by treating the migrants well. Eyewitness accounts by Polish emigrants in Witold Kula, Nina Assorobodraj-Kula, and Marcin Kula, eds., *Listy emigrantów z Brazylii i Stanów Zjednoczonych, 1890–1891* (Warsaw, 1973), 122, 125, passim; English edition of the Kula volume by Josephine Wtulich, *Writing Home: Immigrants in Brazil and the United States, 1890–1891* (Boulder, Colo., 1986). Dirk Hoerder, "Auswandererverschiffung über Bremen/Bremerhaven: Staatliche Schutzmaßnahmen und Erfahrungen der Migranten," *Zeitschrift für Kulturaustausch* 39 (1989): 279–91.

49. Mary Antin, *From Plotzk [recte: Polotzk] to Boston* (1899; reprint, New York, 1986), 22–26, 51–52; Michael Just, *Ost- und südosteuropäische Amerikawanderung 1881–1914: Transitprobleme in Deutschland und Aufnahme in den Vereinigten Staaten* (Wiesbaden, 1988), 44–142; David M. Brownstone et al., *Island of Hope, Island of Tears* (New York, 1986), 168, 204–5, 227; *Reports of the Immigration Commission*, 3:367, 4:122–23.

50. There are only a few reports of women acting as guides.

51. *Reports of the Immigration Commission*, 3:358–59, 362–65. Stieglitz's famous photo "The Steerage" shows return migrants, not, as is often assumed, immigrants.

52. Letter by Ludwik Koronowski, 6 March 1891, in Kula, *Listy*. See also Broughton Brandenburg, *Imported Americans: The Story of the Experiences of a Disguised American and His Wife Studying the Immigration Question* (New York, 1904), chap. 5; Brownstone et al., *Island of Hope*, 147–236.

53. Immigration laws passed between 1875 and 1903. The period of the quota laws will not be dealt with since political changes in Europe and worldwide economic changes reduced the number of migrants anyway. See Roy L. Garis, *Immigration Restriction* (New York, 1927); E. P. Hutchinson, *Legislative History of American Immigration Policy, 1798–1965* (Philadelphia, 1981); "Federal Immigration Legislation," vol. 39 of *Reports of the Immigration Commission*.

54. For the inspection in Europe see Just, *Ost- und südosteuropäische Amerikawanderung*, 97–123; *Reports of the Immigration Commission*, 4:69–134; Brownstone et al., *Island of Hope*, chaps. 5, 6; Brandenburg, *Imported Americans*, 159–70, 198–227.

55. *Reports of the Immigration Commission*, 3:366–71, 4:122–23.

56. Ulrich Herbert, *Geschichte der Ausländerbeschäftigung in Deutschland 1880 bis 1980: Saisonarbeiter, Zwangsarbeiter, Gastarbeiter* (Berlin, 1986); Lothar Elsner and Joachim Lehmann, *Ausländische Arbeiter unter dem deutschen Imperialismus 1900 bis 1985* (Berlin, 1988), statistics in chap. 1.

57. This organization, first named "Zentralstelle zur Beschaffung deutscher Ansiedler und Feldarbeiter," changed its name to "Deutsche Feldarbeiterzentrale" in 1905 and was renamed "Deutsche Arbeiterzentrale" in 1912.

58. The complex administrative and legal relationship between contracts and legitimizing cards cannot be dealt with here.

59. Summary of regulations in Elsner and Lehmann, *Ausländische Arbeiter*, 25–29, 370–75. The southern German states and the Hanse cities of Bremen and Hamburg did not follow the strict Prussian regulations.

60. International conferences to regulate the central European labor market were held in Berlin in 1909 and Budapest in 1910.

61. Dirk Hoerder and Hartmut Keil, "The American Case and German Social Democracy at the Turn of the 20th Century, 1878–1907" in *Why Is There No Socialism in the United States?* ed. Jean Heffer and Jeanine Rovet (Paris, 1988), 141–65; Hoerder, "German Immigrant Workers' Views of 'America'," 17–33.

62. Julianna Puskás, "Transatlantic Migration from a Hungarian Village on the Basis of Oral Testimonies," in Harzig and Hoerder, *The Press of Labor Migrants*, 59–69.

63. David M. Gordon, Richard Edwards, and Michael Reich, *Segmented Work, Divided Workers: The Historical Transformation of Labor in the United States* (Cambridge, 1982).

64. Peter Doeringer and Michael J. Piore, *Internal Labor Markets and Manpower Analysis* (Lexington, Mass., 1971); Clark Kerr, *Markets and Other Essays* (Berkeley, Calif., 1977); Michael J. Piore, *Birds of Passage: Migrant Labor and Industrial Societies* (New York, 1979); Ida Schreuder, "Labor Segmentation, Ethnic Division of Labor, and Residential Segregation in American Cities in the Early Twentieth Century," *Professional Geographer* 41 (1989): 131–43.

65. F. C. Valkenburg and A.M.C. Vissers, "Segmentation of the Labour Market: The Theory of the Dual Labour Market—The Case of the Netherlands," *Netherlands Journal of Sociology* 16 (1980): 155–70; Randy Hodson and Robert L. Kaufmann, "Economic Dualism: A Critical Review," *American Sociological Review* 47 (1982): 727–39; Walter Licht, "Labor Economics and the Labor Historian," *International Labor and Working Class History* 21 (1982): 52–62; B. Harrison, "Human Capital, Black Poverty and 'Radical Economics'," *Industrial Relations* 10 (1971): 285; Edna Bonacich, "A Theory of Ethnic Antagonism: The Split Labor Market," *American Sociological Review* 37 (1972): 547–59; John B. Christiansen, "The Split Labor Market Theory and Filipino Exclusion: 1927–1934," *Phylon* 40 (1979): 66–74; see also Toni Pierenkemper and Richard Tilly, *Historische Arbeitsmarktforschung: Entstehung und Probleme der Vermarktung von Arbeitskraft* (Göttingen, 1982).

66. Victor R. Greene, *The Slavic Community on Strike: Immigrant Labor in Pennsylvania Anthracite* (Notre Dame, Ind., 1968); Michael A. Barendse, *Social Expectations and Perception: The Case of the Slavic Anthracite Workers* (University Park, Pa., 1981).

67. Gutman, *Work, Culture, and Society*, 5–8, 23–24 passim. See also Tamara K. Hareven, *Family Time and Industrial Time: The Relationship between Family and Work in a New England Industrial Community* (Cambridge, 1982).

68. Klaus J. Bade, " 'Preußengänger' und 'Abwehrpolitik': Ausländerbeschäftigung, Ausländerpolitik und Ausländerkontrolle auf dem Arbeitsmarkt in Preußen vor dem Ersten Weltkrieg," *Archiv für Sozialgeschichte* 24 (1984): 91–283, esp. 99–162.

69. Valkenburg and Vissers, "Segmentation," 152.

70. William H. Sewell, Jr., "Natives and Migrants: The Working Class of Revolutionary Marseille, 1848–1951," in *Workers in the Industrial Revolution: Recent Studies of Labor in the United States and Europe*, ed. Peter N. Stearns and Daniel J. Walkowitz (New Brunswick, N.J., 1974), 75–116, shortened version in Hoerder, ed., *Labor Migration*, 225–51; Gisela Bock, *Die andere Arbeiterbewegung in den USA von 1909–1922* (München, 1976); Greene, *The Slavic Community*; Lawrence Schofer, *The Formation of a Modern Labor Force: Upper Silesia, 1865–1914* (Berkeley, Calif., 1975), Klaus Schönhoven, *Expansion und Konzentration: Studien zur Entwicklung der Freien Gewerkschaften im Wilhelminischen Deutschland 1890 bis 1914* (Stuttgart, 1980).

71. This has been the policy of West German unions since the beginning of the "guestworker" migrations.

72. Dirk Hoerder, "The Attitudes of German Trade Unions to Migrant Workers, 1880s to 1914," *Migracijske Teme* 4 (1988): 21–37; David Brody, *Steelworkers in America: the Nonunion Era* (New York, 1960; reprint, 1969).

73. On the cooperation between or conflict among different ethnic groups as well as among migrant and native-born workers in the United States, see Dirk Hoerder, ed., *"Struggle a Hard Battle": Essays on Working-Class Immigrants* (DeKalb, Ill., 1986).

74. Werner Sombart, *Why Is There No Socialism in the United States?* ed. C. T. Husbands (New York, 1976), 106.

75. Some reports indicate difficult, even below-subsistence conditions even for agrarian migrants. See, for example, Christian Gottlob Züge, *Der russische Colonist* (1802; new edition, Bremen, 1988), 88–90, 161–64. See in general Roger W. Bartlett, *Human Capital: The Settlement of Foreigners in Russia, 1762–1804* (Cambridge, 1979).

76. To compare typical buildings and agricultural implements before and after migration, see, for example, the open-air museum of Skansen (Stockholm) and Old World Wisconsin.

77. See the novels by Rölvaag and Moberg; Doris Weatherford, *Foreign and Female: Immigrant Women in America, 1840–1930* (New York, 1986), 157–69 passim.

78. German migrants, in their letters, often asked for additional funds from home. Sometimes one child stayed behind (or had to stay behind) to care for the aging parents. See Wolfgang Helbich, Walter D. Kamphoefner, and Ulrike Sommer, eds., *Briefe aus Amerika: Deutsche Auswanderer schreiben aus der Neuen Welt 1830–1930* (München, 1988), 162, 168, 169 passim.

79. *Historical Statistics of the United States* (Washington, D.C., 1961), series U 183.

80. Shergold, *Working-Class Life*. See also E. H. Phelps Brown and Margaret H. Browne, *A Century of Pay: The Course of Pay and Production in France, Germany, Sweden, the United Kingdom, and the United States of America, 1860–1960* (London, 1968).

81. Peter R. Shergold, " 'Reefs of Roast Beef': The American Worker's Standard of Living in Comparative Perspective," in *American Labor and Immigration History, 1877–1920s: Recent European Research*, ed. Dirk Hoerder (Urbana, Ill., 1983), 100.

82. Alexander Keyssar, *Out of Work: The First Century of Unemployment in Massachusetts* (Cambridge, Mass., 1986). See numerous autobiographical accounts and letters of migrants as well as consular reports to governments in the countries of origin about the status of their citizens as migrant workers.

83. Shergold, " 'Reefs of Roast Beef,' " 101.

84. For this and similar quotes see Gutman, *Work, Culture and Society*, 30, and Ewa Morawska, " 'For Bread with Butter': Life Worlds of Peasant Immigrants from East-Central Europe, 1880–1914," *Journal of Social History* 17 (1983–84): 392. See Brody, *Steelworkers*, 99. "We are treated almost like slaves," letter dated 3 September 1865, in H. Arnold Barton, ed., *Letters from the Promised Land: Swedes in America, 1840–1914* (Minneapolis, 1975), 118–19. See also Hoerder, *"Struggle a Hard Battle,"* 346. See also quotes in Ewa Morawska, *For Bread with Butter: The Life-Worlds of East Central Europeans in Johnstown, Pennsylvania, 1890–1940* (Cambridge, Mass., 1986).

85. Ingeborg Weber-Kellermann, *Landleben im 19. Jahrhundert* (München, 1987), 375–83.

86. Klessmann, "Polish Miners," 253 passim.

87. Joanne J. Meyerowitz, *Women Adrift: Independent Wage Earners in Chicago, 1880–1930* (Chicago, 1988), xix; Richard Klucsarits and Friedrich G. Kürbisch, eds., *Arbeiterinnen kämpfen um ihr Recht: Autobiographische Texte*, 2d ed. (Wuppertal, 1981).

88. Letters did not describe the new society in rosy colors. Friends and relatives migrating in consequence of such misinformation would burden the letterwriter's home and finances (Helbich et al., *Briefe aus Amerika*, 33).

89. Hartmut Kaelble, "Social Mobility in America and Europe: A Comparison of Nineteenth-Century Cities," *Urban History Yearbook, 1981* (Leicester, 1981), 24–38; Williamson and Lindert, *American Inequality*; Helbich, *Auswanderer schreiben*, 110–22.

90. Kaelble, "Social Mobility," 25–31.

91. Ibid., 29, 31. See also Seymour M. Lipset and Reinhard Bendix, *Social Mobility in Industrial Society* (Berkeley, Calif., 1967).

92. Klessmann, "Polish Miners," 272; Claudius H. Riegler, "Emigrationsphasen, Ak-

kulturation und Widerstandsstrategien: Zu einigen Beziehungen der Arbeitsemigration von und nach Schweden, 1850–1930," in *Migration und Wirtschaftsentwicklung,* ed. H. Elsenhans (Frankfurt, 1978), 31–69.

93. The term was used by President Grover Cleveland, Fourth Annual Message, 3 December 1888; 53rd Congress, 2nd sess., House of Representatives, Misc. Doc. 210.

94. Bock, *Die andere Arbeiterbewegung.*

95. The argument is presented in more detail in Hoerder, "German Immigrant Workers' Views of 'America'," in Debouzy, *In the Shadow of Liberty,* esp. 24–31; Dirk Hoerder, ed., *"Plutokraten und Sozialisten": Berichte deutscher Diplomaten und Agenten über die amerikanische Arbeiterbewegung, 1878–1917* (München, 1981); *New Yorker Volkszeitung (NYVZ),* 16 March, 18 April, 1 July, 9 August 1881, 6 and 24 May 1887.

96. *NYVZ* 1881–89; see also Sidney L. Harring, *Policing a Class Society: The Experience of American Cities, 1865–1915* (New Brunswick, N.J., 1983).

97. *Il Proletario,* 14 July 1917, quoted in Rudolph J. Vecoli, " 'Free Country': the American Republic Viewed by the Italian Left, 1880–1920," in Debouzy, *In the Shadow of Liberty,* 35–56.

98. Quoted in Lars-Göran Tedebrand, "America in the Swedish Labor Press, 1880s to 1920s," in Debouzy, *In the Shadow of Liberty,* 72.

99. Continued references to the question of health and strength, as well as to the fear that an illness will force migrants to start again from nothing emerge in Swedish and German immigrant letters (Helbich, ed., *Auswanderer schreiben*; Barton, *Letters*).

100. This definition is influenced by and quoted from Richard Schneirov and John B. Jentz, "Social Republicanism and Socialism: A Multi-Ethnic History of Labor Reform in Chicago, 1848–1877" (unpublished paper), 1–7.

101. For these traditions, see Bruce C. Levine, "In the Heat of Two Revolutions: The Forging of German-American Radicalism," in Hoerder, *"Struggle a Hard Battle,"* 19–45, and Richard Schneirov, "Free Thought and Socialism in the Czech Community in Chicago, 1875–1887," ibid., 121–42.

102. See, for example, John H. M. Laslett, *Nature's Noblemen: The Fortunes of the Independent Collier in Scotland and the American Midwest 1855–1889* (Los Angeles: UCLA Institute of Industrial Relations, 1983).

103. Dick Geary, *European Labour Protest 1849–1939* (New York, 1981); idem, ed., *Labor and Socialist Movements in Europe before 1914* (Oxford, 1989); Hoerder, Blank, and Rössler, *Roots of the Transplanted.*

104. The interpretation of class consciousness from the top down is based on a reading of *New York Times* reports on major strikes, 1877 to 1892. See also the report on the condition of American workers: Philip S. Foner, "The French Trade Union Delegation at the Philadelphia Centennial Exposition, 1876," *Science and Society* 40 (1976): 257–87; Samuel Bernstein, "The Paris Commune in America," in his *The First International in America* (New York, 1965), and his "American Labor and the Paris Commune," *Science and Society* 15 (1951): 144–62. For two case studies see Marianne Debouzy, "Workers' Self-Organization and Resistance in the 1877 Strikes," in Hoerder, *American Labor,* 61–77, and Paul Krause, "Labor Republicanism and 'Za Chlebom': Anglo-American and Slavic Solidarity in Homestead," in Hoerder, *"Struggle a Hard Battle,"* 143–69. Numerous recent monographs deal with these questions. See, for example, James R. Barrett, *Work and Community in the Jungle: Chicago's Packinghouse Workers 1894–1922* (Urbana, Ill., 1987); Richard J. Oestreicher, *Working People and Class Consciousness in Detroit, 1875–1900* (Urbana, Ill., 1986); Leon Fink, *Workingmen's Democracy: The Knights of Labor and American Politics* (Urbana, Ill., 1983). For the German case see Guenther Roth, *The Social Democrats in Imperial Germany: A Study in Working-Class Isolation and National Integration* (Totowa, N.J., 1963); for class consciousness combined with conservative voting patterns in Great Britain see Robert McKensie and Allan Silver, *Angels in Marble: Working-Class Conservatives in Urban England* (London, 1968).

105. This argument has been developed in discussions with the codirectors of the Emigrant Letters Project at the University of Bochum, Wolfgang Helbich and Walter Kamphoefner.

106. Suzanne Sinke, "The International Marriage Market: A Theoretical Essay," in *People in Transit: German Migrations in Comparative Perspective,* ed. Dirk Hoerder and Jörg Nagler (Cambridge, 1995), 227–48.

107. Helbich, *Auswanderer schreiben,* 133, 136 ("could you find a girl and send her over as a partner for me"), 137; Barton, *Letters,* 195, 234; Marie Hall Ets, ed., *Rosa: The Life of an Italian Immigrant* (Minneapolis, 1979), 163, 165, 169.

108. Thomas Dublin, *Women at Work,* for internal migration; Barton, *Letters;* Brownstone et al., *Island of Hope,* 36; Helbich, *Auswanderer schreiben,* 133; Inge Blank, "Polish Folk Culture," in Hoerder et al., *Roots.* See also the description by Yezierska *(Breadgivers)* of a Jewish father bargaining off his daughters.

109. Barton, *Letters,* 42 (see also 256, 285); Martin Andersen Nexö, *Pelle der Eroberer,* 2 vols. (German trans., Berlin, 1949), 1:117, 126–29; Astrid Lindgren, "Sammelaugust," in *Erzählungen* (Hamburg, 1979), 22–31.

110. Margareta R. Matovic, *Stockholmsäktenskap: Familjebildning och partnerval i Stockholm, 1850–1890* (Stockholm, 1984).

111. Weatherford, *Foreign and Female.*

112. Barton, *Letters,* 255.

113. Helbich, *Auswanderer schreiben,* 130, 132–33, 139–40 passim; Barton, *Letters,* 179.

114. Yezierska, *Breadgivers,* 165–72.

115. Hall Ets, *Rosa,* 162–71, 183, 198–200.

116. Christiane Harzig, "The Role of German Women in the German-American Working-Class Movement in Late Nineteenth-Century New York," *Journal of American Ethnic History* 8 (1989): 87–107.

117. Dirk Hoerder, "From Dreams to Evaluation of Possibilities," in Hoerder and Rössler, *Distant Magnets.* For the treatment of migration and migrants' expectations in nineteenth-century German popular literature, see Juliane Mikoletzky, *Die deutsche Amerika-Auswanderung des 19. Jahrhunderts in der zeitgenössischen fiktionalen Literatur* (Tübingen, 1988), esp. 135–43 and 283–93.

118. Herbert, *Ausländerbeschäftigung,* 34–46, quote p. 36; Claudius H. Riegler, *Emigration und Arbeitswanderung aus Schweden nach Norddeutschland, 1868–1914* (Neumünster, 1985), 59–101, 122–219.

119. Christoph Kleßmann, *Polnische Bergarbeiter im Ruhrgebiet 1870–1945* (Göttingen, 1978); Krystyna Murzynowska, *Polskie wychodzstwo zarobkowe w Zaglebiu Ruhry, 1880–1914* [Polish economic emigration in the Ruhr Basin, 1880–1914] (Wroclaw, 1972; German trans., 1979); Monika Glettler, *Die Wiener Tschechen um 1900: Strukturanalyse einer nationalen Minderheit in der Großstadt* (Munich, 1972); Nathan Glazer and Daniel P. Moynihan, *Beyond the Melting Pot: The Negroes, Puerto Ricans, Jews, Italians, and Irish of New York City* (Cambridge, Mass., 1963).

120. The "alien worker" policy was continued and changed to forced labor during the wars until 1945. When postwar West Germany needed foreign workers again (from 1955 onwards), they were intentionally named "guestworkers" to emphasize the break with the past. However, guests are expected to leave.

121. *Historical Statistics,* series C 178–84; Kirk H. Porter, *A History of Suffrage in the United States* (New York, 1918; reprint, 1969); Reed Ueda, "Naturalization and Citizenship," in *Harvard Encyclopedia of American Ethnic Groups,* 734–48.

122. For the general literature, see Francesco Cordasco, *Immigrant Children in American Schools: A Classified and Annotated Bibliography* (New York, 1976); Bernard J. Weiss, ed., *American Education and the European Immigrant, 1840–1940* (Urbana, Ill., 1982). The hostility of parents is attested to by Jerre Mangione, *A Memoir of Italian American Life* (1942;

new ed., New York, 1981). German settlers in several Midwestern states established their own separate German-language schools.

123. This has been described by Lizabeth A. Cohen, "Embellishing a Life of Labor: An Interpretation of the Material Culture of American Working-Class Homes, 1885–1915," in Hoerder, *Labor Migration*, 321–52; Gerd Korman, *Industrialization, Immigrants and Americanizers: Milwaukee 1866–1921* (Madison, 1967), esp. chap. 6, "Americanization at the Factory Gate"; Stephen Meyer, III, *The Five Dollar Day: Labor Management and Social Control in the Ford Motor Company, 1908–1921* (New York, 1981).

124. Sombart, *Why Is There No Socialism*; Husbands' introduction summarizes the debate. See also the essays in Jean Heffer and Jeanine Rovet, eds., *Why Is There No Socialism in the United States?* (Paris, 1988).

125. Historians usually eschew explanations referring simply to facts of geography (and justly so in view of geopolitical claims). But it has to be kept in mind that the European socialist parties never reached over all of Europe. To expect an American program-oriented labor or socialist party to transcend the state level and operate successfully on the national level between New York and San Francisco would imply in European geography that workers from Dublin to Athens can agree on a common program.

126. John H. M. Laslett, *Labor and the Left: A Study of Socialist and Radical Influences in the American Labor Movement, 1881–1924* (New York, 1970); Gerald Rosenblum, *Immigrant Workers: Their Impact on American Labor Radicalism* (New York, 1973); Richard L. Ehrlich, ed., *Immigrants in Industrial America, 1850–1920* (Charlotteville, 1977); Gutman, *Work, Culture and Society*.

127. Kurt B. Mayer, "Die Klassenstruktur in zwei egalitären Gesellschaften: Ein Vergleich zwischen Australien und den Vereinigten Staaten," *Kölner Zeitschrift für Soziologie und Sozialpsychologie* 16 (1964): 660–79; Walter Galenson, "Scandinavia," in idem, ed., *Comparative Labor Movements* (Englewood Cliffs, N.J., 1952), 104–72. See also Gwendolyn Mink, *Old Labor and New Immigrants in American Political Development: Union, Party and State, 1875–1920* (Ithaca, 1986); Nell Irwin Painter, *Standing at Armageddon: The United States, 1877–1919* (New York, 1987). Also Sean Wilentz, "Against Exceptionalism: Class Consciousness and the American Labor Movement," *International Labor and Working Class History* 26 (1984): 1–24, and debate, 25–36; 27 (1985): 35–38; and 28 (1985): 46–55.

128. Dirk Hoerder, "Immigrants, Labor and the Higher Courts from 1877 to the 1920s," *Storia Nordamericana* 4 (1989): 3–29. See also Painter, *Standing at Armageddon*. Income Tax Cases, 1895: see Louis B. Boudin, *Government by Judiciary*, 2 vols. (New York, 1932), quotes on 2:399, 404; Bernard Schwartz, *The Law in America: A History* (New York, 1974); Arnold M. Paul, *Conservative Crisis and the Rule of Law: Attitudes of Bar and Bench, 1887–1895* (1960; reprint, New York, 1969); Felix Frankfurter and Nathan Greene, *The Labor Injunction* (New York, 1930); Edwin Emil Witte, *The Government in Labor Disputes* (New York, 1932; reprint, 1969).

129. Joseph J. Holmes, "The National Guard of Pennsylvania: Policeman of Industry, 1865–1905" (Ph.D. diss., University of Connecticut, 1971); Jerry M. Cooper, *The Army and Civil Disorder: Federal Military Intervention in Labor Disputes, 1887–1900* (Westport, Conn., 1980); William Preston, Jr., *Aliens and Dissenters: Federal Suppression of Radicals, 1903–1933* (Cambridge, Mass., 1963), and, for Canada, Donald Avery, *"Dangerous Foreigners": European Immigrant Workers and Labor Radicalism in Canada, 1896–1932* (Toronto, 1979).

130. Serfdom was abolished in Russia as late as 1861. After emancipation, peasants in Prussia, Austria-Hungary, and Russia had to work for decades to pay indemnity to their former owners; see Peter Kolchin, *Unfree Labor: American Slavery and Russian Serfdom* (Cambridge, Mass., 1987). The *National Labor Tribune* in 1894 talked about Carnegie's "slaves and serfs" (quoted in Gutman, *Work, Culture and Society*, 105).

131. Krause, "Labor Republicanism," 154, 158, 160; *New England Courant*, 1 June 1724,

cited in Dirk Hoerder, *Crowd Action in Revolutionary Massachusetts, 1765–1780* (New York, 1977), 144. See above for the concept of social republicanism.

132. Linda Goldstein Schneider, "American Nationality and Workers' Consciousness in Industrial Conflict: 1870–1920: Three Case Studies" (Ph.D. diss., Columbia University, 1975), and idem, "Republicanism Reinterpreted: American Ironworkers, 1860–1892," in Debouzy, *In the Shadow of Liberty*, 199–214.

133. *New York Sun*, 10 and 11 July 1892, cited in Krause, "Labor Republicanism," 144; Montgomery, "Nationalism, American Patriotism and Class Consciousness among Immigrant Workers in the United States in the Epoch of World War I," 346, and Allen Seager, "Class, Ethnicity, and Politics in the Alberta Coalfields, 1905–1945," in Hoerder, *"Struggle a Hard Battle,"* 304–24 (quote about "Kaisers" in earlier, longer drafts of the essay. For a similar usage in Waterbury, Connecticut, in 1920, see Ferdinando Fasce, "Freedom in the Workplace? Immigrants at the Scovill Manufacturing Company, 1915–1921," in Debouzy, *In the Shadow of Liberty*, 126).

134. Michael Brook et al., "Scandinavians," in *The Immigrant Labor Press in North America, 1840s–1970s: An Annotated Bibliography*, ed. Dirk Hoerder and Christiane Harzig, 3 vols. (New York, 1987), 1:85–117; Jens Bjerre Danielson, "Ethnic Identity, Nationalism and Scandinavism in the Scandinavian Immigrant Socialist Press in the U.S.," ibid., 181–204.

135. The problems of persons entering a new culture without the safety of an ethnic community are described by Panunzio, *The Soul of an Immigrant*, 53–155.

136. Herbert Gutman, "Class, Status and Community Power in Nineteenth-Century Industrial Cities: Paterson, N.J.," reprinted in his *Work, Culture and Society*, 234–92; John Jentz, "Bread and Labor: Chicago's German Bakers Organize," *Chicago History* 12 (1983): 25–35.

137. Frantisek Bielik, "Slovak Newspapers in the U.S. and Their Role in the Acculturation of Slovak Emigrants," in Harzig and Hoerder, *Press of Labor Migrants*, 505–17; Krystyna Murzynowska and Christoph Klessmann, "The Polish Press in the Ruhr District and the Leading Role of *Wiarus Polski*, 1891–1923," ibid., 129–55; David Brundage, "Irish Workers and Western Populism: A Catholic Newspaper in the 1890s," ibid., 369–83.

138. Russian peasant workers in the metal industry in Moscow and St. Petersburg always knew which factories were hiring additional workers. Reginald E. Zelnik, ed., *A Radical Worker in Tsarist Russia: The Autobiography of Semen Ivanovich Kanatchikov* (Stanford, Calif., 1986).

139. Several English and Scottish unions promoted emigration schemes to reduce the labor supply at home. German unions did not encourage migration, but, seeing many of their members leave, provided information on other countries and published warnings not to go to places where employers needed strikebreakers. A sensitive study of networks is John Bodnar, *Immigration and Industrialization: Ethnicity in an American Mill Town, 1870–1940* (Pittsburgh, 1977).

140. Isabelle Bertaux-Wiame, "The Life History Approach to the Study of Internal Migration: How Women and Men Came to Paris between the Wars," in *Our Common History: The Transformation of Europe*, ed. Paul Thompson and Natasha Burchardt (London, 1982), 186–200.

141. The example was reported in the discussion of the symposium "Générations issues de l'immigration, mémoires et devenirs," Lille, 12–14 June 1985 (Groupement de Recherches Coordonnées, Migrations Internationales, de Centre National de Recherches Scientifiques).

142. Thomas Dublin, *Women at Work*; Tamara K. Hareven, "The Laborers of Manchester, New Hampshire, 1912–1922: The Role of Family and Ethnicity in Adjustment to Industrial Life," *Labor History* 14 (1975): 249–65, and idem, "The Dynamics of Kin in Industrial Communities: The Historical Perspective," in *American Journal of Sociology*, spe-

cial issue, *Turning Points: Historical and Sociological Essays on the Family,* ed. John Demos and Sarane Boocock (Chicago, 1978).

143. There is a need for research on role substitution when one gender is absent. It is well known that women took over male roles and jobs during wartime. Letters of some *single* male migrants suggest that they did the networking.

144. Wolfgang Helbich and Ulrike Sommer, "Immigrant Letters as Sources," in Harzig and Hoerder, *The Press of Labor Migrants,* 39–58.

145. The following paragraphs rely on Christiane Harzig, "Frauenarbeit und Familienstrategien: Immigrantinnen in den USA um die Jahrhundertwende," *Gulliver: Deutsch-englische Jahrbücher* 18 (1985): 44–57, and idem, *Familie, Arbeit und weibliche Öffentlichkeit in einer Einwanderungsstadt: Deutschamerikanerinnen in Chicago um die Jahrhundertwende* (St. Katherinen, Germany, 1991).

146. Donna R. Gabaccia, *From Sicily to Elizabeth Street: Housing and Social Change among Italian Immigrants, 1880–1930* (New York, 1984).

147. Tilly and Scott, *Women, Work and Family;* Hans Medick, "Zur strukturellen Funktion von Haushalt und Familie im Übergang von traditioneller Agrargesellschaft zum industriellen Kapitalismus: Die protoindustrielle Familienwirtschaft," in *Sozialgeschichte der Familie in der Neuzeit Europas,* ed. W. Conze (Stuttgart, 1977), 254–82; John Bodnar, *Workers' World: Kinship, Community and Protest in an Industrial Society, 1900–1940* (Baltimore, 1982).

148. This section is based on Hall Ets, *Rosa,* esp. 160–232.

149. Ibid., 158, 162–63.

150. Ibid., 171, 175–76.

151. Ibid., 180 passim.

The Modern Jewish Diaspora: Eastern European Jews in New York, London, and Paris

NANCY L. GREEN

The Comparative Method

Who are more alike, a New York Jew and a Parisian Jew or a Jewish New Yorker and an Italian New Yorker? The comparative question itself shapes the answer in part.[1] In the first half of the question, *Jew* is the noun, *New York* and *Paris* the points of comparison. In the second half, the issue is one of comparative ethnicity within one city. The entire question asks, "What is more important, ethnicity or acculturation, or, in other words, past or present?"

In examining eastern European Jews at three "ports" of arrival, the analysis of the modern Jewish Diaspora raises certain methodological issues from the outset. Migration studies of the last two decades have resurrected the immigrant community in ways crucial to reevaluating the nation-state. Most of these studies have been what can be called linear studies, following the em/immigrant from Poland to Paris or from Italy to New York. The comparison is an implicit one, between past and present, the before and after of the migration experience.[2] A second type of migration study uses a more explicitly comparative approach—a convergent model. Jews and Italians have been the most frequently studied historical neighbors, understandably so, given their proximity both in time (of arrival) and space (the Lower East Side of New York).[3] The questions asked are typically those of comparative social mobility or, more prosaically, success and failure over time. The city is the given, the immigrant "baggage" the explanatory factor.

Each comparative model begins with certain assumptions about similarity and difference. The linear model, not surprisingly, situates difference (and the explanation of that difference) between the Old World and the New.[4] The convergent model postulates difference among ethnic groups at the point of arrival. A third model can be called divergent, tracing paths from Vilna to New York, Paris, and London. Less frequently employed, the divergent comparative study takes an ethnic group as the (or at the) point of (literal) departure and examines the impact of various destinations on ethnicity. This approach, however, raises the problem of disaggregating the diaspora, an uncomfortable premise for some community scholars, as Dominique Schnapper has suggested with regard to Jewish studies.[5]

I would like to explore the divergent paths taken by eastern European Jewish emigrants. This comparison, like all comparisons, has the advantage of generalizing beyond a single linear case. It furthermore has the benefit of challenging an assumption which underlies much of Jewish studies: the similarity of Jews the world over. At one level, the eastern European Jewish "grine" (newcomers) may indeed be more similar to each other, whether in New York, London, or Paris, than they are to first-generation Italians in any of these locations. However, the divergent comparison suggests another level of analysis, one exploring the differentiation of the eastern European Jewish "constant" through space. While the broad lines of eastern European Jewish emigration from the 1880s on are well known, the global description of change from East to West has to be nuanced by confronting variations on the theme.

Before turning to this tale of three cities, two final caveats must be added to the comparative method. First, the level of analysis also necessarily affects the "discovery" of similarity or difference. At a certain level of generality, all eastern European Jews look alike (especially in comparison to native Jews, Polish immigrants, etc.); at a closer level of inquiry, however, differences are more apparent. This is the level which I propose to examine here. Secondly, particularly for questions of acculturation, the time frame chosen will also affect the comparison. If acculturation "works" over the *longue durée,* the comparative question will yield different answers depending on the time period chosen. For the first generation, the category "eastern European Jews" has a greater degree of similarity than two or three generations later. Nevertheless, even by limiting the scope here to the 1880–1924 period, we can still explore the premises of the transformation of eastern European Jews into American, English, and French Jews.[6]

The Linear Paradigm

The movie *Fiddler on the Roof* illustrates the basic model of eastern European Jewish emigration for the period from 1880 to 1914. The final scene portrays the heartbreaking flight after a pogrom. The first step of the move to America is symbolized by a wooden wagon filled with belongings, most of which probably never reached Ellis Island. The popular paradigm of East to West Jewish migration begins with persecution and pogroms and ends with social mobility.

Scholarship of the last two decades has of course nuanced that image, both with regard to the push of emigration and conditions upon arrival. The former was more complex than *Fiddler on the Roof* admits. The latter was not that easy, as even the ruthless success novel, *The Rise of David Levinsky*, by Abraham Cahan, showed.[7] Pogroms were but the most tragic and visible signs of the increasing divorce between Jews and the czarist regime (although not everyone left, and some even returned[8]). Economic difficulties, due to the slow industrialization of the Pale of Settlement (to which the vast majority of Jews were consigned), were seriously aggravated by legislation restricting Jews to a limited number of professions. As jobs and geographic space became increasingly overcrowded, emigration occurred for work as well as for freedom. Consequently, the vast majority of emigrants had not only religion or ethnicity as a community bond, but socioeconomic status as well. Poor, skilled or semiskilled, most of them left with little but a trade *in der hand*.

Whether the destination was New York, London, or Paris, the eastern European Jews (like other immigrants) confronted situations of poverty and hardship upon arrival. They found work in what could be called "immigrant" as well as "Jewish" trades—small-scale commerce and small-scale industry, that is, as peddlers and tailors. They set up organizations for mutual aid and little *shtiblekh* for worship. They began publishing newspapers in Yiddish and debating fiercely, on street corners and in coffee houses or cafés, about the past, present, and future.

To be sure, differentiation within the immigrant communities occurred, as the myriad and often competing organizations attest. Immigrant demands and destinies began to diverge economically, politically, and religiously. Jewish immigrant bosses quickly emerged, although Jewish historians, shy of success story stereotypes, have been reluctant to explore the merciless David Levinskys of the immigrant middle class.[9] Politically, the immigrants imported and developed two ideologies initially problematic for the native-born American, English, or French Jews: Socialism and Zionism. Political differentiation took place within the immigrant "community."

Even in the religious realm, conflicts occurred. While the native Jews often represented all immigrants as either obscurantist preachers or unrepentant anarchists, in fact those who emigrated ran the gamut from traditionalists to freethinkers, and clashes over religious space occurred in all the countries of immigration. The desert-island joke sums it up: A Jew stranded on a desert island builds a synagogue. And then he builds a second one. When he is finally saved, his rescuers, amazed, ask, "Why two?" "One to pray in and one that I never set foot in."

Other, cultural, differences can be traced to immigrant origins. Even in the New World, the haughty Litvaks continued to look down their noses at their uncultivated coreligionists from the south, the Galizianers. And we know that a Galizianer pot roast in the New World is still different from a Litvak one, even two generations removed.[10] Yet more work still needs to be done on the effect of premigration intraethnic differences on life in the New World.

We thus have a linear paradigm of eastern European Jewish communities in the West which, thanks to the last two decades of research, has been increasingly refined. However, the complexification of that model has not been at the expense of a general "eastern European Jewish" construct. On the contrary, it has contributed to enriching it. Differentiation has not seriously questioned the notion of a certain level of "community." As Joshua Fishman and others have suggested, "Jewish" and other ethnic identities were built in the New World as much as if not more so than in the Old.[11] That construction was part of the migration process itself. And ultimately institutional diversification gave way to tactical amalgamation if not actual consolidation. Indeed, the point is that the composite eastern European model includes *all* of the *landsmanshaft* organizations. Their very purpose of differentiation has been analyzed as a characteristic of the entire group. The ethnic community paradigm has emerged as a whole made of diversified but not divisive parts.

The Divergent Challenge

Linear studies of immigrant "community" have not challenged the basic premise that the major difference in experience lies between East and West. In that respect, both East (from Lithuania to Galicia) and West (from New York to London) have, at a certain level, been "homogenized," representing two poles which, like other migration stories, chart the change from tradition to modernity. What happens when we "deconstruct" the West, in examining the eastern European Jew in the modern Diaspora? The location of differentiation shifts. It is no longer solely a comparison of East and West nor is it even one of diversification within the immigrant communities, but an analysis of difference within the New World experience.

The divergent analysis thus has to ask a series of comparative questions which focus on the differences among points of arrival: (1) In what way do perceptions before departure influence the destination decision? (2) To what extent do the numbers (and timing) of migration streams ultimately affect acculturation? (3) How did reception by preexisting Jewish communities affect the adaptation of the newcomers? (4) And how did the different political, cultural, and economic conditions in each country of immigration offer structures that would have a variable impact on the immigrant culture?

Images of Emigration

Roger Ikor, in his prize-winning novel about an immigrant Jewish capmaker in Paris, vividly evoked the late-nineteenth century emigration question: Where to? His hero, Yankel Mykhanowitzki, crossed the Russian-German border with last doubts about his final destination. He goes over the reasons for his choice of France. After eliminating Germany—due to Bismarck, Nietzsche, and Wagner—he turns to England, the United States, and France:

> And England? Ah! England has a lot of good points. . . . But no, not England either. Why? He tried to beat around the bush. The English are rich men, you see, and the poor must not feel very comfortable among them; and they are known to be haughty, imperialist. . . . Liberals, you say? Sure, liberals! But full of prejudices, of tradition, full of dukes sporting monocles. . . . And first of all, why do they still have a king, even an ornamental one? What's his purpose, that parasite?
>
> And Yankel listed all the good reasons for avoiding England. But he forgot the only real one, that England is an island, and he absolutely didn't want to settle on an island. You can never get away from an island, and you never know when you might want to leave.
>
> That left the two Republics, America and France—America meant the United States, of course. Yankel had long hesitated between the two, and he still hesitated, or pretended to. News from New York was encouraging. Emigrant letters talked about masses of money to be earned. But Yankel worried little about money; he had modest needs. Riches as such didn't interest him, or only incidentally. He would easily claim, like his dear Tolstoy, that money corrupts men. What he wanted was a gentle and humane existence. But he had heard of the harshness with which the American immigration officials greeted the newcomers; sure, that was just the first step which had to be gotten over; but it seemed a bad omen. Compared to France, ah! France. . . .
>
> When the word was pronounced in Rakwomir, faces lit up. Victor Hugo, Voltaire, the Rights of Man, the Revolution, the barricades, liberty-equality-fraternity. . . . The tyrants that the French had overthrown! The generous causes for which they had become inflamed! Even their national hymn was that noble *Marseillaise* that democrats, nihilists, socialists and revolutionaries sing, in defiance of autocracy, under the whip of the Cossacks.[12]

Yankel's uncertainty is more suggestive than explanatory. But it raises the important question, to what extend did the predeparture "imaginaire" influence the migration streams? Although the overwhelming number of emigrants followed the streets-paved-with-gold path, we know that there was also a damning flip side to the American myth: "In Europe it has become the custom to view life in America condescendingly. A land of skyscrapers and yellow journalism, a huge circus of business dealing and bluffing—this is all people there [in eastern Europe] know about the United States."[13] The comparative study asks how many people were deterred from

Ellis Island because of bad publicity there or through hearsay about better conditions elsewhere?

About England, we unfortunately have little data. Few immigrant letters or emigrant guidebooks are extant and the composite picture drawn by Lloyd Gartner is not particularly specific to England, except for the symbolic role played by the English Rothschilds (as elsewhere). Indeed, Gartner insists that the emigrants came in spite of warnings about anti-Semitism and difficult working conditions.[14] With regard to France, however, we know that the French Revolution and French civilization remained powerful images a good century after Louis XVI had been toppled. Russian revolutionaries, Italian anarchists, and socialists headed to Paris with 1789 in mind. For Jewish emigrants, the fact that the Jews had been emancipated during the Revolution further enhanced the image of liberty, equality, and fraternity.[15]

At a general level, the United States, England, and France all represented two things that were severely restricted in the East: jobs and freedom. But each country also had its specific character and appeal, which have perhaps been overlooked in the emphasis on linear models of chain migration: Skyscrapers, His Majesty, and the Bastille are but symbolic shorthand for the emigration imagination. This is not to suggest that all of the dreamers and revolutionaries went to France and all of the go-getters went to the United States. Much more work needs to be done on the "destination question" from the perspective of departure. But the comparative emigration study both proves that alternative routes existed to the oft-perceived monolithic choice of America and furthermore suggests that differentiation may have occurred even before emigration. Expectations and images, premigration political and cultural options colored the divergent migration streams before any borders were crossed.

The Impact of Numbers

From 1830 to 1925, over 17 million English, 7 million Germans, and 6 million Italians migrated westward, as did 4 million Jews.[16] Nearly 3 million Jews moved in the 1881–1914 period alone. By 1925, according to Jacob Lestschinsky, 3.5 million eastern European Jews had left their homes, heading primarily for the United States and Canada (2,650,000 and 112,000), England (210,000), Argentina (150,000), and France (100,000).[17]

The overwhelming numbers and overpowering image of migration to America have led some historians to explain the development of the eastern European Jewish communities in England and France as mere by-products of the move across the Atlantic, "leaving behind the sick or more fortunate," according to Michel Roblin.[18] England in particular was a noted country of transmigration. According to Arthur Ruppin's calculations, 114,000 Jews left England for the United States from 1880–1930.[19] An immigrant in 1886 speculated that some 90 percent of those in England planned on continuing to the United States.[20] France also served as an important transit point for emigrants going on to the United States or Argentina. There are stories of families passing through Paris on their way from Odessa to New York, or even from Argentina back to Russia. When the Hamburg port was closed in 1892 due to a cholera epidemic, and the United States slowed immigration that year for fear of typhoid, many transatlantic aspirants got routed through Paris, hoping to get on the next boat out of Le Havre.[21]

The numbers of immigrants alone can in part explain subsequent differences in acculturation patterns. There were some 795,000 eastern European immigrants in New York City in 1910; 63,000 Russian and Russian-Polish immigrants in London in 1911; and approximately 35,000 eastern European Jews in Paris before World War I.[22] The respective populations of these cities circa 1900 being 5.5 million, 6.6 million and 2.7 million, the Jews formed approximately 14 percent of the New York City population, less than 1 percent of the London population, and some 1.3 percent of the Paris population. The massive nature of emigration to the United States can in itself account for a de facto cultural pluralism, while the smaller number of eastern European emigrants in England and France can help explain a greater tendency toward acculturation.

Two corollary factors must mitigate the weight of a purely statistical analysis, however. First, the immigrant neighborhoods, regardless of size, constituted a critical mass for most of the newcomers. It is within their borders that immigrant institutions were formed. (A desert island may suffice.) Second, from the perspective of the natives, absolute size was not always determinant either. The large Jewish Lower East Side of New York was perceived as one (albeit the largest) immigrant neighborhood among others,[23] and the smaller East End of London became a target of attack far beyond its size, while the relatively circumscribed Pletzl of Paris was almost invisible to the unknowing outsider. Thus numbers, while important, are also relative. The massive nature of emigration to America clearly affected the nature of settlement there, but the numbers must also be situated within their larger political and social environment.

Uptown-Downtown, West End and East End, Juifs et Israélites

Jews attract Jews. In each city, immigrant Jews were met by native Jews. The native Jewish communities had two effects on immigration: first, as an implicit (if largely unwilling) "pull"; second, as intermediaries in the acculturation process. The knowledge of Jewish communities in New York, London, and Paris was sufficient in and of itself to attract coreligionists. This "pull" took two forms, one almost mythical, the other more concrete. The most important tangible pull, as for other immigrant groups, came from the letters, money, and boat tickets sent from West to East, a form of "publicity" more powerful than any the boat companies effected. But this was a "pull" essentially between (earlier and later) immigrants. The native Jewish communities exercised a different kind of attraction on the immigrants, and particularly on their imagination. Information concerning conditions in the West included the image of wealthy coreligionists. The Schiffs, Montefiores, Rothschilds, and others symbolized both material and social success. They were also code names for Jewish philanthropy, a safety net in case of need.

But Jewish solidarity had its limits. The western communities (beyond the individuals which represented them) did indeed help eastern European Jews, in czarist Russia as well as in New York, London, and Paris. However, the acculturated western Jews were reluctant to have large groups of poor and foreign Jews settle amongst them and create too-visible "agglomérations" in their "capital" cities. Culture, economics, and even religious practice separated the western Jews from their eastern brethren. Tradition versus modernity, religiosity (or davening fervor) versus secularization (or the calm top-hatted praying that shocked the immigrants), divided West and East in the first generation. Western Jews worried about resurgent anti-Semitism and about community coffers, strained to the limit by the newcomers. The New York, London, and Paris communities all tried various systems to disseminate the newcomers throughout their respective countries, but with little success.[24]

In each country, however, strategies and concerns differed. As Zosa Szajkowski commented, "The principle of every European committee was to facilitate the migration of refugees, but not to their own country."[25] As European committees tried to hasten emigrant departures for the United States, the New York committee tried to avoid their clustering on the East Coast. When the United States began to place restrictions on immigration in 1906, the French Jewish weekly, *Archives Israélites*, complained that this was unjust on the part of such a large and deserted country.[26]

More importantly, the western Jewish communities' concerns were circumscribed by their relationship to the societies in which they lived. The eastern European immigrants arrived in the United States as the debate over "old" and "new" immigrants got under way. Conflicts between ("native") German Jews and Russian Jews can be analyzed as a microversion of the larger debate. Divisions and reciprocal hostilities between the Uptowners (German Jews) and Downtowners (Russian immigrants) reflected not only the ways in which natives perceived immigrants, but the ways in which older immigrants saw the new.

In England, the arrival of the Jewish immigrant poor crystallized worries over two issues more generally gnawing at English society: the debate over the "uses of charity," and concern over unemployment. The English Jews, like English parishes before them, were concerned lest charity itself attract paupers; the "deserving" and "undeserving" poor had to be differentiated.[27] To ward off hardship cases and to prevent increased unemployment, the *Jewish Chronicle* issued warnings about the saturated labor market, while the Jewish Board of Guardians even placed notices in eastern European Jewish newspapers to discourage prospective job seekers.[28]

As for France, the response to the immigrants there, too, was couched in terms specific to the concerns of the native Jews' precarious status within the larger society. The immigrants began to arrive within (and even during) years of the Dreyfus Affair. To be sure, the anti-Semitism surrounding the Affair focused more on rich Jews than on poor ones.[29] But the underlying hypothesis, repeated indefatigably by Edouard Drumont (author of the virulently anti-Semitic and extremely popular *La France Juive*), was that Jews were foreign to the French body politic. The arrival of really foreign Jews *(juifs)* only heightened the French Jews' *(israélites)* concern over their place within French society. The immigrants arrived as the *israélites* reemphasized their allegiance to the state and their identification with the French Republic.

In all three countries, foreign and native Jews eyed each other warily. Yet beyond this similarity, the specifics were rooted in the native Jewish communities' relation to their surrounding environment. The solutions proposed by the American, English, and French Jews took on a similar yet fundamentally dissimilar form in each country. Each community sought to socialize the newcomers. But that socialization was less in conformity to a universal Jewish model than to the local cultural one: to be American in the United States, English in England, more French than the French. The *Settlement Cookbook* not only provided recipes; it prescribed Americanized norms of cleanliness for the immigrant housewives' kitchens.[30] In England, the Jewish Working Men's Club founded in 1872 by Samuel Montagu, sought to eliminate foreign "speech, habits, and views" "repugnant to English feeling and to imbue [the newcomers] with English sentiments and notions."[31] Similarly, the French Jewish weekly *L'Univers Israélite* strongly suggested at the turn of the century that it was necessary "to give this population . . . a very suitable Parisian demeanor, to 'wash away' *(débarbouiller)* that which is exotic and too shocking. . . . We are not suggesting either makeup, nor a disguise, but a sort of material and moral adaptation."[32]

The native Jews, from Paris to London to New York, sought to remake the immigrants in their own image. They promoted the acculturation of the newcomers while protecting their own. In so doing, they provided a crucial first impetus to the subsequent differentiation of eastern European Jews into French, English, and American ones. Their actions reflected, in each case, their status as a minority group within a dominant society. And each society and state had a different perspective on the minority groups within its midst.

Politics and Timing

The American, British, and French contexts, within which the native Jewish welcome was expressed, also affected immigrant adaptation directly. Legislation concerning immigration, which determined arrival and entry, also, I would argue, conditioned subsequent settlement and acculturation. The timing of the immigrant cohorts varied as a result of that legislation, roughly from 1870 to 1905 in England, 1870 to 1924 in the United States, and 1881 to the 1930s in France. And the timing and duration of the cohorts, like the number of those who came, were yet another factor of ultimate differentiation.

The politics of migration differed significantly from one country to another and reflected different political cultures and social attitudes toward the acceptance of foreigners. Two factors are particularly salient in the American case: the wide-open doors of the late nineteenth century and the closing of those doors in the 1920s. In no other country was the schizophrenia about migration so apparent. The result was the creation of mass immigrant communities *before* the gates were closed. And this meant two things. First, the Jewish immigrants to New York settled into a situation of de facto cultural pluralism quite different from that encountered in England or France. The horizons of their acculturation were not just the German Jewish social workers, but also the Italians with whom they shared the Lower East Side. Second, the cut-off which then occurred in the 1920s, I would suggest, both hastened Americanization and also, and importantly, consolidated the eastern European cohort into a model which would serve for future reference.

The English case was quite the opposite. Immigration was halted earlier than anywhere else by the Aliens Act of 1905. Although the Act was perhaps more effective psychologically than legally, its impact, for our purpose, is twofold. First, particularly after it was reinforced in 1914, it limited Jewish immigration before massive and multiple immigrant communities had formed. More importantly, it expressed a political culture which rejected the notion of England as a country of immigration. Through the legislation and debates surrounding the Act, England drew an image of itself as a country of *em*igration, to be sure, and one with more than enough internal immigrants, from Ireland, to fill unskilled jobs. But through the

1905 law, Russian and Polish Jews were pinpointed as undesirables in a culture that dismissed aliens altogether.[33]

France represents an intermediary position. Contradictory currents of immigration policy were always present, but the legal apparatus remained the most generous of all, until the 1930s. By the late nineteenth century, the country was caught in a double demographic bind, wanting more inhabitants but unsure how to go about it. Visions of demographic drought led to a largely unheeded prescriptive literature encouraging French female fertility but also to numerous essays debating which national groups were most apt for assimilation to the French mentality. The open immigration policy was thus underwritten by conflicting tendencies: the need for "arms" to "fill the void" along with concern about which "races" were most appropriate. While the anti-Semitism surrounding the Dreyfus Affair attacked Jews as outsiders to the French nation, it was not as immigrants per se. In Drumont's imagery, the foreignness of the Jews was more diffuse, in the sense of a foreign graft onto an otherwise healthy body.[34] The eastern European immigrants thus arrived in France as worries about the "Frenchness" of French society became increasingly predominant. Yet, at the same time, immigration was a de facto, indeed encouraged, part of French society and public policy.

The impact of these differences in politics, political culture, and the timing of immigrant cohorts needs to be explored further. The different immigration policies not only circumscribed the numbers and timing of the immigration but also expressed and reinforced the political cultures into which the immigrants moved. At a very first level, the laws which aimed at halting immigration into England and the United States perhaps changed the course of some migration routes. How many radicals went to France or the United States after 1905 rather than England, while hoping for an eventual return to Russia? How many Polish Jews went to France instead of the United States in the 1920s?

More importantly, over the long run, politics and timing may also explain the strength of the American Jewish immigrant community compared to the European ones. The creation and maintenance of an ethnic community were perhaps greater in the United States not only by sheer numbers, but, ironically, due to the quota laws of the 1920s. The comparison with England suggests that the later cut-off, *after* greater growth in the United States, meant the consolidation of an eastern European ethnic model which would impart a more specific character to the Americanization which followed. The formation of this immigrant culture was halted earlier in England and in a context of early hostility and limitation on immigration in general, which set the tone for adaptation to English manners. In France, where the progressive opening of French doors was preceded and accompanied by a theory of assimilation, Jewish immigration continued into the 1920s and 1930s, with the arrival of new cohorts of Polish, Turkish, and German Jews.[35] The Jewish immigrant population, still predominantly eastern European, thus also became more diversified.[36]

Comparison forces us to analyze acculturation differently. It is not just a question of adaptation and change from East to West, but also one of relative timing, numbers, and politics. Not only is the melting pot not solely indigenous to the land of skyscrapers, but it was perhaps, for different reasons, even more effective in London and Paris.

The Economics of Divergence

Finally, we can compare the eastern European Jews at work in these three cities. To be sure, there is much similarity in the activities of the Russian and Polish immigrants at home and abroad. The emigrants headed toward economic opportunity in the industrializing West, and, as they congregated in major cities, they entered those light industrial and petty commercial trades which offered easy access for the newcomers. In this respect, Jewish immigrant activity in New York, London, and Paris looks much the same. There were lots of tailors and peddlers.

Table 1 provides some tentative data for a divergent analysis. These figures must be interpreted with care, however, since they are based on censuses and surveys whose categories are not easily comparable. The absence of certain categories (clerks and domestics in London, 1895–1908), for example, may be due to the ways in which the inquiries were conducted or tabulated. In comparing the base population in Russia with the emigrants, two basic characteristics emerge, however: tailors left in much greater numbers than grocers. That is, the emigration from the East is marked first of all by a particularly high number of skilled workers, who left in numbers proportionally far greater than their percentage in Russia. This corresponds both to the reality of stifled opportunity in the East and to expectations regarding potential opportunity in the West. The "settled" figures bear out the fact that there was opportunity for skilled workers in the manufacturing and artisanal trades in the New World.

Second, merchants left in numbers significantly smaller than their proportion in the East (although "declarations" upon arrival may be deceiving—biased in function of expectations and rumors as to what to answer). The disappearance of commercial activity in the "arrival" statistics undoubtedly reflects the greater difficulty of transferring capital stock and clientele (rather than a trade skill) abroad. The reemergence of a commercial sector as the immigrant communities settled in, then, indicates perhaps less a direct carryover from eastern Europe than an entrance into a new field of activity, easy of access for the newcomer—peddling.

Nonetheless, a closer look at the figures shows the diversity of opportunity in the West and the greater the chance that an eastern European Jewish immigrant could become a tailor in New York, a shoemaker in London, or a woodworker in Paris. The figures reflect the specific urban economies of each city. The garment industry, while important in all three metropolises, was, without contest, the major factor of economic life for the Jews of the Lower East Side. By contrast, while there was certainly an abundance of Jewish garment workers in London and Paris as well, Jewish occupations were more evenly distributed in the East End and the Pletzl. Jews became boot and shoe makers ("animal products") in large numbers in London. (There were also some two hundred Jewish umbrella-stick makers—to each city its specialty.[37]) They were cigar and cigarette makers as well ("food industry"), in a country where the trade was not, as in France, a state monopoly. In Paris, many eastern European Jewish immigrants became cabinetmakers, working in the faubourg St.-Antoine furniture district (specializing in the less expensive end of the trade). There were a significant number of goldsmiths and tinsmiths ("metal industry") as well. The other distinguishing characteristic of Paris was the large number of "professionals," that is, students and revolutionaries, who headed there. However, as we see in the "settled" figures, they did not necessarily find jobs in their "field."

These varied options, which if interpreted within the context of a sole country may pale under the predominance of garment making, take on greater importance in a comparative perspective. The economic data clearly show how differentiation reflects the structures on arrival more than the culture of departure. And the importance of these differences is in their challenge to the causality of a linear model. Skill transfer alone is not sufficient to understand either the growth in number of garment workers or the diversification of job opportunities from the Lower East Side to the East End.

Conclusion

The divergent comparative study shifts the analysis from one concerned with difference between East and West to one interested in variations within the immigrants' new worlds. While at one level (compared to other immigrants or natives) eastern European Jews may look alike in the modern diaspora, at another, important, level, the emigrants' itineraries, and their ultimate transformation into American, English and French Jews, were inscribed in the migration project from the very beginning. Self-selection and representations of immigration started the process even before emigration.

More importantly, the divergent comparison locates differentiation and change within the receiving country. In this respect the divergent analysis

Table 1
An Economic Profile of Divergent Migration

	Base Population	Declaration upon Arrival			Settled		
	Russia	U.S.A.	London	Paris	Manhattan	London	Paris
	(1897)	(1889–1914)	(1895–1908)	(1906–12)	(1890)	(1891)	(1910)
	A. All Occupations						
Agriculture	2.8%	2.3%	2.3%	0.6%	0.0%	—	0.0%
Manufacture and Artisanal Trades	37.7	64.0	75.0	76.8	76.9	—	62.1
Commerce	31.4	5.5	22.7	6.6	15.5	—	32.7
Labor and Domestic Service	18.6	21.0	0.0	3.4	0.0	—	0.0
Professions and White Collar Work	5.0	1.3	0.0	12.6	7.6		4.0
Other	4.5	5.9	0.0	0.0	0.0	—	1.2
Total	100.0[a]	100.0[a]	100.0[b]	100.0[c]	100.0[d]	—	100.0[e]

B. Artisanal Trades							
Clothing	37.6	52.2	—	36.3	78.0	32.1	47.2
Animal Products	17.6	8.5	—	22.8	0.5	34.6	16.8
Wood Manufacture and Construction	16.2	15.2	—	12.8	6.1	5.6	15.9
Food Industry	8.4	6.2	—	6.1	9.6	25.0	0.5
Metal Industry	7.1	4.6	—	12.7	5.0	0.9	15.5
Other	13.1	13.3	—	9.3	0.8	1.8	4.1
Total	100.0[a]	100.0[a]	—	100.0[c]	100.0[d]	100.0[f]	100.0[e]

[a]Simon Kuznets, "Immigration of Russian Jews to the United States: Background and Structure," *Perspectives in American History* 10 (1976): 101–2, 110. Kuznets adjusted the Russian figures to conform to the U.S. immigration categories. I have adjusted all other figures to Kuznets's: gainfully employed only; peddling combined with commerce; boots and shoes (classified, as are leather goods, as animal products); and cigars and cigarettes (classified as food products).

[b]Lloyd Gartner, *The Jewish Immigrant in England, 1870–1914* (London: Simon Publications, 1973), 57–58. Derived from declarations made upon arrival at the Poor Jews' Temporary Shelter (*Annual Reports*).

[c]Société philanthropique de l'Asile Israélite de Paris, *Rapports des exercises*, 1906–7, 1909–12; see list in Nancy Green, *The Pletzl of Paris* (New York: Holmes and Meier, 1986), appendix C.

[d]Adapted from Moses Rischin, *The Promised City: New York's Jews, 1870–1914* (New York: Corinth Books, 1964), 272. Derived from Baron de Hirsch study, published in *Geshikhte fun di idishe arbeter bavegung in di feraynikte shtatn*, ed. E. Tcherikower (New York, 1943–45), 1:258–59.

[e]Wolf Speiser, *Kalendar* (Paris: N.p., 1910), 78–80; see list in Green, *Pletzl*, appendix D.

[f]Derived from Léonty Soloweitschik, *Un prolétariat méconnu* (Brussels: Henri Lamertin, 1898), 47–48.

complements the linear one, while bringing into question certain assumptions about culture and skill transfer. Such transfers were affected, from the very first generation, by different opportunities in New York, London, or Paris, just as they were mediated by the receiving societies and by native (Jewish) intermediaries. In this perspective, the "Eastern European Jewish community" in emigration is a construct less dependent on continuity than on change.

Finally, the divergent analysis is also extendable. We have ultimately explored a relatively homogeneous model of urban economies in the industrializing West. What if we compare eastern European Jews in Buenos Aires or Palestine during the same period? New dimensions of difference appear. The eastern European immigrants also became cowboys ("gauchos") and farmers. And even within England, the experience of a Jewish garment worker in (a factory in) Leeds was in many ways quite different from that of his or her compatriot in a small workshop in London.[38]

To study the modern diaspora raises important questions about ethnic unity which need to be addressed. As Caroline Brettell has commented, to study "community" is to find it.[39] By the same token, to study diversity is also to find it. However, both approaches are complementary and need to be addressed in order to properly compare bagels around the world.

Notes

1. Nancy L. Green, "L'histoire comparative et le champ des études migratoires," *Annales: Economies, Sociétés, Civilisations* 6 (November-December 1990): 1335–50. I would like to thank Phyllis Albert and Judith Friedlander for their comments on an earlier draft of this article.

2. John W. Briggs is one of the few to have explicitly questioned this implicit comparison, in "Fertility and Cultural Change among Families in Italy and America," *American Historical Review* 91 (December 1986): 1129–45; see Virginia Yans-McLaughlin, *Family and Community: Italian Immigrants in Buffalo, 1880–1930* (Ithaca: Cornell University Press, 1977).

3. Thomas Kessner, *The Golden Door: Italian and Jewish Immigrant Mobility in New York City, 1880–1915* (New York: Oxford University Press, 1977); Joel Perlmann, *Ethnic Differences: Schooling and Social Structure among the Irish, Italians, Jews, and Blacks in an American City, 1880–1935* (New York: Cambridge University Press, 1988); Dominique Schnapper, "Quelques réflexions sur l'assimilation comparée des travailleurs émigrés italiens et des Juifs en France," *Bulletin de la Société française de sociologie* 3 (July 1976): 11–18; Judith Smith, *Family Connections: A History of Italian and Jewish Immigrant Lives in Providence, Rhode Island, 1900–1940* (Albany: State University of New York Press, 1985). See also Josef Barton, *Peasants and Strangers: Italians, Rumanians, and Slovaks in an American City, 1890–1950* (Cambridge: Harvard University Press, 1975); Ronald H. Bayor, *Neighbors in Conflict: The Irish, Germans, Jews, and Italians of New York City, 1929–41* (Baltimore: Johns Hopkins University Press, 1978); Donald B. Cole, *Immigrant City: Lawrence, Mass., 1845–1921* (Chapel Hill: University of North Carolina Press, 1963); Ewa Morawska, *For Bread with Butter: The Life-Worlds of East Central Europeans in Johnstown, Pennsylvania, 1890–1940*

(New York: Cambridge University Press, 1985); Gary Mormino and George Pozzetta, *The Immigrant World of Ybor City: Italians and their Latin Neighbors in Tampa, 1885–1985.*

4. "New World" here designates the country of immigration, be it transatlantic or trans-European. See Dirk Hoerder on the importance of integrating these different migrations into one conceptual model: "An Introduction to Labor Migration in the Atlantic Economies, 1815–1914," in *Labor Migration in the Atlantic Economies: The European and North American Working Classes during the Period of Industrialization*, ed. Dirk Hoerder (Westport: Greenwood Press, 1985), 3–31.

5. Dominique Schnapper, "Jewish Minorities and the State in the United States, France, and Argentina," in *Center: Ideas and Institutions*, ed. Liah Greenfeld and Michael Mertin (Chicago: University of Chicago Press, 1988), 186–209. There are few examples of the divergent approach applied to the Jewish diaspora: Karin Hofmeester, *Van Talmoed tot Statuut: Joodse Arbeiders en Arbeiders-bewegingen in Amsterdam, Londen en Parijs, 1880–1914* (Amsterdam, IISG, 1990); Andrew S. Reutlinger, "Reflections on the Anglo-American Jewish Experience: Immigrants, Workers, and Entrepreneurs in New York and London, 1870–1914," *American Jewish Historical Quarterly* 66 (June 1977): 473–84; Jack Wertheimer, "Conclusion: A Comparative Perspective," in idem, *Unwelcome Strangers* (New York: Oxford University Press, 1987). Concerning Italians, see Samuel L. Baily, "The Italians and the Development of Organized Labor in Argentina, Brazil and the United States, 1880–1914," *Journal of Social History* 3 (Winter 1969): 123–34; idem, "The Adjustment of Italian Immigrants in Buenos Aires and New York, 1870–1914," *American Historical Review* 88 (April 1983): 281–305; John Briggs, *An Italian Passage: Immigrants to Three American Cities, 1890–1930* (New Haven: Yale University Press, 1978); Donna Gabaccia, *Militants and Migrants: Rural Sicilians Become American Workers* (New Brunswick: Rutgers University Press, 1988); Herbert S. Klein, "The Integration of Italian Immigrants in the United States and Argentina: A Comparative Analysis," *American Historical Review* 88 (April 1983): 306–46; Dominique Schnapper, "Centralisme et fédéralisme culturels: Les émigrés italiens en France et aux Etats-Unis," *Annales: Economies, Sociétés, Civilisations* 29 (September-October 1974): 1141–59. And for a study of Portuguese and West Indians by two anthropologists: Caroline B. Brettell, "Is the Ethnic Community Inevitable? A Comparison of the Settlement Patterns of Portuguese Immigrants in Toronto and Paris," *The Journal of Ethnic Studies* 9 (Autumn 1981): 1–17; Nancy Foner, "West Indians in New York City and London: A Comparative Analysis," *International Migration Review* 13 (Summer 1979): 284–97.

6. In France, for example, the categories of Jewishness have changed continually since the nineteenth century. The "Portuguese" and "German" Jews of the eighteenth century became the "French (and Alsatian) Jews" of the nineteenth century, especially from the perspective of the eastern European newcomers ("Pollacks" to the unkind). Since World War II, the "French (and Polish) Jews" have become the "Ashkenazic" Jews in contrast to the "Sephardic" newcomers from North Africa. (That the latter term is a misnomer, according to the Spanish Jews from Turkey, is another issue.) To an American Jewish visitor, of course, they're all "French." I explored this evolution in the naming of "community" in greater detail in "Jewish Migration to France in the 19th and 20th Centuries: Community or Communities?" *Studia Rosenthaliana* 23 (Fall 1989): 135–53.

7. Abraham Cahan, *The Rise of David Levinsky* (New York: Harper, 1917).

8. Jonathan Sarna, "The Myth of No Return: Jewish Return Migration to Eastern Europe, 1881–1914," in Hoerder, *Labor Migration*, 423–34; Zosa Szajkowski, "Deportation of Jewish Immigrants and Returnees before World War I," *American Jewish Historical Quarterly* 67 (June 1978): 291–306.

9. See Bill Williams, " 'East and West': Class and Community in Manchester Jewry, 1850–1914," in *The Making of Modern Anglo-Jewry*, ed. David Cesarani (Oxford: Basil Blackwell, 1990), 15–33.

10. Judith Friedlander, "Jewish Cooking in the American Melting Pot," *Revue française d'études américaines* 11 (February 1986): 87–98.

11. Joshua Fishman in *The Rise and Fall of the Ethnic Revival*, ed. Joshua Fishman et al. (Berlin: Mouton, 1985); Stephen Steinberg, *The Ethnic Myth* (Boston: Beacon, 1981).

12. Roger Ikor, *Les fils d'Avrom: Les eaux mêlées* (Paris: Albin Michel, 1955), 92–94. The suspension points are Ikor's.

13. Editorial by Abraham Cahan in 1911, cited in Ronald Sanders, *The Downtown Jews* (New York: Signet, New American Library, 1976), 344–45. Much has been written on the eastern European Jews in New York; two classics are Moses Rischin, *The Promised City: New York's Jews, 1870–1914* (New York: Corinth Books, 1964), and Irving Howe, *World of Our Fathers* (New York: Touchstone, Simon and Schuster, 1976).

14. Lloyd P. Gartner, *The Jewish Immigrant in England 1870–1914* (London: Simon Publications, 1973), 26–30. It is a curious historiographical footnote that the supposedly most literate of emigrant groups left no good stock of letters. On eastern European Jewish immigration to England, see also Eugene C. Black, *The Social Politics of Anglo-Jewry, 1880–1920* (Oxford: Basil Blackwell, 1988); Cesarani, *Modern Anglo-Jewry*; David Feldman, *Englishmen and Jews: Social Relations and Political Culture, 1840–1914* (New Haven: Yale University Press, 1994); William J. Fishman, *East End Jewish Radicals, 1875–1914* (London: Duckworth, 1975); Bernard Gainer, *The Alien Invasion* (London: Heinemann, 1972); Vivian D. Lipman, *Social History of the Jews in England, 1850–1950* (London: Watts and Co., 1954); Robert S. Wechsler, "The Jewish Garment Trade in East London, 1875–1914" (Ph.D. diss., Columbia University, 1979); Jerry White, *Rothschild Buildings: Life in an East End Tenement Block, 1887–1920* (London: Routledge, 1980).

15. I have examined this imagery at greater length in "La Révolution dans l'imaginaire des immigrants juifs," in *Histoire politique des Juifs de France*, ed. Pierre Birnbaum (Paris: Presses de la Fondation Nationale des Sciences Politiques, 1990), 153–62, and in Nancy Green, Laura Frader, and Pierre Milza, "Paris: City of Light and Shadow," in *Distant Magnets: Expectations and Realities in the Immigrant Experience*, ed. Dirk Hoerder and Horst Rössler (New York: Holmes and Meier, 1993). On eastern European immigrants in France, see Green, *The Pletzl of Paris: Jewish Immigrant Workers in the Belle Epoque* (New York: Holmes and Meier, 1986); Paula Hyman, *From Dreyfus to Vichy: The Remaking of French Jewry* (New York: Columbia University Press, 1979); and David Weinberg, *A Community on Trial: The Jews of Paris in the 1930s* (Chicago: University of Chicago Press, 1977). For the war period, see Jacques Adler, *The Jews of Paris and the Final Solution: Communal Response and Internal Conflicts, 1940–44* (New York: Oxford University Press, 1987).

16. Jacob Lestschinsky, *Di yidishe vanderung far di letste 25 yor* (Berlin: HIAS-Emigdirekt, 1927), 2.

17. Ibid., 6; see Arthur Ruppin, *Les Juifs dans le monde moderne* (Paris: Payot, 1934), 69.

18. Michel Roblin, *Les Juifs de Paris: Démographie, économie, culture* (Paris: A. et J. Picard et Cie., 1952), 65; see Wechsler, "The Jewish Garment Trade," 231–33, on the effects of transmigration on the Jewish immigrant labor movement in London.

19. Ruppin, *Les Juifs dans le monde moderne*, 69. Some migrants simply passed through English harbors. Others stayed a while (how long?) before moving on. Transmigration and step-migration are subjects that merit further study in themselves. Aubrey Newman has suggested the importance of studying the efforts of shipping companies in regulating the migration flow, in "Trains, Ships and the Jewish Question" (paper delivered at the International Center for University Teaching of Jewish Civilization, Jerusalem, 10 July 1990).

20. Gartner, *The Jewish Immigrant in England*, 44.

21. See Greene, *Pletzl*, 43, 221–22.

22. Rischin, *New York's Jews*, 271; Wechsler, "The Jewish Garment Trade," 57–58; Green, *Pletzl*, 45. Statistics on Jews are notoriously difficult to establish. The *Encyclopedia Judaica* cites two different figures on the same page (albeit in two different articles) concerning the Jews in the East End: 125,000 at the beginning of the twentieth century,

85,000 after World War I (entry "London"), and estimates of only 540,000 Jews on the Lower East Side of New York for 1910 (entry "New York City"). No figures are given for Paris.

23. By 1910, the Jews had become the largest immigrant group in New York City, constituting 41 percent of all foreign-born. The next largest group were Italians, representing 17.5 percent of all foreign-born, followed by the Germans (14 percent) and the Irish (13 percent) (Rischin, *New York's Jews,* 271).

24. The Industrial Removal Office was set up in the United States specifically for this purpose. See ibid., 54; Green, *Pletzl,* 56–58; Gartner, *The Jewish Immigrant in England,* 148–50; and Black, *The Social Politics of Anglo-Jewry,* chap. 9.

25. Zosa Szajkowski, "The European Attitude to Eastern European Jewish Immigration (1881–1893)," *Publications of the American Jewish Historical Society* 41 (December 1951): 127–62.

26. *Archives Israélites,* 29 November 1906.

27. See, for example, Gareth Stedman Jones, *Outcast London* (Oxford: Clarendon Press, 1971), 266; David Owen, *English Philanthropy, 1660–1960* (Cambridge, Mass: Harvard University Press, 1964), chap. 8; Peter Mandler, ed., *The Uses of Charity: The Poor on Relief in the Nineteenth-Century Metropolis* (Philadelphia: University of Pennsylvania Press, 1990); Gartner, *The Jewish Immigrant in England,* 49–56.

28. See, for example, ibid., 25; Wechsler, "The Jewish Garment Trade," 178–79, 187–88. Seasonal unemployment in the garment trades aggravated the issue. From 1872 to 1906, 30 to 40 percent of the casual relief recipients at the Board of Guardians were garment workers. See ibid., 180, 298.

29. Nancy Green, "Transformation de l'ennemi héréditaire: Le cas du Juif en tant qu'étranger chez Drumont," in *Vers des Sociétés pluriculturelles: Études comparatives et situation en France* (Paris: ORSTOM, 1987), 143–49; see also Hyman, *From Dreyfus to Vichy,* and Michael Marrus, *The Politics of Assimilation* (Oxford: Oxford University Press, 1971).

30. For example, Rischin, *New York's Jews,* 99–103, on the Americanization of immigrants.

31. Cited in Wechsler, "The Jewish Garment Trade," 208–9. See also Black, *The Social Politics of Anglo-Jewry,* chap. 9; Gartner, *The Jewish Immigrant in England,* 182. Anglicization was so effective that after World War I the Jewish community began to concern itself with Judaicization. See ibid., 240; Lipman, *Social History of the Jews,* chap. 7.

32. *L'Univers israélite,* 15 February 1907.

33. See Gainer, *The Alien Invasion,* along with J. A. Garrard, *The English and Immigration 1880–1910* (London: Oxford University Press, 1971), and Colin Holmes, *John Bull's Island: Immigration and British Society, 1871–1971* (London: Macmillan, 1988). As Roy B. Helfgott wrote, comparing Jewish immigrants to England and the United States, "legislation affected the quality as well as the quantity of the immigrants" ("Trade Unionism among the Jewish Garment Workers of Britain and the United States," *Labor History* 2 [1961]: 202–14).

34. Edouard Drumont, *La France juive* (Paris: Librairie Blériot, 1888), 27.

35. Annie Benveniste, *Le Bosphore à la Roquette, La communauté judéo-espagnole à Paris, 1914–1940* (Paris: L'Harmattan, 1989); Edgar Morin, *Vidal et les siens* (Paris: Seuil, 1989).

36. The massive deportations of foreign Jews in particular and the post–World War II immigration of North African Jews have, however, done more than anything else to change the internal composition of the French Jewish community.

37. Léonty Soloweitschik, *Un prolétariat méconnu* (Brussels: Henri Lamertin, 1898), 48.

38. See, for example, Anne J. Kershen, "Trade Unionism amongst the Jewish Tailoring Workers of London and Leeds, 1872–1915," in Cesarani, *Modern Anglo-Jewry,* 34–52; cf. Joseph Buckman, *Immigrants and the Class Struggle: The Jewish Immigrant in Leeds* (Manchester: University Press, 1983).

39. Brettell, "Is the Ethnic Community Inevitable?" p. 1.

The Adjustment of Italian Immigrants in Buenos Aires and New York, 1870–1914

SAMUEL L. BAILY

Amedeo Canuti and Giuseppe Trimora left Italy for the Americas at the turn of the past century. Amedeo was born in the tiny Adriatic fishing village of Sirolo in 1865. When the town's fishing industry came upon hard times during the latter part of the nineteenth century, he and his three brothers went to Buenos Aires. In 1894 Amedeo was recorded in the membership lists of a leading mutual aid society as a literate, twenty-nine-year-old sailor who lived with six fellow villagers at 175 Calle La Madrid in the Boca, the center of Argentina's maritime industry. He later married and moved with his family to the nearby town of Quilmes, where he became the owner of a grocery store. Giuseppe's background was somewhat different. As an unmarried Sicilian of thirty-two, he migrated to New York in 1896. The census of 1900 records him as living with eighty other individuals, all but five of whom were Italian, in a tenement house at 228 Elizabeth Street in the heart of one of the city's many Sicilian colonies. Giuseppe could not read, write, or speak English. He listed his occupation as laborer, but at the time of the census he had been unemployed for several months.[1]

Amedeo and Giuseppe were joined by millions of their countrymen who migrated to Argentina and the United States before World War I. Some remained permanently in their adopted country. Others returned home. Still others went back and forth many times. By 1914, however, nearly a million Italians lived in Argentina and a million and a half in the United States. In each country, the Italian immigrants settled primarily in the urban areas, especially in the rapidly growing commercial and industrial port cities of Buenos Aires and New York. When World War I broke out, 312,000 Italians—one-third of the total in Argentina—lived in Buenos Aires, and 370,000 Italians—one-quarter of the total in the United States—lived in New York.

What happened to Amedeo, Giuseppe, and the hundreds of thousands of Italians who went to Buenos Aires and New York at the turn of the century is the central focus of this essay. As these immigrants looked for jobs and housing and attempted to make a better life for themselves and their children, how did they interact with each other and with those already living in the two cities? What were the similarities and differences in the patterns of adjustment? And why?[2]

Scholars in various disciplines have devoted considerable attention to Italian migration to the Americas.[3] Although this cumulative scholarly effort has increased our understanding of the process of Italian migration, it has fallen short in several important respects. Among the most important, the coverage of the subject is uneven. Much more has been written about the United States and Italy than about Argentina, Brazil, or Canada. The literature on the United States, moreover, is not only extensive but also more developed in terms of local and topical studies. A second shortcoming is that this work, with few exceptions, is not comparative. Although the Italians immigrated in substantial numbers to several American countries, few scholars have analyzed more than one receiving country. Furthermore, many students of Italian migration have focused on isolated parts of the subject, unmindful of the interrelatedness of the various aspects of the experience. Some, for example, have written exclusively about the receiving society as though nothing of importance had happened before the immigrants got off the boat. Others have accounted for the development of the process solely in economic terms, with little or no mention of social, cultural, psychological, political, or other noneconomic variables. Finally, authors have frequently confused their readers by using such broad, imprecise, and in general poorly defined terms as assimilation, absorption, and integration.

My own work during the past decade and a half has impressed upon me the difficulty of grasping the complexity of the Italian migration experience.[4] The literature to date provides a base upon which to build, not only because it contains specific information but also because the shortcomings suggest new approaches and directions for future study. Several recent works, whose authors have already approached the subject in new ways, are particularly useful, and I gratefully acknowledge my indebtedness to them.[5] My intent here is to provide a broad comparative overview of one phase of the process of Italian migration, the immigrants' adjustment to Buenos Aires and New York, to identify the important explanatory variables in the process, and to suggest a framework or model that can be applied to immigrant adjustment in other cities.

Because adjustment is an early phase of assimilation, the meaning of "assimilation" must be established. Scholars have, however, used the term in different ways.[6] Is it a process or a fixed condition? How does it differ from absorption or integration? When does it begin or end? How can it be measured? And what is its outcome? I use the term "assimilation" to refer to the long-term, open-ended process of interaction that begins when the immigrants first come into contact with a new environment and with the people living there. Adjustment is the first phase of this process, in which the immigrants develop the knowledge, skill, and organization that enable them to function effectively. The advantage to focusing on adjustment lies in the ease with which it can be identified and in the ability to measure it accurately by how quickly and how easily immigrants are able to find housing and employment, to improve their circumstances, and to develop organizations to protect their interests.

Almost all of the Italians who went to Buenos Aires and New York did so primarily to earn more money than they had in Italy—either to send back home or to improve their living conditions in the New World, or perhaps a combination of both. To earn more, however, they first had to find work and housing. The temporary migrant, who was interested in maximizing his short-term savings, was willing to live in the least expensive housing, no matter how crowded or unhealthy, and to accept any job.[7] Those who decided to remain for some time, however, sought to improve their living and working conditions and to form organizations to protect their interests.[8] Here I am focusing primarily on the permanent migrant. The cumulative search by thousands of Italians in Buenos Aires and New York for jobs and housing, for better living and working conditions, and for collective forms of protection created patterns that can be studied and compared. To the degree that Italians in one city obtained better positions, experienced more occupational and residential upward mobility, and formed more effective community organizations than those in the other city, they "adjusted" more rapidly and successfully to their new environment. Just what were these "patterns"?

Buenos Aires and New York were the leading ports and economic centers of their respective countries at the turn of the century. Although Buenos Aires was a provincial town of 180,000 inhabitants in 1869, it became, during the next forty-five years, a major metropolis with a population of 1.6 million. In 1870, New York was already a leading industrial and commercial city with a population of just under a million people. By 1914, it had grown to more than five million.[9] The success of the Italians in their economic pursuits in these two cities is an important indicator of adjustment.

Foreign workers and owners dominated the commercial and industrial sectors of the Buenos Aires economy. As early as 1887, Italians, who accounted for 32 percent of the population, made up 53 percent of the workers in industry, 57.5 percent of the owners of industrial establishments, 39 percent of the workers in commerce, and 16 percent of the owners of commercial establishments. Native Argentines, who made up 47 percent of the population, represented only slightly more than 20 percent of both workers and owners in commerce, 16 percent of the workers in industry, and less than 10 percent of the owners of industrial establishments. During the next three decades, Italian workers and owners in industry gradually declined to between 35 and 40 percent, largely because second-generation Italians were recorded as Argentines. In commerce, however, although the percentage of Italian workers remained the same, that of owners more than doubled. Throughout the period, the percentage of Italian immigrants active in these areas stayed above that of native Argentines.[10]

In New York, the situation was fundamentally different in large part because the Italians there formed such a small percentage of the total population and, as such, had little chance of dominating any sector of the economy. Although Italians never represented as large a percentage of workers or owners in industry and commerce as did native Americans, they formed a substantial proportion of the workers in personal and domestic service. In 1900, when they accounted for 4.2 percent of the population, they represented 17 percent of the workers in service positions. Most notably, 55 percent of the male barbers and hairdressers and 97 percent of the bootblacks were Italian. Italians were also slightly overrepresented in manufacturing and mechanical pursuits; they accounted for 5.5 percent of the total, including 34 percent of the shoemakers and 18 percent of the masons. And 9 percent of the retail merchants and 16 percent of the peddlers were Italian.[11] Thus, although Italians in New York were numerous in a few occupations, they never dominated any sector of the economy as Italians did in industry and to a lesser extent commerce in Buenos Aires.

The relative distribution of Italians in white- and blue-collar occupations also differed in the two cities. Both in 1880 and in 1905, approximately three-quarters of the Italians in New York were blue-collar workers, most of whom were in unskilled or semiskilled construction, transportation, factory, or domestic service jobs. White-collar peddlers, shopkeepers, and barbers accounted for most of the remaining one-quarter. High white-collar occupations provided only 2 percent of the total. The only significant group of professionals were musicians and teachers of music.[12] Most Italians in Buenos Aires also held blue-collar jobs, but a substantially higher proportion (30 to 35 percent in Buenos Aires versus 13 to 22 percent in New York) were skilled workers. Although approximately one-quarter entered white-collar occupations, as was the case in New York, the distribution differed; many more Italians in Buenos Aires were owners of small industrial and commercial establishments as opposed to peddlers and barbers. Furthermore, although the percentage of high white-collar jobs was small in Buenos Aires, it was twice as large as that in New York (4 percent compared to 2 percent); there were significant numbers of Italians in Buenos Aires among the health, education, and fine arts professionals and among engineers.[13]

The Italian immigrant groups in both cities experienced some upward occupational mobility, but of a different sort. Although there was a substantial increase in semiskilled (7 to 16 percent) and skilled (13 to 22 percent) Italian workers in New York between 1880 and 1905, there was a decline among white-collar workers (25 to 18 percent). In Buenos Aires, the percentage of both skilled and white-collar Italian workers increased slightly between 1895 and 1914. And a few immigrants were able to move into the leadership ranks of the army, the church, and politics. Thus, there was some upward mobility among Italians in New York, but it was confined to blue-collar workers; in Buenos Aires, however, mobility—however slight—extended to white-collar occupations as well.[14]

Italians in Buenos Aires also played a more significant role in local workers' and employers' organizations than did those in New York. Organized labor in Buenos Aires was almost completely the product of the various immigrant groups. In the 1880s and 1890s the immigrants attempted several times to organize national confederations, and by the first decade of the twentieth century they had succeeded in establishing two rival organizations. Italians made up about 40 percent of the organized workers, provided the most important leadership within the movement, and were much more active in labor organizations and in strikes than were native Argentines. In New York, the Italians were slow to organize. The Immigration Commission concluded that southern Italians were less organized than native workers or foreigners in general. Although by 1914 Italian stevedores, garment workers, bricklayers, and barbers had achieved some success at organizing, they never played a leadership role in New York or on the national level.[15]

The same pattern held true for employers' organizations. Italians were influential in the development and growth of the Argentine Industrial Union. From its founding in 1887, at least 20 percent of the administrative council and one of its officers were first- or second-generation Italians, and an Italian was president of the Industrial Union in twenty-one of the thirty-one years between 1905 and 1935. In New York, Italians played no role in the development of the National Association of Manufacturers, and not one of the presidents or members of the executive committee was a first- or second-generation Italian during the first twenty years of the organization's existence (1895–1914).[16]

The patterns of Italian participation in economic life in Buenos Aires and New York were strikingly different. In Buenos Aires, Italians—who accounted for a much larger percentage of the total population—naturally represented a higher percentage of the workers. Yet they were more effective than those in New York in areas where numbers alone did not make the difference. They formed a higher percentage of the skilled and white-collar workers than their relative proportion of the population, as a group experienced greater upward mobility especially among skilled and white-collar workers, were more active than the native Argentines in the economy, and were a major force in the development of workers' and employers' organizations. Italians in New York, in contrast, were less successful than their counterparts in Buenos Aires at obtaining jobs in the upper levels of the occupational structure and at organizing to protect their economic interests.

Housing was another major concern of the Italian immigrants to both cities. Most immigrants started out in the crowded, low-rent districts in the center of the metropolitan area, where living conditions were poor. To improve their situation, many Italians moved to homes they could buy and to residences outside the center city. Italians in Buenos Aires were more dispersed throughout the city in 1887 and in 1904 than those in New York. In 1904, they—like the rest of the population—lived predominantly in the eleven census districts located within a three-mile radius of the downtown business center, and they accounted for at least 14 percent of the total population in every district (see Map 1). They did, nevertheless, cluster somewhat within this area; while 41 percent lived in the five districts on the perimeter of the downtown business center (3, 4, 8, 9, and 19), only 29 percent resided in the six most central districts (10, 11, 12, 13, 14, 20). Italians in New York, however, concentrated in only a few areas. By the 1870s, a substantial number lived in the sixth and fourteenth wards of Manhattan, and they gradually spread out into several neighboring wards and into Harlem, in the area between Second Avenue and 110th Street (see Map 2). In 1890, 64 percent lived in the Bowery colony and another 10 percent in Harlem. Gradually they moved to other areas of the city, but before World War I, they for the most part remained in these areas of Manhattan.[17]

The living conditions of the Italians in both cities were generally poor. Most suffered from the effects of overcrowding, inadequate sanitary facilities, and unsatisfactory health conditions. A description of New York immigrant housing by the Tenement House Department could equally well have applied to Buenos Aires.

> Many cases have been found where plumbing fixtures have been removed and the pipes left open. . . . [T]he tenants have used the dumbwaiter shaft as a chute for the disposal of rubbish, fecal matter and garbage. . . . [T]he water closets have been stopped up for weeks. . . . Often the roofs are not repaired, and after a storm the water soaks through the plastered ceilings. . . . Bedrooms are often festooned with cobwebs hanging from the ceiling.[18]

Yet the Italians in Buenos Aires were somewhat better off. In the Argentine capital, less than one-quarter lived in crowded tenement houses, compared to more than three-quarters in New York. In addition, the population density per acre of the Italian districts in New York was approximately 50 percent higher than it was in Buenos Aires. The remaining, nontenement-house working-class living quarters in Buenos Aires may not have been much better, but at least they were less crowded.[19]

Property ownership was also higher among the Italians in Buenos Aires. In 1887 and in 1904 approximately 12 percent owned their own homes,

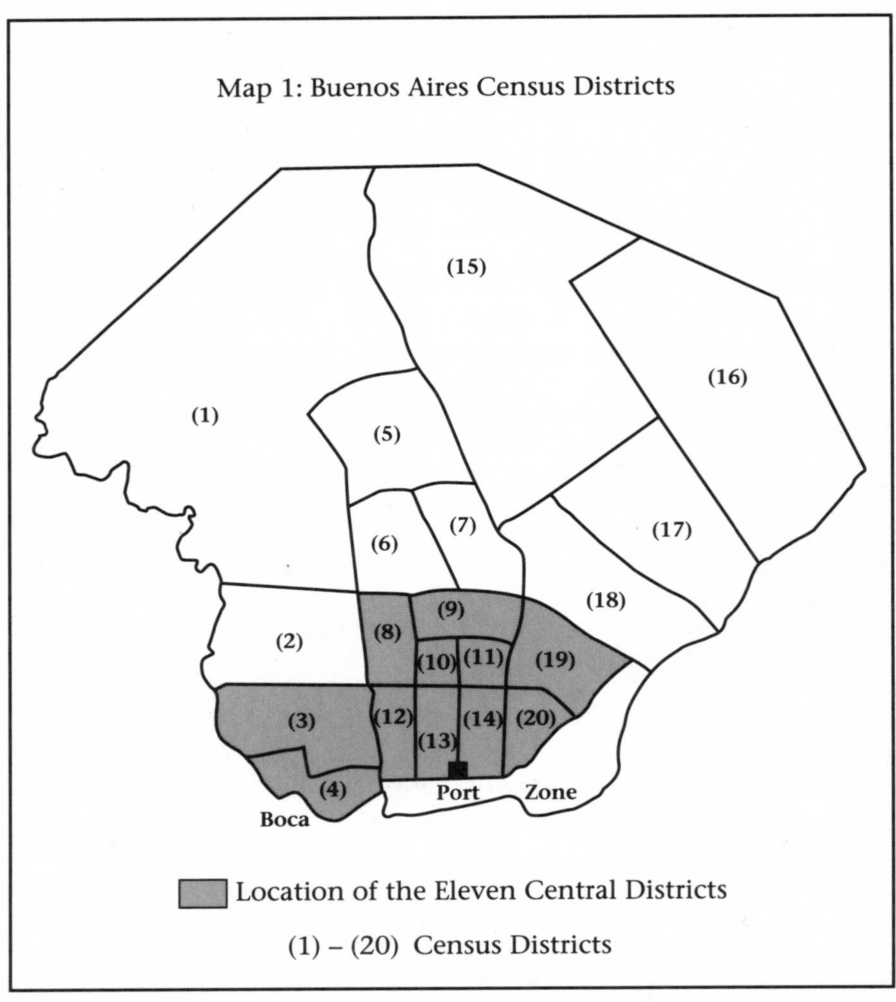

and by 1914 this figure had risen to 17.6 percent. Even in the areas of heaviest concentration, such as the Boca (district 4), the percentage of Italian homeowners was substantial: 8 percent in 1904 and 11 percent in 1914. Data on property ownership in New York are fragmentary but suggestive. The Immigration Commission's survey of 524 households in 1909 indicates that only 1.3 percent of the Italian immigrants owned their homes. Even if that figure were doubled or tripled, to account for the possible underrepresentation of property owners in the sample, it would still be far lower than the percentage for Buenos Aires. Clearly, in the years before World War I, New York Italians were much less successful in achieving the goal of property ownership than were those in Buenos Aires.[20]

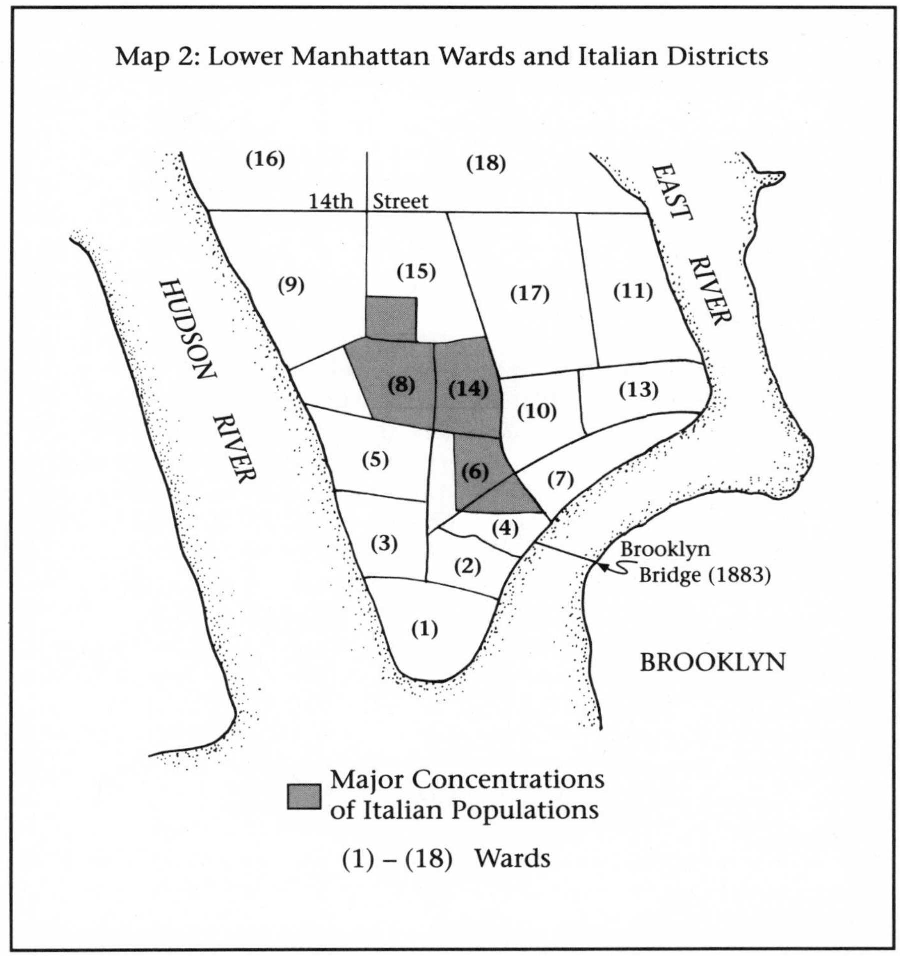

Although Italians in both cities changed their residences frequently, they may not have improved their living conditions by doing so. Many immigrants left New York and Buenos Aires for places in other parts of their adopted country, and others relocated within their own neighborhood. We cannot trace those who left either city, nor can we make any meaningful judgments about the significance of intraneighborhood moves. We can, however, measure the movement to the outer areas of the two cities, where conditions were less congested and the opportunity to purchase a home was greater.[21] In Buenos Aires, Italians at first resided almost completely within the central area; as of 1904, 70 percent still remained there (districts 3, 4, 8, 9, 10, 12, 13, 14, 19, and 20). By 1914, however, only 47 percent lived in the center, and 53 percent lived in the outlying districts. Although

Italians in New York first settled in Manhattan and gradually spread out to Brooklyn and the other boroughs of the city, they moved from the center at a later date than those in Buenos Aires. In 1900, 66 percent lived in Manhattan, and ten years later 59 percent still resided there. Only after World War I did more than half of New York's Italians live outside Manhattan.[22]

Several factors influenced patterns of settlement and dispersion. Italians, especially those who worked long hours for low pay, lived near their places of employment. Italians in New York, therefore, lived below 14th Street in Manhattan, where, as late as 1906, 67 percent of all factory jobs were located. In Buenos Aires, industry and commerce were concentrated in the central area, yet, because the city was not an island, the Italians could spread out and still be close to their jobs. As industry and commerce expanded to other parts of each city, the Italians followed.[23] Although the transportation system influenced where an immigrant might move when he decided to relocate, it did not necessarily determine the timing of his move. Elevated trains began to run from the Battery to Harlem in 1881, which clearly facilitated the development of the Harlem colony. By the early 1900s, however, the subway system connected Brooklyn, Queens, and the Bronx with Manhattan, yet the major outward movement in New York did not occur until after World War I. Although in Buenos Aires the rail system linked various parts of the city, not until the introduction of the electric streetcar and the drastic reduction of fares in the early 1900s did Italians in large numbers begin to move to the outlying districts.[24]

Old-world ties also proved important in determining patterns of settlement. Italians in both cities frequently settled and then moved in village- and language-based clusters.[25] Migrants from Agnone to Buenos Aires, for example, lived in District 14, especially in two nearby clusters on Calle Córdoba. Those from Bagnara also lived in District 14, but in a four-block area between Calles Reconquista and 25 de Mayo. Amedeo Canuti and other Sirolesi lived in three clusters within the Boca (District 4). A second colony of Sirolesi developed in Quilmes, about eleven miles and several train stops away from the Boca. Amedeo and one of his brothers moved to Quilmes, but the other brothers remained in the Boca.[26]

Similarly, Italians in New York generally settled by villages. In 1890 the Neapolitans populated the area of Mulberry Bend, the Genovesi settled on Baxter Street near the Five Points area, and the Sicilians, like Giuseppe Trimora, on Elizabeth Street between Houston and Spring Streets. In 1920, more than two hundred families from Cinisi, Sicily, lived in the area of 6th Street and Avenue A. Other clusters from Cinisi lived in the Bowery, Harlem, and Brooklyn.[27] Presumably, the relationship between the Cinisi colonies in Manhattan and Brooklyn was similar to that of the Sirolo colonies in the Boca and Quilmes.

Although the availability of jobs, inexpensive transportation, and village chains primarily determined patterns of residence and movement, they do not by themselves explain the earlier movement of Italians to outlying areas of Buenos Aires. Circumstantial evidence indicates that the greater ability of the immigrants in Buenos Aires to save does more to account for the early relocation of Italians in the outlying districts of the city. Because more Italians in Buenos Aires held more prestigious, better-paying jobs, they were presumably in a better position to save. Since the main purpose of the move outward was often to buy a house with some land, relocation was postponed until accumulated savings permitted such a purchase. In New York most Italian immigrants were unable to accumulate the necessary savings until after World War I; thus, the move outward came later.[28]

Italians in Buenos Aires were more dispersed, lived in somewhat better physical circumstances, were more successful in acquiring property, and were residentially upwardly mobile at an earlier date than those in New York. This difference must not be overstated. Most Italians in both cities lived in very poor circumstances. Nevertheless, there was a difference. And that difference meant that Italians in Buenos Aires were more likely to have found better housing.

Immigrant institutions often played an important role in the adjustment of the Italians to their new environment. Both in New York and Buenos Aires, the Italians established mutual aid societies, social and recreational clubs, hospitals, banks, chambers of commerce, churches, and newspapers to help them meet their needs.[29] To the extent that these organizations involved the immigrants, had the necessary resources, and developed representative leadership, they could provide social and economic services and a structure that served to integrate and strengthen the community. The stronger and more united the community, the better able it was to defend the interests of its members within the new society.

Mutual aid societies were the most important of these immigrant institutions; more Italians in New York and Buenos Aires joined these societies than any other kind of organization. Some societies recruited members exclusively from a specific village or area of Italy. Others were more broadly based, bringing together individuals from all parts of Italy. Still others were formed by workers in the same occupation. All of them sought to provide essential death, sickness, and unemployment benefits for their members as well as a congenial social environment.

Both the New York and Buenos Aires mutualist movements began in the mid-nineteenth century and expanded with each new wave of immigrants. Although many of the largest and most important societies in Buenos Aires were established before 1880, more were found during the last two decades of the nineteenth century than at any other time. In New York, growth was very gradual, and by far the greatest number of them were established in the decade or so prior to World War I. By 1910, in Buenos Aires there were seventy-five mutual aid societies with approximately 52,000 members out of an Italian population of some 280,000. In New York at about the same time there were as many as two thousand societies with an estimated total membership of 40,000 out of an Italian population of 340,000.[30]

The two movements differed in ways that significantly affected their ability to serve their Italian communities. Divisiveness, based on personal rivalries and old-world ties, typified the mutual aid movement in New York. The overwhelming majority of the societies were small (under five hundred members), poorly financed and managed, and restricted to immigrants from the same town or region of Italy. Although a few societies opened their membership to all Italians, these few never attained the size, wealth, or influence necessary to establish effective leadership of the mutualist movement. Most of the societies were made up of artisans, but the top officers frequently were successful businessmen. Louis V. Fugazy, a noted banker and labor agent, was the prime mover in more than one hundred mutual aid societies and was president of fifty. Beginning in 1905, many societies joined the National Order of the Sons of Italy, and that organization thus gradually gained influence within the community. But the Sons of Italy was really a loose confederation of societies, and it, too, lacked the resources to be of significant help to most immigrants.[31]

In Buenos Aires, however, a number of large societies (one thousand or more members) dominated the movement and provided a distinct kind of leadership. These societies had substantial assets in both buildings and capital reserves. They also performed more extensive services for their members; in addition to the normal insurance and social benefits, they provided schools, medical clinics, hospital care, pharmacies, restaurants, and, in some cases, job placement services. Although skilled artisans formed the largest subgroup of members in most Argentine societies, these organizations also included substantial numbers of semiskilled and white-collar workers. The leaders came almost exclusively from the white-collar members. Furthermore, Italians from all parts of the peninsula joined these societies and rose to positions of leadership within them. Although local ties, politics, and personal rivalries led to some divisions, the large societies were able to develop a relatively united mutualist movement by World War I.[32] The wealthier, better administered, and more unified mutualist movement in Buenos Aires provided more extensive services for a larger percentage of the Italian population than did the movement in New York.

The Italian-language newspaper was probably the second most important immigrant institution in Buenos Aires and New York. No one joined newspapers, but more Italians read them than there were members of mutual aid societies. Tens of thousands of immigrants scanned their columns in search of job opportunities, notices on the activities of community organizations, tips on how to survive and prosper, guidance in understanding and adjusting to the wider community in which they lived, and information on Italy. Since these papers reached more Italians than any other immigrant organization, they were in the best position to unite the community.

In Buenos Aires, the first Italian newspaper was established in the 1860s. Dozens of others were published in subsequent years, but most had small circulation and did not last very long. *La Patria degli Italiani* had by far the largest circulation and continued publishing longer than any other paper. Founded in 1876 by Italian journalist Basilio Cittadini, it reached a circulation of approximately sixty thousand—or 19 percent of the Italian community—in 1914. *La Patria* was a liberal, anticlerical, and moderately antimonarchist morning daily that attempted to serve the interests of immigrants of all social and income levels within the Italian colony in Buenos Aires. It regularly published information on working and living conditions and explained the grievances of workers involved in labor disputes. Every issue included letters from immigrants, who most frequently described their problems and asked for help. The editors of *La Patria* interpreted Argentine society for the Italian immigrants, defended their various interests, arbitrated some of their disputes, and often spoke for them as a community. In addition, the paper performed several, more unusual functions, particularly in the decade prior to World War I: it ran free medical, legal, and agricultural clinics for its subscribers. These services gave *La Patria* something of the character of a mutual aid society and increased its impact on the community.[33]

The first Italian-language newspaper in New York began publication in 1849, and many others of short duration and small circulation appeared in the following half-century. The largest and most long-lived of these was *Il Progresso Italo-Americano*. Established in 1879 by businessman and labor contractor Carlo Barsotti, the paper reached a circulation of roughly eighty thousand—or 22 percent of the Italian community—by the beginning of World War I. *Il Progresso*, however, made little effort to serve the interests of all of the Italians in New York. It was, most significantly, antilabor, probably because Barsotti was afraid that labor unions might undermine his other businesses. Barsotti frequently used the paper as a vehicle to further his personal interests. "Publishers," as one author explained, "used their journals to advertise their own far-flung enterprises, to praise themselves and their friends, to promote projects in which they were interested, and to attack anyone with whom they disagreed."[34] Although *Il Progresso* provided information on the happenings in the Italian community, defended all Italians against attacks by outsiders, and perhaps helped break down village-based provincialism and foster a larger group awareness, it did little to interpret American society to the immigrants or to strengthen the community as a whole. *Il Progresso* supported the needs of some of the Italians in New York, but it opposed that of the large majority of workers.[35] *La Patria* was more effective in serving the Italian immigrants in Buenos Aires than *Il Progresso* was in New York.

The supporting evidence for some parts of this analysis of the adjustment process of Italians in Buenos Aires and New York is not as complete as it is for others. The evidence on housing conditions, home ownership, residential mobility, economic activity, and community organizations does, nevertheless, all point in the same direction. And, although future studies will certainly provide more information on the Italian immigration experience in both cities, they are not likely to alter substantially the basic conclusion. Italians in Buenos Aires adjusted more rapidly and successfully to their new environment than did those in New York.

The earlier and greater success of the Italians of Buenos Aires in adjusting to their new environment is clear. The reasons for the discrepancy are somewhat more complex. Were the Italians in Buenos Aires in some way better prepared for the immigration experience than those who went to New York? Did they encounter a more receptive host society? What, if anything, did they do to improve their chances of success? Although a considerable number of interrelated variables explain the different experiences of the Italians in the two cities, they can be divided into three categories: those relating to the character of the immigrant groups when they migrated, to the kind of societies they found, and to the changing nature of the immigrant community over time.

When Italians migrated to New York and Buenos Aires, they brought with them certain attributes that influenced their ability to find jobs and housing and to organize community groups. Among the most important were not only occupational and organizational skills but also expectations regarding the permanency of the move. Unskilled laborers predominated in both groups: 75 percent of those who went to the United States between 1899 and 1910 and perhaps 60 percent of those who went to Argentina were unskilled farm or common workers. Only 25 percent of those who migrated to the United States and 40 percent of those who migrated to Argentina were listed as skilled or white-collar workers. The statistics do not break down the overall figures for those who went specifically to Buenos Aires and New York; but these centers of economic activity undoubtedly attracted at least the same proportions of skilled and white-collar workers, and most likely an even higher percentage of them than the national norm for each country. Italians in Buenos Aires as a group were also more literate than those in New York; some 60 percent were literate in Buenos Aires compared to about 50 percent in New York.[36]

A larger proportion of the Italians who migrated to Buenos Aires were from northern Italy. They were in general not only more skilled and literate than Italians from the south but also more familiar with organizations such as labor unions and mutual aid societies. While 42 percent of those who went to Argentina came from the north, 46 percent from the south, and 12 percent from the center, 80 percent of those who went to the United States were southerners.[37] And not all of their skills were transferable to their new environments. Skills appropriate to rural occupations such as farming were of little use in urban New York and Buenos Aires; those of artisans and white-collar workers for the most part were. With better occupational skills, higher rates of literacy, and greater familiarity with organizations, the Italians in Buenos Aires had an advantage in finding higher-status jobs and in developing community institutions to protect their interests.

Expectations regarding the permanency of their emigration differed to some extent between those going to the Northern and those to the Southern Hemisphere. Measuring the Italians' intentions when they left their villages and towns for the New World is, of course, impossible. Nevertheless, data on their respective rates of return and on sex and age composition of the migrants are at least indicative of intent. The percentage of Italians who repatriated for the period 1861–1914 is slightly lower for the Argentine immigrants than it is for the U.S. immigrants (47 percent compared to 52 percent). Those who returned to Italy from both countries were overwhelmingly unskilled males, and New York had a larger proportion of unskilled Italian males than did Buenos Aires. Approximately 30 percent of the immigrants repatriated from Buenos Aires during the decade and a half before World War I, whereas approximately 50 percent repatriated from New York during those same years.[38]

Demographic distribution of the Italian immigrants in the two cities according to age and sex provides supporting evidence for the relatively greater permanency of the Italian settlement in Buenos Aires. Italians who migrated to both cities were predominantly males between fourteen and forty-four years old. In Buenos Aires, males represented a little less than two-thirds of the Italian population in 1895 (61 percent) and 1914 (62 percent), and two-thirds of all immigrants (65 percent) were between the ages of fourteen and forty-four. The percentage of Italian males and of fourteen- to forty-four-year-old Italian immigrants was higher in New York. During the three decades before 1910 approximately 77 percent of the Italian immigrants to the United States were males, and nearly 80 percent of these were between fourteen and forty-four years of age. There is no reason to assume that the percentages of New York City were any lower. Therefore, while roughly two out of every three Italians who went to Buenos Aires were males between the ages of fourteen and forty-four, approximately four out of every five Italian immigrants in New York were in these age and sex categories.[39]

These figures, significantly, indicate a higher percentage of women, children, and older people in the Italian population of Buenos Aires. This in turn is suggestive of a larger proportion of family units and probably greater permanence for the immigrant community in Buenos Aires. It is, of course, possible that more Italians got married after they arrived in Argentina than they did in the United States, but it is more likely that a greater number of families migrated to the Argentine capital in the first place. To the degree that rates of return and sex and age composition reflect intentions, it seems that more Italians who migrated to Buenos Aires expected to remain and that more who came to the United States were temporary migrants who planned, when they left Italy, to return.

Although the Italians who arrived in New York and Buenos Aires during the forty-four years under consideration here shared to some extent a similar general culture based on a common language, religion, and set of values, they did not have identical group characteristics. Those who migrated to Buenos Aires included more workers with higher levels of skill and of literacy, more individuals with experience in organization, and more people who intended to stay. These differences gave the Italians in Buenos Aires an initial advantage as they sought to find jobs and to develop community institutions to protect their interests. But these differences do not alone account for the vast difference in the two Italian colonies. The receiving environments the immigrants entered also varied dramatically and significantly affected the immigrants' adjustment. The economy, the host society's perception of the Italians, the culture, and the existing foreign-born community in Buenos Aires contrasted sharply with those in New York.

The economies of the two urban societies were strikingly different. In 1869, at the time of the first national census, Argentina was sparsely populated and economically far less developed than western Europe or the United States. Those who ruled Argentina during the next forty years were determined to replace the stagnant economic and social structures inherited from Spanish colonial rule with the most dynamic and advanced systems to be found anywhere. They sought to institute such sweeping change by encouraging massive immigration, improving the educational system, introducing new technology, modernizing agriculture and livestock breeding, developing a transportation infrastructure (notably railroads and port facilities), and wooing foreign investment capital. By 1914, the export-oriented, landed elite had succeeded in accomplishing most of its objectives. Argentina had, in a relatively short time, become one of the leading agricultural and livestock-breeding countries in the world. It was a major exporter of grains, the leading supplier of beef to England, and a center of industries to process agricultural and pastoral products for export.[40]

The rapidity of Buenos Aires's economic development, which coincided with the wave of Italian migration, provided opportunities at all levels for the new residents. When Argentine development began, the country had no vital middle class, no significant skilled working class, no other numerically important immigrant groups, and no labor movement or employers' organizations. The traditional native elite continued to confine itself primarily to land and politics, which left commerce, industry, and some of the professions and economic organizations to the immigrants, especially to the large Italian community.

The United States had a much larger population and a more highly developed economy in 1870 than did Argentina. During the next forty-four years, the United States expanded both its heavy and light industry, and by World War I had become a major industrial as well as agricultural and commercial country. The Italians who migrated to New York encountered thriving professional, middle, and skilled working classes composed of native-born Americans and previous immigrants. What the New York economy needed was unskilled construction and industrial workers. There were opportunities for Italians, but opportunities of a kind different from those in Buenos Aires. As a result, the Italians entered the economy at the lower levels and had greater difficulty in achieving upward occupational mobility. More restricted economic opportunity in New York limited the growth of upper-level Italian occupational groups, the resources of the Italian community, and the development of immigrant institutions—all of which made adjustment to the new environment more formidable.[41]

The host society's perceptions of the Italians also influenced adjustment. The Argentine elite viewed the immigrants as a means of "civilizing" the country as well as developing its economy. These leaders believed that the native population of the interior—symbolized by the *gaucho* ("cowboy") and the *caudillo* ("charismatic leader")—was backward and inferior. European immigrants would, they thought, intermix with the indigenous population and in time help create a biologically superior population. The tiny Argentine elite may have looked down upon Italian immigrants as social inferiors but still saw them as superior to 95 percent of the native population. In this sense, the Italians were bearers of civilization. By the early 1900s, some members of the elite did become concerned about the dominating influence of the immigrants in Argentina. This concern, however, remained limited as long as the economy continued to grow, and it did not translate into significant restrictions either on immigration or on the opportunities for the immigrants until the Depression of the 1930s.[42]

In contrast, Italians who went to New York were viewed in an entirely different way. Many New Yorkers viewed the immigrants—especially the great mass of southern Italians—as an inferior race that threatened to dilute the good northern European stock and undermine traditional American institutions. The Italians provided the unskilled labor necessary for the growth of the economy, but the native-born elite certainly did not see them as bearers of civilization. The United States had a "superior culture" to which the Italians were expected to adapt if they were to succeed.[43] This negative perception resulted in various types of social and economic discrimination and ultimately in restrictions on Italian immigration. And it reinforced the limitations created by more restricted economic opportunity.

The differences in the cultures of the two receiving societies also had an impact on immigrant adjustment, but these differences were probably of less importance than some scholars have suggested. In Buenos Aires, the Italians entered a Latin culture whose values, language, and religion were similar to their own. Italians in New York, however, confronted a very different culture; there they had problems with the language, were subjected to religious prejudice, and had difficulty understanding some of the values of the host society. As a result, the Italians in Buenos Aires presumably were able to adjust more easily, and their success came more rapidly.[44] Although the cultural explanation is of some significance, it has its limitations. Most important, the Italians in Buenos Aires were successful in economic life precisely because they rejected some important Argentine values. Economic opportunity and the host society's perceptions were more significant.

Furthermore, Italians in Buenos Aires inherited a more extensive, wealthier, and more effective organizational network that had been developed by earlier immigrants. When massive migration began in the 1880s, Buenos Aires already had an Italian community of eighty to ninety thousand immigrants. Its established institutions were capable of helping the newcomers adjust to life in the city. In New York, when massive migration began in the 1890s, the Italian community of forty thousand immigrants did not have as developed or effective an organizational infrastructure and was therefore less able to help subsequent immigrants find their way in their new environment.[45] Thus, the differences in the economies, the host societies' perceptions, cultures, and immigrant institutions worked together to make adjustment in Buenos Aires relatively easier and more rapid.

In addition to the skills and attitudes the Italian immigrants brought with them and the characteristics of the receiving environments, the subsequent development of the two Italian communities influenced adjustment. Continuing immigration in the 1890s and early 1900s modified existing conditions within the communities, and the new conditions themselves became important in the relative speed and degree of immigrant adjustment. Among the most important of these new conditions were the pace of immigration, the concentration and numerical strength of the two groups, and the nature of the emerging Italian elites.

The pace of migration to the two cities varied considerably. The flow of individuals to Buenos Aires was spread out more evenly over the four decades following 1870 than it was to New York. In 1870, 44,000 Italians lived in Buenos Aires, and less than three thousand lived in New York. The Buenos Aires community grew gradually over the next forty-four years; from 1887 to 1914 the annual increase averaged less than 4.3 percent. The New York community, which started with a much smaller base, grew more rapidly throughout the period. Most significantly, 77 percent of all Italian immigrants who went to the United States between 1860 and 1914 arrived during the fifteen years prior to World War I, compared to 50 percent of those who went to Argentina (see Table 1). The larger initial size of the Italian population and the greater effectiveness of immigrant organizations combined with the more even pace of subsequent migration enabled the existing community in Buenos Aires to absorb the newcomers more easily

Table 1
Italian Immigration to Argentina and the United States

Period	Argentina	United States
1861–70	113,554	11,728
1871–80	152,061	55,759
1881–90	493,885	307,309
1891–1900	425,693	651,899
1901–10	796,190	2,104,209
1911–20	347,388	1,165,246
Total Immigrants, 1860–1914	2,270,525	4,083,000
Total Immigrants, 1900–1914	1,137,475	3,156,000
Immigrants 1900–14 as a Percentage of Immigrants 1860–1914	50	77

SOURCES: República Argentina, Dirección de Inmigración, *Resumen estadística del movimiento migratorio en la República Argentina, 1857–1924* (Buenos Aires, 1925); and U.S. Bureau of the Census, *Historical Statistics of the United States, Colonial Times to 1972* (Washington, 1975).

and to help them adjust more readily. But the massive influx of immigrants in a short period of time overwhelmed the less developed and less united existing community in New York and prohibited it from absorbing and guiding the new arrivals.

The consistent relative concentration and numerical strength of the Italians in Buenos Aires further strengthened their position. In 1910 the one and one-third million Italians in the United States represented 1.5 percent of the total population. In Argentina the slightly more than one million Italians in 1914 represented 12.5 percent of the total population. Italians in both countries were concentrated in a relatively few states or provinces and cities, but this concentration, too, was far greater in Argentina. One-third of all of the Italians in Argentina lived in Buenos Aires, and the population of the city was at least 20 percent Italian-born throughout the period (see Table 2). Although approximately one-quarter of all of the Italians in the United States lived in New York, they never accounted for more than 7.1 percent of the city's population (see Table 3). In addition, there were only two major immigrant groups in Argentina compared to at least a half-dozen in the United States: Italians and Spaniards alone made up nearly 80 percent of the total number of immigrants in Buenos Aires before World War I, whereas Russians, Germans, Irish, Austrians, and Italians made up a similar percentage of the total immigrant population of New York in 1900 and 1910.[46] The sheer numerical strength of the Italians in Buenos Aires made them far more difficult to exclude or play off against other nationalities, and their position thus guaranteed them more influence in the local society.

The nature of the emerging Italian elites also influenced adjustment pat-

Table 2
Foreign-Born Italians in Buenos Aires

Year	City's Italian Population	Italian Percentage of City's Total Population	Annual Growth of City's Italian Population during Preceding Period	Buenos Aires's Italians as a Percentage of All Italians in Argentina
1856	11,000	12.0	–	–
1869	44,000	23.6	23.0	–
1887	138,000	31.8	12.0	–
1895	182,000	27.4	3.9	36.9
1904	228,000	24.0	2.8	–
1909	277,000	22.5	4.3	–
1914	312,000	19.8	2.5	33.6
1936	299,000	12.4	–	

NOTE: The number of Italians in Buenos Aires has been rounded off to the nearest thousand.
SOURCES: Buenos Aires and Argentine Censuses, 1856 to 1936.

Table 3
Foreign-Born Italians in New York City

Year	City's Italian Population	Italian Percentage of City's Total Population	Annual Growth of City's Italian Population during Preceding Decade	New York City's Italians as a Percentage of All Italians in the U.S.
1860	1,464	0.1	–	12.5
1870	2,794	0.3	9.1	16.3
1880	12,223	1.0	33.7	27.6
1890	39,951	2.6	23.3	21.9
1900	145,433	4.2	26.3	30.0
1910	340,765	7.1	13.4	25.4
1914	370,000 (estimate)	–	–	–
1920	390,832	7.0	–	24.3
1930	440,200	6.4	–	24.6

NOTE: In 1898, New York City—which until that time had comprised only Manhattan and part of the Bronx—incorporated its neighboring counties to assume its current boundaries: Manhattan, Brooklyn (King's County), Queens (Queens County), Richmond (Staten Island), and the Bronx. Thus, the pre- and post-1900 figures refer to different geographical boundaries of the city.
SOURCES: U.S. Censuses, 1860 to 1930.

terns. Only two functioning social classes developed within the Italian community in New York: the *prominenti*, the tiny group of successful businessmen and professionals who remained in the community, and the mass of blue-collar workers. The differences in the interests of these two groups were too great for the *prominenti* to provide effective leadership for the mass of laborers. There was no strong middle class to provide pressure for reform or to link these two groups. The occupational structure in Buenos Aires, however, provided the basis for the growth of a multiclass society within the Italian community. The middle groups—the skilled and white-collar workers—were more influential in the organizations of the community and, as part of a broader elite, were able to articulate and serve the interests of all Italians.[47]

The differences between the two elites can be seen in a number of areas. The mutualist movement and the leading Italian newspapers in Buenos Aires, unlike those in New York, consistently defended the interests of the blue-collar workers as well as those of the rest of the community. But the differences extended to the degree of cooperation among Italians who originated from different regions. In Buenos Aires both northern and southern Italians joined the same organizations and worked together in ways that they did not in New York. The greater numerical equality of the two groups in Buenos Aires obviously facilitated this cooperation, as did the relative lack of prejudice against southerners in the host society. In New York, the small group of northern Italians sought to escape the negative U.S. stereotype by separating themselves from the southern Italians. But the commitment of the early leaders of major mutual aid societies to a united Italy and the continual reinforcement of this commitment by the leaders of the community were of major importance in the greater ability of Italians from all areas to work together in Buenos Aires. What regional hostility there was never prevented Italians of all origins from working together in the same organizations and from uniting in a community that sought to benefit the interests of all.[48]

In New York the Italians developed two social strata in what was a multiclass society; in Buenos Aires they developed a multilevel social structure in what had been essentially a two-class society. This major difference, along with some of the social, economic, and historical differences, resulted in leadership in Buenos Aires that was more representative, more unified, and better able to develop an effective immigrant institutional structure than that in New York. The interaction among the various social sectors of the two communities was distinct and forms an important part of the explanation of the differing experience.

The more rapid and more successful adjustment of the Italians in Buenos Aires was dependent upon the skills and attitudes the immigrants brought with them, the characteristics of the receiving societies, and the changing nature of the immigrant communities. All of these variables were interrelated. Although the characteristics of the immigrants and the receiving societies were of primary importance at the time of the immigrants' arrival, these two sets of original variables produced a new set of variables that, once in existence, took on a life of its own. The interrelationship of these three categories of variables is fundamental to an understanding of the process of Italian adjustment.

The labor market in Buenos Aires attracted a relatively more skilled and permanent group of Italians who were perceived by the Argentine elite in more positive terms and who encountered a more developed and effective immigrant institutional structure. Thus they had an initial advantage over the Italians in New York as they sought to find jobs and housing, to improve their living conditions, and to organize to protect their collective interests. But once in Buenos Aires the Italians capitalized on their initial advantages to strengthen further the position of the Italian community relative to that in New York. Not only did the Italians in Buenos Aires move into the economy in positions with higher status, but they continued to find better jobs and housing and to develop community organizations. Their efforts were facilitated by the gradual pace of immigration and the concentration and relative numerical strength of the group as a whole. At the same time, the Italian multiclass social structure in Buenos Aires provided the basis for a more representative and effective group of leaders.

I have posited a model of the process of adjustment of Italian immigrants to the Americas based on the important cases of Buenos Aires and New York City. These two cases may well represent the extremes in terms of the speed and success of the process. What we need to do now is to use the model to study other cities and other immigrant groups. Much has, of course, been written on immigrants in cities throughout the world. Unfortunately, few of these studies are comparable. It is my strong conviction that historians of immigration who wish to develop their field successfully must frame their research in such a way as to make the results more readily useful to others. My hope is that the model of the adjustment process developed in this essay will enhance this effort. As the model is systematically applied to other cities and other immigrant groups, we will obtain a sufficient number of comparable cases to be able to understand with greater certainty the fundamental nature of the process itself.

Notes

I wish to thank the American Philosophical Society, the Rutgers University Research Council, and the Social Science Research Council for financial support, which made possible four trips to Argentina and two to Italy to gather data for this study of Italian immigration to Buenos Aires and New York. I also would like to thank Michael Adas, Jane Orttung, Adrienne Scerbak, Mark Wasserman, the members of the Rutgers Social History group, and especially Joan G. Baily for their insightful comments on earlier drafts of this essay. They are not, of course, responsible for any shortcomings that may still remain.

1. Alfredo Canuti, Interview with Samuel L. Baily, Numana, Italy, May 12, 1980; Colonia Italiana, "Libri d'inscrizione dei soci, 1894," Archiv d'Unione e Benevolenza, Bue-

nos Aires; and U.S. Federal Census Schedules, Manuscript, 1900, New York City, enumeration district 128, A2, B2.

2. In this essay, I am dealing with the Italians as a group, not as individuals. Amedeo Canuti and Giuseppe Trimora illustrate some of the characteristics of their respective groups of Italian immigrants, but certainly not all.

3. The literature on Italian migration is extensive. Some representative works on Italians in the United States and Argentina include Robert F. Foerster, *The Italian Emigration of Our Times* (Cambridge, Mass., 1919), and "The Italian Factor in the Race Stock of Argentina," *Quarterly Publications of the American Statistical Association* 16 (1919): 347–60; Luciano J. Iorizzo and Salvatore Mondello, *The Italian Americans* (New York, 1971); Alexander DeConde, *Half Bitter, Half Sweet: An Excursion into Italian American History* (New York, 1971); Silvano M. Tomasi and Madeline H. Engel, eds., *The Italian Experience in the United States* (New York, 1970); Humberto S. Nelli, *Italians in Chicago, 1880–1930* (New York, 1970); Andrew F. Rolle, *The Immigrant Upraised: Adventurers and Colonists in an Expanding America* (Norman, Okla., 1968), and *The Italian Americans: Troubled Roots* (New York, 1980); Edwin Fenton, *Immigrants and Unions—A Case Study: Italians and American Labor, 1870–1920* (New York, 1975); George E. Pozzetta, "The Italians of New York City, 1890–1914" (Ph.D. diss., University of North Carolina, 1971); Carla Bianco, *The Two Rosetos* (Bloomington, Ind., 1974); Leonard Covello, *The Social Background of the Italo-American School Child* (Totowa, N.J., 1972); Thomas Kessner, *The Golden Door: Italian and Jewish Immigrant Mobility in New York City, 1880–1915* (New York, 1977); Grazia Dore, *La Democrazia italiana e l'emigrazione in America* (Brescia, 1964); Gino Germani, *Política y sociedad en una época de transición* (Buenos Aires, 1962), and "Mass Immigration and Modernization in Argentina," in Irving Louis Horowitz, ed., *Masses in Latin America* (New York, 1970), 289–330; Antonio Franceschini, *L'Emigrazione italiana nell'America del Sud* (Rome, 1908); Emilio Zuccarini, *I Lavori degli italiani nell República Argentina* (Buenos Aires, 1910); Carl Solberg, "Mass Migrations in Argentina, 1870–1970," in William H. McNeill and Ruth S. Adams, eds., *Human Migration: Patterns and Politics* (Bloomington, Ind., 1978), 146–70; Gianfausto Rosoli, ed., *Un Secolo di emigrazione italiana* (Rome, 1978); and Ercole Sori, *L'Emigrazione italiana dall'Unità alla Seconda Guerra Mondiale* (Bologna, 1979).

4. This essay forms part of a larger study in progress on Italians in Buenos Aires and New York City during the period of mass migration from 1875 to 1925. For some of my thoughts on the subject, see "The Italians and Organized Labor in the United States and Argentina, 1880–1910," *International Migration Review* [hereafter, *IMR*] 1 (1967): 55–66, "The Italians and the Development of Organized Labor in Argentina, Brazil, and the United States, 1880–1914," *Journal of Social History* 3 (1969): 123–34, "The Role of the Press and the Assimiliation of Italians in Buenos Aires and São Paulo, 1893–1913," *IMR* 12 (1978): 321–40, "Marriage Patterns and Immigrant Assimilation in Buenos Aires, 1882–1923," *Hispanic American Historical Review* 60 (1980): 32–48, "Chain Migration of Italians to Argentina: Case Studies of the Agnonesi and the Sirolesi," *Studi Emigrazione* (Rome) 19 (1982): 73–91, and "Las Sociedades de ayuda mutua y el desarrollo de una comunidad italiana en Buenos Aires, 1858–1918," *Desarrollo Económico* (Buenos Aires) 21 (1982): 485–514.

5. Josef J. Barton, *Peasants and Strangers: Italians, Rumanians, and Slovaks in an American City, 1890–1950* (Cambridge, Mass., 1975); Rudolph M. Bell, *Fate and Honor, Family and Village: Demographic and Cultural Change in Rural Italy since 1800* (Chicago, 1979); John W. Briggs, *An Italian Passage: Immigrants to Three American Cities, 1890–1930* (New Haven, Conn., 1978); Robert F. Harney, "Ambiente and Social Class in North American Little Italies," *Canadian Review of Studies in Nationalism* 2 (1975): 208–24; Frank Sturino, "Inside the Chain: A Case Study of South Italian Migration to North America, 1880–1930" (Ph.D. diss., University of Toronto, 1981); Mark D. Szuchman, *Mobility and Integration in Urban Argentina: Córdoba in the Liberal Era* (Austin, Tex., 1980); and Rudolph J.

Vecoli, "Contadini in Chicago: A Critique of *The Uprooted*," *Journal of American History* 51 (1964): 404–17.

6. For a useful evaluation of the literature on assimilation, see Charles Price, "The Study of Assimilation," in J. A. Jackson, ed., *Migration* (New York, 1969), 181–237. Also see S. N. Eisenstadt, *The Absorption of Immigrants* (London, 1954); Milton M. Gordon, *Assimilation in American Life: The Role of Race, Religion, and National Origins* (New York, 1964); Gino Germani, "Assimilation of Immigrants in Urban Areas," *Working Papers*, Instituto Torcuato di Tella (Buenos Aires, 1966); John Goldlust and A. H. Richmond, "A Multivariate Model of Immigrant Adaptation," *IMR* 8 (1974): 193–227; J. J. Mangalam and H. K. Schwarzweller, "General Theory in the Study of Migration: Current Needs and Difficulties," *IMR* 3 (1968): 3–17, and "Some Theoretical Guidelines to a Sociology of Migration," *IMR* 4 (1970): 5–20.

7. To avoid the cumbersome *he/she, him/her,* and *his/hers,* I use *he, him,* and *his* throughout to refer to any individual immigrant, either male or female.

8. Many scholars make the distinction between temporary migrants (sojourners) and permanent migrants (immigrants). The definition of these terms is, however, often imprecise. I use "temporary migrant" to refer to those migrants who left Italy with the intention of returning or who returned within five years. "Permanent migrant" refers to those who left Italy with the intention of remaining abroad or who did, in fact, remain there for more than five years. See J. D. Gould, "European Inter-Continental Emigration—The Road Home: Return Migration from the U.S.A.," *Journal of European Economic History* 9 (1980): 41–112; and Betty Boyd Caroli, *Italian Repatriation from the United States, 1900–1914* (New York, 1973).

9. Ira Rosenwaike, *Population History of New York City* (Syracuse, N.Y., 1972), 63, 93, 102; and Guy Bourdé, *Urbanisation et immigration en Amérique Latine: Buenos Aires* (Paris, 1974), 174.

10. Manual arts are included in industry. Some of the figures for Argentina are estimates based on Buenos Aires, *Censo general de la Ciudad de Buenos Aires, 1887* (Buenos Aires, 1889) 2:36, 306, 379, and *Censo general de la Ciudad de Buenos Aires, 1909* (Buenos Aires, 1910) 1:132, 135, 150, 155.

11. U.S. Senate, 61st Congress, 3d Session, *Reports of the Immigration Commission* (hereafter, U.S. Immigration Commission, *Reports*), 41 vols. (Washington, 1911), 28:168–76; and U.S. Bureau of the Census, *Special Reports: Occupations at the Twelfth Census* (Washington, 1904), 634–38.

12. U.S. Immigration Commission, *Reports*, 23:168–76; U.S. Bureau of the Census, *Special Reports: Occupations*, 634–38; and Kessner, *The Golden Door*, 52.

13. These figures are estimates based on the data in República Argentina, *Segundo Censo nacional de la República Argentina, 1895* (Buenos Aires, 1898) 2:47–50, and *Tercer Censo nacional de la República Argentina, 1914*, 10 vols. (Buenos Aires, 1916), 4:201–12. Also see Herbert S. Klein, "La Integración de inmigrantes italianos en la Argentina y los Estados Unidos: Un Análisis comparativo," *Desarrollo Ecónomico* (Buenos Aires) 21 (1981): 3–27. Another important set of figures to compare is relative real wages and buying power. Some information exists for both Argentina and the United States, but the comparison is hazardous, and I have not yet worked out a satisfactory analysis. See Roberto Cortes Conde, *El Progreso Argentino, 1880–1914* (Buenos Aires, 1979), 249–69; Paul H. Douglas, *Real Wages in the United States, 1890–1926* (New York, 1966); Clarence D. Long, *Wages and Earnings in the United States, 1860–1890* (Princeton, N.J., 1960); and Albert Rees, *Real Wages in Manufacturing, 1890–1914* (Princeton, N.J., 1961).

14. The Buenos Aires figures are estimates based on República Argentina, *Segundo Censo nacional de . . . 1895*, 47–50, and *Tercer Censo nacional de . . . 1914*, 4:201–12. Also see Kessner, *The Golden Door*, 52; U.S. Bureau of the Census, *Special Reports: Occupations*, 634–38; José Luis de Imaz, *Los Que Mandan* (Albany, N.Y., 1970); Dario Canton, *El Parla-*

mento Argentino en épocas de cambio (Buenos Aires, 1965); and Robert A. Potash, *The Army and Politics in Argentina* (Stanford, 1969). Many second-generation Italians moved rapidly into positions of leadership in Argentine society. One of them, Carlos Pellegrini, was president of the country from 1890 to 1892.

15. Baily, "Italians and Organized Labor" (1967), 55–66; U.S. Immigration Commission, *Reports*, 7:417–19, and 23:368–75; Pozzetta, "The Italians of New York City, 1890–1914," 337–64; and Fenton, *Immigrants and Unions—A Case Study*, 574.

16. Eugene G. Sharkey, "Union Industrial Argentina, 1887–1920: Problems of Industrial Development" (Ph.D. dissertation, Rutgers University, 1978), 46–89. Professor Sharkey very kindly shared with me data on the nationality of the UIA leadership, which is not included in his dissertation. Also see Albert K. Steigerwalt, *The National Association of Manufacturers, 1895–1914: A Study in Business Leadership* (Ann Arbor, Mich., 1964), 175–83.

17. Buenos Aires, *Censo general . . . , 1887*, 33, 65, and *Censo general de la Ciudad de Buenos Aires, 1904* (Buenos Aires, 1906), 6, 84; República Argentina, *Tercer Censo nacional de . . . 1914*, 2:129–48; Kessner, *The Golden Door*, 127–60; U.S. Industrial Commission, *Reports*, 15 (Washington, 1902): 471–74; and U.S. Bureau of the Census, *Vital Statistics of New York and Brooklyn, 1885–1900* (Washington, 1901), 230–37.

18. City of New York, Tenement House Department, *First Report* (New York, 1903) 1:6–7; Luigi Villari, *Gli Stati Uniti d'America e l'emigrazione italiana* (New York, 1975), 212–22; and James R. Scobie, *Buenos Aires: Plaza to Suburb, 1870–1910* (New York, 1974), 146–59.

19. Kessner, *The Golden Door*, 132; Buenos Aires, *Censo general . . . , 1904,* 84; and Charles S. Sargent, *The Spatial Evolution of Greater Buenos Aires, Argentina, 1870–1930* (Tempe, Ariz., 1974), 150.

20. The data of the Immigration Commission are limited to heads of Italian households; they do not apply to the Italian population as a whole. Thus, the percentage of all Italians who owned their own homes in New York may have been as low as or lower than the 1.3 percent figure used in the sample. See U.S. Immigration Commission, *Reports*, 26:209; Kessner, *The Golden Door*, 150–52; and Buenos Aires, *Censo general . . . , 1887*, 104, and *Censo general . . . , 1904,* 84.

21. U.S. Immigration Commission, *Reports*, 26:244; Kessner, *The Golden Door*, 142; and Società Italiana Unione e Benevolenza, "Elenco dei soci, 1895–1902," Archiv d'Unione e Benevolenza, Buenos Aires.

22. Buenos Aires, *Censo general . . . , 1904*, 6, 84; República Argentina, *Tercer Censo nacional de . . . 1914*, 2:129–49; and U.S. Bureau of the Census, *Thirteenth Census of the United States . . . , 1910* (Washington, 1913) 1:824, 827–28, and *Fourteenth Census of the United States . . . , 1920* (Washington, 1922) 2:47, 747–49.

23. Kessner, *The Golden Door*, 150; Scobie, *Buenos Aires: Plaza to Suburb*, 70–113, 135–46; and Sargent, *Greater Buenos Aires, Argentina*, 22–25.

24. Kessner, *The Golden Door*, 148–49; Scobie, *Buenos Aires: Plaza to Suburb*, 160–80; and Sargent, *Greater Buenos Aires, Argentina*, 66–76.

25. These clusters are normally referred to as "chains." The term "chain migration" is subject to differing interpretations, yet most agree on the essential point: informal personal networks of individuals, kinship groups, villagers, and language clusters in the sending and receiving areas were a major influence on how most individual Italians chose their destinations, how they got there, where they settled, how they got jobs, and with whom they associated. For a fuller discussion of this idea, see Baily, "Chain Migration of Italians to Argentina," 73–75.

26. Baily, "Chain Migration of Italians to Argentina," 73–91.

27. U.S. Industrial Commission, *Reports*, 474; Pozzetta, "The Italians of New York City, 1890–1914," 995–97; John Horace Mariano, *The Italian Contribution to American Democ-*

racy (New York, 1975), 19–22; and Robert E. Park and Herbert A. Miller, *Old World Traits Transplanted* (New York, 1921), 146–58.

28. Kessner, *The Golden Door*, 151; and Robert E. Shipley, "On the Outside Looking In: A Social History of the *Porteña* Worker during the 'Golden Age' of Argentine Development, 1914–1930" (Ph.D. diss., Rutgers University, 1977), 173–96. The availability of credit was another factor that influenced the timing of the move outward, but I have not been able to gather sufficient data to make a meaningful comparison of the two cities. See Scobie, *Buenos Aires: Plaza to Suburb*, 182–91, and Anton F. Mannel, "New York City Population Trends Related to Mortgage Lending" (Ph.D. diss., Rutgers University, 1941), 86–117.

29. Pozzetta, "The Italians of New York City, 1890–1914," 231–304; and Zuccarini, *I Lavori degli Italiani*.

30. Figures on the number of mutual aid societies and on their membership vary enormously for New York. Edwin Fenton's figures seem the most reasonable to me; see *Immigrants and Unions—A Case Study*, 50. Also see "L'Elemento italiano rappresentato nelle associazione di New York, Brooklyn, Hoboken, e Newark, 1884," Archive of the Center for Migration, New York; "Le Società italiane all'estero nel 1908," *Bullettino dell'Emigrazione* 24 (1908): 1–147; "Le Società italiane negli Stati Uniti dell'America del Nord," *Bullettino dell'Emigrazione* 4 (1912): 19–54; and Baily, "Las Sociedades de ayuda mutua," 491.

31. Pozzetta, "The Italians of New York City, 1890–1914," 244–65; and Fenton, *Immigrants and Unions—A Case Study*, 49–54.

32. Baily, "Las Sociedades de ayuda mutua," 487–94.

33. Baily, "The Role of the Press and the Assimilation of Italians in Buenos Aires," 321–40.

34. Fenton, *Immigrants and Unions—A Case Study*, 59.

35. Pozzetta, "The Italians of New York City, 1890–1914," 234–42; Fenton, *Immigrants and Unions—A Case Study*, 58–63; and Robert E. Park, *The Immigrant Press and Its Control* (New York, 1922), 449.

36. The literacy figures for Buenos Aires refer to all Italians in the city eight years old or more; the U.S. Immigration Commission figures refer to Italians fourteen years old or more entering the United States or to Italian male heads of households in New York. Thus, the actual difference in literacy was probably greater than I have suggested. See Kessner, *The Golden Door*, 33–36; U.S. Immigration Commission, *Reports*, 3:84, 95–96, 131–38, and 26:238; Juan A. Alsina, *La Inmigración en el primer siglo de la independencia* (Buenos Aires, 1910), 92–93; Mario Nascimbene, "Inmigración y analfabetismo en Argentina: La Corriente Migratoria italiana entre 1876 y 1925," *Sociológica* 1 (1978): 121–70; Buenos Aires, *Censo general . . . , 1887*, 65; and República Argentina, *Tercer Censo nacional de . . . 1914*, 3:321.

37. The pre-1919 regions of Italy were as follows: the north included Piemonte, Lombardia, Trentino, Veneto, Emilia, and Liguria; the center included Toscana, Umbria, Marche, and Lazio; and the south included Abruzzi, Puglia, Basilicata, Calabria, Campania, Sicilia, and Sardegna. For a detailed breakdown of the regional origins of the immigrants, see Commissariato Generale dell'Emigrazione, *Annuario Statistico della emigrazione italiana dal 1876 al 1925* (Rome, 1926), 145–51. On organizations in Italy, see Barton, *Peasants and Strangers*, 64–67; and Briggs, *An Italian Passage*, 15–36.

38. The *golondrinas*—the Italians who went every year to Argentina to harvest the crops—numbered about thirty thousand annually during the decade or so prior to World War I. Because they did not go to Buenos Aires, I have subtracted this number from the total number of returnees to arrive at my estimate. The same cannot, however, be done for the New York Italians. As many temporary migrants went to New York as to other parts of the United States; they apparently remained in the United States for a somewhat longer period than did the temporary migrants to Buenos Aires. Thus, I am using the

same figure for New York as for the United States as a whole. See Gould, "European Inter-Continental Emigration—The Road Home," 41–71; Caroli, *Italian Repatriation from the United States*, 25–50; Mark Jefferson, *Peopling the Argentine Pampa* (New York, 1926), 183; Commissariato Generale dell'Emigrazione, *Annuario Statistico*, 830–913; and República Argentina, Dirección de Inmigración, *Resumen estadística del movimiento en la República Argentina, 1857–1924* (Buenos Aires, 1925), 4–5.

39. República Argentina, *Segundo Censo nacional de . . . 1885*, 15, 28–29, and *Tercer Censo nacional de . . . 1914*, 3:12–13; Massimo Livi-Bacci, *L'Immigrazione e l'assimilazione degli Italiani negli Stati Uniti* (Milan, 1961), 15; U.S. Immigration Commission, *Reports*, 26:176–77; and Commissariato Generale dell'Emigrazione, *Annuario Statistico*, 187–200.

40. James R. Scobie, *Argentina: A City and A Nation* (New York, 1971), 64–135; and Germani, "Mass Immigration and Modernization in Argentina," 289–330.

41. Klein, "La Integración de inmigrantes," 3–27; Peter S. Shergold, "Relative Skill and Income Levels of Native and Foreign-Born Workers: A Re-Examination," *Explorations in Economic History* 13 (1976): 451–61; Paul F. McGouldrick and Michael B. Tannen, "Did American Manufacturers Discriminate against Immigrants before 1914?" *Journal of Economic History* 37 (1977): 723–46; and Gordon W. Kirk, Jr., and Carolyn Tyirin Kirk, "The Immigrant, Economic Opportunity, and Type of Settlement in Nineteenth-Century America," *Journal of Economic History* 38 (1978): 226–34.

42. Scobie, *Argentina*, 174–91; Germani, "Mass Immigration and Modernization in Argentina," 309–11; and Carl Solberg, *Immigration and Nationalism: Argentina and Chile, 1890–1914* (Austin, Tex., 1970), 65–116.

43. Pozzetta, "The Italians of New York City, 1890–1914," 121–60; and John Higham, *Strangers in the Land: Patterns of American Nativism, 1860–1925* (New York, 1975), 68–194.

44. Solberg, "Mass Migrations in Argentina," 146–70; Maxine Seller, *To Seek America: A History of Ethnic Life in the United States* (Englewood Cliffs, N.J., 1977), 105–11; and Tomasi and Engel, *The Italian Experience in the United States*, 77–107.

45. Baily, "Las Sociedades de ayuda mutua," 485–514; and Pozzetta, "The Italians of New York City, 1890–1914," 231–66.

46. Buenos Aires, *Censo general . . . , 1904*, 28; and U.S. Bureau of the Census, *Thirteenth Census of the United States . . . , 1910*, 827.

47. Scobie, *Buenos Aires: Plaza to Suburb*, 208–10; Baily, "Las Sociedades de ayuda mutua," 485–514; and Pozzetta, "The Italians of New York City, 1890–1914," 231–44. Also see note 14, above.

48. Pozzetta, "The Italians of New York City, 1890–1914," 127–28; and Baily, "Las Sociedades de ayuda mutua," 485–514, and "Italians and Organized Labor" (1967), 55–56.

Bibliographical Addendum

Since the original publication of this article in 1983, scholars have produced a number of significant works on the nature of immigration and ethnic history, Italian immigration to the United States and Argentina, and on comparative migration. What follows is a selective list on each of the subjects for those who wish to pursue any or all of these topics.

Theoretical Works on Immigration and Ethnicity: Thomas J. Archdeacon, "Problems and Possibilities in the Study of American Immigration and Ethnic History," *International Migration Review* 19 (Spring 1985): 112–34; Rudolph J. Vecoli, "Return from the Melting Pot: Ethnicity in the United States in the 1980s," *Journal of American Ethnic History* 5 (Fall

1985): 7–20; Olivier Zunz, "American History and the Changing Meaning of Assimilation," *Journal of American Ethnic History*, Spring 1985, 53–84; John Bodnar, *The Transplanted: A History of Immigrants in Urban America* (Bloomington, 1985); Kathleen N. Conzen et al., "The Invention of Ethnicity: A Perspective from the USA," *Altreitalie* 2, no. 3 (April 1990): 37–62; Virginia Yans-McLaughlin, ed., *Immigration Reconsidered: History, Sociology, and Politics* (New York, 1990), especially the article by Ewa Morawska, "The Sociology and Historiography of Immigration"; Rudolph J. Vecoli and Suzanne M. Sinke, eds., *A Century of European Migration, 1830–1930* (Urbana, Ill., 1991); and Samuel L. Baily, "Immigration," in Peter N. Stearns, ed., *Encyclopedia of Social History* (New York, 1993), 340–44.

Italian Immigration to the United States: Samuel L. Baily, "The Future of Italian-American Studies: An Historian's Approach to Research in the Coming Decade," in Lydio F. Tomasi, ed., *Italian Americans: New Perspectives in Italian Immigration and Ethnicity* (New York, 1985), 193–205; Donna Gabaccia, *From Sicily to Elizabeth Street: Housing and Social Change among Italian Immigrants, 1880–1930* (Albany, NY, 1984); George E. Pozzetta, "Immigrants and Ethnics: The State of Italian-American Historiography," *Journal of American Ethnic History* 9, no. 1 (Fall 1989): 67–95; Gary R. Mormino and George E. Pozzetta, *The Immigrant World of Ybor City: Italians and Their Latin Neighbors in Tampa, 1885–1985* (Urbana, Ill., 1987); Donna Gabaccia, *Militants and Migrants: Rural Sicilians Become American Workers* (New Brunswick, 1988); and Samuel L. Baily, "The Village Outward Approach to the Study of Social Networks: A Case Study of the Agnonesi Diaspora Abroad, 1885–1989," *Studi Emigrazione* 29, no. 105 (March 1992): 43–68.

Italian Immigration to Argentina: Diego Armus, "Diez años de la historiografía sobre la inmigración masiva a la Argentina," *Estudios Migratorios Latinoamericanos* 2, no. 4 (December 1986): 431–60; Samuel L. Baily, "Patrones de residencia de los italianos en Buenos Aires y Nueva York: 1880–1914," *Estudios Migratorios Latinoamericanos* 1, no. 1 (December 1985); Fernando J. Devoto and Gianfausto Rosoli, eds., *La inmigración Italiana en la Argentina* (Buenos Aires, 1985); Fernando J. Devoto and Gianfausto Rosoli, eds., *L'Italia nella Società Argentina* (Rome, 1988); Fernando J. Devoto, *Movimientos migratorios: Historiografía y problemas* (Buenos Aires, 1992); Fernando J. Devoto and Eduardo J. Miguez, eds., *Asociacionismo, trabajo e identidad éthnica: Los italianos en America Latina en una perspective comparada* (Buenos Aires, 1992); and Gianfausto Rosoli, ed., *Identità degli Italiani in Argentina: Reti sociali, Famiglia, Lavoro* (Roma, 1993). The pioneering scholarly journal, *Estudios Migratorios Latinoamericanos*, founded in 1985 by the Centro de Estudios Migratorios Latino Americanos of Buenos Aires and edited by Luigi Favero and Fernando J. Devoto, regularly publishes articles that deal with various aspects of Argentine and Latin American immigration.

Comparative Migration: Samuel L. Baily, "Cross-Cultural Comparison and the Writing of Migration History: Some Thoughts on How to Study Italians in the New World," in Yans-McLaughlin, ed., *Immigration Reconsidered*, 241–53; Nancy Green, "L'histoire comparative et le champ des études migratoires," *Annales: Economies, Sociétés, Civilisations* 6 (November-December 1990), 1336–50; Walter Nugent, *Crossings: The Great Transatlantic Migrations, 1870–1914* (Bloomington, 1992); Nancy Green, "The Comparative Method and Poststructural Structuralism—New Perspectives for Migration Studies," *Journal of American Ethnic History* 13, no. 4 (Summer 1994): 3–20.

Select Bibliography

Anderson, Barbara A. *Internal Migration during Modernization in Late Nineteenth-Century Russia*. Princeton, 1980.

Antin, Mary. *From Plotzk (recte: Polotzk) to Boston*. Boston, 1899. Reprint, New York, 1986.

Archdeacon, Thomas J. *Becoming American: An Ethnic History*. New York, 1983.

Avery, Donald. *"Dangerous Foreigners": European Immigrant Workers and Labor Radicalism in Canada, 1896–1932*. Toronto, 1979.

Bade, Klaus. "German Emigration to the United States and Continental Immigration to Germany, 1879-1914." *Central European History* 13 (1980): 348–77.

———. "Altes Handwerk, Wanderzwang und Gute Policey: Gesellenwanderung zwischen Zunftökonomie und Gewerbereform." *Vierteljahrschrift für Sozial- und Wirtschaftsgeschichte* 69 (1982): 1–37.

———. " 'Preußengänger' und 'Abwehrpolitik': Ausländerbeschäftigung, Ausländerpolitik und Ausländerkontrolle auf dem Arbeitsmarkt in Preußen vor dem Ersten Weltkrieg." *Archiv für Sozialgeschichte* 24 (1984): 91–283.

———, ed. *Population, Labour and Migration in 19th and 20th Century Germany*. New York, 1986.

Baily, Samuel L., and Franco Ramella, eds. *One Family, Two Worlds: An Italian Family's Correspondence across the Atlantic, 1901–1922*. New Brunswick, N.J., 1988.

Bailyn, Bernard. *The Peopling of British North America: An Introduction*. New York, 1986.

———. *Voyagers to the West: A Passage in the Peopling of America on the Eve of the Revolution*. New York, 1986.

Baines, Dudley. *Migration in a Mature Economy: Emigration and Internal Migration in England and Wales, 1861–1900*. New York, 1985.

Barendse, Michael A. *Social Expectations and Perception: The Case of the Slavic Anthracite Workers*. University Park, Pa., 1981.

Barrett, James R. *Work and Community in the Jungle: Chicago's Packinghouse Workers, 1894–1922*. Urbana, Ill., 1987.

Bartlett, Roger W. *Human Capital: The Settlement of Foreigners in Russia, 1762–1804*. Cambridge, 1979.

Barton, H. Arnold, ed. *Letters from the Promised Land: Swedes in America, 1840–1914*. Minneapolis, 1975.

Barton, Josef J. *Peasants and Strangers: Italians, Rumanians, and Slovaks in an American City, 1890–1950*. Cambridge, Mass., 1975.

Beijer, G., et al. *Characteristics of Overseas Migrants*. The Hague, 1961.

Berend, T. Ivan, and Gÿorgi Ranki. *Economic Development in East Central Europe in the 19th and 20th Centuries*. New York, 1974.

———. *The European Periphery and Industrialization, 1780–1914*. New York, 1982.

Berkner, Lutz, and Franklin Mendels. "Inheritance Systems, Family Structure, and Demographic Patterns in Western Europe, 1700–1900." In Charles Tilly, ed., *Historical Studies of Changing Fertility*, 209–23. Princeton, 1978.

Bobińska, Celina, and Andrzej Pilch, eds. *Employment-Seeking Emigrations of the Poles World Wide, XIXc and XXc*. Kraków, 1975.

Bodnar, John. *Immigration and Industrialization: Ethnicity in an American Mill Town, 1870–1940*. Pittsburgh, 1977.

———. "Immigration, Kinship and the Rise of Working-Class Realism in Industrial America." *Journal of Social History* 14 (1980): 45–65.

———. *Workers' World: Kinship, Community and Protest in an Industrial Society, 1900–1940*. Baltimore, 1982.

———. *The Transplanted: A History of Immigrants in Urban America*. Bloomington, Ind., 1985.

Brettell, Caroline. *Men Who Migrate, Women Who Wait*. Princeton, 1987.

Britschgi-Schimmer, Ina. *Die wirtschaftliche und soziale Lage der italienischen Arbeiter in Deutschland*. Karlsruhe, 1916.

Brownstone, David M., et al. *Island of Hope, Island of Tears*. New York, 1986.

Campbell, Persia Crawford. *Chinese Coolie Emigration to Countries within the British Empire*. London, 1923.

Castells, M. "Immigrant Workers and Class Struggles in Advanced Capitalism: The Western European Experience." *Politics and Society* 5 (1975): 33–66.

Castles, Stephen, et al. *Here for Good: Western Europe's New Ethnic Minorities*. London, 1984.

———. "Migrations et domesticité feminine urbaine en France, XVIIIe siècle–XXe siècle." *Revue d'histoire économique et sociale* 4 (1969): 506–28.

Chatelain, Abel. *Les migrants temporaires en France de 1800 à 1914*. 2 vols. Lille, 1976.

Cheng, Lucie, and Edna Bonacich, eds. *Labor Migration under Capitalism: Asian Workers in the United States before World War II*. Berkeley, Calif., 1984.

Cinel, Dino. "The Seasonal Emigration of Italians in the Nineteenth Century: From Internal to International Destinations." *Journal of Ethnic Studies* 10 (1982): 43–68.

Clark, Peter. "Migration in England during the Late Seventeenth and Early Eighteenth Centuries." *Past and Present*, no. 83 (1979): 57–90.

Cohen, Robin. *The New Helots: Migrants in the International Division of Labour*. Aldershot, England, 1987.

Coleman, Terry. *The Railway Navvies*. London, 1965.

Cordasco, Francesco. *Immigrant Children in American Schools: A Classified and Annotated Bibliography*. New York, 1976.

Corris, Peter. *Passage, Port and Plantation: A History of Solomon Islands Labour Migration, 1870–1914*. Melbourne, 1973.

Craig, R. B. *The Bracero Program*. Austin, Tex., 1971.

Curtin, Philip D. *The Rise and Fall of the Plantation Complex: Essays in Atlantic History*. Cambridge, 1990.

Daniels, Roger. *Asian America: Chinese and Japanese in the United States since 1850*. Seattle, 1988.

De Jong, Gordon F., and Robert W. Gardner, eds. *Migration Decision Making*. Elmsford, N.Y., 1981.

de Vries, Jan. *European Urbanization, 1500–1800*. Cambridge, Mass., 1984.

Debouzy, Marianne, ed. *In the Shadow of the Statue of Liberty: Immigrants, Workers, and Citizens in the American Republic, 1880–1920*. Paris, 1988.

Dickinson, Joan Younger. *The Role of the Immigrant Women in the U.S. Labor Force, 1890–1910*. Reprint, New York, 1980.

Diner, Hasia R. *Erin's Daughters in America: Irish Immigrant Women in the Nineteenth Century*. Baltimore, 1983.

Ehrlich, Richard L., ed. *Immigrants in Industrial America, 1850–1920*. Charlottesville, Va., 1977.

Elsner, Lothar. "Foreign Workers and Forced Labor in Germany during the First World War." In Dirk Hoerder, ed., *Labor Migration in the Atlantic Economies*, 189–222. Westport, Conn., 1985.

Elsner, Lothar, and Joachim Lehmann. *Ausländische Arbeiter unter dem deutschen Imperialismus, 1900–1985*. Berlin, 1988.

Eltis, David. "Free and Coerced Transatlantic Migrations: Some Comparisons." *American Historical Review* 88 (1983): 252–55.

Ets, Marie Hall. *Rosa: The Story of an Italian Immigrant*. Minneapolis, 1979.

Fenske, Hans. "International Migration: Germany in the Eighteenth Century." *Central European History* 13 (1980): 332–47.

Fenton, Edwin. *Immigrants and Unions—A Case Study: Italians and American Labor, 1870–1920*. New York, 1975.

Fink, Leon. *Workingmen's Democracy: The Knights of Labor and American Politics*. Urbana, Ill., 1983.

Foerster, Robert F. *The Italian Emigration of Our Times*, 2d ed. Cambridge, Mass., 1924.

Fuchs, Rachel, and Leslie Page Moch. "Pregnant, Single, and Far from Home: Migrant Women in Nineteenth-Century Paris." *American Historical Review* 95 (1990): 1007–31.

Gabaccia, Donna. *From Sicily to Elizabeth Street: Housing and Social Change among Italian Immigrants, 1880–1930*. New York, 1984.

———. *Militants and Migrants: Rural Sicilians Become American Workers*. New Brunswick, N.J., 1988.

———, comp. *Immigrant Women in the United States: A Selectively Annoted Multidisciplinary Bibliography*. Westport, Conn., 1989.

Garis, Roy L. *Immigration Restriction*. New York, 1927.

Geary, Dick. *European Labour Protest, 1849–1939*. New York, 1981.

———, ed. *Labor and Socialist Movements in Europe before 1914*. Oxford, 1989.

Gjerde, Jon. *From Peasants to Farmers: The Migration from Balestrand, Norway, to the Upper Middle West*. New York, 1985.

Glazer, Nathan, and Daniel P. Moynihan. *Beyond the Melting Pot: The Negroes, Puerto Ricans, Jews, Italians, and Irish of New York City*. Cambridge, Mass., 1963.

Glazier, Ira, and Luigi de Rosa, eds. *Migration across Time and Nations: Population Mobility in Historical Context*. New York, 1986.

Glenn, Evelyn Nakano. *Issei, Nisei, Warbride: Three Generations of Japanese American Women in Domestic Service*. Philadelphia, 1986.

Glenn, Susan A. *Daughters of the Shtetl: Life and Labor in the Immigrant Generation*. Ithaca, 1990.

Glettler, Monika. *Die Wiener Tschechen um 1900: Strukturanalyse einer nationalen Minderheit in der Großstadt*. Munich, 1972.

Goldlust, John, and Anthony H. Richmond. "A Multivariate Model of Immigrant Adaptation." *International Migration Review* 8 (1974): 193–225.

Gordon, David M., Richard Edwards, and Michael Reich. *Segmented Work, Divided Workers: The Historical Transformation of Labor in the United States*. Cambridge, 1982.

Gordon, Milton M. *Assimilation in American Life: The Role of Race, Religion, and National Origins*. New York, 1964.

Gould, J. D. "European Inter-Continental Emigration, 1815–1914: Patterns and Causes." *Journal of European Economic History* 8 (Winter 1979): 593–679.

———. "European Inter-Continental Emigration—The Road Home: Return Migration from the U.S.A." *Journal of European Economic History* 9 (1980): 41–112.

Gray, Malcolm. "Scottish Emigration: The Social Impact of Agrarian Change in the Rural Lowlands, 1775–1885." *Perspectives in American History* 7 (1973): 95–174.

Graziosi, Andrea. "Foreign Workers in Soviet Russia, 1920–1940: Their Experience and Their Legacy." *International Labor and Working-Class History* 33 (1988): 38–59.

Green, Nancy L. "L'histoire comparative et le champ des études migratoires." *Annales: Economies, Sociétés, Civilisations* 6 (November-December 1990): 1335–50.

Greene, Victor R. *The Slavic Community on Strike: Immigrant Labor in Pennsylvania Anthracite*. Notre Dame, Ind., 1968.

Gribaudi, Maurizio. *Itinéraires ouvriers: Espaces et groupes sociaux à Turin au début du XXe siècle*. Paris, 1987.

Gullickson, Gay. *Spinners and Wavers of Auffay: Rural Industry and the Sexual Division of Labor in a French Village, 1750–1850*. Cambridge, 1986.

Gutman, Herbert G. *Work, Culture, and Society in Industrializing America*. New York, 1976.

Gutmann, Myron. *Toward the Modern Economy: Early Industry in Europe, 1500–1800*. New York, 1988.

Hareven, Tamara K. *Family Time and Industrial Time: The Relationship between Family and Work in a New England Industrial Community*. Cambridge, 1982.

Harney, Robert F., and J. Vincenza Scarpaci, eds. *Little Italies in North America*. Toronto, 1981.

Harzig, Christiane. "The Role of German Women in the German-American Working-Class Movement in Late Nineteenth-Century New York." *Journal of American Ethnic History* 8 (1989): 87–107.

Harzig, Christiane, and Dirk Hoerder, eds. *The Press of Labor Migrants in Europe and North America, 1880s to 1930s*. Labor Migration Project, University of Bremen. Bremen, 1985.

Heffer, Jean, and Jeanine Rovet, eds. *Why Is There No Socialism in the United States?* Paris, 1988.

Helbich, Wolfgang, Walter D. Kamphoefner, and Ulrike Sommer, eds. *Briefe aus Amerika: Deutsche Auswanderer schreiben aus der Neuen Welt, 1830–1930*. Munich, 1988.

Henri, Florette. *Black Migration: The Movement North, 1900–1920*. Garden City, N.Y., 1976.

Herbert, Ulrich. *A History of Foreign Labor in Germany, 1880–1980*. Ann Arbor, 1990. German original 1986.

Higham, John. *Strangers in the Land: Patterns of American Nativism, 1860–1925*, 2d. ed. New York, 1975.

Hippel, Wolfgang von. *Auswanderung aus Südwestdeutschland: Studien zur Württembergischen Auswanderung und Auswanderungspolitik im 18. und 19. Jahrhundert*. Stuttgart, 1984.

Hochstadt, Steve. "Migration and Industrialization in Germany, 1815–1977." *Social Science History* 5 (Fall 1981): 445–68.

———. "Migration in Preindustrial Germany." *Central European History* 16 (1983): 195–224.

———. "Urban Migration in Imperial Germany: Towards a Quantitative Model." *Historical Papers / Communications Historiques, 1986* (1987): 200–204.

Hoerder, Dirk. "Immigration and the Working Class: The Remigration Factor." *International Labor and Working Class History* 21 (1982): 28–41.

———. "German Immigrant Workers' Views of 'America' in the 1880s." In Marianne Debouzy, ed., *In the Shadow of the Statue of Liberty: Immigrants, Workers, and Citizens in the American Republic, 1880–1920*. Paris, 1988.

———, ed. *American Labor and Immigration History, 1877–1920s: Recent European Research*. Urbana, Ill., 1983.

———, ed. *Labor Migration in the Atlantic Economies: The European and North American Working Classes during the Period of Industrialization*. Westport, Conn., 1985.

———, ed. *"Struggle a Hard Battle": Essays on Working Class Immigrants*. De Kalb, Ill., 1986.

Hoerder, Dirk, Inge Blank, and Horst Rössler, eds. *Roots of the Transplanted: East Central and Southeastern Europe*. 2 vols. New York, 1994.

Hoerder, Dirk, and Horst Rössler, eds. *Distant Magnets: Expectations and Realities in the Immigrant Experience*. New York, 1993.

Hohenberg, Paul M., and Lynn Hollen Lees. *The Making of Urban Europe, 1000–1950*. Cambridge, Mass., 1985.

Holloway, Thomas H. *Immigrants on the Land: Coffee and Society in São Paulo, 1886–1934*. Chapel Hill, 1980.

Houstoun, Marion F., et al. "Female Predominance of Immigration to the United States since 1930: A First Look." *International Migration Review* 28 (Winter 1984): 908–63.

Huggins, Nathan I. *Black Odyssey*. New York, 1979.

Hutchinson, E. P. *Legislative History of American Immigration Policy, 1798–1965*. Philadelphia, 1981.

Ichioka, Yuji. *The Issei: The World of the First Generation Japanese Immigrants, 1885–1924*. New York, 1988.

Jackson, James, Jr. "Migration in Duisburg, 1867–1890: Occupational and Familial Contexts." *Journal of Urban History* 8 (1982): 235–70.

Jackson, Pauline. "Women in 19th Century Irish Emigration." *International Migration Review* 28 (Winter 1984): 1004–20.

Jensen, Joan M. *Passage from India: Asian Indian Immigrants in North America*. New Haven, 1988.

Jerome, Harry. *Migration and Business Cycles*. New York, 1926.

Just, Michael. *Ost- und südosteuropäische Amerikawanderung, 1881–1914: Transitprobleme in Deutschland und Aufnahme in den Vereinigten Staaten*. Wiesbaden, 1988.

Kaelble, Hartmut. *Historical Research on Social Mobility: Western Europe and the USA in the Nineteenth and Twentieth Centuries*. New York, 1981.

Kaiser, Dolf. *Fast ein Volk von Zuckerbäckern? Bündner Konditoren, Cafetiers und Hoteliers in europäischen Ländern bis zum ersten Weltkrieg*. Zürich, 1985.

Kamphoefner, Walter D. *The Westfalians: From Germany to Missouri*. Princeton, 1987.

Karni, Michael, ed. *The Finnish Experience in the Western Great Lakes Region: New Perspectives*. Vammala, Finland, 1975.

Katzmann, David M., and William M. Tuttle, Jr., eds. *Plain Folk: The Life Stories of Undistinguished Americans*. Urbana, Ill., 1982.

Keil, Hartmut, and John B. Jentz, eds. *German Workers in Industrial Chicago, 1850–1910: A Comparative Perspective*. De Kalb, Ill., 1983.

Kennedy, Robert E., Jr. *The Irish: Emigration, Marriage, and Fertility*. Berkeley, Calif., 1971.

Kero, Reino. "The Canadian Finns in Soviet Karelia in the 1930s." In Michael Karni, ed., *Finnish Diaspora*. Toronto, 1981.

Kleßmann, Christoph. *Polnische Bergarbeiter im Ruhrgebiet, 1870–1945*. Göttingen, 1978.

Kloosterboer, Willemina. *Involuntary Labour since the Abolition of Slavery: A Survey of Compulsory Labour throughout the World*. Leiden, 1960.

Köllmann, Wolfgang, and Peter Marschalck. "German Emigration to the United States." *Perspectives in American History* 7, special issue, *Dislocation and Emigration: The Social Background of American Immigration* (1973): 499–544.

Korman, Gerd. *Industrialization, Immigrants and Americanizers: Milwaukee, 1866–1921*. Madison, 1967.

Kriedte, Peter, Hans Medick, and Jürgen Schlumbohm. *Industrialization before Industrialization*. Cambridge, 1981. German original 1977.

Kritz, Mary, Charles B. Keely, and Silvano M. Tomasi, eds. *Global Trends in Migration: Theory and Research on International Population Movements*. New York, 1983.

Kula, Witold, Nina Assorobodraj-Kula, and Marcin Kula, eds. *Listy emigrantów z Brazylii i Stanów Zjednoczonych, 1890–1891*. Warsaw, 1973.

Kussmaul, Ann. *Servants in Husbandry in Early Modern England*. Cambridge, 1981.

Langewiesche, Dieter. "Wanderungsbewegungen in der Hochindustrialisierungsperiode: Regionale, interstädtische und innerstädtische Mobilität in Deutschland, 1880–1914." *Vierteljahrschrift für Sozial- und Wirtschaftsgeschichte* 64 (1977): 1–40.

Laslett, John H. M. *Nature's Noblemen: The Fortunes of the Independent Collier in Scotland and the American Midwest, 1855–1889*. Los Angeles, 1983.

Leeds, Anthony. "Women in the Migratory Process: A Reductionist Outlook." *Anthropological Quarterly* 49 (1976): 69–76.

LeMay, Michael C. *From Open Door to Dutch Door: An Analysis of U.S. Immigration Policy since 1820*. New York, 1987.

Lintelman, Joy. " 'America is the Woman's Promised Land': Swedish Immigrant Women and American Domestic Service." *Journal of American Ethnic History* 8 (Spring 1989): 9–23.

Lis, Catarina, and Hugh Soly. *Poverty and Capitalism in Pre-Industrial Europe*. Atlantic Highlands, N.J., 1979.

Lucassen, Jan. *Migrant Labour in Europe, 1600–1900: The Drift to the North Sea*. Beckenham, England, 1986. Dutch original 1984.

Lucassen, Jan, and Rinus Penninx. *Nieuwkomers, Immigranten en hun nakomelingen in Nederland, 1550–1985*. Amsterdam, 1985.

Marschalck, Peter. *Deutsche Überseewanderung im 19. Jahrhundert: Ein Beitrag zur soziologischen Theorie der Bevölkerung*. Stuttgart, 1973.

Martellone, Anna Maria. "Italian Mass Emigration to the United States, 1876–1930: A Historical Survey." *Perspectives in American History*, n.s., 1 (1984): 379–423.

Matovic, Margareta R. *Stockholmsäktenskap: Familjebildning och partnerval i Stockholm, 1850–1890*. Stockholm, 1984.

Mayer, Kurt B. "Die Klassenstruktur in zwei egalitären Gesellschaften: Ein Vergleich zwischen Australien und den Vereinigten Staaten." *Kölner Zeitschrift für Soziologie und Sozialpsychologie* 16 (1964): 660–79.

Meyer, Stephen. *The Five Dollar Day: Labor Management and Social Control in the Ford Motor Company, 1908–1921*. New York, 1981.

Meyerowitz, Joanne J. *Women Adrift: Independent Wage Earners in Chicago, 1880–1930*. Chicago, 1988.

Les migrations internationales de la fin du XVIIIe siècle à nos jours. Paris, 1980.

Mikoletzky, Juliane. *Die deutsche Amerika-Auswanderung des 19. Jahrhunderts in der zeitgenössischen fiktionalen Literatur*. Tübingen, 1988.

Miller, Kerby. *Emigrants and Exiles: Ireland and the Irish Exodus to North America*. New York, 1985.

Mink, Gwendolyn. *Old Labor and New Immigrants in American Political Development: Union, Party and State, 1875–1920*. Ithaca, 1986.

Moch, Leslie Page. *Paths to the City: Regional Migration in Nineteenth-Century France*. Beverly Hills, Calif., 1983.

———. *Moving Europeans: Migration in Western Europe since 1650*. Bloomington, Ind., 1992.

Montelius, S. "Recruitment and Conditions of Life of Swedish Ironworkers during the 18th and 19th Centuries." *Scandinavian Economic History Review* 14 (1966): 1–17.

Morawska, Ewa. *For Bread with Butter: The Life-Worlds of East Central Europeans in Johnstown, Pennsylvania, 1890–1940*. New York, 1985.

———. "The Sociology and Historiography of Immigration." In Yans-McLaughlin, *Immigration Reconsidered*.

Morokvasic, Mirjana. "Women in Migration: Beyond the Reductionist Outlook." In Annie Phizacklea, ed., *One Way Ticket: Migration and Female Labour*. London, 1983.

———. "Birds of Passage Are also Women." *International Migration Review* 28 (Winter 1984): 886–907.

Mueller, Charles F. *The Economics of Labor Migration*. New York, 1982.

Murzynowska, Krystyna. *Polskie wychodzstwo zarobkowe w Zaglebiu Ruhry, 1880–1914* (Polish economic emigration in the Ruhr Basin, 1880–1914). Wroclaw, 1972. German translation, 1979.

Nichtweiß, Johannes. *Die ausländischen Saisonarbeiter in der Landwirtschaft der östlichen und mittleren Gebiete des Deutschen Reiches*. Berlin, 1959.

Nolan, Janet A. *Ourselves Alone: Women's Emigration from Ireland, 1885–1920*. Knoxville, 1989.
Nugent, Walter. *Crossings: The Great Transatlantic Migrations, 1870–1914*. Bloomington, Ind., 1992.
Oestreicher, Richard J. *Working People and Class Consciousness in Detroit, 1875–1900*. Urbana, Ill., 1986.
Olson, James Stuart. *The Ethnic Dimension in American History*. New York, 1979.
Ostergren, Robert C. *A Community Transplanted: The Trans-Atlantic Experience of a Swedish Immigrant Settlement in the Upper Midwest, 1835–1915*. Madison, 1988.
Piore, Michael J. *Birds of Passage: Migrant Labor and Industrial Societies*. New York, 1979.
Poitrineau, Abel. *Remues d'hommes: Essai sur les migrations montagnardes en France aux XVIIe et XVIIIe siècles*. Paris, 1983.
Portes, Alejandro. "Migration and Underdevelopment." *Politics and Society* 8, no. 7 (1978): 1–48.
Portes, Alejandro, and John Walton. *Labor, Class and International System*. New York, 1981.
Puskás, Julianna. *From Hungary to the United States, 1880–1914*. Budapest, 1982.
Riegler, Claudius H. *Emigration und Arbeitswanderung aus Schweden nach Norddeutschland, 1868–1914*. Neumünster, 1985.
Rosander, Göran. *Herrarbete*. Uppsala, 1967.
Rosenblum, Gerald. *Immigrant Workers: Their Impact on American Labor Radicalism*. New York, 1973.
Rosoli, Gianfausto, ed. *Un secolo di emigrazione italiana, 1876–1976*. Rome, 1980.
Ross, Carl, and K. Marianne Wargelin, eds. *Women Who Dared: The History of Finnish American Women*. St. Paul, 1986.
Roth, Guenther. *The Social Democrats in Imperial Germany: A Study in Working-Class Isolation and National Integration*. Totowa, N.J., 1963.
Runblom, Harald, and Hans Norman. *From Sweden to America: A History of the Migration*. Minneapolis, 1976.
Sassen-Koob, Saskia. "The Internalization of the Labor Force." *Studies in Comparative International Development* 15, no. 4 (Winter 1980): 3–26.
Schäfer, Hermann. "Italienische 'Gastarbeiter' im Deutschen Kaiserreich (1890–1914)." *Zeitschrift für Unternehmensgeschichte*, 1982, 192–214.
Schelbert, Leo. "On Becoming an Emigrant: A Structural View of Eighteenth- and Nineteenth-Century Swiss Data." *Perspectives in American History* 7 (1973): 441–95.
Schmidtbauer, Peter. "Households and Household Forms of Viennese Jews in 1857." *Journal of Family History* 5 (Winter 1980).
Schofer, Lawrence. *The Formation of a Modern Labor Force: Upper Silesia, 1865–1914*. Berkeley, Calif., 1975.
Scott, Franklin D., ed. *World Migration in Modern Times*. Englewood Cliffs, N.J., 1968.
Seller, Maxine Schwartz. *To Seek America: A History of Ethnic Life in the United States*. Englewood, N.J., 1988.
Sewell, William H. *Work and Revolution in France*. Cambridge, 1980.
Shaw, Paul R. *Migration Theory and Fact: A Review and Bibliography of Current Literature*. Philadelphia, 1975.
Shergold, Peter R. *Working-Class Life: The "American Standard" in Comparative Perspective, 1899–1913*. Pittsburgh, 1982.
Simmons, Alan, Sergio Diaz-Briquets, and Aprodicio A. Laquian. *Social Change and Internal Migration: A Review of Research Findings from Africa, Asia, and Latin America*. Ottawa, 1977.
Simon, Rita James, and Caroline B. Brettell, eds. *International Migration: The Female Experience*. Totowa: N.J., 1986.
Souden, David. "Movers and Stayers in Family Reconstitution Populations, 1660–1780." *Local Population Studies* 33 (1984): 11–28.

Swierenga, Robert P. "Dutch Immigrant Demography, 1820–1880." *Journal of Family History* 5 (Winter 1980): 390–405.

———. *They Came to Stay: Essays on Dutch Immigration and Settlement in America.* New Brunswick, N.J., 1988.

Takaki, Ronald. *Strangers from A Different Shore: A History of Asian Americans.* Boston, 1989.

Taylor, Philip. *The Distant Magnet: European Emigration to the U.S.A.* New York, 1971.

Thistlethwaite, Frank. "Migration from Europe Overseas in the Nineteenth and Twentieth Centuries." In *XIe Congrès International des Sciences Historiques: Rapports,* vol. 5. Gŏteborg, 1960.

Thomas, Brinley. *Migration and Economic Growth: A Study of Great Britain and the Atlantic Economy.* Cambridge, 1954.

Thomas, William I., and Florian Znaniecki. *The Polish Peasant in Europe and America.* 5 vols. Chicago and Boston, 1918–1920. Reprint in several different editions.

Tilly, Charles. "Migration in Modern European History." In William H. McNeill and Ruth S. Adams, eds., *Human Migration: Patterns and Policies,* 48–72. Bloomington, Ind., 1978.

———. "Demographic Origins of the European Proletariat." In D. Levine, ed., *Proletarianization and Family History,* 1–85. Orlando, Fla., 1984.

———. "Transplanted Networks." In Yans-McLaughlin, *Immigration Reconsidered,* 79–90.

Tilly, Louise A., and Joan Scott. *Women, Work and Family.* New York, 1978.

Tinker, H. *A New System of Slavery: The Export of Indian Labour Overseas, 1830–1920.* London, 1974.

Todaro, Michael P. *Internal Migration in Developing Countries: A Review of Theory, Evidence, Methodology, and Research Priorities.* Geneva, 1976.

Todd, Emmanuel. "Mobilité géographique et cycle de vie en Artois et en Toscane au XVIIIe siècle." *Annales: Economies, Sociétés, Civilisations* 30 (1975): 726–44.

Treadgold, Donald W. *The Great Siberian Migration: Government and Peasant in Resettlement from Emancipation to the First World War.* Princeton, 1957.

Truant, Cynthia M. "Solidarity and Symbolism among Journeymen Artisans: The Case of Compagnonnage." *Comparative Studies in Society and History* 21 (1979): 214–26.

Tyree, Andrea, and Katharine M. Donato. "The Sex Composition of Legal Immigrants to the United States." *Sociology and Social Research* 69 (July 1985): 577–84.

———. "A Demographic Overview of the International Migration of Women." In Rita James Simon and Caroline Brettell, eds., *International Migration: The Female Experience.* Totowa, N.J., 1986.

———. "Family Reunification, Health Professionals and the Sex Composition of Immigrants to the United States." *Sociology and Social Research* 70 (1986): 226–30.

Vecoli, Rudolph J. "*Contadini* in Chicago: A Critique of *The Uprooted.*" *Journal of American History* 51 (1964–65): 404–17.

Wakatsuki, Yasuo. "Japanese Emigration to the United States, 1866–1924: A Monograph," *Perspectives in American History,* 12 (1979): 387–516.

Weatherford, Doris. *Foreign and Female: Immigrant Women in America, 1840–1930.* New York, 1986.

Weinberg, Sydney Stahl. *The World of Our Mothers: The Lives of Jewish Immigrant Women.* New York, 1988.

Weiss, Bernard J., ed. *American Education and the European Immigrant, 1840–1940.* Urbana, Ill., 1982.

White, Paul E., and Robert Woods, eds. *The Geographical Impact of Migration.* London, 1980.

Willcox, Walter F., and Imre Ferenczi. *International Migrations.* 2 vols. New York, 1929, 1931.

Williamson, Jeffrey, and Peter Lindert. *American Inequality: A Macroeconomic History.* New York, 1980.

Wilson, Francis. *Migrant Labor in South Africa.* Johannesburg, 1972.
Yans-McLaughlin, Virginia. *Family and Community: Italian Immigrants in Buffalo, 1880–1930.* Ithaca, 1977.
Yans-McLaughlin, Virginia, ed. *Immigration Reconsidered: History, Sociology, and Politics.* New York, 1990.

Contributors

Samuel Baily, Professor of History, Rutgers University, is the author of *Labor, Nationalism, and Politics in Argentina* (1967) and *The United States and the Development of South America, 1945–1975* (1976). He completed and edited the late James Scobie's *Secondary Cities of Argentina* (1988) and edited, with Franco Ramella, *One Family, Two Worlds: An Italian Family's Correspondence across the Atlantic, 1901–1922* (1988).

Donna Gabaccia, Stone Professor of American History, University of North Carolina-Charlotte, is the author of *From Sicily to Elizabeth Street: Housing and Social Change among Italian Immigrants, 1880–1930* (1984), *Militants and Migrants: Rural Sicilians Become American Workers* (1988), *Immigrant Women in the United States: A Selectively Annotated Multidisciplinary Bibliography* (1989), and *From the Other Side: Women, Gender, and Immigrant Life in the U.S. 1820–1990* (1994).

Nancy Green, Directeur d'Etudes, Centre de Recherches Historiques, Ecole des Hautes Etudes en Sciences Sociales, is the author of *The Pletzl of Paris: Jewish Immigrant Workers in the "Belle Epoque"* (1986). Her articles include "The Comparative Method and Poststructural Structuralism—New Perspectives for Migration Studies," *Journal of American Ethnic History* 13 (1994).

Steve Hochstadt, Associate Professor of History, Bates College, is writing a history of migration in Germany. His best-known articles are "Migration and Industrialization in Germany, 1815–1977," *Social Science History* 5 (1981), and "Migration in Preindustrial Germany," *Central European History* 16 (1983).

Dirk Hoerder is Professor of History at Universität Bremen. Since Professor Hoerder published *Crowd Action in Revolutionary Massachusetts, 1765–1780* (1977), his work has included eight English-language essay collections and bibliographies on the American labor movement, the labor press, and labor migrations, including *Labor Migration in the Atlantic Economies* (1985).

James Jackson, Jr., Associate Professor of History and Political Science, Point Loma College, is completing a manuscript titled "Migration and Urbanization in the Ruhr Valley, 1820–1910." His article "Migration in Duisburg, 1867–1890: Occupational and Familial Contexts," *Journal of Urban History* 8 (1982) received the biennial award for best article from the Conference Group on Central European History of the American Historical Association.

Leslie Page Moch, Professor of History, University of Michigan-Flint, is the author of *Paths to the City: Regional Migration in Nineteenth-Century France* (1983) and *Moving Europeans: Migration in Western Europe since 1650* (1992).

Ewa Morawska, Professor of Sociology and History, University of Pennsylvania, is the author of *For Bread with Butter: The Life-Worlds of East Central Europeans in Johns-*

town, Pennsylvania, 1890–1940 (1985) and *Insecure Prosperity: Jews in Small-town Industrial America, 1880–1940* (forthcoming).

Walter Nugent is the Andrew V. Tackes Chair in History at the University of Notre Dame. Since the publication of *The Tolerant Populists* (1963), Professor Nugent has written many books, including *Money and American Society, 1865–1880* (1968), *Structures of American Social History* (1981), and *Crossings: The Great Transatlantic Migrations, 1870–1914* (1992).

Index